PAWKA'S STORY

Lima-Charlie 5 X 5

NOEL TAYLOR CHESSÉ

authorHOUSE®

AuthorHouse™
1663 Liberty Drive
Bloomington, IN 47403
www.authorhouse.com
Phone: 1 (800) 839-8640

Published by AuthorHouse 06/14/2019

ISBN: 978-1-7283-1400-6 (sc)
ISBN: 978-1-7283-1399-3 (e)

Print information available on the last page.

This book is printed on acid-free paper.

DEDICATION

This book is dedicated to all my family, living and dead, especially to the memory of my late wife, Scharlene H. Chesse'. It also is dedicated to my sons, Andre' & Nicholas Chesse' and to all my grandchildren. Gabrielle, Harmony, Jaden. Alexis, (Chole & Jaxon). And to Sebastian & Nathan, my wonderful "step grandchildren".

I further dedicate this work to the 58,479 of my "Brothers-in Arms" who gave their lives during the Vietnam War.

It is also dedicated to all the "Baby-Boomers" of my generation and their families.

Lastly, a special thanks to a wonderful "Kentucky Lady", Linda Cole Hopkins who gave this author the time, unconditional love, space and undying support for this project.

SIT BACK, GET COMFORTABLE. READ AND
ENJOY THIS TIME AND MEMORY TRAVEL SAGA TOGETHER,
THANK YOU !

INTRODUCTION

We are about to take a journey through time together. This project began in 2005 after the death of my wife of 34 years, Scharlene. I began to think of her and all of the other family members, living and dead that all had stories to tell, yet nobody recorded those tales to share with the world. The writing was started but lost on several computers over time.

I will tell you of my life from the early 1950s through the Cold War, Vietnam and beyond. I tried to recreate the times as they were experienced my me and my family. Particular attention was given to my military experiences and to the equipment of the times. There is very little left of the Army of my day. That of today, seems very foreign to me.

In recent years dedicated people have tried to record the stories of World War II veterans and the Holocaust survivors. It is vital that we do not loose these personal histories before they are all gone. Today, the Korean War Veterans and the Vietnam Veterans are all getting much older and their stories will also be lost, if not recorded. I have written for the Library of Congress for their "Veterans Project", a multi-media presentation and record of the American Veteran and our collective stories.

It then occurred to me that I owe it to my sons and grandchildren, my story and that of several of my family members. It is also my intent to leave this piece of work to the history students and history buffs who want a firsthand view of history from a participant.

All of us living today have a part in shaping history by all of our collective actions, no matter how small or how big those actions may seem to be to us. It all adds up over time. Sometimes it is even the lack of the action that will dominate and shape history. Think then, of Germany in the 1930s or the Japanese people who watched their nation become militarized over a period of eighty years or so.

To me, we all are involved in the "butterfly effect". That is, that the flapping of a butterfly's wings in the Chinese Emperor's beautiful garden hundreds of miles away from his invasion fleet which was sailing across the Sea of Japan. Those gentle breezes created by those tiny wings added in a small way to the winds of the great typhoon that destroyed that massive invasion fleet.

This project has actually been a work in progress since my high school days when I kept a journal. It continued through my military service, up to my leaving Vietnam in 1971. During those years, I kept my journal current daily. Not only did I write about my "adventures", but I also began to draft "character profiles" of some of the most interesting people who found themselves in the Army during those years. The Army was a demographic profile of America. As my travels widened, I took notes and was fascinated with the histories of the places that I visited and people I met as well as those who have passed those same roads before me. Sadly, my early journals are lost forever.

History and the social sciences have always fascinated me. Throughout the years. I would allow my imagination to travel through time and visit all those places and peoples of the past. I would try to reconstruct their lives and how the people lived in any given era, from pre-historic beginnings throughout history. It occupied me for hours, trying to piece all those fragments of history together trying to figure out how we got to our present situations. I also tried to envision the world in the future as a result of our actions in the present. In many ways time seems to be circular.

I am a firm believer in the statement: "Those who do not learn from history, are doomed to repeat it.". I also can understand and relate to the analogy of the four different people, each standing on one corner of an intersection, when a traffic accident occurs before them. When the police and the reporters interview each person separately, four different versions of the event are told. It also goes to say that "The victors write the history."; and "To the victors, go the spoils.".

FEEL FREE TO FLIP TO THE APPENDIX TO REVIEW THE HEADLINES AND STORIES FROM AROUND THE NATION AND THE WORLD IN A SERIES OF TIMELINES AND FACT CHECKER.

So, I ask you to get comfortable, relax and enjoy these tales from this time and history traveler.

CHAPTER ONE

Have you ever as a child or young adult listened to your parents or grandparents tell the same old stories over and over again, theirs or the family stories, boring you to death? You wanted to run? Years later, when perhaps they have died, have you thought of these stories and wondered why you never wrote them down or somehow recorded these tales? Many times, one's memory does not convey the story the same as Grandpa did. I have attempted here to capture the family's stories as well as my own. This phase of contemporary history is the one that I have lived through. Here it is, our story for the family, both past and present. Or perhaps it will help a future child to relate to a grandparent or perhaps a great-grandparent?

Every person alive today, as well as all those who have gone before, have shared two things in common, other than the basics of Life & Death. These being: the time spent on this Earth and where their travels that have taken them. We live in both the physical and spiritual worlds. Some of these travelers have gone far, and others have not in both realms These comments are not meant to judge or categorize these travelers, for I am one of these. We face challenges in this life and how we manage them becomes our stories and history. Birth and death are not of our control, but how we proceed in life is. We become a part of the events that surround us.

It is no wonder, that this traveler began his journey in the similar way as all the humans before him. I do not know the specifics of my mother's pregnancy, labor and delivery, but I do know the circumstances and conditions surrounding my birth.

My mother was 41 at the time of my birth. Many of the details elude me, as I was born at quite an early age. The world around me was filled with excitement and events that affect even the world of today. Once this rather rough eviction, called Birth is over, will all be well in paradise?

The lightning flashed one more time and the thunder rolled over the San Francisco Bay Area. The fog horns moaned their sad refrain and at their distance, welcomed a tiny human into this world. The rain came down in torrents. The night was darkened by both the storm and my arrival. Would this new life be as dark and stormy as the night of his birth?

I was born on the 27th of November 1951 in San Francisco, the Tuesday before Thanksgiving at the Children's Hospital on California Street. Ah, San Francisco: aka: *"The City"*, *"San Fran"*, *"The City by The Bay"*, *"The City That Knows How"*, *"Bagdad by The Bay"*. Herb Caen, a columnist and city icon, coined the "Bagdad" term due to the City's glamor, multi-cultures, mystery, the night life, being a trade and travel hub, as well as her seven hills. He also later coined the term *"Beatnik"*, the Godfathers of the later *"Hippies"*. I would call *"The City"*, my hometown forever.

From what I was told later, it was a very stormy, raining and windy evening, not fit for man nor beast to venture out into the raging storm. These weather conditions were not typical of San Francisco's fall weather pattern. I was born a month early. I only knew that I was born ready at the time. (Knowing what I know today, I should have stayed inside safe and secure.). Elsewhere in the world, the following was happening.

General Douglas MacArthur was relieved of his command in Korea after he criticized his Commander-in Chief, President Harry S. Truman. The general felt that we should pursue the war past the Yalu River into China. He felt that if we did dot defeat the communists then in Asia, we would be forced to fight them later on. (We did in Vietnam and elsewhere in Southeast Asia.) An overall stalemate is being fought in Korea, with heavy losses on both sides. No real gains were achieved by either side. Today, it is estimated that the total cost of this war in human lives only, all sides, military and civilian was over 1.2 million lives. Was it worth it? (Today, 2018, a state of war technically remains in place between the two Koreas.)

Other headlines and events before and during my birth included: the passing of the 22nd Amendment to the US Constitution, limiting the President to two terms. (FDR was elected to 4 !) Tony Bennett sang the #1 song on the charts that night, "Cold, Cold Heart". (On a cold, cold stormy night.) Others who topped the charts in 1951 were Perry Como, Mario Lanza and Nat King Cole. Cleveland disc jockey, named Allan Friedman, coins the phrase "Rock & Roll", a term that would define a youth movement for decades to come. Today it is just *"rock"*.

Television was in its infancy and the most popular programs were: "I Love Lucy" on CBS premiering on October 15th (It was based on her previous radio show.), and "What's My Line", (First debuting on the BBC network.). World news was available in every household with a picture, for the households that had television. The rest of us still caught the news via radio.

In 1950 there were 1.5 million TV sets in the US. By 1951 there were 15 million sets in use nationwide. The broadcasting in color was introduced, but it was not until the 1960s that color sets dominated the market. Edward R. Murrow and Walter Cronkite fed America with the evening news. In the US, corporate taxation rate was 32%. Today it is at < 10%. The world was shrinking. The comic strip character "Dennis the Menace" was introduced to the nation.

The Korean War was a year old, beginning in November of 1950, when the communist forces of North Korea and Communist China invaded the pro-Western forces of South Korea. After a few short weeks the enemies were capturing the capital city of Seoul. Their southern push was finally halted. The United Nations sanctioned an intervention, as the Soviet Union boycotted the UN. General Douglas MacArthur became the Supreme Commander of the UN forces, Korea.

Americans enjoyed and made the following movies classics for years to come: "An American in Paris", "The African Queen", and "A Streetcar Named Desire". The science fiction movie, "The Day the Earth Stood Still" was playing across the nation's movie theatres.

Events around the world overshadowed my gestation period and my birth in 1951. The first commercial computer in the commercial market was called The UNIVAC manufactured by Remington Rand Corp. That computer would later be used by pollsters to predict the outcome of the 1952 Presidential election. The first electricity from a nuclear power plant occurred in Arcon, Idaho and joined the American power grid. The US tests nuclear weapons in Nevada and the South Pacific. The development of the Hydrogen bomb is just about complete. The Soviet Union develops its own nuclear arsenal and arms its submarines with nuclear missiles. The West feels threatened. (I felt secure.)

Julius and Ethel Rosenberg are convicted of espionage against the US and for selling classified atomic and weapons secrets to the Soviet Union. They both receive the death penalty but are not executed until 1953. Unemployment fell to 3.3%, average family income was $3,700 per year, gasoline cost $0.19 per gallon, and cars now had bigger engines and more powerful than earlier. Car manufacturers offered two tone paint jobs as well as many new accessories.

I was born on the Tuesday before the Thanksgiving holiday in 1951.

I learned the history of my "City By The Bay" much later in life. These highlights chronicle some of the most important events and stories in San Francisco history. It is fascinating to explore the colorful history of my hometown.

I ARRIVED HEAD FIRST INTO THE SAN FRANCISCO CULTURE AND HISTORY:

In many ways *The City's* history had a big influence on my life. I will share some of my oldest and fondest memories of "my city by the bay" throughout this narrative. San Francisco will always be my cosmopolitan city and my cherished hometown, in spite of the crazy politics of recent times, especially as of this writing. (Please refer to the Appendix, Notes & Timelines at the end of this narrative for a more historical background.)

CHAPTER TWO

THE EARLY YEARS

Time did not mean much to me at that time, as I had a lot going on during those first few days of life. I should have stayed in my secure environment until the time of my expected birth which was around Christmas. My name was picked out beforehand and has remained a part of me ever since. These conditions might have been omens for life and events later on in life.

I have been told that the family name, Chesse' dates back to the 13th century in France where a family feud within an older family occurred. Chesalle (or spelling variant) lived in the area around the city of La Salle, France. The family had ties to the various metal crafts and ship chandelling. The roots of this old family can be traced to Roman times and the conquest of Gaul. After this feud, the family was split and our branch, Chesse's left to be on their own. It is also thought that the word, "chesse", can mean a *true, faithful, and loyal friend*" with origins in Celtic roots.

My father, Roland Peter Chesse' (born Jan. 19, 1903) was out to sea at the time of my birth, as he was a uniformed Navy civilian aboard a troop ship, the USNS Sultan (Or was it the USNS Patrick? It could also have been the USNS Buckner), transporting troops and their dependents to the various Pacific duty stations from the San Francisco to the far-flung ports of call: Japan, Korea, Philippines, Guam, Midway, etc., and at times the various atomic test sites in the Pacific. At that time, it was called MSTS (Military Sea Transportation Service, at one time earlier, it was a part of the US Army's Transportation Corps today it is called: The Sealift Command.)

He was the equivalent of a "mess officer". He was responsible for the menus and overall rationing, preparation and food service for the troops as well as their dependents. He was also responsible for the overall mess / galley operations aboard ship and crew.

It took several days for him to arrive home to see me and his loving wife. He had to "island – hop" back across the Pacific to San Francisco. Knowing today, what military planes were in service at the time; it must have been a bone rattling, extremely ear shattering experience, due to the prop engines of the time. It was a sleepless journey for him. He was forty-eight at the time and the trip had to have been more of a stress on him than the young troops and sailors that he hitched a flight with. He would remain mostly "at sea" throughout most of my childhood until his death at home ten years later. He did finally make it home to greet me into this world. Andrew Taylor, my grandfather, was the one who brought me home with my mother.

Andrew Taylor was a led a very interesting and varied life. He was born in 1874 in a small town of Doncaster, just outside of Yorkshire, England. He was the son of a fish monger, John Taylor and Lucy Scope. He was the eldest of 12 children. (He outlived all his siblings, his wife and children.) When he was about ten or so John Taylor, his father, immigrated to America and settled in Buffalo, New York.

My grandfather often tells the story of his crossing the Atlantic on a ship that was a combination steam and wind power. He relates the story of his sneaking out of the family's cabin and venturing out on deck during a brutal storm, totally mortifying the parents who, when Andrew was noted missing, searched the ship for him. They feared that Andrew had been washed overboard. They were very thankful to the sailor who reunited him with his family.

As Andrew Taylor grew up, he studied geometry and art. He later became an ornamental plasterer creating by hand the ornate ceiling fixtures and wall moldings in the Victorian style and era. He was quite the artist in plaster. For years we had in my childhood home, a plaster bust of John the Baptist as a child, all done by his hand.

He got married to May Mc Donald in Buffalo, New York. My mother was born in 1910 in Buffalo, New York. The growing family also had a son, Glenhall Taylor Sr., and another daughter, Anne. He continued to work in plaster and planned to become a contractor in that trade. It was very exacting and demanding work. He remained in the Plasterer's Union for over fifty years. The union gave him a real gold card for his "retirement" while I was a teenager.

He also played a very difficult musical instrument, the Zither, and played in a small band at the time. He also boasted about sleeping in a coffin at a funeral home of one of his friends in the band after a late-night gig. He did comment on how comfortable his sleeping arrangement was but did not look forward to "sleeping" in it for longer periods of time.

My grandfather later moved with his wife, son and daughters to San Francisco, California years after the "Big Quake of 1906" because there was plenty of works rebuilding the "City". He boasted about working on the new City Hall, where his work can still be seen today. A back injury ended his active plastering career. He tells of seeing a chiropractor to relieve his back pains where the medical arts had failed him. He decided to become a Doctor of Chiropractic Medicine.

He maintained his disdain for the medical profession until the day he died. He made a life altering decision to become a chiropractor and moved to Des Moines, Iowa and attended the Palmer College of Chiropractic where he got his doctorate. He returned to San Francisco with his son Glenhall, daughter, Florence, and second daughter, Anne.

He established his chiropractic practice in (at that time a very middle-class neighborhood), the Fillmore District. In the later years that district became one of San Francisco's toughest ghettos. Andrew Taylor would take the city bus only so far, and then walk the last two miles to open his office early every morning. It became a very tough neighborhood to venture in, but he seemed to command the residents' respect for a man of his age and stature. He braved that setting until he closed his office and retired at age 90.

He was later able to purchase a house out in the "Avenues", the Richmond District of San Francisco. That address was: 654 21st Avenue, between Balboa Street, and Cabrillo Street. His eldest child, Glenhall Taylor left home and headed to Los Angeles as soon as he was able.

He remained estranged from his father, until Andrew's death in 1971. Glenhall Taylor Sr. died Hawaii in 1998.

Glenhall Taylor Sr. was active in the radio industry at the time. Glenhall wrote for the radio industry. Some of the programs that he directed and wrote for included: Burns & Allen Radio Show, Ozzie & Harriet Show, The Adventures of Sherlock Holmes, Blondie, The Dorothy Lamour Show, Dinah Shore's Open House, The Jimmy Durante Show, and Silver Threads. Later he wrote for the television programs: Death Valley Days, hosted by Ronald Reagan. He later wrote two books: The Golden Years of Radio, and Before Television-The Radio Years. Both Andrew's wife and daughter, Anne died there in that "654" house.

I always, as a small child, felt as if there were ghosts in the house, especially under the stairs, in the basement. I was raised in that house until I left for Army Basic Training at age 17.

At one time my father was a renter in Andrew's house, when he wasn't away at sea. Roland was dating my mother at the time, as they seemed to have had a very long secret engagement. My parents were secretly married for about two years. (Some family claims that it was 20 years.) When my mother became pregnant with me, the jig was up, confession time. The two Taylor daughters were both secretly married at the time, not even telling each other until my birth. Anne's husband, Benny, owned a liquor store on Geary Street & 27th Avenue. My father would frequent that establishment quite often in later years. I only knew him as "Uncle Benny".

Overall, my grandfather loved me very much and raised me with his second wife, Jessie Mc Gregor-Walker. She was his physical therapist in his Chiropractic practice. They married after the deaths of my parents. They married very late in life to raise me.

A long custody battle ensued. It pitted the Chesse' side of the family, Henry & Marcelle Arian to be exact, against the Taylor side of my family. My grandfather and his "new bride", Jessie, eventually won full custody of me. The Chesse' side of the family obtained visitation rights.

My father was a die-hard "Rebel" and boasted his Louisianan roots and heritage. When rather drunk, he and my grandfather seemed to refight the Civil War. My grandfather was a stout English-Yankee. My father's side of the family traced their roots back to 1830 to a French-Creole heritage when my ancestor, Alexander Chesse' fell in love and married one of his slave ladies. By French law, she became a French citizen. They fled the Caribbean and set out for New Orleans, when slave unrest became a threat to the French colonists on the islands. Napoleon could not get his armies to the area in time. Alexander's off-spring married into Celtic stock, forming today's physical look in the family.

Passé Blanc became a racial barrier for many. These "Jim Crow" and racial identity laws presented many challenges in our family, especially during Reconstruction after the Civil War. My great grandparents maintained that they were white French folks. My father remained a die-hard white "rebel" until his death often denying any Black blood. We later found that there was a "black" Corporal in the Confederate Army in our family tree. There will be more on my father in a narrative from my older cousin, Bruce K. Chesse' later in this writing.

My mother, Florence Scope Chesse' (Taylor was her maiden name, and thusly my middle name) was a very loving and caring woman. People had no problem in liking her and loving her for all her good traits. She was born in Buffalo, New York in April of 1910. I have very little recollection of her, except that she loved me a lot and was a very attentive mother. Somehow she may have foreseen her untimely death and exposed me at a very young age to as many wonders of the world and to San Francisco's wonderful diversity and history that she could. She was blond and blue-eyed, in contrast to my father's dark features.

My mother was very well educated and proof-read for San Francisco's noted publishing houses, (Mc Graw-Hill, for one); she made her living proof reading and she enjoyed that profession. It was unusual for a "stay-at-home" mom to have a career during the 1950s. We were middle class by having two incomes in one household at the time. (Not including my Grandfather's income.) I recall our dining room table being filled with the galley metal proof holders. Many of her proof readings were for scientific and technical manuals. I never recall her scolding me for interfering with work. She was never disturbed by my interrupting her work. She cared for me early on and I am very sure that loved me very much.

One noted author at the time was Oscar Lewis for which my mother did some of his proof reading. He was an ambulance driver in France during W W I. Lewis wrote extensively about the American West and the gold and silver rushes of California and Nevada. Some of his many books included: <u>The Town That Died Laughing</u>, <u>The Children of Sanchez</u>, <u>La Vida, Hawaii, Gem of The Pacific, The Big Four, Silver Kings: (The Lives and Times of Mac Kay, Fair, Flood and O'Brien) Lords of the Nevada Comstock Lode, Bay Window Bohemia, and, but not the last of his 28+ books and essays,</u> San Francisco: Mission to Metropolis.

She loved art and was very good at it herself, often doodling fashion sketches. She was fond of the theatre and was involved with my Uncle Ralph's marionette theatre and marionette production of the TV series "Brother Buzz", which was a weekly children's program dedicated to the prevention of cruelty towards animals. That program would later be syndicated in animation form for a short run. It was sponsored by the Latham Foundation. My mother was loved by both sides of the family. (There will be more on my parents later in this narrative.) The Chesse' family, Uncle Ralph, and cousins, Dion and Bruce Chesse' were all artists and Shakespearian actors. My cousin Peter Albin went on to become the bass player with the 1960s band: Big Brother & The Holding Company, featuring Janis Joplin. His older brother, Rodney Albin played in a blue grass band named "Dinosaur". I recall being exposed to the theatre as soon as I could sit still for a while under the watchful eye of my mother.

I further recall, my mother taking me to the YWCA, (Young Women's Christian Association), and taking me to the swimming classes at a very early age. I do recall how the pool smelled strongly of chlorine. I also remember her taking me to her beauty shop. (Helen Baker's Beauty Shop, on Geary St.). That smell was worse than the "Y". I became popular with the other ladies very quickly. I also remember playing with those hair "bobbing clips"; as I thought they reminded me of smiling alligators. The wire curlers reminded me of automobile springs.

There was a rather large colorful calendar that hung on a big cabinet door in our kitchen. That calendar was given to the family from the insurance salesman during one of his yearly appointments at our house. It was from the 'Bernard S. Greendorfer Insurance Company. I recall it vividly, as it was one of my first introductions to history. That calendar seemed to have every other day of the year, colorfully marked for some important occasion. It displayed such events as national and state holidays, the first steamboat run, National Carpenters' Day, Groundhog Day, BBQ Day, Robert E. Lee's birthday, Decoration Day, Pearl Harbor Day,

Armistice Day, Germany's surrenders (both wars), etc., and a whole lot of days which had something of note to be reminded of.

My mother took me all over San Francisco with her and I still recall those images from Chinatown to Ocean Beach. We explored Fisherman's Warf to the city limits along Mission Street to Daly City. She took me for cable car rides from one end of the line to the other. When I was a bit older, she held me as we helped turn the cable car around on the turn table located on the intersection of Market St. and Powell St. (At that time, women could not ride outside of the cable car on its running boards because their skirts or dresses might be blown up by the wind causing traffic accidents.)

Later we would go to Woolworth's for an ice cream treat. Many times, she would take me out to a more formal lunch at such famous eateries at the time, City of Paris, Blum's and Manning's. I became well-versed in proper table and the proper social graces. She gave me every experience in "The City" that she could. She always wore a scarf and ladies white gloves when in public. (This was before scarves and head wraps became an offensive public display of Islam.)

She exposed me to every culture in the city at the time and it remained a part of me, being open to all cultures, people and places. With this exposure, in my later years, Germany, and Vietnam were not cultural shocks to me as they were for many American GIs at the time.

We also rode on the "Iron Horse" (they still had 'cow-catchers' on the front) street cars that ran along Geary St. from downtown to Ocean Beach. Those old electric trolleys were very loud as they clanged along their route. There were sliding doors between the cars that often slid back and forth as the car rocked from side to side. At those times, the public transportation system smelled of cheap whiskey, beer as well as cigarette and cigar / pipe smoke. I was often compensated with an ice cream from "Awful Fresh, Mac Farlland's on Geary St. on the way home. This was, at the time, before Baskin Robbins' 31 Flavor. I thought our ice cream store had every flavor in the world. I do not recall all of my early childhood experiences with my loving mother, other than images and the spoken word that I heard later in life.

There was an "Art- Décor", grey lamp that illuminated my "changings" in my parent's bedroom. We had "Dy-dee Wash" Service at the time, soiled cloth diapers out, clean ones in, on our front porch, in the morning. Cotton diapers were recycled long before the disposable kind filled our present landfills. My father tried to work for this service, but alas, he went back to "sea", perhaps thinking that there would never be a "baby-boom".

My family was especially fond of Chinese food and often we would "order-in" from Quan's, also on Geary St. I grew up with the owner's son and ate both at their restaurant and in their home. My fondness for Oriental food continues to this day from those experiences.

Sometimes when my father was home from sea, we would have dinner parties and my parents would invite friends and family over for a wonderful meal from Quan's. There was liquor served when my father was in town. I would sneak a few drinks from the guests, undetected, or after the party, from the partially filled glasses. (Perhaps this was when I got my taste for liquor.) My father was always the court jester (after a few good drinks), and the life of the party, both at these and other various family reunions of functions.

(With permission from my cousin, Bruce K. Chesse',
the following narrative is presented.)

(Many of the punctuation corrections are mine, as well
as minor date corrections, and the parentheses items
are solely mine apart from the original text.)

Roland and Florence Taylor Chesse'

A Profile

To talk about my aunt or uncle, it is necessary to first speak of the respective families they came from and the circumstances that, I feel, influenced them both. Who they were was a part and parcel of the home environments they were born into. Each had fathers whose strength of character created a lasting effect on the choices they made in life.

<u>Florence Taylor Chesse'</u>

Florence Taylor Chesse' came from a long line of Scots Presbyterians. Her father, Andrew Taylor was a difficult man in many ways with a strong Victorian reserve. He ruled his family with an iron will and brooked no argument when it came to making decisions for the family. At one time he was a plasterer (ornamental). My earliest memory of him was when he, and other family members plastered the upper floors of our house on Uranus Terrace in San Francisco.

He was a chiropractor by profession with a great distrust of doctors. He had a wife, two daughters, a son, and son-in-law (my Dad), all of whom he outlived, dying himself at 97. Curiously all died at home under his care, with the exception of his son, Glenn Taylor Sr., from whom he (Andrew) was estranged, once he (Glenn) was old enough to leave home. (In one sense he was dead to him as well.) His presence was so formidable that both daughters, living at home, married secretly and never told their family, or each other for over two years.

Florence was a very well-educated person with the same strength of purpose as her father. Professionally, she was a proof reader for McGraw-Hill publishers, editing and proof reading scientific publications. With the deaths of her mother and sister she took responsibility for caring for her father. She spent her entire life in her father's house. She met my uncle, Roland in her early twenties, while working in my father's puppet theatres. She befriended my mother Josie, and my father's three sisters: Yvonne, Leslie and "Ding". There was a bond between all of them that lasted their entire lives. My greatest memories were the interrelationships that existed between them and the joy and laughter they shared with each other. All of them had one or more children and the cousins would spend every summer at their grandparent's house on the Russian River in Camp Meeker, Ca. in Sonoma County. (North of San Francisco)

The aunts would take turns in caring for all the cousins each summer and Florence, who was the last to have children, usually came up with Roland on the weekends. It seems to me that the extended Chesse' family filled a gap in Florence's life and was a relief from the sterner atmosphere in her father's house.

She married my uncle (Roland) when she was in her early twenties (much later, as I was told. Author's comment.) and like my mother, it was the family she was marrying into that gave her great pleasure and an additional sense of belonging. Because my family lived in San Francisco, as she and Roland did, we saw more of them that my father's sisters, who lived down the Peninsula and the East Bay.

I believe that theirs was a great love between her and my uncle in the early years. Prior to their marriage, my uncle Roland lived with Florence's family and when they were secretly married, they kept it to themselves for two years. After they told the family, they continued to live with them and suffered stoically through the losses of her mother and sister. My uncle, working as a merchant seaman, (Army Transportation Corps) came and went, shipping in and out throughout World War II and on until his death. (The author believes that he was enlisted Navy during the war, possibly working in the San Francisco Naval Purchasing Office, as he had the enlisted sleeve rank stripes & rating of an E-6, Petty Officer First Class Storekeeper among his personal belongings discovered after his death. There was also a family photograph of him in an enlisted uniform.). He was a functional alcoholic for most of the time; Florence must have put up with a great deal in their married life, but I never heard her complain. We cousins had some inkling of Roland's problem, but it didn't become apparent to us until later in life when we became teenagers.

Florence, childless, was very attentive to my twin sister and me down through the years. She always took us out to lunch at least once every two months and I was always a source of entertainment to her. I was what might be classified as ADD and hyper child, but one with an animated sense of humor and enormous energy I had. When I became frustrated with my inability to communicate with my father, she was always there with a comforting thought. She was the most caring person I knew growing up, next to my mother. I could always talk to her about any concern.

She was the least judgmental person I knew. The greatest thing I remember was when she explained my name to me. Because my sister and brother were better students than I; my self-esteem suffered under the comparisons. One day, she told me the story of Robert the Bruce, who united Scotland with the help of a spider. She said I was named after him and that he was able to unite the Scots, when on the eve of the battle (he lost most of them prior to this time); he watched a spider spinning a web, only to have his attempts fail time and time again. In persistence, the spider finally overcomes the problem and completes his web; the moral being never give up but pick yourself up and try, try again until you succeed. Needless to say, Bruce won the final battle, freeing the Scots from the tyranny of the English king. I never forgot the story and subsequently have never given up on myself, always working through the stumbling blocks we meet in life. As a teenager, I spent a lot of time with Florence, trying to get an understanding of who I was. It was through her good graces that I survived adolescence.

In 1951, about the time I was graduating from high school, Florence gave birth to Noel Taylor Chesse'. This was a time for great celebration. It was something Florence had longed for some time. What was most interesting though was that this planned decision to have a child was hers alone. As with her marriage, she told no one readily about her pregnancy until the last minute, not even Roland, who by this time was in his fifties (actually 48), or my mother, father, aunts and uncles. It was a surprise to everyone, but pleasant at that time on.

She put everything she had into raising Noel, while Roland was in shock and had great difficulties adjusting to becoming a parent so late in life. All her energies went into raising Noel and giving him every experience possible.

The next years, until her death were devoted to Noel and preparing him for adulthood. As luck (fate) would have it, she came down with breast cancer, depriving her of seeing her son pass through his adolescent years and come of age in the tumult years of the 1960's and the Vietnam War. (Of which he fought in)

The circumstances of her death were painful to all of us in the family. Because her father was a chiropractor, her early symptoms were ignored, and doctors were not called in until the cancer had taken a firm hold. The extended families were not given a lot of the details and I was told only after she had been admitted to the Laguna Honda Home on Sloat Boulevard. By this time, there was very little that could be done. She was in great pain when I visited her there and her father was still giving her chiropractic treatments until the very end. I sat with her several times, trying to comfort her at best. I could, knowing that the end was near. I promised her I would look after Noel. But, even in the end, she had enormous strength. She was ever the stoic and never complained, even with the pain she was in; she managed to meet her death with great dignity. It was a devastating thing to experience her deterioration, for me, she was always the most beautiful of women and the most loving and caring person I knew. Life seemed very unfair to me at the time. Her funeral was hard for all of us to get through. Roland, in particular, seemed very lost. She was his primary support system throughout his married life to be a single parent.

Roland Peter Chesse'

There were two events that had a momentous effect on the Chesse' family. One left them in a state of denial and the other with a sense of guilt that permeated the psyche of all the male members of my father's 'immediate family'.

The Chesse's immigrated to Louisiana in America from France in the late 1700's (some say by the way of Santo Domingo.) Our branch of the family was descended from Joseph Alexander Chesse', 1802-1862 and Justine Oliver 1800-1866. They were married or cohabitated in 1830 (we have only the census records). Justine was a slave brought to Louisiana in 1830 by Joseph Alexander's uncle, Jean Jacque Chesse' in 1822. The census records have Joseph Alexander's family listed as black. They married in 1830. This parentage haunted the family until the present day and was a subject of denial for Roland's father, Alexander Laurent Chesse' II, and my grandfather who was a silver plater; this was not brought to light until the 1960's when relatives came over from France and began doing a genealogical search of the family.

Joseph Alexander Chesse' committed suicide in 1862, when his son, Leon stole the family gold and fled to France. (Note: the Civil War was being fought at the time of Joseph's suicide.) The newspapers falsely credited the theft to two of Joseph's black servants, but it was Leon who stole the gold and it was his relatives, the Lambert family, who contacted my father in the 1960's.

The subsequent denial of our black heritage came about in two ways. The first being the fact that the family considered themselves French (by French law at the time.), first and foremost, color was immaterial; French was their first language, as it was Roland's. In addition, parts of the extended family were slave holders. Secondly, after the Civil War and the institution of "Jim Crow" laws, those who passed as white did so out of fear and necessity. Some members of this, such as my grandfather's sister, Florentine, married into "colored" families and strengthened their black gene pool, whereas my grandfather married Marie Ticoulete gene pool, whose father was from France and her mother, from Ireland strengthening their white gene pool.

So, today, we find a both black and white families strongly represented.

Roland's father considered himself French, as did his wife. (The father's wife.). His children all spoke French initially, but never felt the need to hold on to their language skills, with some exceptions. Roland lost all of his command of the language, while my father retained his. My grandfather and grandmother always spoke to each other in French. They had three girls and three boys who survived childhood.

The second event that was to have a lasting effect on the family was the loss of their eldest male child, Marcel, to appendicitis when he was thirteen years old. "Marce", as they called him, was the light of his father's life. He was a prodigy on the violin and excelled in everything that he attempted. His death was due to inept doctors and a diagnosis that delayed proper medical treatment. In today's world, he would have survived the peritonitis that killed him.

This single event created a guilt in both the minds of my father and Roland that they were never able to escape. Their father mourned the loss of his favorite son to the degree of guilt for being the ones to have survived. Their father never was able to confront his grief and had a problem with confronting anything else in life. My father always told the story of walking down the streets with his father and having to cross the street to the other side whenever people who owed him money would approach.

His self-image was such that he was embarrassed to ask for what was due him. This was passed on to Roland, my father, and sadly my brother as well. All had great difficulty in sticking up for themselves and were very conscious of making a good impression on everyone. Anything you did was considered a reflection on themselves. My grandfather never accepted the fact that my father chose to be an artist. To him, it was not a worthy profession. Roland too, felt he let his father down and had not lived up to his potential. Neither learned to accept compliments, or they tended to disparage their own efforts in life.

In his early years (Roland) he displayed great mechanical skills and was known to be able to fix anything. As children, he was always making us things like wagons, coasters and kites, which he took great delights in demonstrating for us. Roland, of all the uncles was the one who was most like a child and took a delight in getting down on our level and playing with us. He charmed us all and as a young man he charmed all the ladies as well. With the death of Marce, it was my father who tried to make up the loss for everyone and become a male role model for everyone else. When he decided to leave New Orleans and settle in San Francisco, the whole family followed, including Roland. When my father began running his puppet (and marionette) theatres in San Francisco, all of his siblings worked in them with him. Of them, Roland was the least interested until he met his future wife to be, Florence Taylor, whom he courted at the same time, renting a room in her father's house so as he could be nearer to her.

At the same time, he found jobs with UPS (United Parcel Service) and the "Dy-dee Wash" people. He single handedly created the routing for both concerns, but when the responsibilities became too much for him, he managed to get himself fired, often for drinking. In French families, wine is a staple food found on every dinner table, so the taste for liquor was quickly cultivated. Equally evident in the family was the occasional alcoholic, this was something that Roland quickly slipped into.

With the loss of several jobs, Roland drifted into the maritime service, where he remained for the rest of his working life. In the late twenties, he got my father a job on the ships which took them to the Orient for the first and last time of his life. (Ralph's) Roland found the merchant marine life was the ideal lifestyle with little responsibility. It afforded him a casual lifestyle with the benefits of visiting the various ports of call, where he could drink, if he wanted to, three square meals a day, and a clean bed to sleep on every night. For a man with little ambition, it was the best of all possible worlds. When he came home from a trip, his wife was patiently waiting for him, at the same time; he had a house without the responsibility of ownership. Occasionally, on dry land, he overdid it (The drinking) He never wanted for a place to come home to.

When Florence became pregnant, his entire world changed. The responsibility of a child was not something he could escape from. I can't begin to imagine what he went through psychologically. On the ships, his tenure also brought additional responsibilities. At one point he was promoted to Chief Purser. This was so overwhelming that he had to be demoted.

At the same time, his drinking increased and began to affect his work and his home life. When Florence died, he lost the glue that held him together. His downhill slide began at this time. His relationship with his father-in-law became increasingly difficult; exacerbated, his drinking problem and health. He saw his son and father-in-law only between trips at sea, and his drinking became constant.

The last memory I have of him was an appearance at a party at our house where he arrived very drunk, after driving his son, Noel, and Andrew Taylor from their house. He was forbidden to return, unless sober. Shortly after, it had become obvious that the alcohol was affecting comprehension.

He was relieved of duty with MSTS and died not too long after from a heart attack, brought on by his alcohol abuse. Given, the distrust that existed with the respect to the medical doctors, in our family, the problems went undetected; he sadly died alone in his sleep in a chair in his living room at 58 years old. Irrespective of the demons that haunted him, Roland was a kind and generous person whom we all loved very deeply. Of all of the uncles, he took the time to play and laugh with us when we were young. My sister and I always looked forward to his visits, he was our favorite.

I sent a copy of this profile to Norman Rush, (three years older that I, Bruce. 70 at the time.), he had this to say:

Norman Rush's Narrative

"This is really interesting work Bruce and good of you too. It brought back a memory from the deep past of going out with "Ro" (Roland), when he was driving for a diaper service, on
one of his runs. I remember how much fun it was. He drove very fast and was very jolly and friendly. I envied the Chesse' kids and their closeness to Roland. I believe he would take you guys out horseback riding in Golden Gate Park. One thing about "Ro" was that he seemed to keep up with my evolving interests and enthusiasms: astronomy,

world explorations, deep sea diving, that sort of thing. He Always gave books for Christmas presents, when he was around, and they were always right on target, though now I think about it, "Flo" may have been in charge of buying those gifts.

It was Florence who sent the books. She always made sure to remember the birthdays of all of the older cousins. Her workplace made her favor the scientific publications that she proof-read. She never forgot us at those important times. That there was a great love between them was always very evident. Renee' and I remember them both with great fondness."

The above are narratives by my cousins, Bruce Chesse' and Norman Rush. These were presented to me in later years. I do hope that they it shed a light on my further writings and the events that occurred after. In reviewing these writings, I can see clearly where a lot of my perceptions and actions had a root in. It is in the present that I can fully appreciate their writings and reflections. At this point I shall proceed to my early child hood, and the previous references will become more apparent.

CHAPTER THREE

The world continued on in those post war years with the growing competition and hostility between the Communist and non-communist nations and the many aspects of the Cold War may have directly or perhaps indirectly affected my life. The year was 1952. Dwight D. Eisenhower, famed general of World War II, was elected the Republican president of the United States. Volkswagens arrive on the American shores and were received with mixed reactions. Japan regains its freedom after six years of Allied occupation. Japan has a democratic constitution outlawing war as a political option and enters into a mutual defense pact with its former enemy, the United States. Our former enemy is now one of our strongest allies in the cold war.

The Soviet Union with its Eastern Bloc allies occupies Eastern Europe. Germany enters into an agreement with the new nation of Israel to compensate the Jews for the Holocaust. Palestinians continue to be expelled from Israel, should they choose not to become Israeli citizens. Queen Elizabeth II in Great Britain ascends the throne while Mother Teresa opens The Home for Dying Destitutes in Calcutta, India.

The Korean War ends in 1953 after three years of a bloody stalemated war which was not very popular in the United States. The two nations were divided along the 38th Parallel. It remains so today, the most militarized DMZ (De-Militarized Zone) in the world today. Cambodia declares its independence from France as the French continue to fight to retain their colony. Nikita Khrushchev takes over power after the Death of Joseph Stalin in the Soviet Union and remains in power until 1964. The Soviets celebrate 1953 by exploding their first hydrogen bomb. The arms race is in full speed ahead. The surgeon general declares cigarette smoking may be harmful to health. DNA is discovered by a British scientist, Francis Crick and an American James Watson. Sir Edmund Hillary and Sherpa Tenzing Norgay reach the peak of Mount Everest.

I continue to grow with the unconditional love and care of my mother. I have my grandfather as my male role model, perhaps in contrast to my father, who is in and out of my life in between his sea trips. I continue to grow not really wanting for anything and my mother is very devoted to my care and upbringing. The world on the outside is becoming more and more hostile as the world plays cat and mouse with its nuclear arsenals pointed at each other.

The year is 1954. President Eisenhower formulates and makes public the political theory of foreign policy which was titled *"The Domino Theory"*, in which nations will fall to communism one by one as each fall on its own. This finally led to President Lyndon Johnson escalating the Vietnam War years later in order to save Southeast Asia and Australia from communist domination. The French are defeated at Dien Bien Phu and eventually withdraw from Southeast Asia and her former colonies. The country, like Korea is divided into two nations, North and South Vietnam. Other pro-Western nations in the region form SEATO of which the United States is the principle nation. It is modeled after NATO in Europe. "Containment" becomes a goal of foreign policy. The US sends *"advisors"* to South Vietnam.

The year, 1955 saw the *"Iron Curtain"*, as Winston Churchill called it; that wall descended over Europe, dividing the East and West. Rosa Parks refuses to "ride in the back" of the bus, forcing integration of the Montgomery public transportation system after a boycott of that system. This event is often heralded as the beginning of the Civil Rights movement.

RCA introduces mass produced color television sets that a majority of the consumers can afford now. Perhaps these sets will eventually bring the future Vietnam War to American's living rooms in the future "in living color". The world market is flooded by the industrious Japanese, with a new electronic device, the transistor portable radio. Tokyo Telecommunications Engineering becomes "Sony" in 1955.

The next year, 1956 saw the signing to the Interstate Highway System into law and the nation embarked on a mass nationwide construction project, connecting every city in the United States by highway when it is completed. The second Arab-Israeli war is fought. Nikita Khrushchev declares to the West in his famous UN Speech, pounding the podium with his shoe and declaring "We will bury you!" Elvis Presley released the first of his 170+ recordings, "Heartbreak Hotel"

The very next year, 1957, was not much different, in that major events continued to shape the world that I was growing into. Some of these events were the famous Brown vs. The Board of Education, forcing the issue of integration, as the National Guard in Arkansas is mobilized to prevent that continued segregation of the school system. Martin Luther King Jr. established the Southern Christian Leadership Conference to fight for equal rights for all American citizens.

This year, 1957 saw our "Baby Boomer" population swell to 4.3 million+ and was growing by leaps and crawls. By the end of that decade, our ranks swelled to over 29 million. The Soviets launch Sputnik I, man's first artificial satellite on 26 Oct 1957. It broadcasted a radio message to the world, but sinisterly it proved the Soviet's capability to launch intercontinental weapon systems, known as ICBMs targeting any city in North America.

From my earlier years:, I now move forward to grammar school in 1956. I was ready for school, in that my mother read to me, played games to further intelligence and mental growth from an early age. School was not as traumatic for me as, perhaps it was for my mother.

My Grammar school was at the Argonne Elementary School, San Francisco. The pledge of allegiance with the presentation of the flag was mandatory every morning in school in those days. The school was a brick fortress dedicated to the famous battle of WW I. (The Battle of the Argonne.) Before mandated bussing, we all walked to and from school and, with a note, went home for lunch

When we stayed at school for lunch, the Blacks ate with the Blacks, the Asians and Latinos ate separately, the Whites also, for the most part ate together. What did bussing prove?

I recall eating paste (tasted like mint) during "cut, fold & paste"; never being able to sleep during "nap time" and not sharing during "graham crackers & milk". Sometimes we would have "barf" contests, to see who could eat the gram crackers and "chug" the milk the fastest.

Unknown to me, my mother was dying of breast cancer and was in hospice care. While my mother was at the Laguna Honda Home, I spent about a year and a half living with the Rush family and my cousins down in the San Francisco suburb of Belmont, Ca. I was the youngest of thirteen cousins and was often the brunt of their teasing and jokes.

This was in 1957 when the discovery of the California *"Big Foot's"* massive footprints and evidence of the elusive beast living in the area of Humboldt County, in Northern California. That discovery had us all concerned that *"Bigfoot"* would make the trip to Belmont to terrorize us. I also recall watching the original "Godzilla" movie, starring Raymond Burr. I also thought that "Godzilla" would cross the Pacific Ocean and join up with the *"Big Foot"* monster in San Mateo County, Ca. I was further concerned that "Godzilla" would sink my father's ship at sea.

I was scared to some extent, as my cousins did not help much with their jokes and teasing. I slept in the downstairs family room and was convinced that the *"Big Foot"* would break the glass outside door and kidnap me. There were enough of wooded areas around that even walking to school we passed through these green areas and crossed a small creek to get to school. Ironically, the school was named "Louis Barrett", later my father's last ship to serve on. I enjoyed these settings yet kept a watchful eye out for the big hairy one. Luck remained with me, no *"Big Foot"* kidnappings occurred in Belmont or San Mateo County.

Overall, the Rush family loved me and treated me very well. They introduced me to a lot of things that were not a part of my home life in San Francisco. My older cousin, Robert was an Egyptologist and often he would read stories to us from copies of the hieroglyphic scrolls and books. We attended church on a regular basis. The whole Christian experience as strange as it seemed to this young boy, and the teachings were slowly becoming a part of my upbringing. The family would often meditate together, complete with burning incense and *"Om"* chanting; we would pray together, often for my mother's recovery. Unbeknownst to us, she was terminal at this point. (After her death, I no longer believed in a kind and just God.)

The summer vacations up at the Camp Meeker summer home were a mixed bag of experiences and feelings. I slept out on an open porch and kept a watchful eye for "Big Foot". I enjoyed the outdoors, the river swimming trips on the Russian River as well as the long hiking trips deep into the woods.

There was a small creek a short walk from the family summer home and we would venture up and down this creek exploring and communing with nature. We went fishing and Cray-fishing with our light fishing gear. This was a new experience for me, as my father did not take me fishing until much later. It was quite an experience for me to eat the fish and cray fish that we had caught. Being surrounded by the redwood trees and nature; the tree house, which was built between three of these magnificent trees on the property all became a retreat for me.

Art was a very big part of the family' life, both at the Belmont home, as well as "up in the country". All of the members of the family were very talented and put my primitive art to shame. I perhaps, never pursued my art because of this. The laundry room in the family house was plastered with the children's art.

At one point, I recalled that the cousins got together and produced a small newspaper, complete with their own comic strips. My uncle, Roger Rush, was in the business machine industry, so we had copy machine in the house. (IBM or Xerox, I believe). The cousins had an old wire recorder, that we had a lot of fun playing with. They had made a silent 16mm movie and upon getting this wire recorder, produced the sound track for that movie. I was intrigued by all this, yet never went into any of these fields.

The United States and Canada jointly and quickly develop and build the North American Air Defense system, or NORAD as an early warning radar system against any Soviet rocket attack launched over the North Pole or from the oceans. I recall watching the "Santa Claus" progress on Christmas Eve on television, brought to us by NORAD. This year, 1958 also saw Cuban revolutionary, Fidel Castro lead the revolution fighting dictator Batista. NASA is created, and the manned Mercury project begins. The United States develops the technology that later puts two monkeys into space and safely returns them to Earth in 1959.

These were the last days of the decade of the 1950's, although I was the youngest, I recall that, much to my aunt & uncle's objections, *Rock & Roll"* music was here to stay. I remember a couple of "dance" parties at the Rush house. The 'Doo-Wop", "Rock- a- Billy", "Street Corner A-Capella", the "Blues" and "Folk" all became new musical genres. All are my musical staples today. The teen aged girls who attended these parties soon caught my eye and interest at the time.

The Elvis Presley performance on the Ed Sullivan Show was only seen from his waist up. Many churches held record burnings, denouncing the *"Devil's Music"* and *"Race"* music. The "Red Scare", the "Domino Theory" was in full swing. We were made aware of the "Communist Menace" running rampant in the world. The Rush family was very pacifist in their views and actions and these views and practices were carried out throughout the Vietnam War and the Anti-War movements of the 1960's and 1970's.

War movies were banned in the household, in spite of a few sneak viewings. "Victory at Sea" which was one of my favorite documentaries. There were a couple of very graphic books about the two world wars that left an impression on my young mind. My father, on the other hand, would encourage me to join the military when I got older. The country, on the whole, was still glowing in the aftermath of World War II, minus a slight set back after the Korean War. He wanted me to become a US Marine. I wanted to be a sailor and follow in his footsteps. (Ironically, I did neither and joined the US Army.) The pacifists in the family were all in the majority and those views later led to an estranged situation from the entire family for many years for me due to my fighting in the Vietnam War.

The next summer, I was returned back to my grandparents' home in time for my mother's final days. We lived at 654 21st Ave, in the Richmond District of San Francisco, home to me of my earlier years. I was able to visit her for the last few times and did not really recognize that frail woman in the hospital bed. She died that August 1959, to my grief and disbelief. My father was notified of his wife's passing and once again, it took several days for him to return home. My sadness and sense of loss followed me throughout my life.

My grandfather informed me of my mother's death at his chiropractic office on that overcast summer day. I recall him telling me that my beloved mother had *"...gone to sleep."* I was unsure what he meant, but managed to blurt out, "She's Dead!" I was numb and wanted to cry, but I recalled my macho upbringing and my father wanting me to become a brave Marine; I managed to hold back the tears until much later when I was alone. Like other events relating to death, I did not know how to act. I never learned to grieve.

This was true of my father's later death, grandparents' deaths, other family members dying; my daughter's and later my own wife's death. The combat deaths became blurred as well. I was not allowed to attend my mother's funeral. It was thought to be too much for me. I turned away from God in anger.

The overcast and foggy weather mirrored my internal mood at the time. I was happy to see my father, when he returned from sea, but he was never the same jovial man I originally knew as "Dad". My father would be in a downhill slide after my mother's passing until his own death in 1961.

The mood and lifestyle with my grandparents were a lot different than the upbeat mood and generally "fun" atmosphere that I had enjoyed with my cousins. My step-grandmother "Jessie" was my grandfather's physical therapist for years and I knew her as *"aunt"* Jessie. By the time they got married to raise me, she was in her seventies and my grandfather in his eighties.

I do not know a lot about Jessie,(aka Jessie McGregor Walker) other than she had been my grandfather's physical therapist for as long as he had his chiropractic practice and she was always involved with the family. As a child I merely knew her as "Aunt Jessie". She hailed from Glasgow, Scotland and was fiercely Scottish. I recall her teaching me 500 Rummy at a very early age and in a gentle way taught me how to be a good sport when she beat me at cards. She was quite the housekeeper after she moved into our house and had me do a lot of the things around the house to help. For example; I recall having to wax and polish the hardwood floors that were not covered by carpet. The garbage was always my responsibility, both to take the trash downstairs to the big can, and to take the large can out on the Tuesday trash day. It was required that I line the big garbage can with old newspapers when the can was brought in after being picked up.

Jessie loved me a lot in spite of my rebellious nature at times. This lady was always "proper" in her nature and actions. She was rather "plump" and had her waist length reddish-brown hair braided and pinned atop of her head. She always wore a veiled hat when out in public and wore white gloves. As far as I knew, she never married, nor had any children. Her past was always a secret to me.

Her older sister was Catherine Walker (aka Catherine McGregor Walker.). Catherine had led a very interesting life. She was a retired RAF officer, Nursing Corps who traced her career to before World War I. She spent most of the time in the Middle East to include tours in Egypt, Palestine, Trans Jordan, Iraq, Iran and Basra. She knew Lawrence of Arabia in person. She had many gifts from the royal households of kings Feisal & Farouq. Some of these gifts included silverware decorated by the process known as Damascus Silver in which the metal is blackened to create the design images on the metal. Her legacy included teaching the women in the various harems the basics of nursing, which became the Red Cross' equivalent, the Red Crescent of today in the Middle East. Her career saw her through World War II, and she retired after the war and immigrated to America to be closer to her sister, Jessie.

Catherine bought a large Victorian mansion on First Street in a tree-covered neighborhood in San Jose and ran a nursing home. That proud Victorian had a wooden porch which ran around ¾ of the house. There were several wicker rocking chairs out on the covered porch for the resident's leisure. I also recalled that there were two rooms that were converted to bath rooms which and boasted large clawed tubs and Jacuzzi pumps. Those bath rooms always smelled of mustard, sulphur or chlorine (after being cleaned.) We would go down to her place on weekends and help out where we could. I recall my grandfather, even at his advanced age, doing plaster work on that old place.

She would eventually sell that old Victorian and move up to San Francisco to be with her sister, Jessie. I learned years later that she was really the money power in the family. She died in1973 and unknown to me had an estate worth about ½ a million. Much of her worth came from the Middle Eastern artifacts, stamp and coin collections as well as the remainder of the funds from the sale of the San Jose property. Since she had no formal notarized will, the probate court found a very distant relative in England or Scotland and they got the estate proceedings. My aunt and uncle, the Arians, tried to get me the estate, but were unsuccessful.

Jessie always had reminders of our British heritage all around the house. For some reason, my grandparents had me use the name "Neil" instead of "Noel" to emphasize the British side of me. I did this through junior high school but reclaimed my French roots from the freshman year of high school on. Other examples of this Anglo mania were that we always had "Lyle's Golden Syrup" in the house. It was a thick golden syrup wonderfully delicious on pancakes, scones and English muffins. (Lyle's was also "…by appointment to the queen", making it an authentic Scottish product.) We would always have English butter cookies in the kitchen; but, I better not to get caught with my little hand in the colorful printed tin that the cookies came in. On occasions there was also an English beer snack, called "Twigs". They were somewhat like pretzels, but straight, bumpy, salty, with its unique taste. A souvenir plate of Queen Elizabeth's coronation stared out of the class china case in the dining room. The queen's image always seemed to be holding court in the dining room.

If there was a *"generation gap"* among my peers and their parents, mine was the Grand Canyon of gaps. They were very strict, and they did the best they could in raising me. I often resented their strictness and could not understand why my friends could do and get so much more than I. there was love abundant, yet I saw a much different home life than that of my childhood friends and neighbors. I was often scolded for expressing my feelings and views on many issues, both inside and outside the house. Perhaps this is why, even today, why I internalize so much.

Aside from my mother's death that year, the world saw Fidel Castro victorious in his revolution and he established the first communist regime in the Western hemisphere. Cuba is only 90 miles from the Key West in Florida and was perceived as a major threat to American security. Many Cubans fled the horrors of the revolution and established themselves in Miami, Florida as well as Cuban communities across the nation.

Alaska and Hawaii become the 49th & 50th states. Yasser Arafat establishes the militant revolutionary group al-Fatah, dedicating itself in establishing the Palestinian state and the destruction of Israel. Middle East tensions increase. We kids heard of all these events, but really did not understand them. The air raid drills continued, and our young ears always were attuned to the world's "next crisis". The Soviets launched an unmanned spacecraft, Luna 2 and hit the moon. We launched and retrieved the "space monkeys".

There was a rather bitter guardianship fight between my grandparents and my father's side of family for my future care. I mentioned this earlier for contrast. I was mainly kept in the dark over these proceedings. My views were basically that I did not want to be transplanted or passed off to others again. I remembered my stay with the Rush family and the cousins. I was drawn between the present security and the open and freer atmosphere enjoyed with my father's side of the family. To the best of my knowledge, this case was not finally resolved until closer to the time of my father's death about two years later.

My father's returns from sea became holidays for me, much akin to Christmas. He would shower me with toys and gifts. We were amazed at how ingenious the Japanese made such toys, mechanical, wind up, sound activated, and generally fascinating for young and old alike. He would go grocery shopping and bring home many treats that were forbidden under my grandparents rein. I was allowed root beer, ginger ale, the breakfast cereals of my choice. I recall a lot of good food as well from the old "Mom & Pop neighborhood delis and bakeries.

We would take weekend trips to Clear Lake, or to Monterey Bay, fishing at both. I loved being with him. Bed times were more to my liking when he was home. He would take me and my friends to the famous amusement park, the Whitney Brothers' Playland at the beach in San Francisco. A small fortune was spent on the "forbidden foods". Playland, to this kid, had the best burgers, hot-dogs, chili dogs, {which barked at night}, cotton candy, salt water taffy, corn dogs in all of "The City". We rode all the rides and played the games of skill and chance. This was before I knew that most "Carney" games were rigged.

I would admire the servicemen who were able to use their marksmanship skills to beat the carnies. I would always look forward to his return, just as I looked forward to his letters from the various ports of call. He always slipped a couple of dollars in the envelope, which I was not to show my grandparents. In many ways, he was spoiling me, often as a mask for his drinking.

I was a rebel in elementary school after my mother's death. At one point, I had to travel to the other side of town to see a school district child psychologist for my unacceptable behavior both in school and at home. All involved did not fully understand how the loss of my mother and my father's absence affected me. In the 3rd grade I was suspended for fighting. I became the toughest guy in school for cold cocking the resident *"bad ass"*. That event was forgotten over the years until my Army "Top Secret" clearance was returned with the notation that was suspended from school. I was not declared a national security risk over that incident that occurred in the 3rd grade.

I recall the integration of the races, not at lunch time, but on the school yard. It was not really until junior high school, did we see more integration of the student body. I could not understand why, when the neighborhood schools disappeared and in place was a vast transportation system; the races still ate separately at lunch. In the neighborhood we had many Oriental, Latin and other nationalities' families living the middle-class life style at the time. Those integrations seemed normal to me. This was not the simple racial truths I experienced that were demonstrated in other parts of the country in the early days of the Civil Rights movement.

For the most part, I walked to Elementary school, Jr. High School, and high school, when the weather was permitting. Public transportation was available to both my junior high school and sr. high school. When parents were available for a ride, we rode, and we did not have to walk.

I did not do very well in elementary school and continued to be a discipline problem. I was always told by my grandparents to "wait until your father gets home." Seldom was his justice carried out, although my grandparents dealt their brand of justice swiftly.

The space race was in its early years and I became very interested science at the time. I recall working on a large "mural" drawn on a roll of butcher paper in the hall of my schoolroom. I drew moonscapes, rockets, stars and scenes from other planets. As long as I stayed out of trouble, I was allowed to work on *my* project. Other pupils would help under my direction. I felt worthwhile and important. It seemed to work for the most part, the trips to the principal's office declined. I began to keep science scrap books with all the space news of the time. This creative distraction held my interest and lessened the disciplinary infractions for the time being.

The beauty of the neighborhood school system was that a child kept friends for a long time. Many times, these friendships lasted through high school graduation and beyond in life. We walked to and from school together, played after school together and had a general sense of community, to even include the parents. Often, if a kid misbehaved, the parents mysteriously knew about it even before the kid returned home. I have had friends all through the school years, from kindergarten through high school we remained together. Once in a while a family would move out of the neighborhood, and it seemed a great loss at the time. I often had dinner over at a friend's house and savored the different foods, from Oriental to Latin, as well as good 'ole American home cooking.

Most of my Japanese friends had fathers who served in the famed 442nd Infantry Regiment, the Nisei unit formed from out of the Japanese internment camps established at the start of WW II. While these brave young men fought throughout Europe; their families remained behind American barbed wire. The 442nd was one of the most highly decorated units of the European Theatre. They suffered heavy causalities rescuing an encircled Texan unit, known as "The Lost Division".

CHAPTER FOUR

It was a different world back then than it is today. Every neighborhood in San Francisco had within walking distance every store and service needed in those "modern" times. Within a four-square block area, we had the following available: A hardware store, a liquor store, a furniture store, a "fix-it man shop", a barber shop, seven grocery stores (only two had a butcher's counter), two dry cleaners / seamstress services, a TV repair shop and small electrical appliance repair, and one bar. Walk a few more blocks to Geary Street, and much more was available, without getting on the bus yet.

Neighborhood beat cops still walked their beats twirling their night sticks and periodically reporting in from those small blue call boxes scattered around the neighborhood. A horse-mounted cop stood guard at the elementary school. A short walk of a block and a half put me into the Golden Gate Park. On Sundays, my grandfather and I would walk to Strawberry Hill in Golden Gate Park, which was in the middle of Stow Lake. We would feed the ducks with stale bread and watch the boaters sail around the lake. I was told that the hill was made from the debris of the 1906 earthquake. There was also a man-made waterfall which flowed from the top of the hill where a city water reservoir was located. Often kids would pour laundry soap in the water and the "water-falls" became a "bubbles-fall". Somewhere in the general area, there was an old pair of marble columns and entrance to a long destroyed Victorian mansion from the '06 earthquake. It was called "The Portales of the Past", remembering the devastating earthquake. I often envisioned that, if I walked through these old columns, I would be transported into the past. It was my time machine. It, in reality only transported me to "lunch time" when a brown bag lunch was eaten.

The neighborhood kids would invade the park in-mass for our games and military maneuvers. We rode our bicycles everywhere, a few times, even across the Golden Gate Bridge to Sausalito for an afternoon of fishing. I have also walked the same route over the bridge.

The Municipal Railroad System (included all the busses, streetcars, cable cars, and trolley buses.) provided excellent transportation. For $ 0.15 one had two transfer privileges for connecting bus routes. One was never more than two blocks from any address in the city. The student card cost us $0.50 for ten rides with the transfer privileges as well. We could go anywhere in the city by walking, bicycling or taking the bus. Public transportation was always an opportunity for me to amusingly "people watch". The drunks and winos were always both annoying as well as comical. I often got stuck sitting next to the "sleeping drunk" on the bench seats, slipping over to my shoulder. It took my careful repositioning of him not to wake him up.

Many remnants of the war years remained during those days. We still were under the impression that a Soviet attack was inevitable. The city air-raid sirens were tested daily during the work week at 8:00 AM, 12 Noon and 5:00 PM, signaling the start of the work day, lunch time and quitting time, (to many, cocktails and happy hours). Church bells still rang out on Sunday morning, calling the faithful to worship. Today, I believe, they would violate the noise abatement ordinances. Perhaps some would try to sue the churches over the bells, and the nativity scenes at Christmas.

We still had air raid drills at school on a random schedule, especially after Sputnik's success. I found it amazing that we believed that if one got under his or her small school desk, one could survive a nuclear blast. (And earthquakes better that the '06 shaker.)The *curtain monitor* was instructed that when the air raid siren sounded, he or she was to get up and pull down the blackout shades, (these shades were used when movies were shown in the classroom.) to prevent the rest of the class from being blinded by the nuclear blast. The curtain monitor would have surely been blinded or killed before the curtain task was completed. This was an unlikely survival scenario.

There were supposedly military rations and 55-gallon barrels of water stored somewhere in the school. We never knew where to look, even if we survived. Our school did not have cafeteria service, at the time of those threats, so there were no other foodstuffs that we could raid. Perhaps, we could eat the dead kids' lunches. Armed with that survival information, I began burying gallon bottles of water in my back yard. I had a Japanese bayonet that my dad brought home from one of his overseas trips, a war souvenir, so I was ready for the Soviet invasion of San Francisco.

The daily routine at the house remained pretty much the same throughout the years. It was get up early in the morning and get ready for school. My grandfather had been long gone, headed to his chiropractic office 143 Fillmore St. It was located a couple of blocks from Haight St. of later 1960's fame, north of Dubose St., with the street car tracks and tunnel. Up on a hill above a supermarket was the San Francisco Mint. Safeway was one of the first supermarkets.

My grandfather was known to take the bus within approximately two miles of his office and walk the remaining distance every working day. By this time, the neighborhood in which his office was located was becoming a ghetto, as the once middle-class families moved out to the suburban developments. It took two buses to reach his office.

I hated the Saturday trips to the office, since I could not be left alone at the 21st Ave home, unless my grandmother was home. I would bring some toys to play with. My grandfather had a huge library in the office and I often found something of interest to read. He had many anatomical books with a lot of pictures that held both my interest and curiosity as a child. The anatomical charts on his walls graphically showed me the dissected human body. On a wall hung an actual human spine, which he used as a patient training aid when describing the spine to his patients. Saturday was usually the shopping day and laden with grocery bags my grandmother and I would take the two busses and trudge home. I hated my friends seeing me as a beast of burden.

As crime started to invade the ghetto, I often feared for my safety as new racial tensions and demographics arose. We (white folks) had become the minority in this changing neighborhood. I was glad when, years later my grandfather closed his Fillmore office and moved all to the "654" location. He "retired" at 90, but still saw occasional patients at home.

After eating a breakfast, laid out the night before by my grandmother,

I got ready for school and left through the "tradesman entrance" common in many of the houses in the city. When I finally had to get glasses, I would hide and leave the pair in that entrance to the house until I came home. I was reprimanded when my deception was unmasked by a well-meaning teacher who noted my constantly having to go up close to the blackboard to see clearly. I made it through the dreaded school day and looked forward to that 3:10 final school bell.

After school, I returned via the same route and changed into my "play" clothes. If my grandmother was not at home yet, I was to call my grandfather to let him know that I was home safely. I was to do any homework and household chores before going out to play with my friends, and usually had to wait until my Grandmother got home. I was allowed to play outside, providing that I let my grandmother know who I was with, what were we going to do, and if need be where we were going. Now, to a kid, that was an opportunity for some creative story telling. In those days, for the most part, we could stay out until the sun went down or until dinner was ready, always subject to change. My grandmother would summon me home with a brass Indian temple bell. I caught plenty of flack and teasing from my friends over that. Somehow, none of my friends wound up on milk cartons. That "missing" tactic came much later.

We kids kept busy with a vast amount of activities. There were always our bicycles, wagons, scooters, coasters, as well as those whose parents gave them the coveted "Flexi" wheeled sled to ride. Many times, if we were not riding we were building and "customizing" our bicycles. We were always on the lookout for new construction sites or a remodeling project and a debris box for scrap wood and anything else for our construction projects. A wagon or two would be dispatched to pick up our spoils. It never was a crime, in those days, to pick up scrap.

There was a host of "street" games we played, such as: baseball, football, hand ball, (until the apartment residents shooed us away.) We played: "tag" hide and seek, (with neighborhood limits.), dodge ball, "monkey" in the middle, keep away, running bases, "stair baseball", (until the neighbor, whose stairs we were using complained.) "Red Rover", catch (both baseball and football versions) and two squares. We also had races with our various vehicles, usually around the block. Then there were always the traditional foot races, sprints as well as a predetermined distance, or course. The kids of those days always seemed to be doing something physical, always in motion. Television altered that picture as more and more families got television sets into their homes.

I recall one time that I both became a neighbor legend (and later in a lot of trouble). I had this sturdy wagon that my father had made for me. I had nailed a big juice can to the bottom rear of the wagon punched holes in the bottom of the can, which faced forward, and filled it with rags soaked in a flammable liquid. I then pushed my "rocket wagon" to the top of the hill at the end of the block. We posted a "road guard at the bottom of this hill at the cross street as was the practice when we were coasting down the hill. He would stop any cars as we shot across the intersection. I lit my "rocket fuel" and headed down the hill with huge colorful flames shooting out of the back of my wagon much to the awe and amazement of my friends. (And to the horror of a motorist who had stopped at the intersection as this kid, on a flaming wagon, shot across the intersection.)When word of my exploits reached my grandparents, I was severely punished. (It was still cool.)

When television was first introduced on the block, only a couple of the well-off families had the new invention. In response we kids, became like nomadic wanderers, going to the house that had a TV and whose parents allowed the living room invasion. Depending on which program we choose, determined whose house we went to. It took several years until the TV became commonplace on the block. For the most part, radio still reigned supreme; the transistor portable radio (usually made in Japan) extended radio's rein a little longer.

When I finally was "called home" by my grandmother for dinner I had to remain in the house. (Some exceptions were granted in the summer time after dinner to go out again) I had to set the table and any other kitchen tasks assigned. There was always the garbage to take down and on the evening before collection, put the can out. We also bundled up the old newspapers and tied the bundle with string. (Yes, we kept a "ball of string".) That was the extent of our re-cycling in those days, other than calling the "scrap" man to haul off discarded appliances, or us kids roaming the neighborhoods looking for soda bottles, which were worth $0.03 each and $0.05 for the larger sized bottle at the corner stores. I usually had some free time before my Grandfather came home for dinner.

Unless I was needed in the kitchen, then it was off to my room for some free time.

We would welcome my grandfather home. I was often the "lookout" for my grandmother, announcing my grandfather's progress down the block from the bus stop. Once we had washed up and my grandfather had settled in, dinner was served. There were practically no prepared foods. We usually had soup and / or salad, a main course and at times dessert. I would be quizzed about school, current events and how my day, in general, went. There were always these family discussion times always followed by the evening news on the radio. We had two radios.

When dinner was done, dishes cleared washed, we retreated to the living room for the evening radio entertainment. I recall some of these popular broadcasts: "The Shadow" (re-runs), "The Lone Ranger", "Dragnet", as well as the musical and variety programs broadcast live from "Top of The Mark", "The Conga Room" "The Tonga Room" and other popular night spots and restaurants in "The City".

At that time my grandfather would retreat to read the evening paper. He would mark articles he liked, cut them out and save them. If I had no chores to do, I was free to disappear to my room. All homework was inspected, and if it was a "no-go" it had to be redone. I had very bad cursive writing and was always rewriting my work. Even to this day, I print all my writing.

Over time I came to hate the multiplication "flash" cards and the chalk board that I had to master. I never became proficient in, nor liked math much. There were always plenty of books available in the house and at a young age. I love to read. It used to bother me that if I did not understand a word and asked what it meant, I was told to "look it up" on the huge dictionary that we had, which sat on its own special stand in the living room. That edition of the unabridged dictionary must have weighed as much as I did at the time. If I was doing a writing assignment for school and did not know how to spell a word; I was told to "look it up". This response, to me did not make any sense. If I did not know how to spell it, how could I look it up? The standard response was "sound it out". English phonetics is not that easy. Then for me, it was, once again off to the monster dictionary. (Today, thank God and Microsoft for "spell-check". It is how I got this far in this narrative.

When my mother was still alive, and I was just starting kindergarten, she bought the complete set of the World Book Encyclopedias (and subsequent Year Books). I would spend many hours merely reading and looking at the many pictures, from each volume, "A' to "Z". Those precious volumes would last through high school. (I always had to embarrassingly, site my information / references with those, outdated encyclopedia's information.) My mother instilled a sense of the importance of a good education that did not really take hold until high school, when I took her advice seriously.

I grew up on plenty of the "Tom Swift" and "Hardy Boys" novels at the time. The girls enjoyed the "Nancy Drew" mystery series just as much. I guess those were the "Harry Potter" series of that time. They all encouraged children to read more. Comic books, on the other hand, became our mainstay. My comic books and my baseball cards would have come in handy in my retirement, supplementing or providing a retirement nest egg. Had they been kept I would be rich now.

Some progressive parents had the children read for a given amount of time, before they could even watch television. To my recollection, the TV did not become the "electronic babysitter" until much later. A few years later we got an old Hoffman TV. It was complete with AM / FM radio and record player from my cousin's family. It was a monstrous device in a massive hardwood cabinet. Two cabinet doors were closed when the set was not in use. (In a subsequent TV set, a modern floor model, my grandmother would cover the screen with a prayer rug at the end of the viewing evening at night so that "they" couldn't see us.)

The Hoffman had a 12-inch screen and, it seemed that it had a hundred glowing tubes inside, once the set "warmed up". If any one of those critical tubes blew out, a frantic call was made to our neighborhood TV repairman. He must have done quite well in those days. Even the supermarkets got into the act and had "tube testers" installed in the stores, so one could bring in the questionable tubes and test them free of charge. Needless to say, they could sell you a replacement from their limited stock. A store clerk with his key had to open the cabinet to get you the new tube.

We had no remotes in those days. I was the remote for my grandparents. Later when the remote was introduced, it was an audio activated device emitting a "clicking" sound as each different function was pressed on the hand set, ergo: "the Clicker" as another name for the remote. Those old TVs had "rabbit" ear antennas, which were always under adjustment by this "remote". Whenever one of those telescoping arms broke, a wire coat hanger would serve as an antennae (sometimes serving better than the original.) until a new one could be purchased. I soon learned that I too, could be an antenna. By holding on to the antennae, I could alter the reception of the TV set. (I was impressed.)

There are many programs which aired during those early days of television, that are classic today. I do not recall all of them. My grandparents were pretty strict on my viewing. The following are some of the programs that I recall. They are presented in no particular order, chronological order or in any kind of preference order on my part. (**Refer to the Appendix, Notes & Timelines for the complete list.**)

I am quite sure that that list is not complete and may be expanded in the future. As one can see, these shows have become classics over the years. There were many more programs as I got older and watched when access to my own TV had been provided. I do not recall the exact times or days that these were broadcast. The same goes for which network these were shown on. Perhaps a bunch of old TV Guides would sort those questions out.

Sundays were always a change of pace for our household. My grandfather, or my father, when he was home, would cook a huge breakfast. I recall a large iron skillet platter would be placed over all four burners on the old Wedgewood gas stove. That stove had a firebox on the right side which was always fired up to keep the cooked food warm and heat the kitchen. They would make pancakes, eggs, sausage and bacon. The kitchen would be a symphony of sizzling, popping, snapping and hissing indicating breakfast was well on its way. There would be toast or toasted English muffins. At times, fresh pastries straight from the bakery would be a welcome treat. The coffee was brewed in the old percolator coffee pot on the top of the stove, filling the room with the smell of strong coffee. Maple syrup came in a tin can in the shape of a log cabin. (Log Cabin brand, of course). The syrup was heated and mixed with fresh butter (before Mrs. Butterworth brand came out). After breakfast, I would listen to the radio show "Big John and Sparkie". The radio characters would read the Sunday paper's comic section while we kids would follow along, paper in hand. The kitchen always seemed to be the social and domestic center of the family. (When my sons were little we tried to keep those Sunday traditions going, giving my wife a break on Sunday.) The rest of the Sunday would be dedicated to the various chores, tasks and projects left over from that week. Sometimes Sunday was lazy, on others very busy.

Dinners on Sundays were often a more of a traditional affair, that is to say fried chicken, or some other style of chicken, mashed potatoes and vegetables. Today, I must agree with the Southern saying that a chicken was the "gospel bird", served on Sunday after the gospel meeting or church service. In those times, there were very little prepared foods. Most all of what we ate was made from scratch from soups & salads to desserts.

TV dinners came much later, not in use in our house, but were with my cousins. They had the traditional 1950's "TV tray / table. That was a big contrast to what I was used to, in that the TV could not be turned on during dinner in my house. The strict rule at mealtime was "eat it all or go hungry and no dessert." Drink after the meal, not with it. Bread was not usually served, unless French garlic bread with spaghetti.

The only other variations for meals came when my father was home, and I was treated to a "drive-in" for lunch. The favorites in the city for us were either: "Hals" or "Mel's", on lower Geary Street, located towards the huge Sears & Roebucks store, on Divisadero St.; at the base of College Hill, before heading down Geary St. towards downtown. On occasion, a stop at the "Doggie Diner" was in order.

Lunches during the school days for me, usually consisted of peanut butter and jelly / preserve sandwiches, a fruit and a sweet roll or raisin snail. It was not until Junior High School and Sr. High School that I was allowed to buy my lunch at school. We paid weekly for milk at school, for the morning break and lunch. This was way before the Federal lunch programs. In both Jr. & Sr. High schools there were "mom & pop" stores nearby where we could buy sandwiches, sodas and other treats. I seldom had the money for these luxuries until the start of high school, by which time I was working part-time.

CHAPTER FIVE

Other things kept me busy in those early days before high school. Our back yard was always my domain. I did almost all of the cultivating, pruning and care of the many plants out back there. The larger branches and tree stumps made for lots of firewood for the house. There was a plum tree and several acacia trees that every year had to be trimmed and pruned.

I found an interest in caring for these plants and at times, experimented with grafting one flower type to another and was amazed at what developed. (Some of my hybrids are probably still there). One of my chores was to clean the fireplace in the living room and the firebox of the old Wedgewood kitchen stove. For years, those ashes were turned over in the ground, along with the leaves and garden debris. The soil out there became very rich compared to the sand dune that the house was built on. We were able to raise vegetables in the backyard. It was always a treat when our vegetables were harvested for dinner. They always tasted better than the "store-bought" varieties. I planted many "Victory" gardens out back during those years.

The plum tree, in the center of the backyard, provided bushels of fruit every year. My grandmother would prepare preserves and jellies from the plum harvest. In spring time, the plum tree was ablaze in bright blossoms, rivaling the "Cherry Blossoms" celebrated elsewhere.

I always seemed to be digging out there. I would dig "foxholes" and make "forts" for the war games that my friends and I would wage out there. Those holes were often filled in with throw-away things from the house and garage cleaning projects. (Archeologists in the future will have much to study from our era from my back yard.) The little green army men of my time left the same mysterious relics as the "Legos" of today, left buried in many countless yards.). There also was an old hen house out in the very back corner of the yard that dating back to the depression years, when chickens and rabbits could be raised within the city limits, it too, became a part of our area of operation during our war games.

There was a clothes line pole made from a sturdy 6x6 pole, about15 feet tall, complete with sturdy climbing rungs, or so, that was next to the "hen house". At one time, clothes were put out to dry from my bedroom window as there were pulleys at both ends as well as a rope clothes line. (This set-up would later serve as an antennae mast for my future radio projects.) The acacia trees obscured the top of the pole, so it became an excellent "lookouts' post "for us, keeping a constant vigil out for our enemies imaged or real as well as the rest of the neighborhood back yards.

When I was very young, I recall my father bringing home a big white duck, named "Donald Dina". She had free reign in the back yard. I do not remember what happened to that duck, but I do know that she kept the yard free of the snails. He also brought home a black cocker spaniel mutt, who was a stowaway on the ship. We named the dog "Buck", as he was found on the USNS Buckner. One time, much to my mother's horror, I painted that dog yellow because I wanted a lion after I had been taken to see a circus. We kept that dog until I left for Belmont and my cousins. I remember being caught sharing and eating dog treats with the dog. (My teeth were kept clean though.) Years later, my father went down to Chinatown and rescued two chickens from becoming Kung Pao Chicken.

The chickens earned the free run of the back yard. The "chicken droppings" that I cleaned up made for great fertilizer. They were named "Whitey" and "Goldie" after their coloring. These two hens provided brown eggs for us. I was responsible for their care and feeding. Those brown eggs were very rich in flavor and provided a welcome break from the "Store-bought" eggs that I was used to. We kept those hens for a couple of years, until the neighbors complained. These hens were donated to the San Francisco Zoo. I do not know of their fate after their delivery.

Other bits and pieces of these early years continue to flood back to me. My mother would often take old toys away from me, when the new ones appeared. Later, if I was good, the old ones would be magically reappearing to me. Old friends and I would be reunited. It was like being at a re-union with old friends all again and Christmas all rolled into one.

In those days every neighborhood had a "Five & Dime" store. It was like a mini-mini Wal-Mart and Dollar Tree rolled into in one. They seemed to have everything a household could need. They would stock sewing notions, household cleaning supplies, cloth, hardware, tools, and toys. On occasion, my mother and I would venture down to our local "Five & Dime" on Geary St. for something that was needed for the household. Once in a while she would buy me a small toy, usually a painted lead toy soldier (of WW I era.) or a plastic dinosaur. Today those toy soldiers are worth a lot.

I think just about every young boy goes through the "dinosaur stage". We became fascinated with these ancient animals. A collection of these beasts soon grew in numbers in a variety of sizes. They could be found in plastic, wax or rubber. I had several books on the subject and read all that I could on dinosaurs. My mother would encourage this phase of my interests also to include other fields of science. (I guess it was from her proof reading of scientific books.)

One Christmas, after my parents had died, I got a chemistry set from my other relatives, and coupled with the microscope and slides that my father had made for me earlier, I became a scientist. I learned a lot and in retrospect should have pursued those interests. I also do recall producing smells that were quite offensive. I also made a color solution that when poured on a burning fire, produced a rainbow of different colors as the chemicals soaked into the wood and burned in the fireplace. Luckily, I had not made any explosives.

At other times, I was a builder and engineer, building wonderful creations with the following "must have" toys of the 1950's & early 1960's: Tinker Toys, Lincoln Logs and the white building blocks that were similar to Legos, but not as big, Castle Blocks I believe they were called. That set contained, in addition to the basic blocks: green cap pieces, clear blocks to simulate the glass mason blocks popular in the 1950's, "L" shaped foundation pieces and green window pieces. Then there was the ever popular "Erector Set", complete with small electric motors to power a variety of machines. One could build a functional Ferris wheel. The Erector Set was assembled with small bolts, nuts and screws.

There was even tin castle set which was assembled with small metal fold tabs which joined the walls of the castle. My grandfather cut wood to fit inside the castle walls to strengthen the castle and then mounted it on a board. He also built a box to house this wonder and put away when it was not in use. I had a huge collection of toy knights and "Robin Hood" plastic figures to provide hours of play. All of these toys were not only very entertaining they sparked the young imaginations and prompted creativity. I somehow never went into the sciences. (at least until I went into nursing at age 53.)

Another element in developing my imagination and creativity, when I was much older, was model building. My father used to build ship and army armor models. I preferred to build model cars. (a hobby I still enjoy today.) The most popular was the AMT 1/25th scale series that offered the builder the option to build the model one of three ways: stock, custom or competition versions. The beauty of these model kits was twofold; one could mix or match the parts to create a model car that was totally unique and by saving the extra parts one could add to the next kit for an even more unique creation. I would often collect all three of the same year and make and make all three versions. The ample decal sheets could also be saved and used on subsequent projects.

A more expensive version was made all in metal; hence AMT meant "all metal toys" in that with fully rotating wheels and a functional steering wheel. They actually could be used as a toy instead of just a display model. Later on, I built the most expensive model kit, the 1/8th "Big 'T' 1925 Ford Model "T" bucket hot rod roadster. I did not stop until I entered the Army and gave my entire collection away, along with all my childhood toys. I even gave away all of my baseball card collection, which in today's dollars could have aided in funding my retirement. I did not pick up this hobby again until I was in my 50's and in rehabilitation. That collection was also given away. Today I am just starting that hobby and collecting over. To my shock, those model kits that cost $1.49 when I was a kid, now cost $20.00 or more in today's dollars. The young sales clerk looked at me as if I was the village idiot when I told him that. It all costs more to assemble these model kits when one considers paint, glue, tools and accessories. It still is something that I enjoy today and hope to continue in the future.

CHAPTER SIX

More stuff from the deep memory vaults:

The Fog Horns were always haunting sounds of the city. When the thick fog rolled in, the fog horns would signal a warning to the ships passing in and out of the Golden Gate Straits. They would sing their mournful sound. The "Papa" (which was on our side of the bay.) would sound his long bass sound: BOOOOOO…Ya. The "baby" would sound off from the far side of the bay a few seconds later with his Beee,OP….. Beee…O. At times the concert would go all night long. GPS and improved radar ended all that. I still miss those vanished sounds, as I miss the haunting train whistle sounds.

Everybody paid cash back then for just about everything. There were no credit cards or debit cards in those days. Checks were written usually for those bills that had to be mailed or in rare occasions when one did not have enough cash in hand. It seemed that most services for the house came in person to collect either at the end of the month or within the first few days of the new month. They all seemed to arrive on our doorstep around dinnertime, as the telemarketers of today, to interrupt the evening meal. The newsboys collected by themselves and it was only when the account became <u>very</u> past due did his manager pound on the door.

We used to leave our dry cleaning and special laundry (dress shirts, table cloths, napkins, blouses, etc.) in a white mesh laundry bag that the Chinese laundry man would pick up a couple of times a week. "No tickee, no laundry", he would greet us with, because at his shop that was the unwritten rule. He would show up right on time to collect his bill.

The large Italian "garbage-a-man", would collect for his due. (Sunset Scavengers, in the Richmond). He was too intimidating to refuse. I do believe some Mafia connection, in that there were only two garbage companies in the city at the time and we got the Italians. The Borden's milk man also collected in person.

We used a "flag" system placed on the porch in an empty milk bottle. There were multiple little flip up flags in the shape of a "key" with a smiling cut-out of "Elsie" the cow. One could order just about every dairy product in this manner. One could order eggs, milk, and chocolate milk, quarts or half gallons, yogurts, cream, whipping or half & half, butter, etc.; special orders had to be called in advance. Notes were usually included indicating the quantities requested, rather redundant, but very effective at the time. If one subscribed to the "Dy-Dee" wash service, he too would be at the door to collect. Any other vendors or service men who advanced any credit would be there as well. (My Scottish grandmother never used the cursed credit to the best of my knowledge.).

Shopping in general was always done with cash. Many times, I would be sent to the store up the block with a pocket full of change to pay for my purchase. My grandmother had a keen memory for what the grocer was charging, and I seldom returned with any change. (Perhaps, I kept a few pennies, but never a nickel or bigger.) The mortgage, the utilities, water, my father's car payment, insurance and any other major expense were all paid for with a check.

Telephone service back then was like something out of the Flintstones compared to today's cell, smart phones, and other telephonic services. In those days people have not grown that extra appendage growing out of their head, nor stared down at their moving fingers madly flying over a small screen.

We were on a "party line", meaning that several households shared a common phone line instead of an exclusive private dedicated line. When one wished to make a call, one would have to first check to see if anybody else was on the line. If the line was clear, one could proceed to place their call. Any important or emergency calls were always allowed after a friendly apology.

I still remember the phones and the phone numbers of my childhood. All the phone numbers in the city had a prefix, which was sounded as an actual word, such as: KLondike, SKyline, and EVergreen, Mission, FIllmore, etc. Those "prefixes" were the number of the Dial Central Office for that area or neighborhood. Our first number was simply BAview 6715. That number was dialed 22-6715. It was later expanded to BAview-1-6715, dialed as 221-6715. Many years later the area code was added to the number and the simple 22-6715 became 415-221-6715.

There were no "911" or "411" numbers in those days. There was no speed dialing or voice mail either. The operator was needed to summon the police, fire service or to send an ambulance. One could also have the operator connect you directly with the desired number, it would go like this: "Operator, please give me BAyview 6715." Operator assisted calls cost a little more. If you needed an unknown number, the operator was called, and she would transfer the caller to the "directory assistance operator" who looked up the needed number.

Toll calls were measured and charged by the distance from the originating phone. For example, calls to the East Bay or down the peninsula were "toll" calls for us. Long distance was, again, measured by the distance to the receiving city, and the operator would assist in making those calls by getting the main switchboard for the distant city. After many years, we got our own private line and gone was the party line, which made eavesdropping as easy as simply picking up the receiver very gently and listening. One had to be very watchful of any background noise which would expose the eavesdroppers. Above all, there was only one phone company, today known as "Ma-Bell" nation-wide. The regional variants were Southern Bell, Mountain Bell, etc., as well as all the other regional units. Ours was Pacific Bell or "Pac-Bell".

The telephone was central to both the family as well architecture of the time. Phones connected families and friends. No E-mail or Facebook in those days. Social networking was always done in person. To "delete" someone, one simply took the phone off of the cradle, so that any caller would only get the "busy" signal.

Most houses, flats and apartments all had a "phone nook" built into the design of the structure. The nook could be as simple as a corner shelf which held the phone or something a bit more elaborate. Many houses had a phone nook similar to ours. It consisted of a small shelf built into the wall which held the phone and your own small private phone book. Above that there was another cabinet which held the large city phone book. Lastly, there was a small seat that pulled out of the wall so one could sit down to use the phone. Some houses had a very elaborate "phone nook" almost like having a "mini" phone booth of one's own.

The phones of my childhood were the old rotary dial type. They were upright with the dial facing forward at a convenient angle. They were heavy as well. Each number was dialed on a circular dial in a clockwise direction. One would remove the finger from the hole for that number and let the dial return to its original position automatically. The phones seldom came with enough wire. It seemed as if we were tethered like a dog on a short chain. Since the caller could not often move too far away from the phone, the "phone nook" was stocked with a note pad and a pen or pencil. Our pencil was on a string attached to the wall.

The central telephone office had the "X" "Y" mechanical switching systems. While dialing, the caller would hear the traditional: "Whoosh… click, click, click…ta, ta ta…" as the rotors clicked into place and selecting the dialed number at the Dial Central Office. This process would be repeated until the entire number was completed.

When out of the house, phone calls were not as easy to make as today. First, one had to find a pay phone or phone booth. Both were abundant, but it always seemed, never when one had to make an important call or an emergency arose. One would also hope to have enough change in one's pocket or purse to make the given call.

For the longest time, local calls were only a thin dime, hence the expression "…it's your dime." That is an expression that is still in use today. Those old pay phones would take nickels, dimes and quarters. As the coins were dropped into the correct slot, there were emitted from the phone a series of bells and "clanks" as the coins were registered. If one was short the mechanical voice of a female operator would come on the line and inform the caller: "please deposit another fifty cents for the next three minutes." and so on. A person, if caught short, could request from the operator that the call be billed to another number, such as a home or business number providing the phone bill of the requested number was paid to current. One could also make collect calls, but they had to begin with a dime. Now phone service is right in the palm of your hand. The odd thing is that in many ways "texting" has replaced talking. I guess the loss of the art of conversation is upon us.

San Francisco boasted many newspapers during my childhood. We got the bulk of the news in print form. We subscribed to the evening paper. (Its name changed as some papers merged with another, while some merely went bankrupt.) The newspapers were competing with that new device, the television for the news. Today there are only two main papers: The Chronicle, (morning) and the Examiner, (evening). The papers that I recall are many. **(Listed in their entirety in the Appendix.)**

Also available were all of the major newspapers from every major city in the United States as well as the world. Some received these other papers in the mail and were not as current as the local papers. Some people kept up their tradition of reading the monstrous New York Times, (Sunday edition) over a Sunday Brunch, or curled up in bed on a foggy Sunday morning.

Hundreds of *"newsies"* or commonly known as 'newspaper boys' delivered most of the major papers all over the city. When I was older, I also delivered papers for my friends. (I charged a nominal fee, of course.)I was not always up-front with my grandmother as how much I had earned. The Sunday editions were big. We "assembled" them on Friday with all the advertisements and inserts. The actual "news" was added early Sunday Morning.

At those times, we all were well read and to augment the above newspapers, there were hundreds of magazine and trade journals available. There were several major book publishing houses located in "The City" and around the Bay Area.

There are so many things that are no longer a part of the contemporary scene. Another such thing is the "door to door" salesman". I recall many of these people doing, just that, door to door selling. The two most iconic and recognized of these are "The Fuller Brush Man", and the (Bing Bong)... "Avon Lady". Then there were the others: "The Vacuum Cleaner Man", "The Book Salesman", "Encyclopedia Salesman" "Insurance Salesman", "The Jehovah's Witnesses" (I had no idea then what they were selling, those pamphlets, I guess.) They still go door to door today. They would talk their way into your living room and began to show and demonstrate their products. In the case of the Jehovah's Witnesses, they attempted a theological discussion on the porch. Many times, the housewife would buy the product merely to get rid of the sales person. It was a good tactic for its day. When they came to my door there would be an awkward exchange that went something like this.

The Door Bell Rings!

Salesman: "Hello sonny, I'm here to show our new line of products, I'm with ACME, is your mommy home?"
Me: "No, she's dead."
Salesman: "Oh, I am so sorry to hear that"
Me: "That's OK."
Salesman: "Well then young man, is your father at home?"
Me: "No, he's still out to sea."
Salesman: "Oh, he's in the Navy?"
Me: "No, MSTS".
Salesman:" Hum mm ... Well then are you home alone?"
Me: "No"
Salesman: "You must be with the babysitter then."
Me: "NO, I'm too old for a baby sitter."
Salesman: "Ok, sonny who is at home that I can talk to?"
Me: "My grandmother."
   (Off in the distance from the back of the house, my
      grandmother shouts "Who's at the door?")
Me: (Turning away from the salesman, answering my grandmother)
   "It's some guy with ACME! He's selling something."
      (Off in the distance: "Tell him to go away. We
         don't want any; *And close the door.*")
Me: "Ok, My grandmother says that we don't want any."
Salesman: "But, but, well...."
Me: "Thank you..." I close the door.

That is to say, no sale that day for that salesman from our household, although at times my grandmother would entertain the Avon lady. Today those methods of sale are rare. Most of that is done on line today and when a salesman comes to your door, more than likely, you invited him / her to do so. (Fill out any surveys lately?)

Other merchants of sorts came into our neighborhood in the form of a "drive-by". Oh, not the shooting and killing type, they were mobile vendors. There was quite a variety of these entrepreneurs. These were my favorites. There was still the "Ice Man", dressed in leather, carrying the blocks of ice with huge ice tongs to his various customers, or he would sell a block of ice to you for your party if you asked. There was also an ancient open, but canvas covered flatbed truck which would drive slowly down the street. Mounted on the back were several grinding wheels. On the sides he displayed new cutlery. This man would be the "Sharp Man". He would call out in a very loud and deep voice announcing his arrival and his products. The neighbors would come to him to have their knives, shears, scissors, and lawn mowers and any other tool that needed a new sharp edge put on it. He went to work with fervor and a bead of sweat on his brow. We kids would be fascinated by the wall of sparks that he generated.

There were also produce vendors, patrolling the neighborhoods selling farm fresh fruits and vegetables. Another salesman drove in the same slow ritualistic manner harping "Fresh Berries, fresh berries here... Got all kinds here...Farm Fresh... Got Raspberries, Raspberries!!"

We called him, of course "The Raspberry Man". As he passed we would give him a big "raspberry", commonly known as "The Bronx Cheer". PUSSSSSSTTTTTT! (Or however one spells the sound of that famous cheer.) There was also a unique guy that arrived with a pickup truck and a horse trailer, usually on a weekend in the summer. He would set up at the end of the block, his camera equipment, and then unload a saddled pony and clothing rack loaded with an array of Western / Cowboy & Indian costumes. We could also dress up on our own. We would bring our parents (guardians) with a dollar or so in order that we get our photo taken posing as a Cowboy or Indian. This guy was so cool, and he even cleaned up the pony droppings!

Today, we put out our specially designed garbage cans and re-cycle cans. On present day collection day, the truck drove by and with its large mechanical arm, picked up the can and dumped it into the belly of the truck.

We had very large, smelly and open prehistoric red dinosaurs as our garbage trucks. The cab was open with a pair of stairs on each side behind the driver leading up to the large platform which faced the walled bed of the truck. The garbage men, wearing long leather knee length aprons and leather gloves, would go down the street with a very large wheeled can, pick up our smaller garbage cans and dump it into his large can. One man worked on each side of the street. He would do this for several houses and then return to the truck. Then he would let out a horrible grunt and climb the stairs to the platform and dump his large heavy can into the belly of the beast. Often riding atop of the garbage was a guy who raked the recent dumps to the back of the truck. At times, a strong smell followed both the truck and its crew.

In the summer, the flies also followed the trucks. Only the most daring of seagulls attempted to rob from that garbage truck. These men had to be very big and muscular to do this labor-intensive work. It seemed that it only took this team a few minutes to cover one block. They usually made their rounds very early in the morning. I think that it was company policy of sorts that they had eight hours to make their rounds and when done they could go home, regardless of how long it took. I think some held two jobs because they were so quick making their pick-ups. It was no wonder that the garbage bill was always paid on time after seeing these he-men work. We also made fun of their thick Italian accents, but never in their presence, for the above reason.

Another wonder of my early days was the "Street Sweepers", (not the mechanical street Zambonies of today), who usually made it every other week or so, following the garbage collection days. A pickup truck (Probably driven by a supervisor.) would drive slowly ahead of the sweepers with large cans in the back to pick up the sweepings and any other debris left in the street. The whole crews were city workers because of the city markings on the doors of the pickup truck. These guys were usually black men who worked one side of the street each. It was fun to hear them joke and carry on as they rhythmically swept the street. They would often stop and talk briefly and kindly to us kids, as they kept an eye on the pickup. These were the first black people I recall ever meeting. They were armed with big stiff brooms with longer than normal bristles and a wide shovel that they kept on the truck until they were ready to pick up their sweepings. Attached to the base platform of the broom was a bent piece of angle metal, used as a scraper. The sweeping made a distinct sound caused by those stiff brooms. It was only in the downtown areas at that time did the monstrous street sweeping trucks patrol the city streets. These trucks eventually took over the entire city, and I guess these guys were out of work.

I was introduced to national politics during the 1960 presidential campaign between John F. Kennedy and Richard Nixon. (It was a lot different than the 1956 days of "I Like Ike"!) I recall watching the presidential debates with the family, not fully comprehending what was going on and where there was confusion of my part, and my grandparents tried their best to clarify things for me. At this time, I thought that if Nixon was Vice President once, he would make a good president. (Needless to say, years later when I was able to vote at 18, I was surely fooled.) Leonid Brezhnev became the president of the Soviet Union and JFK became the elected US President. "Tricky Dick", the loser sort of sulked off into the political sunset. "You won't have Richard Nixon to kick around anymore." that he was once quoted as saying. (He would emerge years later.)

One of our high flying new "spy" planes, the U-2 was shot down over the Soviet Union and its pilot, Francis Gary Powers was captured. The Soviets threatened to put him on trial and possibly execute him as a "spy" I thought we were going to go to war over this incident. Later he would be exchanged for a Soviet spy that we held, Rudolf Abel.

The Irish Republican Army is formed and begins its guerrilla war in Northern Ireland against British rule. It becomes a religious war, Catholics against Protestants in addition to the political goals. I did not understand this at all because I had family roots that were of English, Scottish and Irish decent. I knew of the Protestants, but the Catholics were like the kids that went to the Catholic schools in the neighborhood. They were like me, except they wore corduroy pants, a shirt and tie, sometimes a sweater that had an embroidered emblem on the chest to school. I could not understand why people hated each other over this difference. Northern Ireland was quite more complicated than my simple observation in the neighborhood.

The civil rights movement was growing in the nation and as a child in San Francisco, a non-segregated city; I could not understand the conditions in the South. Some descriptions of the protests, "sit-ins", "freedom riders" and all the civil unrest seemed to be something from a foreign country, not my America. Too many, me included; it came as a cultural shock when we first traveled in the South. (For me, years later, when I was in the Army all this was realized. It seemed like I was traveling in another time and another country.) Some of the racial identity then remains clouded as what the correct term for those of African descent. What should we white folk use and not offend anybody? (Negro, Colored, Black, African-American) The "N" word usually was reserved for the word *no* and did not for us have the same connotation as it does today.

Although I was not quite aware of "the birds & the bees' at the time, I learned many years later that the contraception pill was developed that year and simply became known as "The Pill".

I was aware of some of the history of the Holocaust and the Nazi horrors and the death camps (We had next-door neighbors who were survivors of the camps.). That year Israeli agents captured SS officer Adolf Eichmann in South America. He was returned to Israel and stood trial for his war crimes. He was convicted and later he was hung in 1962.

In the late summer of 1961 in August, my father came home from the ship and I thought it would be just like any of his other homecomings. This one would prove to be different. I did not know that he was on administrative leave, pending his termination hearing. His ship had sailed without him. He had missed a ship's sailing, similar to a soldier missing a troop movement. He was basically AWOL from duty.

He would be terminated from the MSTS for his drinking. At first it all seemed normal and that evening proved quite different. He came home drunk and continued to drink. He got into a major argument with my grandparents. Things quieted down after a while and I came out of my room to join the family. He would get up and leave for a while and return. His breath was a strong smell of bourbon with each trip out of the room. The rest of the evening went uneventful. I went to bed that night hoping all would be well in the morning.

I recall getting up early the next morning and as I went out to meet my friends, I saw my father still sitting in the tan leather chair that he was sitting in the night before. It was not until later that morning that my friends and I saw the ambulance and the police cars in front of my house. I knew then that something was not right. I could not go into my house at that time. Later, when the police and medics left, and I was informed that my father was dead. I was nine years old and both parents were dead.

My world collapsed. We, as a nation, also survived the "Bay of Pigs" crisis in Cuba. I would survive as well.

In June of 1962, four men attempted an escape from the Federal prison on Alcatraz Island, known as "The Rock," in the middle of the San Francisco Bay. One never left the island. Three convicts made it off of the island. They were Clarence Anglin, his brother, John Anglin and their buddy, Frank Morris. All the law enforcement and the Coast Guard searched the bay and surrounding land for these dangerous escapees. They were never recaptured, nor their bodies found. After quite a lengthy search, they were declared dead by drowning and presumed missing.

But before that announcement, I felt scared that the escapees would break into our house.

To this day, their case is still open by the US Marshal Service. There were 14 attempts over the years to escape "The Rock", resulting in 23 being recaptured, 6 killed 2 confirmed drowning, and finally 5 listed as missing. One man in Florida, on his death bed, under an alias claimed to have been one of the escapees. Supposedly there were post cards sent to a mother from South America, it was never confirmed.

Only one man survived his escape. John Paul Scott made his escape in December of 1962 but was captured in a weak condition on the rocks near Fort Point on the south side of the Golden Gate Bridge quite a while after the escape.

In September, I returned to Argonne elementary and finished the next semester quite depressed. I really did not feel life was good anymore. Things settled into a dismal routine for the next year or so. Events in the world just kept on happening regardless of my understandings.

As grammar school at Argonne Elementary School drew to its completion for me, I had settled down, and was no longer the discipline problem that I had been earlier. Perhaps I had adjusted to my father's death.

I had been on the school safety patrol for about a year and enjoyed those new duties and responsibilities, assisting other students crossing the four intersections surrounding the school. At that time, it was "boys" only, although the all-girl Catholic schools had their own, Safety Patrols as well. Our uniform was simple. We had a white belt which went around our waist and over one shoulder. This belt had to be brilliant white, so on weekends it was taken home, washed and bleached.) We also had an orange military style overseas cap made out of cotton that we washed and starched very heavily. That cap would stand up on its own when done. (Made me think later, of *"breaking Starch"* in the Army.)

We were armed with a paddle **"STOP"** sign and would check traffic, if safe, would step out to the outside of the crosswalk in a semi-military manner, holding out the **"STOP"** sign to halt any approaching traffic. These duties boosted my sense of being and having a meaningful duty to carry out. It made me feel good to assist my fellow students, as well as being able to tell a grown-up to stop.

It was both an honor and privilege to serve on the safety patrol squad. We got out of class early so we could be on our post on time at the appointed times. We would be on duty before school, early releases, lunch time and the dismissal times. At full strength there would be four "patrolmen" on each of the four corners immediately surrounding the school there were about 18 posted for the arrival to school and dismissal times. During early release and lunch, we posted two per corner. If we were short personnel, there would be posted two per intersection. The two would be posted on each end of a diagonal, one near the school and the other on the arriving corner.

There was also a *"chain-of-command"* for the safety squad. The whole unit was headed by a Captain. A Lieutenant acted as the "executive officer" to the captain. The *"Louie"* would also act as the captain, should the captain be absent. There were also two Sergeants who helped out wherever needed and trained the new members of the squad. The rest of us were the *"grunts"*.

Usually one of the junior officers would act as a "shift leader" for the middle tours. They would walk around the block that the school was on and kept an eye on those on that watch. The roving patrolman would also keep an eye on the neighborhood in general. Anything out of the ordinary would be reported. There was always the ever-present mounted police officer at the same corner of Balboa and 17th Ave. The faithful officer would usually remain until after the last lunch period.

The sergeants would insure that the patrolmen followed the proper procedures, remained at their posts, and were in "proper uniform". Most of the patrolmen carried out their duties in a semi-military manner, parade rest when not actively crossing students, snapping to attention when students approached to cross, then ready, checking traffic from his post before stepping out to the crosswalk to complete the cycle. The "all clear" and "off duty" signal would be waved from the porch of the main entrance to the school with the orange cap. It was the captain who waved the troops back.

In the morning before going on duty, the patrol was lined up, military fashion and inspected by the captain and lieutenant. If all was in order, the patrolmen would be marched to their respective posts by the sergeants to the north and south corners.

Should the weather turn foul; we were prepared. The school kept a huge stock of rain gear. They had the traditional yellow rain slickers in many sizes. (There was always the little kid who wound up looking like a yellow traffic cone.) There was always the black rubber "Galoshes", which also came in many sizes. Both the foul weather coats and boots had those clumsy "hook & snap" fasteners.

Every year the city would honor the school safety patrols with a big parade and review in Golden Gate Park at the polo field. Many of the city officials, the police high command, and anybody who was anybody in the city would be there. (It was more of a photo op. for them than for us patrol kids.) The media was out in full force. Hundreds (if not thousands) of parents and family members would be there to share in the pride of having their boy (or Catholic girl) on display. The event was the high point of the safety patrol's year. It was held just prior to the summer break.

Before we set out for that event we would be drilled properly by the district's high school ROTC cadets for a couple of weeks prior. Our squad was pretty good in drill and ceremonies, so the drilling became more of free time for us after the cadets ran us through the proper drill movements and procedures. The only real new thing with the drill and ceremonies was the use of the guidon. We formed up by size; the smaller guys were on the right, with the tallest in front and to the left. This was done to provide a uniform view from the reviewing stand. Needless to say, we looked sharp, and I got my photo in the city paper my final semester on the squad.

Algeria became independent. The Cuban missile crisis occurred in which the US Navy blockaded Cuba and directly challenged Soviet shipping in and out of Cuba in 1962. (We still had the air raid drills more frequently then.). Algeria became independent from France, ending their eight-year war of independence. France was still licking her wounds from Dien Bien Phu. Over all, the European nations were losing their former colonies because Europe was still rebuilding and recovering from World War II. Nelson Mandela was jailed in South Africa for his stand against apartheid.

The next semester, my last at Argonne and grammar school (February 1963), I became the Safety Patrol Captain. I have no Idea who was behind this, but it really changed my life. I think that the uniformity and the semi-military aspect of this service prepared me for my future, both in the military and in service to others. I finished out of trouble and with improved grades. I still had a long way to go.

America put its astronaut, John Glenn into orbit around the Earth. We were beaten by the Soviets in 1961, as they put their cosmonaut, Yuri Gagarin into space before us, beating us by only one month. Our first man in space was Alan Sheppard.

Sam Walton established the retail giant Wal-Mart when he opened his first store in Bentonville, Arkansas. The US Supreme Court ruled against prayers in public schools that same year. Telstar became the first telecommunications satellite. Two years later, the Tokyo Olympics would be televised worldwide.

The next main chapter would be Junior High School at Presidio Jr. High School, 29th and Geary Blvd. (7th to 9th grades). It would be about a 12-block walk to school. I didn't mind moving on. There were a lot of friends who also would be going to Presidio, plus a couple of girlfriends. I would not be alone, and we vowed to stick together to face the rumors of the hazing of the new "scrubs", which we would become in the fall. That summer passed as usual, although I seemed a little freer as my grandparents eased up some on the rules and regulations.

CHAPTER SEVEN

The biggest cultural shock and change in Jr. High School from elementary school was the changing of classrooms. Instead of being taught all of our subjects by one teacher in one room, we were taught six subjects in six different class rooms that we had to go to each period. Lunch made up one of the seven periods.

We started in a "homeroom" where all the administrative stuff was handled, announcements were made and usually any problems or questions could be handled, or at least brought to light. My "homeroom" was in a classroom in which a home economics sewing, and fashion class was held. The first teacher we saw in that room in the morning was a small Chinese lady, (a Miss Yee, if I recall.) For the first couple of days, it was not unusual for us to wind up in the wrong classroom, at least through roll call. A locker was issued to us, so we could keep with us only the books we needed for the next class or two.

The scrubbing didn't stop, for me; the worst was that an upperclassman would knock the books out of my hands amidst a lot of teasing and laughter. I guess the tough guy in me resurfaced, and after standing up to a couple of these guys, the harassment seemed to stop. We did hear of *"scrubs"* being stuffed into a garbage can and rolled down the hill next to the school or be given a *"wedgies'"*. After what seemed like a long time we got accustomed to life in junior high school, where we would be for the next three years. The hazing stopped almost as quickly as it started. Many of the horrible hazing stories proved to be merely "Urban Myths".

To many, but not me, gym class was traumatic, changing and showering with a bunch of guys as we went through the awkwardness' of puberty was not easy. We had another locker for, (of course in the locker room) the gym class. We also had to have a "gym" uniform, consisting of khaki gym trunks, a grey sweat shirt, a "jock" strap, white socks and sneakers.

My grandmother was with me when we went to buy the gym uniform. All was going well until it came to the "jock" strap fitting. The sales girl asked me what size I needed; well that did it, I tried to show her how big my penis was; much to the shock of both my grandmother and the sales girl I was about to demonstrate the size of my penis. In horror the sales girl screamed "oh, no, they are sold by waist size!!" (People all turned to look.) Oh, now I understand how to buy my next "jock strap", properly termed "an athletic supporter"; it is by waist size, not schlong size, thank you.

It seemed that the male gym teachers were all former Drill Sergeants. We also wondered about the female gym teachers. They all had the same gruffness as one would expect of a drill sergeant. Their sexual orientation did not enter into the picture in those days. Some displayed that military persona constantly, others it seemed to come out from time to time. They all had the very short military style haircuts. (The female instructors usually wore their hair pulled back in a tight bun.) They all wore a whistle around their necks as a badge of office. The ever-present clip board completed trappings of office. The gym teachers all seemed to follow a uniform dress code, consisting of a Tee-shirt (in warm weather), or a sweat shirt (in the cooler weather). They wore grey sweat pants or khaki pants most of the time. There was always the ever-present satin wind breaker. They all had "cool" looking athletic shoes, before it became a fashion statement.

These guys were never "politically correct". In fact, that term was not in use for years to come, long after we left school altogether. Also, I am sure that they never took "sensitivity training", (I've heard that the drill instructors of today must take that training.), as they, the gym teachers, were sometimes very harsh on the kids who were not as physically fit and agile as the majority of the class. Many kids cried. It seemed that the punishment for infractions or failure to make the grade was to make the student "do laps" around the school yard or gym or to "drop" for push-ups. Those terms and practices resonated to me years later in the Army, when the real Drill Sergeants would meet out similar punishments.

There was always the dreaded rope climb in the gym where the student was required to climb a rope suspended from the girders of the gym. (It seemed a mile but was only about twenty feet or so.). Those kids who were overweight had a lot of trouble in doing these tasks. Not many kids were overweight in those days, as compared to today's youth of similar age. The fat ones had so much trouble. They only were able to jump up a little way and hang on to the rope. Their fat little legs would be flaying back and forth, trying to get a foot hold on the rope in order to begin their climb. After several failed attempts, they were sent to do laps around the gym. It would not be uncommon to see a couple of *"chubbiest"* jogging and waddling around the gym, as the rest of the class scampered up and down the ropes on command. I seemed to do this quite naturally and had no problem in doing so.

There was another instrument of agony for those not as fit as they should be. That was the "peg board". The participant would be given two large dowel-type wooden pieces. There was a large, thick board attached firmly to the gym wall with nine holes drilled into it. These holes would just be big enough to accommodate the "dowels". The object of this drill was for the student to jump up driving one of the "dowels" into the hole in the board, pull himself up and place the second "dowel" into another hole. With a good hand hold in place, he would move around the wall board for as long as he could or until the gym teacher was satisfied that the performance was acceptable. Sometimes the given holes were assigned a point value and the one who had the highest score won. The winner was sometimes allowed to leave the class early and leave the class early to shower. The dowels were removed and passed on to the next contestant. Needless to say, this was even worse to the "fatsos" than the ropes. I had no problem with this either.

Overall, I did well in all the sports, except basketball. Even today, I do not venture near a basketball court. As hard as the gym teacher tried, I did not do well in basketball. I could shoot pretty well, dribble in place, but my inability to put it all together proved that I was a dismal failure at that sport. While playing basketball, I usually would be sent to the center of the court, where I would be passed the ball. I was one of the tallest kids in the class at the time, a big target. The smaller kids would be jumping up and down at my feet trying to steal the ball away from me. On cue, I would pass the ball in enough time for my team members to get in place where they could make a basket.

Every year we had to complete a "fitness" test, similar to the military's annual physical fitness test. There were so many events we had to pass for our final PE grade. I do not recall the exact events, but it was designed to test every aspect of our fitness. Some events, like the 50-yard dash and the 660-yard run were timed events. I saw this PE thing as being very patriotic, as President Kennedy was a big supporter of physical fitness in the school, as well being prepared physically for the military.

The final act of the gym class was the shower. Many sprouting adolescents were very shy and embarrassed in having to undress, suit-up, and shower with so many other boys of various stages development watching. The gym teachers would try, for hygiene reasons, try to ensure that everyone showered. (And to ensure that one did not go to the next class smelling badly.) He was also on guard for the frequent "wet towel snapping", which was a frequent sport during that time in the locker room. Cutting the showers was an offense punishable by detention. Some guy who was excused from participating in that day's gym class would be assigned to hand out the bleach smelling, crisp rough towels. It was during this final part of PE that many of us would keep a bottle of aftershave in our locker, to further insure that we smelled good for the next class, as well as the girls that we were becoming more and more interested in. (It seemed that most of the girls grew new boobs over that past summer, nice.)

There was some teasing going on, but in general we got through it. Finally, it was from this locker room that we heard of President Kennedy's assignation from one of the gym teachers. That event shook the nation as well as the world. I recall watching all the events of the killing up to and including his state funeral on TV, both in school as well as home. I could not help but to lose some innocence at that point, realizing that we all were vulnerable and mortal.

For the boys, one of the requirements was to take shop classes. There was Wood Shop, Metal Shop, Print Shop, Mechanical Drafting and the Electronic Shop. The full semester would be divided into "beginner" & advanced" levels for each shop.

For the girls, they would take home economics which included teaching the cooking skills, sewing and fashion design, as well as the general budgeting and domestic management. The seventh graders were not given the initial choice of a shop or which shop or home economics class for the girls.

I wound up with Wood Shop. I was already pretty versed in working with the various tools and the fabrication of items made out of wood from my father's and grandfather's shop in our basement. I excelled in this shop and was encouraged by a wonderful Black man, Maxwell Gillette. (He would later become my electronics teacher.) He was a Korean War veteran of a medium stature. Unlike some of the gym teachers, by contrast, he was very patient and understanding. He took the time to teach the finer points of woodworking as well as encouraging his students to excel in all of the other academic disciplines. I still have, to this day an enthusiasm for wood working. I love the smell of fresh cut wood, the sawdust and in general the feel of a fine crafted wood piece. (Later in life, I would work in a cabinet shop and in general construction, many times as the *"cut man"*.)

Each semester we had a couple of minimum projects to complete for our grade. If done well, and ahead of schedule, one could go on to continue making other wooden items. I made several things in wood shop that endured for many years to come. I only recall a gravity-held book rack and a shadow box. The city held an Industrial Arts show every year where the schools would display the best examples of the various crafts. I had one item entered but did not place. I got an honorable mention which I thought was great.

The next shop that I was required to take was print shop, not of my choosing. There were three old presses which rumbled and seemed to shake the floor when they were running. There was a constant "sticky" sound as the rollers picked up the ink off of the palette and rolled over the galley plate. Those presses seemed to create their own rhythm; Ka chunk, stch, stch. Ra ta ta ta. Sometimes they were printing student projects and at other times official work for the school itself. I did not like the print shop.

The Print Shop teacher was a crusty, bitter old man who seemed to have the demeanor of W.C. Fields when dealing with us kids. Mr. McCarthy, I believe his name was. I remember a little bespectacled Chinese kid who had to leave early because he was on the library staff after school and was required to be at the library by the time when the final bill rang. He had the proper hall pass that McCarthy had to honor, but it pissed him off to do so. Mr. McCarthy would belittle this poor kid and send him off telling him to "…and kiss all the books good night for me! ". That old guy must have been weaned on pickles. He wore an ink stained apron, and wire rimmed glassed that made him look more like a leprechaun than his name would let you believe. The seats in that shop were on tiers, like an amphitheater with the teacher's podium off center. Mr. McCarthy ruled his shop with an iron fist, especially at clean-up time. I had him for 7th period and he demanded that the shop be in a top clean condition before we were released for the day.

There were several type cabinet / holders containing all the letters of the alphabet plus all the punctuation marks used in the English language. The type for the "p" and "q" looked the same if one was not careful. (Thus, came the saying, from the printing industry: "Watch your "p"'s and "q"'s".!)

For each different font and print size (pica) an entirely different type rack was required to hold the hundreds of separate types. The shop had many of these print holders stacked around the shop. They were quite heavy when loaded with the lead type. The first assignments involved setting and re-setting the same type in a rack in such a manner that it came out evenly as the printing became more spaced out. Many of these racks were hurled against the floor in Mr. McCarthy's rage as the student cowered over not getting the assignment correct. When this first test of our typesetting skill was finalized we moved on to other more appealing projects. Every project had to be "proof read" by the master himself before being put on the press for mass production. It had to be letter perfect.

There was the cutting of a linoleum block into our own initials with very sharp knives. (Yes, there was a first aid kit on hand.) Once it passed Herr McCarthy's high-quality standards we were allowed to print, and bind note pads for ourselves. We went on to print more note tablets with our name on different colored note paper. Lastly, (Today, I have totally forgotten the technique and method) for making these stamps.), we made a rubber stamp with our name and address on it. I used that stamp for years to come. That was my last souvenir of print shop.

One of the dirtiest jobs in the shop was that of "the salvage". There seemed to be an endless supply of lead type from the shops around the city when they replaced their old type with new type; they would donate the old type to the schools. If assigned to the salvage operation we had to clean the old type in a solvent with a toothbrush. Then the clean type was segregated into its proper size and font style before being put back into the proper type galley cabinet.

I would come home with ink stained hands and it took a good scrubbing with Lava soap and Dutch Cleanser to be ready for dinner when coming home from the salvage operation of that day. Although I did not care for the Print Shop, I did acquire a keen understanding of my mother's proof reading jobs as she read the galley proofs that came off of the press in a real printing shop of a major publisher. Like Mr. McCarthy, my mother's proof reading had to be perfect. The printer would have to reset his galley to make the corrections that my mother had noted.

The last and the best shop that I attended was the Electronics shop, taught by my former Wood shop teacher, Mr. Gillette. It was my most favorite shop, in that there was always a "spark" in the air. (Bad Pun, not intended.) Not only did we learn about electricity and electronics, we were encouraged to excel in the other academic subjects and do well in all aspects of our lives. Mr. Gillette became a mentor to many and for many of his students; he was the inspiration to remain in school.

The shop always had a slight smell of the hot melted resin, which was used in soldering, and the fresh smell of wood and sawdust. The same shop was used for both classes. At times there would be the accidental smell of an electrical charred wire. It is hard to describe, but it was that smell we sometimes ask "...do you smell something electrical burning?" That is almost a universally recognized smell. There was never any danger, as our instructor was always on top of these things.

The shop routine was a combination of lecture and practical hands on work in the shop. The lecture portion of the class covered electrical and electronic theory, shop procedures and safety requirements. Included would also be some history of the industry to include the famous names associated with inventions and science of electricity. It also would include the career fields and paths within the industry.

The "hands on" portion of the class was always my favorite time. The shop had an abundance of old radios, televisions and small electrical appliances on hand, either for parts or a project to restore the ailing unit. The shop had an abundance of tools to work with. I enjoyed working with my hands and made many "cool" things. I once made a radio fit into a match box, which at that time seemed an accomplishment in miniaturization by the standards of the day.

I put together a "all band / short-wave" Heath Radio Kit both at home and in the shop. That radio, when hooked up at home with my larger antenna, was able to pick up radio signals nation and worldwide on atmospheric skip signals. I kept a log with the call signs and locations of most of the stations I received.

There was a very simple project, the "magnetizer" and "de-magnetizer" made by wrapping a magnet wire around an old empty toilet paper roll. Depending on which direction the wire was wrapped, determined whether the device would magnetize or de-magnetize. This was based on the principles of electro-magnetic flux and magnetic fields. The fuse for this device was a simple tin foil chewing gum wrapper placed between the input contacts from the AC line.

One of the most complicated projects to come out of that simple shop was a laser. Yes, a laser built in about 1965 by a Japanese student who came from a wealthy family that could finance this major project. Needless to say, that laser swept every (not literally) category and won top prizes in the Industrial Arts shows. My little radio felt sad.

The shop curriculum came with a text book that the course followed. It was a good textbook and it included various projects complete with schematics, symbols, and a glossary of electronic terms in the back of the book. We had to learn the various terminology and the electronic symbols and abbreviations. We learned the color code by memorizing the following: "Bad Boys Rape Our Young Girls But Violet Gives Willingly" Translation: Black, Brown, Red, Orange, Yellow, Green, Blue, Violet, Grey, and White. (Gold & Silver had 5% and 10% tolerances.)

Each color represented a number, 0 through 10. They were colored bands on a resistor. For example, a resistor with an ohm rating of 525 ohms would be indicated by the colored bands of: Yellow, Red, Yellow and perhaps a tolerance of 10% with a fourth band of silver. The color code also applied to other elements of the electronic components and wires. Wires used a similar system by using a base color with up to three stripes to indicate a numerical value for that wire. For example, wire # 58 would be a Yellow wire with a violet stripe on it. (Little did know then, but I would later work in a wire and cable shop doing just the color coding wire.)

Junior high school was not just gym and shop. We carried a full curriculum with math, English, social studies, history (world and US) and usually one other academic type of elective. I began to have a great interest in history and the social sciences. I found the events in history fascinating in that I tended to see the connections between multiple events along a given time line or in a geographical location.

I loved ancient history in that I found it easy for me to see and feel the lives of the past. I was always in awe on how the ancient peoples made such huge stone structures such as the pyramids in Egypt and elsewhere in ways that still baffle today's engineers. I was also fascinated with evolution and the extremely old remains that were found in Africa by such scientists as Dr. Leakey with his discovery of the early humanoid, "Lucy". (Alien intervention was not even thought of back then.)

Sometimes I would not be too popular with some of my teachers and class mates with some of my observations and conclusions. For an example: The American Civil War, to me, it was not a "civil war" in that the South was not trying to overthrow the Federal government. Was Lincoln more motivated to either free the slaves, or to preserve the union? Was the "Civil War" a major result of disputes of State vs. Federal law and jurisdiction? These thoughts were not popular with the growing Civil Rights movement that was sweeping the nation at the time. It became quite clear to me over these formative years how a given action in one place could have such major results and consequences elsewhere, either in the nation and / or the world. Many of my early historical theories and observations would not be fully developed until high school and college. Even today my television always seems to be tuned to the History Channel, the Discovery Channel and the Learning Channel. Alternative history was fascinating with all of the "what ifs".

The social studies per se, covered other aspects of the human experience. Some of the lessons covered the other countries and cultures. I became fascinated once again with different people and cultures, both contemporary and ancient. Geography was fun in that I liked drawing maps and with these maps, I would plot many worldwide adventures of my own. I liked, envisioning the people, cultures and societies of the various points on the maps. It set up within me a need to travel and explore.

English, in the traditional form of instruction, always had its silly exercise of diagramming a sentence. (It bored me to death to do so.). I saw no point in doing so if subject and predicate made any sense and that subject and verb matched. Any and all adverbs and adjectives could then be generously applied to clarify a given verb or noun to further clarify again a given idea that was committed to paper. Some complicated sentences, which when diagramed, looked like the organizational chart of a Mongolian Horde. The best part of English and the related courses and subjects were the inspiration to me, such as creative writing. (Such as this project.).

The beauty and challenge of any language that, when written, is to be able to take an idea and project in such a manner that a second person can visualize and understand that idea as close as it possibly can to the writer's original. It is perhaps the same paradox as when one has read a book and when the movie is seen, they don't seem the same. Two readers both came up with different interpretations of the same idea. In many ways the writer, the original reader, the screenplay writer, and finally the movie director all shared and interpreted the same idea differently in some ways.

The cornerstone of civilization is mathematics. Without it, many of man's creations would not be as magnificent or even still standing today. The ancient structures could not have been constructed with such accuracy without some deep-rooted understanding of mathematics and geometry. That is perhaps why I did not build any ancient structures. I was horrible at math and struggled with it all my life. I still do today.

I managed to do all right with the basic math, but when I got to elementary algebra in the ninth grade, I was shot down in flames. My grades and understanding of the subject inspired my grandparents to hire me a tutor after school just to keep up in class. I would sit a few times a week with this guy in an attempt to improve my understanding of math with letters. When my grades finally rose to a "C" average, the tutoring ceased. He was good at math and I did manage to learn from him. Overall, math remained a sore subject for me, even through college, where I took only the required amount of credits for my degree. My very last math subject was College Algebra. I had to take that class on a "pass / fail" basis as not to damage my overall GPA at the time. I did get my degree anyway with the minimum of math. I did take some math later in College; those classes were accounting 101 and statistics 101 and then called it quits, as those subjects were required for my minor.

I recall that at the time, the algebra tutor was the only person allowed to smoke the house by my grandmother. The smell of the cigarette smoke was promptly covered up with air freshener before my grandfather came home.

Science is what made the modern world of today what it is. Much to my dismay, science is based on a sound foundation of mathematics, ah there lies the rub. In junior high school we had to take what was called General Science or Biology. I choose the General Science course over Biology. General Science was just that, a class providing a basic understanding of several major disciplines of science. It was an overview of the scientific principles of investigation and study. I did manage to do well in this class, and while my other peers were cutting up dead frogs in Biology; I was exploring the stars and planets when we learned about the solar system and the universe.

Aside from the academics of Junior High School, the major purpose of this experience was socialization. Physically it was the growing into adulthood. Sexual awakenings and the raging hormones for both sexes both confused and amused us as well. The girls usually got their periods at that time and grew breasts; while we boys were experiencing NRB's (No reason boners) experienced hair growth, deepening voices, which were known to "crack" embarrassingly at times) and growth spurts. In general, we all had to deal with some form of acne and skin problems while the body chemistry was being altered. It was a great opportunity to become immersed in the entire teenaged experience and the pop culture of the time. It was also an awkward period of life as we entered into the teen years and lived out those same years.

There was a whirlwind of both physical and emotional changes going on within us. We also had to adjust and for the most part to confirm to a different norm that was laid out by our parents. It was a time of immense peer pressure. Sometimes loyalty was split between friends and family. There was also the ever-present power of the media. The advertisers bombarded a vast youth population with non-stop advertising and marketing strategies, competing for our attention and dollars.

The pop culture bombarded us constantly, telling us how we should dress, what we should eat and drink (or not to drink). It was a time to discover one's self and create the image that was no longer a "child". Those years kept us captive through high school. It was a seven-year process. To many, these years were years of rebellion, against the establishment, parents and for some even the Madison Avenue image of an American teenager.

Some adapted quite well, while others it was a traumatic experience. Luckily, those teen years only lasted for seven years. As I later told my sons, "Next time I am going to meet you on the other side of those years." For some, even in their later years seem to be stuck in those years permanently. I later noticed this when on occasion when I was on leave from the Army; many of my friends were still acting as if they were still in high school, although we were drinking in a bar at twenty-one.

CHAPTER EIGHT

At this point in time, America was invaded, and we teenagers welcomed the invaders with open arms, to many, to the shock and disapproval of their parents. The Defense Department did not react to this invasion in any manner of a military response. This invasion took several years to complete and perhaps, laid the foundation to the American Counterculture. I was there, and I was in Junior High school (1963-1966) when the first invaders landed on our shores. Our ears were attacked a long time before the ground troops hit our shores. We young Americans were still enjoying our brand of "Rock & Roll" and the emerging "Folk" music genres.

Meanwhile in England, a new form of music was emerging, influenced by American "Rock & Roll", Country, Jazz, and "The Blues". The vanguard of this movement emerged out of Liverpool, England with a sound which became known as "The Merseybeat". The invasion forces tended to fall into two distinct categories, modeled after the British youth movements at that time, known as "The Mods" (short for "the moderns", a bit more conservative in appearance than their counterparts), and "The Rockers", (kind of a variant of the James Dean look) more rebellious in appearance and behavior.

Probably the first to be recognized of the vanguard was a Liverpool group, formerly known as "The Quarrymen", renamed "The Beatles" (after the "beat boom" as their music was called in England.) The Beatles music hit the British charts in late 1962. The British instrumental "Telstar" topped the American pop charts at the same time. That was merely a "recon" mission.

The British charts boasted songs featuring the hits from the following groups: The Searchers, Gerry & The Pacemakers, and Billy J. Kramer & The Dakotas, to mention a few. Americans were listening, and many radio stations began airing these new sounds.

By early 1963 the first wave hit our shores featuring music by the following groups: The Rolling Stones (still together in 2015), The Yardbirds, (from which Jimmy Page would form Led Zeppelin years later), The Kinks, The Crickets (no relation to the Beatle) The Pretty Things, Dusty Springfield, Peter & Gordon, Chad& Jeremy, and The Merseybeats. Emerging in the forefront of this wave to challenge The Beatles was, The Dave Clark Five. There would be fierce jousting between those two groups for musical supremacy, chart topping and fan loyalty.

The second wave, many emerging from other English cities, to augment the Liverpool advance guard were such groups as: The Hollies, The Crickets, Wayne Fontana & The Mindbenders, Freddie & The Dreamers, and Herman's Hermits. Newcastle fielded Eric Burdon & The Animals. Birmingham followed suit with The Spencer Davis Group (featuring Stevie Winwood) and The Moody Blues. Ireland was not to be left out they sent Them (the springboard group for Van Morrison). From St. Albans came The Zombies.

The year 1963 proved to be the testing ground for this British musical invasion of the American "Top-40" charts. America was listening, but not really buying in huge numbers until about January 1964 when, on the Jack Parr television show, he aired concert footage of a Beatles' concert. Two weeks later, the Beatles song "I Want to Hold Your Hand" skyrocketed to the #1 position on the American Top 40 charts. These phenomena became known as "Beatlemania". The Beatles first appeared a few weeks later, February 9th, 1963, on the Ed Sullivan Show. It is estimated that 45% of American households tuned in and watched that broadcast. The Beatle tours brought thousands of screaming, hysterical, fainting and swooning young teenage girls to frenzied heights before, during and after the performances.

This musical revolution and invasion continued, roughly throughout my Junior High School years until about 1966 when the music blended, and the American counter attack was launched coinciding with the "Hippie Movement", "The Anti-War Movement" and the emergence of our "West Coast Sound" (San Francisco and the Los Angeles versions.)

America responded with its first line of defense, Paul Revere & the Raiders, complete with American Continental Army uniforms.

The post Beatle British reinforcements which came to the front included: Petula Clark, The Troggs, Donovan, Small Faces, The Honeycombs, The Who, as well as a whole string of "one hit wonders". By May of 1965 the invaders claimed all but the #2 spot of the American Top 10. The musical history of just these few years could fill volumes and changed society as a whole. Many musical genres were blended or fused together. Many new genres emerged over the next few years to include: "Soul", "Funk", "Urban Funk, "Latin Soul", "Latin Funk", "Underground Rock" and "Protest".

For me, gone were the days when there was only music on the radio dial could be very clearly classified as: "Top 40", "Soul", "Country & Western" and "Classical" (The original "long-haired" music.), and the news / talk programs. Today, there are 307 distinct types of music disciplines and genres that are recognized.

In the midst of this musical experience, I laid down my own form of rebellion when my grandmother began to listen to and like the Beatles. She also commented how it was a Godsend to have the Beatles pouring so much into the coffers of the British Treasury through their taxes. She was ecstatic when the members of The Beatles were later knighted. In response, I preferred the "bad" boys, i.e.: The Rolling Stones, The Animals, etc., as well as turning to my American roots with The Blues. These genres still hold my preference today.

The American music industry responded with a myriad of artists and groups. Emerging from the Civil Rights movement, many Black artists were able to break into the mainstream recording industry. "Motown Records" rose to meet the challenge as well. This Black enterprise promoted the new genre of "Soul" music. Many white youths embraced this music as well. Many of the headliners of the American music scene were overshadowed by these emerging musical genres.

The British musical invasion brought with it a whole new reshaping of the youth market. The "Mod" look became the new rage. Nehru jackets became popular along with bell bottom pants, wide wale corduroy pants, wide belts, the mini skirt, boots, starched button-down collar shirts, Paisley shirts, polka-dot shirts, "Dino shirts", the Romeo "puffed sleeved shirts", satin shirts, Greek fisherman caps (ala: John Lennon of The Beatles), variants on and to include surplus military uniforms, and perhaps above all vibrant colors were the rage.

With the onset of the *"Beatle mop haircuts"*, males across society began to grow their hair longer, rejecting Dad's military crew cut. Many traditional barbershops closed during the next decade or so as a result of this trend in grooming. Females began to take on the "Go-Go" dancer look, complete with the mini-shirt and knee-high boots. Their longer hair was ironed straight or put up in a massive bee-hive bouffant. Their blouses and tops also became as revealing as the mini-skirt. Leather and suede became very popular and was no longer just for the outlaw bikers, cops and bomber pilots. Many boutiques featured their own line of leather styles.

The fashion industry cashed in on this transformation of the youthful look. The retail "boutique" became the "in" place to shop for one's clothing, usually at very high prices. To keep up with the latest styles and trends coming out of Europe, one needed a lot of money. The mainstream clothing retailers scrambled to introduce the latest clothing lines trying to follow the latest "in" styles.

As teenagers during both the 1950's and 1960's, to go alongside the music was the dance craze. A teen was not cool if the latest dance step was not learned and mastered. It seemed that for us, a new dance was born every week. Many a teen would practice to American Bandstand's dance party on TV, hosted by the "eternal teenager", Dick Clark. The list of dances was just as varied and colorful and to the older generation, strange. Not only did we practice these dance steps, we also played the "broom" guitar or the "air" guitar in front of a mirror getting ready for that big show business break as the newest rock star. That also included dance steps of sorts.

The list could be much larger, but for argument sake, here is a partial list of some of the dances that were sweeping the nation during this time: "The Stroll", (a '50's spill over), "The Twist", (The dance that revolutionized dancing in general.), "The Mash","The Mashed Potatoes", (followed by), "The Monster Mash", "The Monkey", "The Dog", (followed by), "Walking The Dog", "The Madison", (Cleveland Ohio), "The Hully Gully", "The Watusi", "The Pony","The Fish", (which led to), "The Swim", "The Hitch Hike", "The Freddie" (from Freddie & The Dreamers), "The Frug", and finally the coolest for me, "The Temptation Walk". Sometimes we mixed and matched and by the end of the 1960's we danced our own style and gone were the rigid steps and routines. Slow dancing with a girl was always the best as the young bodies clung and swayed rhythmically to the slow beats. With the lights turned down low, a long kiss was at times in order. Not only did it feel good, it sometimes allowed for other physical contacts. (A NRB had to be avoided, if possible.) Also refer to my Appendix in this narrative.

During The two summers between 7th & 8th grades, my grandparents decided to send me to summer camp for two weeks each. I wound up going to The Salvation Army's Youth Camp each year. At first, I resisted, thinking it was a retreat for ghetto inner-city youth, but when I got into the swing of things, I really enjoyed myself and it was a good character building experience.

The camp was located in the Santa Cruz Mountains on California's coast. It was nestled among the redwood trees and beautiful country settings. The cabins and the other buildings on the grounds were all done in an old rustic country style. It was a kind of a faux log cabin exteriors and knotty pine paneled interiors. There was a large fire pit where there would nightly entertainment and "hootenanny" sing along. Nearby was an amphitheater and stage where talent shows were held, skits and more structured lectures, sermons or general entertainment were held.

Overall, I felt this more of a spiritual experience than a religious one. The nature walks and just the simple being in the country, fresh air away from family and the city was very invigorating. The night sky, without the city glare, was the most awesome spectacle I had ever seen. The vastness of the night sky left me in wonder and realizing how very small we really are. The summer meteor showers were fireworks for free.

The Salvation Army, at least at this camp, did not put on a heavy religious program, although there were mandatory Sunday services. I accepted Christ that summer, not really understanding the doctrines or the teachings. I think that I did so out of peer pressure and the fact that one of my "girlfriends" did so first. The camp counselors were probably Salvation Army youth, or adherents. I recall the loudspeaker system aside from the daily program announcements and pages, often played a mixture of soft music and often very melodic and haunting African choral and choir arrangements on Sunday.

My grandmother sent me off to camp with some money that I was to use sparingly, as we had canteen sales at camp for candy, food treats and toiletries. Overall, I made it through this limited funding with little trouble, although I wished I had more money to treat the girls with. I could not but to think that a lot of these underprivileged kids sure came with plenty of money for the canteen though.

The camp also offered other growing and learning experiences. The camp was co-ed so we older kids had quite an interest in the opposite sex quite naturally. There would be long walks together and those awkward social interactions. There was the late night sneaking out in the moonlight to the girl's cabins. There was always the failed "panty raid". We always managed to evade being caught. At times I thought that some of the counselors of both sexes really did not care, in that we got away with a lot. There was the usual pairing some was more intense than others. I had a couple of female friends and we took it very slow, as we all were quite inexperienced in all of this. Because of some of these "summer romances", the social life at school in the fall was not as awkward to me. I had a good time that summer and looked forward to returning the next year.

During the summer of 1964, two American destroyers were allegedly attacked without provocation in the Gulf of Tonkin by North Vietnamese patrol boats. When I heard this, I felt that we were going to war. (We were). Responding to this, President Johnson pushes through Congress the Gulf of Tonkin Resolution allowing him to greatly increase the US troop strength in Vietnam. By 1964, unknown to many, 50,000 military personnel had already served in that country since 1954. Many of these newer troops were not strictly "advisors", many were Special Forces, which technically did not carry out offensive operations against the Viet Cong or the NVA.

The Civil Rights Act is passed and becomes Federal law. Reactions across the country are met with mixed responses. Old ways are hard to end merely by the stroke of a president's pen. The Equal Employment Opportunity Commission is created. (The EOC). In future years "equal opportunity" is really given a bad rap by non-minority citizens. That is to also raise the question of "Who is a minority?" In many ways just about everybody can find come reason that they can prove their minority status, for instance, at one time being Jewish alone qualified one as being a minority. (Today is a minority a: White, Anglo-Saxon, Protestant, college educated Vietnam Veteran?".

When The Beatles made their television debut on The Ed Sullivan show and in some ways, they proved the nay-Sayers wrong. Theirs was not just a fad and they proved the statements wrong that were circulating at the time: "It's just a fad. They couldn't carry a tune across the Atlantic. It won't last." Etc. The subsequent British invasion, as mentioned earlier, turned the American music scene on its ear and helped reshape contemporary society.

France and China explode their own atomic weapons. The nuclear club no longer has an exclusive membership. By proxy and alliances, the entire world is blanketed by nuclear weapons in such quantities as to overkill everybody in the entire world several times over. The world is divided into two armed camps. (Not counting the underdeveloped 3rd world nations who were either being wooed by either side, or non-committed or aligned.) Mutual total destruction becomes a cornerstone of foreign policy. Simply put, if you try to eliminate me with a nuclear attack, my response will be so destructive you will never recover. We all are going to die and suffer regardless of who began the conflict. The nuclear arms race continues in spite of this. Other nations are also trying to develop this technology. At the same time the conventional arms races continued. A simple but popular expression was, and still is, simply "Nuke 'Em" or turn (fill in the blank, name of the offending nation) into a huge parking lot.

Young people began to both fear and oppose this insane arms race and militarization; it became clear that survival of a massive nuclear exchange would be futile. If one people survived the initial nuclear exchange, the 'nuclear winter' would take care of the rest as the world would be just a little better than reduced to a level, perhaps at the Stone or Bronze Ages. The "Peaceniks" replaced the "Beatniks" of the late 1940's and the 1950's. These movements later evolved into the "Hippies" of the mid to late 1960's (the "Hippies evolved into the "Yuppies" of the 1980s.) The "Anti-War" movement eventually ended the Vietnam War in 1975 with the fall of Saigon that April. The official end of the war is May 7th, 1975, by many historians.

Society always seems to be in flux and changing. In spite of how we think that it's all "the same old shit"; it is not static and there is change and movement all around, even though one may not be aware of it. Those formative years up to this point made this fact quite apparent. In many ways, I felt my own change, as I rejected much of my parents and now grandparents' world. I was striving to fit in both with my peers, please my grandparents and family while trying to form my own person, personae. I began to develop my own ideas, views and theories about the world that I will be inheriting.

It seemed to me, that time was beginning to move faster and what seemed like a very long time when I was, but a small child just passed so quickly. I was in my last year of junior high school and now that we were the upperclassmen time seemed to wiz by. I may have "scrubbed" a few, but could not continue to do so, as I felt their pain and embarrassment. I stopped that and any other form of the hazing that went on.

We were in the 9th grade in 1966, at the junior high school; technically we had become the freshman class of high school. It seemed odd that we were not attending the high school at the High School. From the physical location of Presidio Junior High School, we could simply look to the next block and up to the top of the hill to see George Washington Senior High School. We were king of the hill down here, but would, once again, be at the bottom of the food chain in high school.

By this time my grades were getting better, but still seemed to struggle with math. The liberal classes, the history classes, social study classes were all holding my interest and good performance. I got my first series of "As" in these social studies classes. At this point in time, the teachers, counselors and my grandparents all began to both inquire and to push me to think and perhaps commit to a college curriculum and perhaps a college or university to strive towards. I had no clue. In those days it seemed one's choices were an education geared towards college, business or the blue-collar workforce. I actually enjoyed elements of all options.

It was about this time that I started working odd jobs to earn my own spending money. I had to keep up with the fashions, music and the girls. There was a summer youth jobs program and promotion in the city. I ran an advertisement in the small neighborhood "throw-away" newspaper, The San Francisco Progress that summer, and got a good response from it. I had to go get my social security card at that time. In those days, the social security card was not issued at birth, but rather when one began to work. I found myself doing car washing, yard work, house cleaning and general "handy-kid" work. One customer I kept on an irregular basis until I went into the Army. I enjoyed the work and the gaining of more independence from my grandparents. They also demanded a portion of my earnings. (For room and board, I suspect.) I even sent them an allotment when I was in the Army.

Events around the world resonated with me those years. President Johnson announced "The Great Society" program. Medicare was created, and the "War on Poverty" was declared.

Congress passed the Voting Rights Act, targeting unfair voting registrations and poll taxes, primarily in the South. In spite of these expensive programs, he refused to raise taxes.

That summer, 1965, President Johnson sent 3,500 combat Marines to the air base at Da Nang. These were full combat troops whose mission was the defense of that air base. They had limited offensive authority. The rules of engagement remained very ambiguous, confusing and hated by the military throughout the war.

Dr. Martin Luther King Jr. led 4,000+ people on a "freedom" march from Selma, Alabama to Montgomery, Alabama demanding their equal civil rights and treatment in society. The marchers were met with hostility and violence along the route. Approximately 600 of these marchers are attacked brutally by state and local law enforcement. Many were arrested. The march reached its goal in Montgomery. Not all of the other goals could be met at that time. Sadly, enough change comes very slowly and not without some major resistances.

In New York, Black Muslim leader Malcolm "X" is assassinated after his pilgrimage to Mecca, where he saw that Muslims from around the world come in every racial and national identity. He heard of the peace of Islam. He tried to tame down his racial venom against the white and other races. His changes did not seat well with the more militant within his organization. These differences led to his death. His death was noted among the Black students and there were some minor confrontations in and around the school. Nationwide, the Black reaction sparked some racial violence. Some believed that the "race war" was on.

The Soviet cosmonaut, Alexi Leonov, becomes the first human to walk in space with his excursion, lasting about ten minutes, outside the Voskhod spaceship. The United States follows with the spectacular Gemini missions who also included a spacewalk by astronaut Ed White and the space rendezvous of two spacecraft. All the events in space kept my interest and held me in awe of these feats. Back down here on Earth, the St. Louis Arch is completed.

That summer was also known as "The Long Hot Summer" after nationwide racial riots erupted following the riot in Los Angeles, known as The Watts Riots or, to some, The Watts Rebellion? It was a time when it seemed that the peaceful civil rights movement had failed, and the nation was on the brink of a race war. The riots that took place in San Francisco were not as severe as those in the other parts of the country. For the most part it was contained in a few neighborhoods by the police and California National Guard. I was scared to ever go through the Fillmore District. My grandfather closed his office forever at 143 Fillmore St. after those riots.

The Watts riots took place in that neighborhood in Los Angeles from August 11th to August 17th, 1965. It all began when a white California Highway Patrol officer stopped a black motorist, Marquette Frye, 21 years old, for driving his mother's 1955 Buick recklessly and a possible drunk driving charge. The CHP officer, Lee Minikus, performed the routine field sobriety test Frye was placed under arrest. The driver's brother Ronald, who was a passenger, walked to their nearby house and returned with their mother, Rena Price. She reprimanded her son for driving drunk. A roadside argument soon erupted. A back up unit arrived on the scene

A crowd soon gathered and there was pushing, shoving, the throwing of objects, and spitting directed towards the officers. The backup officer was forced to display force by displaying his riot shotgun. The two Frye brothers and their mother were arrested and transported to county jail. Later as the crowd grew more responding police officers were met with thrown bottles and rocks. The riot was on as the crowd began to move throughout the neighborhood spreading violence and destruction.

Soon Watts was to become a combat zone. A 119 square block or 46 square miles of Los Angeles and Watts were affected. Black civic leaders tried to hold a town meeting on August 12th to quell the unrest, but that resulted in failure and increasing rioting, looting, violence and death continued.

Martial law was declared as the California National Guard's 40th Armored Brigade was diverted from going to their summer camp at

Camp Roberts, they had all their vehicles and weapons with them. At full deployment, 3,900 guardsmen took to the streets, first creating a secure perimeter around the area in conjunction with 934 Los Angeles police officers and 718 Los County Sherriff deputies. At times the Los Angeles fire Department was overwhelmed and retreated, letting burning buildings just burn as even the fire trucks and ambulances were met with rocks, bottles and gunfire.

By the time the riot was quelled and the residents returned home the following costs and damages were realized: $40 million+ in damages, primarily white owned business were looted and destroyed, (most never returned) 258 buildings burned or destroyed, 192 looted, 14 public buildings destroyed or damaged, 34 deaths directly related to the riots (I later served with a Chief Warrant Officer who was there as an enlisted man, and he told of firing a .50 Caliber machine gun at a car that tried to run a road check point, the occupants were cut in half by the machine gun fire.), 1032 were injured, 3,438 were arrested. Parts of the damaged area looked like Europe after WW II. Much remained so for decades.

Perhaps we Californians were not really prepared for the scope of the destruction of Watts and an awareness of the severity of the racial and economic inequality that existed in the Golden State. We did not consider ourselves as racist or biased, but those riots awakened an underlying racial hostility for both the Black and White communities.

That fall, in September 1965, we entered our last year of Junior High School, finally. Now we were at the top of the social pyramid in our school. Overall it went well for me. The grades held fast but the mounting pressure to improve and head towards college weighed on me. I really did not have a clue of what I wanted to do in the immediate future or with my life. All the events of my young life up to this point helped shape my personality, my personae, my self-image, my views and perhaps my political leanings, and continued to keep me seeking a greater perspective and meaning of life and the universe. I ran on the track team that last semester earned "letters" in both sports and service.

CHAPTER NINE

High School & Beyond

Our neighborhood was largely Latin, Russian, Jewish, Asian, with a large portion being Chinese. Many of these Chinese maintained relationships to the mainland China which was under communist rule. Their parents and grandparents often spoke of the horrors inflicted upon the Chinese population by the radical communists. Thousands were executed, tortured and / or imprisoned without due process of law. Many fled to Taiwan.

In 1966 Chairman Mao launches the Cultural Revolution in a massive movement to reshape the Chinese society. There was a lot of violence and death as the youthful followers of their beloved chairman terrorized the citizenry. Many of our neighbors were deeply concerned with those developments in China. Many feared for their families and loved ones trapped in the turmoil and violence.

Things were going pretty well in the closing months of that year I had a few girlfriends and our dates usually consisted of a long walk home and perhaps a cup of coffee at Donut World on Geary St. on the corner of 18th Avenue. In retrospect, from then on, just about all of my girlfriends were Oriental, or Latin. This trend continued through high school and culminated in my marriage to Scharlene Martin who, herself, was half Japanese & American years later. Asian women are beautiful in my eyes.

I often met resistance for my being with an Oriental girl. Much of this racial bias came from World War II, which was only 21 years in the past. Other resistance came from the girl's family not wanting their daughter seen with a white boy. My grandparents would sometimes comment on my preferences. I was later told by my grandmother's sister that I had married *"below my station in life"* because my wife was half Japanese. Catherine was a staunch British colonialist.

In September 1966 the Class of 1969 enters its sophomore year at George Washington Senior High School. We are now going to high school at the actual high school. There was not as much real adjusting, as it was in the lower school. There was still the changing of classes and the adjusting to a much larger student body comprising of students from other Junior High Schools. We stood a little taller than before; we were in high school, finally.

There were still the gym classes, but an alternative was also offered, Jr. ROTC (Reserve Officers Training Corps). ROTC could be taken in lieu of the traditional gym classes or as an elective course. Many of the less fit choose to take the military courses. It was not uncommon to have many of the physically marginal in the ranks of the cadets. Later a physical fitness program was introduced into the cadet curriculum. Others choose to take ROTC, as perhaps I did, out of a sense of patriotism and maybe in the pursuit of a military career, being physically fit to do so.

There was a very strong opposition to having the military on campus at that time. The anti-war movement was in full swing in society and at my high school. The "Height-Asbury", "Hippie" youth movement was in full bloom then. I felt the peer pressure, but in many ways, my decision to take the ROTC program shaped many actions and decisions in my future life.

Upon entering the cadet corps, I felt a purpose, in spite of many of my peers' opposition. I also found a good mentor in the Senior Military Instructor, Sergeant Major Walters (Ret.) He was a decorated veteran of WWII and Korea. His assistant instructor was a SFC Perkins (Ret) also a combat veteran of WWII and Korea. In spite of being a good soldier and instructor, SFC Perkins was believed to be quite the alcoholic. He and the janitor would frequently disappear to the boiler room for a "boiler".

This cadet experience would prove to be a major turning point in my life, as the instructors encouraged all of the cadets to excel in all areas of their lives in academics or otherwise, whether or not they were headed towards the military service or not. I learned a new discipline and a proclamation to improve my grades and get an eye on college.

We were issued the Army dress green uniform, the same as the active duty, with the exception that the lapels had blue felt sewn on them. The cadet officers wore the garrison cap, (the saucer hat.), while the enlisted ranked cadets wore the flat overseas cap. The officers' brass was different from the enlisted. Both stood out. The rank insignia was worn on the shoulder epaulet. The officers wore silver "pips". The enlisted and NCO rank equivalents were a black material with gold chevrons indicating the rank and snapped on over the epaulet.

The Cadet Corps had a strict chain of command. The entire public high school system consisted of ten high schools which comprised The Cadet Brigade, commanded by a Cadet Colonel. The Brigade had its own staff officers, usually Cadet Lieutenant Colonels or Cadet Majors. Each separate high school was a Cadet Battalion, commanded by a Cadet Lieutenant Colonel. The Battalion had its own staff officers, usually Cadet Majors or Cadet Captains. Each battalion was comprised of from two to five companies. Each company was commanded by a Cadet Captain. The company Executive Officer was a Cadet 1st Lieutenant. A Company consisted of two to four platoons, led by a Cadet 2nd Lieutenant. The NCO ranks were like that of the Army from Cadet Sergeant Major at the Brigade and the Battalion levels, to Cadet First Sergeants at each company. Cadet Sergeants First Class ran each platoon; squads were led by Cadet Staff Sergeants or Cadet Sergeants. There were also the Cadet Corporals, and Cadet Private First Classes. The rest of the enlisted were merely the Cadet Privates.

The overall ROTC program and curriculum covered the three years of high school. It covered many aspects of the military training and activities. The program became more demanding and comprehensive as the cadet progressed with each school year. The advanced course was in the senior year. With each passing semester it was encouraged that the cadets do well academically both in the ROTC program as well as the other academic classes in school. Promotions in the Cadet Corps were based on performance and participation. All cadets up for a promotion, faced a formal promotion board, comprised of the cadet officers and a cadet Sr. NCO. The Military instructor oversaw the proceedings. When a cadet broke into the officer ranks, more responsibilities were required, often requiring the cadet to use his free time and extra duties to accomplish his assignments.

The program included many extracurricular activities which included: The Drum & Bugle Corps, The Drill Team, The Color Guard, The Honor Guard and the Rifle Team. All of these activities required a lot of practice time before and after the regular school hours.

We participated in many civic activities and parades. Cadets earned ribbons for many of these activities. By the senior year, many cadets touted a full chest of ribbons. We earned marksmanship medals and there were several actual medals that were available such as the one the Daughters of the American Revolution (DAR) presented at year's end to an outstanding cadet. There were a couple of others, which elude me now.

We were versed in the Army's history and traditions, organization, drill and ceremonies, leadership, tactics, map reading, first aid, CBS training, physical training, instructor training. With the parents' approval, basic rifle marksmanship on the indoor .22 Caliber range with the target rifles. The best shooters usually wound up on the rifle team. The rifle team was also open to non-ROTC students as well.

It was required every Wednesday (uniform day) to polish the brass and shoes and wear the uniform, pressed and with a well starched khaki shirt, all day at school. We always got mixed reactions in public, as some people thought that we were active duty and either going to or returning from Vietnam. At times, we used the sympathy card to our benefit to those who did not know the differences in the uniforms.

The worst reaction was in school. We were teased and taunted, and some fights broke out over this. We had just as much right to our choices as the others had in protesting ours. There was the battalion parade on the athletic once a month field in the morning before school. It was mandatory to attend, as roll call was taken, and an inspection took place. These activities were a part of our grade. By the end of that first semester, I was promoted to Cadet Staff Sergeant and decided to remain in the program, as I was beginning to have doubts about continuing, but decided to continue. It was my right to study as I choose, and ROTC was my choice. In one way, I began my military career as that ROTC cadet.

At the end of each school year the 91st Training Division (US Army Reserve) held the annual drill competition at the San Francisco Civic

Center. Each high school fielded a drill team, a standard close order drill platoon and a drum & bugle corps performance. The grading was very strict and by the book. The drill teams were scored on their precision and the complexity of their drills and routines. I enjoyed the thrill of these competitions and the camaraderie and esprit-de-corps we shared. Many times, it seemed that it was "us" against "them", as the atmosphere in society at the time was very anti-military. These same feelings were carried on through the active military experience. In returning home from Vietnam, we were spit upon and cursed.

Other events of that year continued to reshape society and had their effect on the youth, and my peers. The Soviets land an unmanned spaceship, the Luna 9, on the moon. The US lands the Surveyor 1 also on the moon and transmits images of the lunar surface back to the world. The Miranda Act becomes law, requiring the police to read a suspect his / her rights and the right to legal counsel and protects the accused from self-incrimination. Sony produces the first integrated electronic circuits. Betty Friedan and 27 other women establish NOW (National Organization for Women) Indira Gandhi becomes the prime minister of India. The feminist movement was in its infancy waiting to shake up the society. It will take several years to really take hold and make major changes.

The first year of high school was very good year for me. I was on the "college-bound" academic track. I took the required and advanced courses. There was to my recollection (not in any order), a geometry class (which I did poorly in due to the math involved), English, and English Literature, American History, Chemistry, (also did not do very well due to the math involved) and ROTC. I had two girlfriends who were interested in me as well as many of the other girls who we hung out with. I tended to have my "good-time girls", regulars and a few I could get serious with. I was rather clumsy, awkward and naïve teen at that time. I guess that I made up for it later.

There was always the ROTC "groupies" (of which, one I later married) that we ran around with. I earned a lot more freedom from my grandparents and continued to earn my own spending cash from the "odd" jobs. Much improvement was due to my grandparents and SGM Walters constant encouragements. The grades were improving at a decent pace. I even went to summer school to pick up extra credits and improve the overall GPA. I recall taking Black history in summer school; (much to most everybody's shock) I did well in that class but did put up with a lot of harassment from both the Whites as well as most of the Blacks. It was worth it, I got an "A" and the extra history credits. I learned a lot and overall enjoyed the class.

I had one Japanese girlfriend that I had known since kindergarten that was my first serious teenage love. I will refer to her as "Nancy". We would take long walks, often through Golden Gate Park and spent a lot of time at the Japanese Tea Garden there in the park. I was head over heels over her and thought it would last forever as most teenaged love affairs go. I took her to the school dances (Slow dancing was a piece of Heaven on Earth for me.) We went out to dinner several times. Her parents liked me a lot. Her father had served in the 442nd during WW II, so he had the respect for the military and my pursuing both the military studies and a possible future career. The only racial indifferences that I experienced were from my own family and, at times bigoted people in public. We got along very well for that first year and I thought that this love would be forever. She did not object to my being in ROTC and in fact, we often were out in public while I was in uniform. (It was, to me, like something straight out of a James Michener novel, East meets West.). It was not until the next year that this illusion of true love was shattered.

The next year, 1967 we completed the sophomore year of high school by that summer. All was going well for me, both academically and at home. I enjoyed more freedom at home. I began to realize that world events were destined to have an effect on my future. Upon entering the junior year of high school, I had decided that I was going to go to college and at that time had my eye on a commission as an officer in the Army. The search and applications began later in the year. The world and the war would have to wait for me.

By the end of that year, the United States had over 480,000 troops in Vietnam. The US began mining the rivers in North Vietnam (In the opinion of many, something that should have been done much earlier in the war, to perhaps include mining the Haiphong Harbor and perhaps, a naval blockade as a better solution.) The Vietnam War is on television nightly and by this time the casualties are announced with such coldness, merely being a statistical number.

In Washington D.C. over 50,000 people protested the Vietnam War at the Lincoln Memorial. Student unrest sweeps the nation as thousands burn their draft cards in protest. Many Vietnam Veterans turn in their medals as well. Mohammad Ali is stripped of his heavyweight boxing title for refusing military service based on his Muslim faith.

The third Arab-Israeli war is fought (That war became known as the Six Day War.) after Egyptian President Nasser begins remilitarizing the Sinai Peninsula. Israel is victorious, routing the Arab forces of Egypt, Jordon and Syria. Israeli forces capture and occupy old Jerusalem, the Sinai, the West Bank, and the Golan Heights. After this short war boundaries are redrawn, and the Suez Canal is closed for security reasons. It is not reopened until 1975.

The first Super Bowl was played that year on January 15th. The Green Bay Packers defeated the Kansas City Chiefs by a score of 35-10.

Both sides fighting each other in the Nigerian Civil War, call for and honor a cease fire for 48 hours so that the soldiers could watch Pele' play in an exhibition match in the city of Lagos.

I was a lot of different things this year. I held on to many opposing views and lifestyles of that era. Overall it was a great period to have lived through with all the changes reshaping contemporary society. I lived in some ways, a duel life.

During the week, I was the typical high school student and ROTC cadet headed with eyes towards attending college to pursue more traditional careers. I broke with tradition on the weekends, or whenever possible. I would put on my Greek fisherman cap, to hide my short hair, and head to the Haight; I was the emerging rebel and the "hippie". The youth movement was headed towards changes. This movement seemed to have its epicenter located on the intersection of Haight St. and Asbury Ave. in San Francisco. I was in the thick of it all on a part time basis.

The music was the biggest draw for many. I was exposed to just about every major and minor West Coast band that emerged at the time. My cousin, Peter Albin, was the bass player for a new band, "Big Brother and the Holding Company, Featuring Janis Joplin. There were many free concerts in Golden Gate Park and in the Panhandle area of Golden Gate Park, near the Haight. I would go to see these events whenever possible. I would go to the original Fillmore Auditorium, The Matrix, The Avalon Ballroom for dancing and the psychedelic light shows.

The FM radio dial was beginning to change and feature this new "underground rock". This new form was slowly being invading the FM dial. Classic music and "elevator" music stations began to disappear off of the FM band dial. Many of us teen agers listened these genres of music, Soul, R&B, Top 40 and the emerging "underground rock", just to maintain our cool. Teenagers of all races also listened and danced to the Motown hits. Many other bands and artists got their start in the '60s but did not hit the top of the charts until the next decade. There were many more "Soul" groups and artists on other record labels (such as James Brown). I merely highlighted Motown in this narrative. **Refer to the Appendix, List**

The above list is far from being complete and my apologies to any band or artist who was not mentioned here. It was amazing to me today how quickly that list came to mind. It is in no way presented in any chronological order and spans more than only one year. I have also tried here to show a variety of musical styles and is no way a presentation of strictly the author's preference.

The music was great, and many aspiring groups were formed. This was the origin of the *"garage bands"*. It seemed that on every block and neighborhood in The City, young people were practicing and rocking the world. I learned basic guitar and was going to be in a famous band and the next San Francisco teen idol. I even went to guitar classes in the old neighborhood that my grandfather had his office, except that the studio was closer to Van Ness Ave.

My overall musical career did involve several attempts to master an instrument. I tried to learn to play the "song flute", violin, piano and cello in elementary school. Even with lessons, I did not excel in music. These endeavors did not last too long, as an almost severed finger from earlier in childhood hampered my fingering of the strings on all but the piano and flute.

Yet, all of these different and diversified musical styles we always enjoyed going to the high school dances. The high school circuit bands always tried to play a variety of music as not or alienate the races. Music played an important role in the sixties; in that it brought the youth together in spite of growing racial awareness and identity. It seemed that even many of the white teens abandoned their racial indifferences to dance to a good Motown slow dance.

Summer, 1967-"The Summer of Love"

The youth movement rocked the society and a generation was often defined by the events of this summer in San Francisco. The Counter Culture questioned the very foundations of the society. This period for me, was an eye-opening experience. As many of my peers did, I questioned religion, and explored new religions, primarily the Eastern religions. The military-industrial complex, American corporations, politics in general and especially the American War in Vietnam, traditional Western history, family and sexual morality, all come under scrutiny and question. Drugs use also was commonplace among the youth. Psychedelic drugs (such as LSD) came into vogue as Professor Timothy Leary, (kicked off of the Harvard's psychology school's faculty) preached "Tune in, Turn on, and Drop out." That phrase became a mantra for the developing *"Hippies"*. Some sought spiritual experiences through the use of drugs, others abused the drugs.

Although similar movements occurred around the nation, Greenwich Village in New York and in many college towns, it all seemed to come together in San Francisco as the epicenter of the "movement". The prelude to the mass summer migration was the much publicized "Human Be-In", January 14, 1967. (I was there as a *"wanna-be"* hippie, Greek Fisherman hat covering my short hair.)

As the lyrics of the Scott McKenzie song beckoned American youth nation-wide; "If you are going to San Francisco, be sure to wear flowers in your hair." "Flower power" was born. It was estimated that 100,000+ young people flocked to "The City". It was also called "The Gathering of the Tribes". It was a time to wear a "costume" of one's own creation. There was color everywhere. It was the time of Free Love, shared drugs and an attempt at peace. (Love, Peace and Happiness).

The Monterey Pop Festival, June 1967, drew many more people estimated to be between 30,000 and 50,000 to Northern California. There was also the Fantasy Fair and Magic Mountain Music Festival in Marin County, north of San Francisco also in June. Many of the bands listed earlier, played to huge crowds at these festivals. It was, perhaps the granddaddy of Woodstock, held later in New York in 1969.

The mainstream media had a field day with this colorful and strange neighborhood and its inhabitants. I even recall that the Grayline tour busses would take tourists through the Haight-Ashbury as a special trip, (no pun intended.). We would offer the tourists free apples and other fruit in the spirit of sharing. Most was refused, thinking that our offerings were laced with LSD. Those tour busses crawled down Haight Street, as often the street was packed with people.

Different types of music floated through the air along with the exciting smells of incense mixed with marijuana and hashish smoke. The tourists would close the windows on the bus. We would hand out handbills for events, light shows, musical and cabaret dancing at "The Fillmore Auditorium", "The Matrix", "Longshoremen's Hall" and "The Avalon Ball Room".

Psychedelic light shows became another art form as strobe lights and overhead projections of oil and colored water ebbed and flowed on the walls and ceilings. Multi-media projections filled these auditoriums with an artificial psychedelic "trip" (if one was not stoned enough). As Eric Burdon sang, "...strobe lights beam, creates dreams...walls move, and minds do too...on the San Francisco Nights...".

Many free concerts were also advertised in this manner. The psychedelic posters advertising became the decoration of many a teen's room. Today these posters command very high prices. Black light posters also became very popular. Day-Glo paint became quite popular as well. "Lava" lights would amuse the watcher, especially if stoned, as the wax changed shape.

Many of the city's services, such as, sanitation, law enforcement, health services, food banks, housing and other social services were simply overwhelmed by this huge and often quick influx of people. It may have taken a couple of years for the transformation to take effect, but hit its zenith during this summer.

The hippie community came together with the "Diggers" and The Haight Street Free Clinic. Several churches opened up "soup kitchens" and food pantries. They gave donated clothing to these new arrivals. There was a great atmosphere of sharing and caring for each other. Many people formed communes and many people lived together in hundreds of the large multi-roomed Victorian houses in the neighborhood. Many of these classic houses were re-painted in bright colors. These became known as "the painted ladies". The most famous were photographed thousands of times and featured in the hit TV series, "Full House". Those rows of Victorian houses were off of Grove Street and the Hayes Valley Park.

In the early days all was chaotic in some ways, yet peaceful most of the time, until later when the "hard" drugs (heroine, speed, meth, illegal prescription drugs) flooded the community. It is said that organized crime was behind the flood of these drugs. Local street gangs preyed on the unfortunate youth, often along racial lines. The neighborhood began its down fall and deterioration. What seemed to have taken a couple of years to create, ended rather quickly. The neighborhood fell into dis-repair and reverted to its former ghetto status. The human toll was great, many became victims of street crime, drug abuse, and health other issues.

As the summer faded and the weather began to grow colder, many "homeless", stoned, burned-out young people, wrapped themselves in old blankets and with blank looks on their dirty young faces and wandered the streets often begging for life's essentials. They became known as "The Blanket People". The end was near for the "Hashbury". The once Utopian dreams died harshly and relatively quickly.

Love, Peace and Happiness was no longer the mantra of the youth. The Haight-Asbury became a necropolis. I too, felt that the movement failed in that it did not provide a viable alternative for the Post-Industrial Society.

Many of these youth returned home to their middle-class homes, colleges, jobs and families. Students returned to school in the fall. Others were drafted and went to Vietnam. Many of the older hippies packed it all up and moved out to the country. Some began cultivating a new cash crop, marijuana, especially in the northern county of Humboldt (of Bigfoot fame). Others reopened their boutiques and specialty shops elsewhere in the city. Antique furniture became the rage and showed up in vast numbers in the shops around the city. Many items were "taken" from the old Victorian houses.

It is often said that the "Hippies" evolved into "The Yuppies" as they graduated from their various colleges and universities. And years later poured new money back into the area transforming the former condemned Victorians into multi-million-dollar pieces of property.

There was a symbolic funeral for the Haight-Ashbury and the "hippie". This mock funeral and public statement was called "The Death of the Hippie". It was the brainchild of activist Mary Kasper. The funeral notices were published and spread around the city. The event was held October 6, 1967 at Buena Vista Park in the city. Mary Kasper is quoted as saying:

"We wanted to signal that this was the end of it, to stay where you are, bring the revolution to where you live and don't come here because it's over and done with."

There were 40th & 50th Anniversary celebrations held in San Francisco years later to commemorate that era in the city's history.

That fall, I resumed my scholastic pursuits and strived to raise my. My true love, "N", had moved out of the city after she dumped me for a cadet officer, a "big man on campus" in other aspects. (I learned later that she had a child out of wedlock and her BMOC left for college.)

I was quite hurt by the loss of my "true love" but was soon revived because another girl had won me over. Her name was Scharlene. (I would later marry her.) She was half -Japanese and held me in awe and wonder. She danced in the Sakura Cherry Blossom Festival, kimono and traditional Japanese music, arts and crafts. It was called "Oban Odori". We went together pretty much until the last semester of my senior year. I became a Cadet Captain later that semester and was appointed as one of the battalion's company commanders.

I do not recall all the classes or the sequence that I took them in both my Junior and Senior years. A few come to mind. These were:

- French (two years),
- World History,
- American History,
- Civics,
- World Literature,
- English Literature,
- American Literature,
- Asian History.
- Black History (in summer school).
- Chemistry,
- Geometry,
- Creative Writing,

- Art, (Sketching)
- Track & Field as my PE elective, in addition to ROTC.
- Journalism.

For a project in journalism, I interviewed my cousin's band, Big Brother & The Holding Company and Janis Joplin. The interview was held in an old Victorian near the corner of Haight & Stanyan Streets. I recorded the interview on a small battery-operated tape recorder. All went well, yes we drank some, smoked some great weed while the drummer played a continuous rhythm on the empties. We all had a good time and I had an excellent interview. I wrote my article and presented the tape as my back-up for the interview. For reasons unknown I never got that tape back. (It probably would be worth quite a bit if it was made available today.) Neither did it ever surface again. My article was not published in the school newspaper, <u>The Eagle</u>, citing that it was too risqué and improper for the student body.

The world experienced a lot of changes. The Vietnam War continued to be fought on the battlefields as well as being protested and fought against on American streets and in the universities and colleges across the nation. The evening news reported the causalities as very routine and often compared the Allied losses to the enemy's losses. At some point I thought with these (inflated numbers); there should be no enemy soldiers or Vietnamese population left.

North Korean armed patrol boats capture the USS Pueblo, an intelligence gathering ship (spy ship). They took the 83-man crew prisoner and threatened to put them on trial as spies, which the punishment would be death. We thought we would open up another theatre of war. It was alleged that the US ship had violated the North Korean waters which extended 12 miles from shore. This foreign policy SNAFU would haunt the US for the next 11 months. The crew was finally released on December 22nd.

On January 31, 1968 the North Vietnamese and the Viet Cong launch a massive offensive throughout South Vietnam. This offensive coincided with the celebration of the Lunar (Chinese) New Year. This is now known as the "Tet Offensive". The US Embassy was invaded and held until 9:15

that morning when US Marines finally was able to secure the embassy again. Losses are heavy on both sides, but the US forces repel the attacks.

In later years, General Giap commander of the North Vietnamese forces, in his memoirs secretly admitted defeat, and was quite surprised that the United States did not capitalize on their victory. The US was caught by surprise by both the suddenness, massiveness, of the attacks and the enemy's temporary gains. Both the US and South Vietnamese were basically demoralized by the enemy's actions and never truly recovered from the enemy's bold move during "Tet". Ironically it was our victory, as the enemy suffered massive losses that took a long time to rebuild back up to their combat strength levels. The US lost its 10,000[th] aircraft fighting during the war.

The first ATM (Automatic Teller Machine) is put into service at the Barclay's bank in London. Years later these debit cards could be used at the POS (Point of Sale) almost everywhere. Credit cards grew exponentially as their use and ownership grew to almost eight cards per American household. American credit card debt was at $8 Billion+ in 2015 dollars.

Dr. Christian Barnard performs the first successful heart transplant in Cape Town, South Africa. He is assisted by a black doctor, Hamilton Nali, who was a self-taught surgeon. Dr. Naki finally received an "honorary" Doctor of Medicine. South African society is still organized under the theory and practice of Apartheid, denying Blacks and "colored" full social standing and recognition. Thurmond Marshall becomes America's first African-American Supreme Court Justice.

On March 16th, at the Vietnamese village of My Lai, US forces under the command of Lieutenant William Calley massacre 347 Vietnamese men, women and children. He is court-marshaled later. The US troop strength "in-country", peaks at 541,000. The secretary of defense announces that 24,500 reservists will be activated. This is the first action calling on the reserve forces. Ironically, at the Newport Folk Festival, July 24th, Arlo Guthrie performs the 20-minute version of the song that will become the anthem for the anti-war movement, Alice's Restraunt. The Movie followed later. (Even today, Alice's Restaurant is played almost non-stop on Thanksgiving by many radio stations.)

The 1968 Presidential election both heats up and is polarized between the "Hawks" (Who want the Vietnam War to be fought to victory.) and the "Doves" (Who want peace at any cost.) The nation was divided over Vietnam and both sides appealed to "The Silent Majority".

President Johnson shocks the nation when he announces that he will not run for re-election and will refuse any attempted nomination by his party. Robert F. Kennedy enters the race and wins the California Primary in June. On his way to a speech accepting the nomination, he is assassinated by an angry 24-year-old Jordanian, Sirhan Sirhan over remarks Kennedy said about his (Kennedy's) support of Israel.

The Democratic Party nominates Hubert Humphrey as their candidate. The convention in Chicago is marred by often violent protests and the leaders later go on trial as "The Chicago Seven". "The Yippies" have landed in Chicago and Mayor Daly gears up for the August Democratic Convention. A bitter campaign is fought until Richard Nixon wins the November election with his promises to win in Vietnam with honors. (He repeats this slogan while expanding the war itself.)

The United States passed the Civil Rights Act of 1968 which in part outlaws housing and other discrimination based on race or religion. In spite of the Civil Rights Act passing, on April 4th, Dr. Martin Luther King Jr. is assassinated in Memphis, Tennessee at the Lorraine Motel by a white radical named James Earl Ray. (Ray is later convicted of King's murder; he dies in prison in 1998.) Immediately afterwards, race riots erupt across the nation. Forty-six are killed across the country during these riots. The nation is still embroiled with the JFK assassination conspiracy theories, the Dr. King assassination gives the country yet another conspiracy to unravel. Both continue today to remain unanswered. Once again race relations in the country are very strained and at times violent.

Student protests continue around the country, while in Paris, France students take to the streets protesting inequalities of the French educational system. They block streets and run wild in the streets until the French police contain the protestors and finally restore calm. The student demands are taken under official advisement.

In spite of the Sexual Revolution sweeping the world, as "The Pill" is used by most women at this point in time also is the use of condoms; Pope Paul VI issues an encyclical against "artificial means of contraception". He further demands priestly celibacy as fundamental doctrine of the Roman Catholic Church. He re-issues this same demand in 1970. Many priests begin to come under investigation for pedophilic acts. Catholic Church attendance declines.

As a vital part of my quest for a college scholarship, I must demonstrate community service. I join the youth branch of The American Red Cross in the spring and was chosen to attend the Youth Leadership Summer Camp. It was held in the Santa Cruz Mountains which was the same location, but different camp site, as the Salvation Army summer camp that I attended earlier. To say the least, aside from the leadership training, I found another girlfriend, which I continued to see, in spite of my dating my future wife. After a hot and heavy semester, I got rather scared because her mother came across as wanting to get the daughter "hitched-up" with someone with promise, perhaps marriage in mind at such an early age. I also recall there was always plenty of liquor waiting for my visits to see the daughter. It was hot and heavy, and that young lady taught me a lot. I remained involved with the American Red Cross throughout my high school days. I had it made, a steady girlfriend and one across town. The two would never know about each other.

Apollo 7 is launched from Florida on its eleven-day mission in space. They orbit the Earth a total 163 times. Apollo 8 follows on December 21st on a mission to orbit the moon.

Once again in my short young life on August 20th, I thought that another war was going to break out as the Soviet Union and its Eastern Bloc Aligned nations invade Czechoslovakia with 200,000 + troops and armor to stop the popular uprising, known as "The Prague Spring", that was sweeping that nation. The troops remain in full occupation enforcing an oppressive program of "normalization". American forces in Europe remain on high alert during the initial phases of the Soviet action.

Less than a week later, Mayor Richard Daly opens the Democratic National Convention in Chicago. There were plenty of protestors on hand. For the most part, the early demonstrations were peaceful compared what would follow. Mayor Daly immediately orders an 11:00 PM curfew. (Did that apply equally to the conventioneers?) On August 28th,

Daly unleashes the police to quell the demonstrations which are making Chicago "look bad" in the nation's eyes. By most accounts, the police reacted without provocation, sending 100+ to the emergency rooms and arresting 175. Hubert Humphrey is nominated, and later on

September 1st, kicks off his presidential campaign during New York's Labor Day Parade. Later, on September 7th The Women's Liberation groups, to include the National Organization of Women (NOW) protests The Miss America Pageant. Their actions included the iconic "bra-burnings". The bra-burnings experienced an excited titter in society. Governor George Wallace also is making presidential bids amidst a lot of racial overtones. He chooses General Curtis LeMay as his running mate.

The Summer Olympics Games open in Mexico City on October 12th. Earlier that month, October 2nd, the Mexican Army massacred, killing and wounding hundreds of student protesters at the Plaza of the Three Cultures (Tlatelolco Square).

At the Summer Olympics two African-American sprinters Tommie Smith and John Carlos give the Black Panther Power Salute after receiving their medals as the Star-Spangled Banner is played in their honor and that of the United States. Many whites are outraged at their display. Blacks now embrace the "power salute" and the ritualistic hand shaking known as "dapping" emerges in the Black culture as a sign of solidarity and brotherhood. Many whites find this ritual as offensive.

November 5th, is Election Day in the country. When the votes were tallied the results were:

> Popular vote} 31,770,000 for Nixon, 43.4 % of the total, 31,270,000 or 42.7 % for Humphrey and an astonishing 9,906,000 or 13.5% for Wallace with 0.4 % going to other candidates.

The year ended with a few historical tid-bits they are as follows: November 14 becomes "National Burn Your Draft Card Day", which did involve several protests mainly on college and university campuses nationwide. November 26 after much stalling and delays the South Vietnamese government decides to join the Paris talks. On December 11th, Veterans Day, a 3.3% unemployment rate is announced. On November 27th, I turned 17, old enough to enlist.

My own young life was moving along at incredible speed. Lyndon Johnson was the US president. Hubert Humphrey was the Vice President.

Ronald Regan was our governor. The 90th Congress would convene on January 3rd. The war still raged on. We had entered the last year of high school in September of 1968.

Ours was the mighty George Washington Senior High School, Eagle Class of 1969, known as **"The Class of the Century".** We were not only the senior class; we were at the top of the school system with less than a year to go until we were "free". "No more school, no more books, no more teacher's dirty looks…" Well, at least for some. Many seniors would be heading off to the various colleges and universities, both here in San Francisco and elsewhere in California and the nation. Others would be venturing to vocational schools or apprenticeships in the various trades. Still others, simply would join the job market in some form.

I had applied to and had been accepted at the following universities: The University of Hawaii, The University of Oregon, The University of Washington and The University of Idaho.

By this time, my grades were straight "A" s with extra units completed. The last semester would basically all extra credit and I declined to graduate early. I joined the track team and became the running long jumper. I did not star in a lot of events but was placed on the various teams as a utility man and as "filler" which gave the team points in a given event for fielding a full team. I was just about at the peak of my physical fitness. Our Eagle team won the San Francisco All City Track & Field Championship. I had earned my varsity letter and jacket. (Never picked them up though.). The extra activities and community services added to my resume'.

I had also applied for a full 6th US Army ROTC scholarship which would have covered all of my expenses plus giving me a monthly stipend almost equivalent to a Buck Sergeant, E-5. I was the JROTC San Francisco Brigade commander (Cadet Colonel) and had many letters of recommendation, both from the Military Science instructors as well as my other civilian teachers and administrators. It really looked as if I would be selected at the HQs. 6th US Army right there at the Presidio of San Francisco. I had a "plan "B" ready in the wings if all this fell through. I would be 17 in November of that year and with my grandparent's signature, I could enlist in the military. For the next few months I would play a long and anxious waiting game for the scholarship. All that would be needed would be my choice of university and for my sending that school a letter of acceptance.

In those days the ROTC scholarship was very political and very connected due in part to the Vietnam War. Middle class American parents were trying to get their sons into college with a deferment for at least four years. They were wagering that the war would be ended on Nixon's timetable. Having a son in ROTC was almost guaranteed to keep him in college, avoiding the draft. (Unless the grades fell too low or, failed the ROTC program then it was back into the draft pool.)

Most though, avoided the military all together and would take their chances with the draft or perhaps relocate to Canada or Sweden. Some even would go to prison for refusing. The Anti-War movement was reaching its heights and there was often unrest in the streets. Many protests were held at the recruiting stations and at the ROTC units on the various college campuses nationwide. (One ROTC building was bombed as well.)

I still was keenly aware of what was going on worldwide as the cold war dragged on and at times very tensely. The war in Vietnam to be never-ending, but I was prepared either way to join the military. I perhaps had hoped that if the ROTC scholarship came through that I could be commissioned, complete my officer training and head to Vietnam. (It was the only war that the United States had going at the time, and in a patriotic way I did not want to be left out.)

I had a good friend whom I worked with at the bakery who dropped out of school as a junior and enlisted in the US Marine Corps. They made him a baker and sent him to Vietnam. He hated both with a passion. I was also corresponding with another friend from the Red Cross who was also in Vietnam. He also did not report favorably either on the Marines or the war itself.

Many cadets both from my high school and the brigade wound up going to the different military academies. (West Point, Annapolis, the Air Force Academy, the Coast Guard Academy and the Maritime Academy.) Others were accepted into the 6th US Army ROTC program. I only recall about six or so of my class who enlisted either in our senior year or within the year after graduation. I continued to wait on news of my scholarship. I decided to enlist at 17. After convincing my grandparents, after a long argument, they agreed to sign me into the Army. I enlisted soon after my 17th birthday on the Delayed Entry program in 1969. That plan, with the provision that should the scholarship come through, I would be immediately enrolled in the ROTC program as an enlisted reservist.

My friend, Bill Garrett, and I made many trips to the recruiters in our junior year. Ironically, the Marine recruiter almost had us almost convinced to join until he mentioned our friend who had earlier enlisted through that recruiter's office. When the recruiter mentioned his name and how the Marine Corps had made him a baker, we were no longer interested since we knew how much our friend hated baking for the Marines in Vietnam. That recruiter sealed our rejection when he commented something along the lines that "…well you guys have skills from your work experience that the Marine Corps needs." (Thanks, but no thanks.) We went to see the Army recruiter where I was offered one stripe (PVT, E-2) for enlisting on the delayed entry program as well as my three years of JROTC. The other advantage would be that with a three-year RA enlistment, one could select the training that one was qualified for. (Pick a long school as being drafted one would be at the mercy of the needs of the Army.)

The Bakery:

Other things from my senior year of high school that I recall; I had a good job (at the time) and I had been working in Knopp's Bakery on Geary Street, between 17th & 18th Avenues for about a year with four of my classmates. (One had later dropped out of high school to join the US Marine Corps; they made him a baker.) If I recall correctly, we made $1.50 an hour. We worked a few hours after school several days a week and quite often on the weekends. It gave me plenty of spending money and some cash to give to my grandparents. (At that time, I thought that they really needed my money.) I did not know that for the most part they were financially secure. I even had the Army send them an allotment check later out of my military pay every month.

The owner was a German immigrant who had served in the US Army after the war. The building was old at the time, in that the Richmond district was developed from the late 1800's. I do not know when it was built, but there was plenty of plumbing and electrical issues that had to be taken care of. Heinz had a wife and a small cute little daughter. The family lived in an apartment above the bakery and store. He was quite the strict boss and perfectionist in the disciplined Germanic military tradition. His heavy accent often reminded us of a Nazi SS officer. He was firm, but fair in his treatment of his employees.

We began our career cleaning up the bakery when we got off of school. He would leave a note or instructions with his wife, who passed us our instructions. He usually was already upstairs asleep, as he began his work day very early in the morning. We would rotate the various assignments in the bakery. We had all the pots and pans, as well as the various utensils and machine parts to wash. There was a mountain of pie, sheet pans and cake pans to grease for the next morning's use. All the equipment had to be washed as well as the walls.

The hardest job was when two of us (usually) wound up having to scrape the floor, on our hands and knees, from one end of the work area to the other of dry, caked on dough, which had been ground into the old wooden floors. We were armed with a metal scraper with a thick wooden handle and a shop whisk broom. Under the fear of Mr. Knopps' wrath, we were to strictly "Scrape und brush, nine brush und scrape…" The wooden floors were old and in many places warped and or uneven. Not only did we have to scrape the floors, the cracks between the boards had to be clean as well. Once the floor had been scraped, it was washed down with disinfectant.

We would periodically have to clean the refrigerators which were of the industrial type with two levels and a separate door for each level. There were about six or eight separate double sections. It got gross at times, as the mold would build up along the seams and we discovered food stuffs that had been forgotten since the last cleaning. It was a science project away from school.

We had a lot of fun working there, as we all went to school together, except for one guy who was a high school dropout and was quite into the drug scene. To put it simply, Bob was stoned most of the time. We never went hungry, as there were plenty of "day-old" pastries and other goodies that we could have. Many times, we could go home with a bag of bakery goods. Not only did we once eat a cheese cake apiece, we often took one home.

After I had been working there at the bakery for about six months or more, the baker began teaching me some baking skills. He had me come in early on Sunday to help with his biggest day. I would love arriving at work on a wet and cold morning entering the bakery to the smells of the baking and strong "cowboy coffee" which was always brewing on another ancient gas burner. The hot bakery on those cold mornings was greatly appreciated. (Until we got working hard.) We were offered a cup of the brew and a Danish pastry that we brushed with a good coating of melted butter that was kept in a metal bowl in front of the oven. Sometimes we would drizzle the pastry with a powdered sugar glaze. Hot cross buns were always a favorite at Easter.

He catered to a very large Sunday church crowd from Saint Monica Catholic Church and school who would always buy bakery goods after church. He taught me how to cook the fruit fillings and cheese cake toppings. It was cooked in a very large copper kettle over an old large gas burner mounted on old cast-iron legs. I would make strawberry, blueberry, raspberry, pineapple and custard fillings and toppings. I would also mix a huge batch of whipped cream with either vanilla or rum. When nobody was looking I would consume large amounts of the whipped cream, especially the rum flavor. I loved that assignment. As time passed I would be making simple cakes, pastries, cookies as well as being the "hot man" removing the baked goods from the huge industrial oven. The oven had rotating shelves and we had to be quick in removing the finished products. The pans were removed with a large wooden paddle similar to what one would see in a pizza shop, or with heavy oven gloves. The finished goods were then placed on the cooling racks. It was long and hot work, especially in the warmer summer months. Overall I enjoyed the job.

Once the baker was satisfied with our skills, he would often leave us alone to work as he disappeared upstairs and usually, if not sleeping, he was drinking beer and his schnapps. We usually got along just fine when he would make a surprise inspection and super-visionary visit because we had found the case of rum that he kept in the cellar which was used in his recipes. At other times, we would share a joint or a bottle ourselves.

During one of these times Bob brought in a large bag of marijuana to be dried out in the oven at a low temperature with the oven shelves rotating. The oven and the bakery were ventilated by a large exhaust system which exited the bakery just outside of the baker's upstairs apartment. My friend forgot about his weed and it proceeded to be slowly "baked". When he realized his error, it was too late. Both Bob and his stash were very well baked. The baker's wife came down in quite a good mood, giggling all the way to the front of the store. Another time my rather stoned friend was making a batch of cookies and dropped his bag of weed into the mixer. Most of his weed spilled out into the mixing bowl and joined the cookie dough. It all became well mixed. Much later when the cookies were sold, one of the sales girls commented about an old lady who kept returning to the bakery to buy just a few of the same cookies at a time with each trip. We never were caught and the neither the baker nor his wife said anything about those strange incidents occurring.

I continued to work there all the way until graduation and would later stop by to visit when I was home on leave from the Army. The owner would later bake my multi-tiered wedding cake the next year and he gave it to me and my bride as a wedding gift. That work experience was invaluable and helped me to build a strong work ethic.

During that last semester in high school, a good friend and I bought a car together. We bought this car off of one of our other friend's Dad. For $50.00, we became the proud owners of a stock 1953 Mercury "woody" station wagon. It was rather beat up and sported a huge dented rusty hood that shook when we were driving about town. Patches of rust flaked off before we could begin to Bondo the rust spots. At times it left a smoke cloud in its wake. While we did not have the "cool" car or the hot rod as others in our class had, we were still very happy we had a car. We could load a few of us in that big car. Besides all the teasing that we got, we were mobile and could care fewer what others thought of our ride. It beat walking or taking the bus. The vehicle was illegal as hell. The license plate was good for a year. (In California, the license plate remained with the vehicle.) We had neither insurance nor even a license ourselves. We drove very well and often prayed that the smoke screen would not be blown out near a cop.

We were able to tune it up and change the oil as well as make minor repairs. We cleaned it up quite a bit and were able to keep gas in the tank. One time I wanted to take my girlfriend out driving, but the crew insisted on tagging along. We stopped at the San Francisco Memorial at Land's End and had planned to park and make out. The crew all bailed out to afford us some privacy but ruined the mood by constantly trying to nonchalantly stroll by trying not to peek. The mood was broken, and we regrouped and headed off to other destinations. That old car served us well and when my friend Bill and I got our report dates for the Army's BCT (Basic Combat Training), the friend's father who had sold us the car in the first place, felt bad for us and bought the car back from us with a profit. The year, 1969 saw many more historic events that still influence life today. I felt that I was in the middle of it all. Some of these events are listed in the **Appendix** for simplicity sake:

As the end of the high school days were nearing their end, the world events seemed more relative to me. I would soon be considered a man before my time in many ways. The military, for many of us, would become our "rite of passage" into adulthood. I also had a tentative reporting date for my final enlistment process and report date for BCT.

My love life takes a major turn, as Scharlene discovers that I had been secretly seeing my former girlfriend, "Nancy" and thanks to my good friend "Bill", who is a very bad liar, we break-up. I do have two senior prom tickets in my possession, and I turn right around and ask "Nancy" to the George Washington Senior Prom. She then asks me to hers. The two senior proms were just wonderful. We enjoyed a two very exclusive dinners, two romantic evenings together. I even hired a cab to take us to the top of "Telegraph Hill" where Coit Tower in Pioneer Park, is located in San Francisco, and we were mesmerized by the city and Bay Area night lights. We shocked many people at my prom in that they knew of the history of my two girlfriends. The rumors flew. We parted from those two enchanting evenings promising to remain true to each other and, of course remain in contact, as it would not be long until I would be in the Army and she would be going to college. We continue to see each other as my report date drew nearer.

The class of George Washington Senior High School was graduated in the second week of June 1969. **"FREE AT LAST !** "I spent the last few weeks getting rid of my childhood toys, unwanted clothing and souvenirs, either donating them or giving them to the younger kids in the neighborhood. I was counting down my last days as a civilian. I do believe that at some time in those last months, my scholarship rejection notice arrived. I was Army bound much to the dismay and sadness of my grandparents. They had signed for me, yet also realized that if they had not have done so, I would merely have to wait until my 18th birthday in November when I could enlist on my own.

My report date was June 27th at the Oakland AFES (Armed Forces Entry Station). There would be one more physical to pass and my good friend Bill (He would report two weeks after I did.) would be ready to be sworn in on our report date.

I made my rounds and said good bye to all of my friends and class mates the week before my reporting. Everybody swore that they would stay in contact with me while I was in the Army.

I was now, very much in tune with the world situation and the events that were unfolding before me. With the Army so close to be my life I had to take another stock of events.

CHAPTER TEN

The Armed Forces Entry Station & BCT: June 27, 1969

The armed forces entry station in 1969 was nothing like it is today. Today we have the all-volunteer military and no draft. Not so in 1969 where 24.9% of the military was drafted, primarily for the Army and Marine Corps. Between 1964 and 1969, 1,857,304 men were drafted. The Navy, The Air Force and The Coast Guard only selected those very few who had very special skills already developed and in use at the time of their induction. Those few who had a college degree were usually offered OCS School (Officer Candidate School).

I reported on June 27th, 1969 to the Oakland, Ca. induction / entry station very early that morning. I was already qualified for Signal School. I would become a tactical communications repairman. I would become a Field General COMSEC Repairman (Communication Security, Crypto, MOS [Military Occupational Specialty] 31S20.) I had only a few things packed and in a small over-night bag, as the Army did not want a trainee to have very much when he reached the Reception Battalion in basic training. I was tired even before the day started; a day that seemed to never end. It would all begin in Oakland. I caught the Muni buses and then the trans-bay bus over to Oakland and on to AFES.

First off, there was a small army of protestors on hand to greet us, even at that un-Godly hour, urging us not to enter the building. One young lady even bared her breasts with a smile. They handed out leaflets (Which were deposited inside the building in a large trash barrel.)Many were here only for their initial physical and determination of their draft status. Others either had previously been drafted and were reporting to ship out to basic training, or like myself, were enlisted, waiting final processing.

Once inside, the military staff tried to keep us in order and moving through a seemingly endless maze of lines, stations, paperwork, physicals and, of course the traditional "hurry-up and wait." All of the armed services were represented and when a specific function was required for that branch we were separated.

Many of those there were trying to get out of military service, period. A couple of perspective draftees showed up *"in-drag"*. (The shrinks cleared them; they were not really gay; they were more like Klinger from the MASH episodes.) Another gentleman showed up in black pajamas wearing a bamboo conical hat (like the VC wear). He had a large bull's eye target painted on his back. He kept yelling "...shoot me, SHOOT ME !!" He did not follow instructions quite well. The military personnel took him aside and a bit later a Federal Policeman arrived and that was the last we saw of "Charlie". We suspected a Federal citation was issued and he was given another chance to be drafted after his court appearance.

The circus was just getting underway. Those of us who were actually trying to enlist were getting rather angry yet amused. Another guy, after he was already inducted went up to a medic and pulled out a large knife (how he got the knife in was a mystery, other than there were no metal detectors in use at Federal buildings at that time.) and cut off his right index finger stating "...I cannot shoot a rifle now!", as he waved this bleeding hand all about. The medics rushed in, stopped the bleeding and bandaged up the stump. That did not get him out of the military, as an older master sergeant came out a bit later and announced to us "It was a nice try! ...we'll just have to teach him to shoot left handed."

Others tried other methods, like faking convulsions, masturbating, simply acting like the village idiot, messing up deliberately on paper work and the written tests. The most creative attempt that I saw that morning was when about 100 of us were in a large room stripped down to our skivvies getting our physicals and an individual when ordered to "...drop 'em, and spread your cheeks (buttocks; yes, there were those who spread their facial cheeks.) did so; and his buttocks, anus and inside legs were covered with a brown substance. This guy then, to our shock, began to wipe his finger over the brown mess and then lick his finger. Needless to say, those around him quickly moved away from him. A couple of rather large NCOs grabbed this man and bodily escorted him out of the room and to the shrink's office.

A while later one of the sergeants returned to announce to us that basically"…peanut butter is not shit!" I guess this guy got an "A" for his creativity and effort but was drafted anyway. Even after all that while we were still standing around very exposed, some joker yanked on the curtain cord and opened the blinds to show the employees of the office building across the street our "junk". (I'm quite sure those office workers were very used to this by now.)

I was not then, nor am I now a psychologist, but an aware that the psychology tests and profiling tests are designed with the same type of question being asked in many different ways. What comes to mind would go something like this: Do you like camping? *No!* Do you like the outdoors? *No!* Do you like hiking? *No!* Do you like to walk along the beach in the summer with your girlfriend? *Yes!* Busted, he'll probably wind up in the infantry any way. There were many variations to these lines of questioning that when analyzed, revealed the truth.

Some tried to indicate that they still wet the bed, others claimed to be sleep walkers. Yet others indicated that they talked in their sleep. (As I learned later in Crypto School, those who readily talked in their sleep were security risks.) Some tried to indicate that they were gay. Weight was not always a factor back then, unless diagnosed as morbidly obese. Those who qualified in all categories, but weight, usually found themselves in "special training" companies upon arrival at basic training. In many cases the Army saved many lives this way and improved the overall health of the "fatsos" Others tried to fake all sorts of symptoms to be rejected and classified as 4-F, unfit for military service.

The "jocks" were sometimes the funniest to me with all of their "macho bravado". I recall this one very muscular young man in particular. In the course of the usual small talk (what branch? Drafted or enlisting? What will your job be? Where are you from? Etc.) he revealed that he was enlisting for Airborne Infantry, with the Ranger, Special Forces option. He came across as a John Wayne on steroids. When the medic pulled out the needle to draw a blood sample, this one man killing machine, with blood and guts and veins between his teeth (thank you Arlo) turned whiter that a sheet collapsed, passed out in a cold dead faint, falling into a scrambled hunk of America's finest killing machine. We don't know what happened to him afterwards. (Maybe he should have tried the Peace Corps.)

We broke for lunch and with an Army issued meal ticket were escorted across the street through the protestor's lines to a large restaurant and with a dollar limit, had our first meal on Uncle Sam.

After lunch we returned to the AFES building and by mid-afternoon, we were ready for the last phase of our first day in the military. We were all marched into a large room and lined up in what would be our first formation. We then were sworn in. We had a travel packet issued, containing our travel orders, as well as a basic set of paperwork to be handed over when we reached the Reception Battalion at our Basic Training station. Most of us "army guys" would be going to Ft. Lewis, Wa. The marines would be going to San Diego, Ca. for their 'boot' camp.

We were put at ease. Then out of the blue we were called back to attention and a couple of mean looking Marines came out and went down the rank counting: "One, Two, Three, Four...Marine!" If we had the paperwork that indicated that we were "RA" (Regular Army, meaning that we had enlisted) we were safe. Everyone that the Marines called out had their paperwork pulled and their travel orders were changed to indicate San Diego bound. That is when I saw several draftees break down and cry.

I don't know what time it was, sometime in the later part of the afternoon, we were all called together again in that large room. Those with orders for Ft. Lewis were separated out into our movement orders. We were now officially in the US Army and subject to the UCMJ (Uniform Code of Military Justice); after a roll call, we were led downstairs to a waiting army bus, another roll call taken and then loaded onto the bus. So far, no one had escaped. We would be transported to the Oakland International Airport for our trip to Seattle, Wa., and on to Ft. Lewis.

Soon, I don't know how long it actually was, as time now did not have the same meaning for those on their way to basic training, we arrived at the Oakland International Airport.

The bus delivered about 50 +/- of us to the terminal and we were marched (not really marched, sort of an orderly meander.) to the waiting area for our flight to Seattle.

As we walked through the terminal we got many odd looks and

comments from the other civilian passengers. Some knew what we were all about and flashed us the "V" peace sign. Servicemen in uniform from all the branches, walked by, some shook their heads, others wished us luck; others merely flashed us the peace sign. One soldier simply flipped off the NCO who was in charge of us, with the traditional "bird", or the "one finger salute". That vet must have known that we were Basic Training bound, He was back from the 'Nam as he had a chest full of ribbons.

When we sat around the boarding / waiting area we continued to be observed and commented upon as somewhat of an oddity. We were allowed to visit the snack bar, and gift shop, but could not wander too far, as we were under the constant surveillance of our "Troop Movement NCO". The armed services maintained a courtesy patrol at the airport, usually comprised of a mix of the services. Their function was to insure that military personnel were in the proper uniform and were behaving properly. We did not have any uniforms yet, so we were safe.

We probably were too tired or bored to behave badly. Many returning G.I.s from Vietnam walked by with their ribbons and badges displayed. Quite a few of these veterans were drunk by now. I could not but to think how these young men looked as they were about our ages. It was understandable for the older NCOs and officers to look older, as they were. Once again, more waiting made time drag by. We were getting used to this "hurry-up and wait" routine already.

After what seemed like an eternity, our flight was announced, and we headed to the boarding gate. We were allowed to board first because the clerk had been informed that we were "America's future soldiers". Some waiting passengers clapped and wished us well. The "movement NCO" checked off our names and wished us well, as we boarded the aircraft. Another NCO replaced the first one and collected all the necessary paperwork. Number two would accompany us for the rest of the trip. We were finally on our way. No one had escaped.

Our contingent did not fill the plane, but we took up the majority of the seats. The plane shuddered and rumbled as it was towed out to the tarmac. The tow tractor disconnected, and the jet fired up its engines and began its slow taxi towards the runway. There was no turning back now. The stewardesses gave us the traditional safety briefing and emphasized we would be over water during most all of the flight and of importance of the flotation devises, should we have to ditch over water. That really gave me confidence for the aircraft and the piloting skills of the crew. I was already nervous, and we were not allowed to consume any liquor per the Army's directives. A few of us had quite a bit earlier.*(Thanks a bunch Uncle Sam, you are not helping this kid.)*

I was quite nervous, as this would be my first airplane ride. I was afforded a window seat near the wing. I had a good view of the outside from my vantage point. The plane finally reached its ready point on the take-off runway. The engines burst into a great roar and we could feel the aircraft strain on its set brakes. The jets reached the approximated maximum RPMs and like magic, we surged forward when the pilot released the brakes. We all shakes rattled and rolled down the runway at an ever-increasing speed. I was forced all the way back into my seat as the "G" force increased. All of a sudden with a great "thump" we were bounced into the air. We were airborne. I thought how magical this was. I recall looking down at the Alameda Naval Air Station and saw a huge aircraft carrier down below; it looked like a bath toy to me.

The captain came on the cabin intercom and introduced himself. He informed us and the other passengers that we were on board, brand new Army recruits headed to basic training. He then told us that he was going to bank the air craft and circle the San Francisco Bay one more time. The captain continued on telling us that he would be headed out over the Pacific Ocean and will be flying up the Pacific Coast to Seattle. (Perhaps for some, their very last view of the Bay, as I suspected that they would be in Vietnam in about four months or so, and not all of them would make it home alive.)

We continued to head west, steadily climbing towards our cruising altitude over the Pacific. The Golden Gate Bridge slipped past my window and I felt rather sad having to say good bye to my city by the bay. Other than a couple of trips to Reno, Nv. With the family, I had never been out of California in my 17 years. This was going to be an adventure in more ways than one.

My sad feelings soon passed as we flew through several clouds and I was amazed. It looked like pink cotton candy as the sun began its decent into the horizon, giving the clouds a pink hue. It seemed as if I just could reach out of the window and grab a hand full of that cotton candy. We banked right and headed north. The San Francisco Bay Area slipped way behind me.

For the first leg of the flight I was fascinated taking in all of the new feelings and generally the experience of just being up in the air, seemingly unsupported. I watched the tip of the wing rise and fall. My feelings were mixed about this in that a little thought kept telling me that the wing was going to fall off. I kept my feelings and thoughts to myself and kept telling myself that everything would be OK and that I was a soldier now. (Actually, a maggot trainee, as I would soon learn, as well as some other colorful descriptions the drill sergeants would lay on us.)

A traditional airline dinner was served which for me, was both a new experience, and a welcome one at that. We had green peas with the meal. (I would later conclude with my continued flying experiences, that when green peas are served, the plane would always hit a bit of turbulence on that flight.) We hit a small amount of turbulence. The aircraft shook a bit and bounced just enough to force some of the green peas into my lap. I survived my first airborne turbulence.

We continued flying up the West Coast as evening closed in about us. The dinner trays were cleared, and we were on the last leg of the flight. It was a quiet time and I could not but think of all that went before this moment in my young life. At this point of the experience, I felt like an experienced flying veteran. When I first used the in-flight toilet, I thought that I would be sucked down into the bowels of the aircraft when the toilet flushed with a great roar and blue/green liquid swirled down the trap door.

{The whole flight seemed to take forever then, but in researching the aircraft speeds today, the total flight time would be around 1 hour and 45 minutes cruising at an average air speed of 500 MPH. I do not recall the model of the aircraft taken at the time, but a 707 would carry 110 passengers and a crew of 8 at a top speed of 570 MPH and a DC-8 would cruise at a top speed of 588 MPH with 124 passengers and a crew of 6. We may have even been on some other type of aircraft at the time as well.}

Soon the captain announced our decent into in Seattle / Tacoma International Airport. I felt the plane bank and it began its decent. My ears popped. We could also feel the plane slow considerably. It was an incredible sight as we broke through the cloud cover and the lush green panorama of Washington and the Cascade Mountains spread before us. Soon the metropolis of Seattle / Tacoma spread out before us. Seattle proper was to our northeast, Tacoma and Ft. Lewis were to our south west. Mt. Olympus was to the North West and Mt. Rainer was to the northeast. We continued towards the airport and as we got lower, I could see the cars, houses roads and buildings rise up to meet us as we descended. They looked like toys until we were just about to land things returned to their normal size.

The plane continued its decent. I looked out of the window and saw the flaps drop towards the ground and the air brakes pop up from the wing. With a jolt, we dropped, and I heard the tires scream with the first contact with the tarmac. I was lunged forward, as if pushed by magical invisible hands. There was a huge *"whooshing"* sound as the aircraft continued to slow with the brakes slowly being applied bringing us to a normal speed. The jets were reversed to bring us in. It seemed as if we were going to run out of runway. The engines now were only making a gentle whine as we turned around and taxied towards the terminal.

With a few small bumps we slowly pulled up to the waiting terminal. The plane shuddered as we came to a complete stop, parked at the terminal gate. (The aircraft seemed to sigh as the lights flickered and the air conditioning briefly shut off.) In a blink lights and A/C was restored being that we were now connected to the auxiliary outside power terminal. People began to stand up and gather their carry-on baggage and personal items. The front door was opened by the stewardesses. The smell of spent aviation fuel soon became apparent to us. (That smell would remain with me throughout my life, especially in Vietnam.) We began to exit the plane.

There were more sergeants in starched Khaki summer uniforms waiting to direct us to a large seating area near the main front of the terminal. There seemed to be more groups of young men with small overnight bags sitting patiently waiting for something to happen. There were more NCOs about with these groups as well. It was now well into the evening.

Soon several OD green army busses pulled up to the terminal and opened their doors. The drivers dressed in army green fatigues stepped out by the doors of the busses. Some lit their cigarettes. We all really wanted one as well ourselves. These groups slowly stood up and headed towards the waiting busses. One good sergeant allowed his groups a smoke break outside. One by one the rest of the groups went outside for the same luxury of nicotine and Seattle / Tacoma air.

Our group was next and having seen what was allowed the other groups, many scrambled for their smokes. Those who did not have any cigarettes bummed one from a travel companion. We were led outside and enjoyed our break. Our sergeant took another roll call, checking off our names as we boarded the bus and we ditched the last of our cigarette.

Waiting with the driver was another NCO. Instead of the overseas cap, he wore a painted fiberglass helmet liner with a decal of his rank in front and a colored stripe running around the helmet liner. Our "movement NCO" handed his paperwork over to this new sergeant. This looked serious as the helmeted one barked instructions to us and reminded us that "We were in the Army now!"

At this time Interstate 5 was not complete between the airport and Ft. Lewis so I do not recall the route taken. I do not remember how long it took to make this journey, but then, it seemed a long time and even longer as we entered the post and headed towards the Reception Station. (Probably on North Fort, where all the Basic training was held, three brigades worth in 1969.). On the map, it is 37.3 miles of today's travel between the two locations. Ft Lewis is also 9.1 miles south, south west of Tacoma. This leg of the interstate would not be completed until November of that year. We were "rubber-necking" all the new sights as we headed to our new home.

We pulled into Ft. Lewis at some point that night. A lot of history preceded us as we headed towards the Reception Station. I do not recall the route, other that once on post, we were told that we would be headed towards North Fort, and for more processing and then on to Basic Training. The post was divided into two main parts, the older North Fort, north of I-5 and the newer Main Post, Ft. Lewis.

Fort Lewis was established in 1917 as Camp Lewis and became the home of the 91st Infantry Division. (Years after WW II, the 91st would be the 91st Training Division and assisted in a lot of my reserve training.) It was the largest military post on the West Coast covering over 87,000 acres. It was named after Col. Meriwether Lewis of the Lewis & Clark expedition in the early 19th Century. It became Ft. Lewis during WWII and was a major training and deployment staging site for the Pacific Theatre, as well as preparing other troops for the African and the European Theatres. The 4th Infantry trained there until its departure for Vietnam in 1966. Army Reserve and National Guard also trained there. Other active duty units also trained there as well as the nearby Yakima Firing Range.

Basic training was held on North Fort from 1966 until 1971 until the 9th Infantry Division was re-activated in 1971 after Vietnam and remained the premier unit until 1991when the 9th Division was, once again de-activated. The 9th Division had several nick-names over the years. They were known as "Old Reliable" (official), "the Varsity", and in Vietnam; known as "Flower Power", "Flaming Assholes", as well as the "Psychedelic Cookies".

We finally pulled into the Reception Station. It was night time at this point. We were greeted this time by a friendly Drill Sergeant. He wore the Campaign Hat, or what was called "The Smokey the Bear Hat", the trademark of a DI. He carried a swagger stick. On second thought, he was not that friendly. First of all, he and his assistant kept reminding us that we were interfering with their Friday night and their serious drinking time. He rushed us over to a slab of concrete which had neat yellow footprints and a number painted on it in the correct foot position for the position of attention. We must have been too slow as he kept yelling **"…MOVE IT, MOVE IT! … Faster…Quickly Ladies!"** Another roll call was taken. (No one had escaped yet.).

The DI also used a stream of profanities that probably will not be published here. He probably out did the drunken sailor with Tourette's syndrome. He called us to attention and that was not good enough for him. He put us at ease and used his assistant (The guy with the helmet liner.) to demonstrate the proper position of attention, as dictated by FM 22-5 (Field Manual 22-5, Drill & Ceremonies). He ran through this a few times until we seemed to have it correct. He then went through the same procedure for the commands of "At Ease" and "Parade Rest". We also were taught "Right Face" and "Left Face". Needless to say, this initial drilling would become greatly improved upon in the next nine weeks. His ADI (assistant drill instructor) moved through the ranks correcting any incorrect movement or body positioning. The same was going on with the other groups that had joined us at the airport. I guessed that all of us combined would make up a company of about 200 men.

We were marched to a mess hall (Dining Facility in today's Army parlance.) where we were given a box lunch and 15 minutes to eat. When we had finished our first Army meal, we were instructed to *"Fall In"* back on the concrete slab down the road. We had to *"Double Time"* (run) it down to our formation site. Some of us were lucky, in that if we were the first ones down to the formation area, we were allowed a smoke break.

Next, we were marched down to an old wooden WWII two story style barracks. Then by file we marched to a nearby long wooden shed which was the supply room and issued our bedding, two blankets, two sheets, one white towel, one pillow, and one pillow case. We had to sign for this government property. When this was done, with our arms full, we were led to our barracks and the sergeant assigned us to our bunk bed. Ah, at last bedtime, as we were exhausted. Not so fast *"trainee"*. More training was in order, and one had better pay attention to the sergeant.

We would now spend the next couple hours or so receiving instructions on how to properly make up our bunk. The DI and his assistant were quite thorough. Our bunks were to have crisp 45-degree hospital corners on each sheet and the blanket. The second blanket was to be folded into a proper dust cover over the pillow. We then scrambled over to our bunk. We had to make our bunk up under the watchful eyes of the DI and his assistant. If not done properly, the bedding was ripped off and the trainee had to start all over again. I was amazed at how many of these young men had never made their bed in their entire life. (God bless Mama.)

I could see that this was going to be a very long night as more and more bunks were being remade. Those of us who passed this first block of instruction were allowed to go outside for a smoke break. We, under the fear of the two pissed off sergeants' wrath, could not even think of leaving the barracks area. After a while when the NCOs were satisfied with how the bunks were made, we had some free time before the lights would be turned off. I had no idea at what time it was as it seemed that most of the post had called it a day and for the most part all was dark. Fire guards were assigned and the rest of us crashed for the night (morning). I decided that I would sleep on top of the covers as not having to go through the bed making ritual again. Sleep came swiftly for me. For others they were wide-awake tired.

From out of a deep restful sleep, we were awakened very rudely at something like 5:00AM. (That would soon become 0500 in military time.) There was a flood of lights, a terrible banging and clanging on an empty garbage can with a toilet brush. The Assistant DI walked through the barracks shaking the bunks and throwing off the blankets of those who did not respond fast enough. We were informed that we had a half an hour to shit, shower and shave. Brooms and mops were thrown into the center of the bay and we then heard an empty bucket being thrown down the center of the bay. "You maggots will have to clean my barracks from now until we form up for chow. And you will have a half hour after chow to finish cleaning my barracks."

At 0530 we were formed up and were marched a little way down the road to the mess hall. It was still dark out, but the smell of the bacon and the coffee seemed to make it worthwhile. We were hungry and tired. I recall that "hungry & tired" often described Basic Training for me. In front of every mess hall was a set of "monkey bars" which had to be traversed before the trainee could eat. The fat boys always ate last, since they were not able to cross the obstacle. Those who were overweight or unfit always ate last because they would have to jog around to the end of the chow line and try again. As good as the breakfast seemed at the time; we were only allotted 5 minutes to eat and then forced to run back to the barracks to finish cleaning the place up. As always, someone always threw up during the run so soon after scarfing down the meal. This routine would be repeated for the duration of basic training.

Some of us caught on to the psychology playing out here (introduction to team work) some immediately grabbed a broom, others reluctantly a mop or began cleaning the latrine (bathroom / toilet area.). At first it was those of us who enlisted took the lead in both organizing and executing the "G.I. Party". Many of the draftees were reluctant to do anything at all. It would not take long until they went along with the program or wound up in the stockade. (Military jail)

At about 0630 or so the Drill Instructor returned, and he had his assistant in tow with him. Whistles were blown, and we were formed up again. We began our "zero" week on a Saturday and there was not a lot that could be done, since most of the regulars had the weekend off. Most offices and warehouses were closed. The real in-processes would be on Monday. This did not stop the cadre from keeping us busy.

We were marched to a large field and were lined up one abreast at double arm's length apart. This would be our first "police-call". (Trash removal) A few trainees were issued plastic trash bags and fell out to the rear of this long line. It was a big field. We were instructed to pick up anything that did not grow. The cadre sergeant then asked the group who was from California. Many hands went up to respond to the question. "All right you hippie faggots, you and you alone will pull up all the daisies and dandelions…you piss poor flower children!" We were then given a "forward march" at a slow pace. "Get it all! All I want to see is assholes and elbows." Was yelled by the cadre sergeant. We picked up cigarette butts, paper trash, beer cans as well as things we could not identify. At the end of the field we turned around and repeated the "police call".

The cadre personnel seemed to have a very keen eye for everything that was missed on our first pass. Sometimes this whole process was repeated. The sun was up by now and climbing up in the bright Washington summer sky.

Ft. Lewis was quite alive and awake by now. We could see other trainees running in cadence up and down the distant streets and roads. They must be happy we thought because they all were singing. We could not make exactly what they were singing about, but it had a definite beats and rhythms to it. We were reformed after our police call and marched back to the barracks. Just as we were halted and faced the barracks building, the DI stepped out and greeted us with his dissatisfaction on the condition of his barracks. We had no idea about what he was talking and cussing about. It had seemed that we had done a pretty good job at cleaning the barracks. We were instructed to get busy and have the building "standing tall and looking good" for his inspection.

The formation was dismissed, and we rushed into the barracks to see what all the fuss was all about, and to our horror it looked as if a bomb had gone off inside there in our absence. Bunks were torn apart with bedding strewn all over the place. Some bunks were turned over, trash was all over the place (No one told us where to dump the garbage cans that morning.) There was shaving cream sprayed all over the latrine, as some fool had left his can of shaving cream in the latrine. The cadre troop simply opened the outside supply shed. There were plenty of cleaning tools, brooms, mops, toilet brushes and chemical cleaning supplies. He simply informed us to get busy before the sergeants returned. He also pointed out where the dumpster was located. Out of the cadre room he produced a buffing machine, buffing pads and floor wax. After a brief instructional block, he departed outside to have a smoke.

We were dumbfounded. This sure has been one hell of a way to welcome us into the Army. I resigned myself that these next nine weeks not only were going to be very long, they were either going to "make or break" me. We allotted ourselves a break and then slowly got busy straightening out the mess of our barracks that the DI had done to us.

The cadre man hung around the area and would periodically check on our progress. Soon others in our platoon took to cleaning things that we would not have thought of, such as the rafters over the bay on the second floor. Some guys even began to do things, perhaps just out of boredom and a need to participate. Things were looking better than when we first began. The floors were waxed and buffed, the latrine was spotless, someone attempted the windows, but we had no glass cleaner. Our lockers were empty other than our personal stuff. They were very empty, and we would later learn how organized they would have to be when we got our full issue. For now, we were still in our civilian clothes.

After a couple of hours or so, we were done, and the cadre man gave us a good review and a passing evaluation. We were informed that after lunch, there would be a formation at 13:00 hours in front of the barracks. Later we were marched to the mess hall and the same monkey bar drill was performed. After lunch and at 1300hrs, we were in formation as instructed.

At this formation, the cadre man issued us a "post-locator" card that we were to fill out and return to him. This document would acknowledge that we were on post at Ft. Lewis, should any inquiries be made as to our location while in the military. (This would be done in the future for every new post that we would be assigned to.) We also had the option to have a formal USPS (United States Postal Service) change of address form. A few ball point US Government pens were handed out to a few men in the platoon. (Without saying it, we were encouraged to share.)

The cadre man sat outside on our pick-nick table collecting the paperwork, while he enjoyed a smoke. It was interesting to note how he knew when the last man turned in his "post locator card". Some of us who had completed this assignment enjoyed a smoke break in the barracks. Yes, we could smoke in the barracks back then, as every upright post in the barracks had a big, #10 coffee can which was painted bright red, with some water in it, nailed at the proper height uniformly throughout the barracks, to be used as a "butt can".

A little while later a whistle was blown and that meant another formation. We were formed up and the cadre man marched us.(This time he counted cadence, 'Left, Right, Left Right…and began to sing a song that we were to repeat or answer him. We learned our first *"Jodie song".)* The platoon wound up at what was at one time a movie theater. We filed in and to our amazement; there must have been hundreds of civilians in there. (Oh, yeah, there were more of us.) Some 2nd Lieutenant got up to the podium, (Could not have been older that 22 or 23.) tested the sound system and then began his "briefing". I'm not sure even what it was all about as he just rolled on in a semi monotone (some dozed off) introducing us to Ft. Lewis, informing us not to leave our company area at any time, under the threat of disciplinary action, as there was a spinal meningitis outbreak on post. (This was good news?) He did stress that there would be a white canvas strip sewn on the right front of our fatigues over the U.S. Army strip indicating that we were Basic Trainees and were to be isolated from the main bodies of other troops. (This became known as a "maggot tag".)

Back at the company area, the company clerk had more paperwork for us to fill out and return to our cadre man. I recall that one question asked what our religious preference was. I did not know, but it was for our dog tags, not for Sunday. I still have my dog tags and that "No Preference" was meant to indicate that when I die, I really do not mind which man of the cloth says my last rites. I'm sure that this was only the first couple of tips to a paperwork iceberg.

Once again we were formed up and taken out to the very same large field that we had preciously policed up, and (you guessed it, we were to police it again). We spread out once more and made our sweeps of that field. I could hardly find anything to pick up, so I managed to get a few daisies and dandelions. I was to come to learn that this was the military method of accomplishment, that is if a given task is done over repeatedly, it is about to be done right at some point. It is known as "Accomplishment through redundancy.")

The platoon was re-formed, and we marched back, to our company area singing our *"Jodie"* songs. That, I must admit did start to feel as if I was in the Army. We passed a company of trainees who sang in part: "One more week and we'll be through…I'll be glad and so will you…Bring it on down…" I wanted to learn that one just about now.

The rest of the afternoon was spent as follows: First the cadre decided to take us on a "short run". I did not mind, as the letter in track and field was not that old, but it sure shook out those who were not quite as fit. Once again we were returned to the company and the cadre gave us some basic drill, as we would be marching quite a bit in the next week. Between paperwork and the cadre trying to keep us busy, the afternoon passed rather quickly.

Off in the distance we heard a large "boom" and wondered if there was an explosion somewhere else on post. We happened to be in a formation at the time and the cadre halted us and faced us in the direction of the sound. We later learned that that was the signal for "retreat", the end of the work / training day and that the American flag at main post was being lowered. Since we had no uniforms yet, we did not have to salute. This routine was repeated daily. I could not but to ponder why we were facing and saluting a flag that that we could not even see. I would later learn that it was the principle that was involved, not the practicality involved. This would become an ongoing military principle and daily practice.

We had some free time before dinner, chowtime and we made the best of it. Once again we were formed up and marched off to the mess / chow hall. The same routine was performed as to the monkey bars. There must not have been too much else to end our first real day in the Army, as I do not recall it. I also do not recall how the rest of the evening was spent, other than when I finally hit the pillow, it was quite welcome, and sleep came rapidly.

Sunday was a bit eased as compared to our first Saturday. I do recall hearing reveille being sounded on a mysterious unseen post-wide sound system. We would come to appreciate how easy these first two days were. We were allowed to sleep in an hour on Sunday. We still had the same barracks cleaning duties to perform before and after breakfast. Once again, we were marched down to the mess hall, and it seemed that we had a bit more time to eat. A while later, the CQ (Charge of Quarters) runner came by and asked who wanted to go to church. A roster was made up dividing the church goers between Catholic and Protestant. The cadre marched the group to a nearby chapel two times, once for each denomination. We were allowed outside and could enjoy a smoke or two. We still did not experience the drill sergeants return. I do believe that the DI's initial appearance was for its shock & awe potential, a psychological move. From what I recall, we did not see the drill sergeant again until we actually reached our BCT Company after this "Zero" week of processing.

The cadre personnel seemed to have taken over and for the rest of the week; they were the ones who escorted us around as we processed in. It seemed that we had things to do on Sunday and were kept somewhat busy, but not at the earlier frantic pace. By the time we heard "Call to Quarters" (lights out, 23:00) and a bit later "Taps", we were ready for sleep and I recall drifting off to sleep being a bit anxious and wondering what Monday would bring.(I would learn later that during a normal duty there are actually 25 bugle calls authorized. On Sunday 9 bugle calls are authorized. It is up to the post commanders which are to be used. I even to this day I only can recognize six: Reveille, Recall, and Call to Quarters, Taps and Adjutant's Call, [parades only].) KPs (Kitchen Police) were assigned; a fire guard roster was posted.

Well, that peaceful sleep did not last long. The morning was started in the usual fashion, lights, noise and sergeants who have had way too much coffee already, waking up the platoon. We had the same amount of time to get ready as previously. After breakfast and a thorough cleaning of the barracks, we were formed up and would begin the long week of in-processing.

I do not recall the specific order, or where the specific functions took place, but I do recall that we marched, ran or were transported by "cattle car / truck" all over Ft. Lewis to accomplish all the required in- processing functions. It seemed that different routes were taken as to confuse our sense of bearing and location. (Canada was basically due north of us.) This tactic seemed to last all the way through basic training itself. All the days blended into one with the same daily routines. We were slowly becoming acclimated to both the North West climate and the Army itself.

The very first stop was the barber shop. More waiting, for a haircut which would only take less than a couple of minutes? The "hair cut" was simply a cut to the bare scalp. There must have been a half a dozen barber chairs or so and what seemed like a mountain of hair of all different colors and textures. The barbers had fun with the trainees who had shoulder-length hair. First the top would be cut off, then the sides from ear to ear. Others they made look like "Friar Tuck". A sudden rush of cold air encompassed our head. Everyone came out of the barber shop simply rubbing their hand over what stubble was left. (Many were uttering all kinds of profanities after losing their "hippie hair".)This same hair cut would be the same standard cut, "the number one", every week until the middle of Basic Training, when only the sides were shorn down. (At least at this point, we did not have to pay for those haircuts.)

We received a small advance pay from Finance, which took a very long time as we were to fill out all the paperwork for our pay, taxes, allotments and any charitable contributions that we wished to come out of our pay. At that time a "buck" private made $97.50 a month. Since I entered as a Private E-2, I made a whopping $127.50 a month. (At that time, if I recall, the Army pay scale, that was one of biggest increases between the ranks.) I forget the order of the pay whether or not we were paid in advance or in arrears. I'm not sure how this "advance pay was handled.

After we had finished with the finance section, we were taken to a small PX (Post Exchange). Under the watchful eye of the cadre, who stood guard at the check-out stand, we were instructed **not to** buy sodas, candy or snack food. We could buy a few packs of cigarettes though. Our regular pay-day was only a few days away. We were instructed to buy specific items of hygiene and items required for our foot locker display (even if we did not use them). It was highly recommended to buy a shoe polish kit, a bundle of wire coat hangers, and a padlock.

One of the first stops was the Quartermaster warehouse where we were sized up, measured, fitted for our uniforms and foot wear. We were measured from head to toe for: 3 types of headgear, O.D. green fatigues, shirts and pants, dress uniforms (summer lightweight poplin and the heavy wool winter dress greens) dress poplin shirts, 2 sets of summer Khakis, a heavy wool overcoat, a grey raincoat, 2 pairs of combat boots, dress shoes known as "low quarters", underwear (damn boxers), socks etc. We were issued a bundle of white handkerchiefs, towels and wash cloths. Anything that was either out of stock or had to be tailored would be issued on the next trip. We started this shopping trip with just an empty OD green duffel bag, which was bulging when we got finished hours later. When we returned to our barracks, the cadre issued us a diagram on how our wall locker should look and the proper footlocker display. (To me this seemed redundant, as in less than a week; we would be tearing all this down, repacking it and repeating all this effort when we reached our Basic Training unit.).

There was a lot of time spent in the personnel office as our permanent records were constructed (The 201 File) containing all of our personal information, biography, and home of record, next of kin information, emergency contact information, education and contract information if we were enlisted as opposed to have been drafted. I became RA 19835953.

That week also saw us spending a lot of class room time in that old movie theater, learning all about the Army and our role in it. We were briefed on the world situation and American foreign policy. (Vietnam was emphasized.) I also learned about venereal diseases and the proper use of a condom. We also learned about the Army rank structure and who to salute (when in uniforms) and who not to. The insignias of the different branches of the army were instructed as well. A lot of this would, of course, be repeated throughout the upcoming weeks of basic.

The week seemed to both zipping by as well as dragging by with all the lines, paperwork, the "hurry-up" and wait routine as well as the constant encouragement from the staff personnel. We saw the dentist and an initial assessment was made in our dental chart (which also would become another military file folder.) and future requirements. Once again we saw the medics and were further charted, and our initial entry physical condition was noted. As with the dental charting, our medical folder was being constructed. If, I recall correctly; we were also given the first if many inoculations that we would receive during our stay at Ft. Lewis. We were also "blood-typed" which that blood type identified and would be stamped on our dog tags, should we need a "field transfusion" in the future. (In combat, back then, the medic would simply call out for a blood type and we were obligated to donate in the field.)

Final trips were made to the quartermaster to pick up any items of clothing that were not issued on the first trip. Any follow-up appointments were met and by the end of the week, we were in uniform, and were packing our bags for the transportation to our actual basic training company for the official start of training. I do not recall the day that we were done in processing.

Our final formation was held at the Reception Station. Names were called out and we were reformed into what would be our BCT Company. We would become E-1-1, which is "Echo" Company, 1st Battalion, 1st Brigade: Basic Combat Training. When the bus stopped, and the door opened up, our young lives would change forever. We were off loaded with all due haste under the encouragement of our drill sergeant. We were carrying our heavy duffle bag with all of our new issue. We had to "double-time it" (run) at all times when in the company area. There was a lot of yelling and confusion. The profanity was overwhelming. We had one drill sergeant and a cadre, permanent party NCO to herd us along. We were introduced to our new Drill Sergeant, SSG Zeek, and his assistant SGT Tarn and to our new home. As our name was called out, we were assigned a bunk. Even the distinction between top and bottom was made clear. It was always head to toe, that is one member, let's say on the bottom bunk had his head to the right, the upper bunkmate had his head to the left.

Once inside the old WW II wooden barracks, we were to stand by our bunks at attention. It was made clear that these old wooden structures had about a 5-minute life span should a fire get started. There will be a fire guard on each floor on duty from lights out until reveille. They would also be responsible for the outside building security. They were to be issued a baseball bat for a weapon. The duty roster would be posted after the evening meal.

The Drill Sergeant continued to take stock of his newest trainees. The only thing we seemed to have going for us was that for some unknown reason, we were all "RA"s. (Regular Army, volunteers.). Our DI liked this but seemed not too happy to see us. I guess that we had to earn his respect and be promoted from our present "maggot" status. We soon filed by to pick up our bedding.

We were given another diagram to show how our wall and footlocker would be arranged. Our bunks were also to meet the same high standard that was instructed at the Reception Station. There would no exceptions and no deviations from the layout. We were further introduced to the cleaning supplies, the mops, brooms, and the buffing machine. All would be used quite frequently and professionally in the next few weeks. At the order of the Drill Sergeant, we had only a certain amount of time to get all of our issue "squared away" we would expect an inspection. In a flurry, we were released to carry out this new order and set of instructions. Both floors of the barracks became a whirlwind of activity.

The DI had us clean the barracks, it looked spotless when we arrived, more military redundancy, I would guess. The DI stormed off, leaving us under the watchful eye of his assistant. We got to work cleaning the spotless barracks.

A few hours later, SSG Zeek returned as we were putting the finishing touches on the barracks. He was not too happy, as we were not completely finished within his timetable. Once again, we were ordered to stand by our bunks with our wall locker and foot locker open and ready for inspection. The inspection began downstairs, since I was on the second floor, I felt a bit relaxed. We could hear the shouting and noise as the DI went through the downstairs bay. Apparently, those defects were noted as the offending bunk, wall locker or foot locker was torn apart. It was our turn after a while, and we were treated to the same routine. For most of us there was little damage to our displays and only minor corrections were to be made. It would be in our best interest to have all these corrections made and the barracks in immaculate order in the morning. After the inspection, whistles were blown, and we were to fall in out on our concrete slab.

We were reminded that we would run every time that we were in the company area. It was also pointed out where the mess hall was, on the company street, the orderly room, the supply room / arms room. The soda machine outside the orderly room was for permanent party personnel only. Any trainee even attempting to use it would be dealt with in a severe manner.

Next on the agenda, was our first real drill instruction. The good sergeant and his assistant demonstrated the positions and movements related to each drill movement. We began with the stationary positions: attention, parade rest, at ease, and rest. After moving through all these positions and constant harassments and corrections, we were ready for the marching movements. Every movement and position would be gone over repeatedly, and corrections were applied swiftly. As would be the standard practice throughout Basic Training, minor infractions usually were met with the trainee doing 25 or 50 pushups.

In what seemed like a totally random selection process, four trainees were called out and SGT Tarn issued them a black arm band with buck sergeant's stripes. These were to be our squad leaders. They were to move into the respected two open NCO rooms at one end of the bay. They were to move in with all of their belongings. Next, one trainee was called out and he became our trainee platoon sergeant. He wore the stripes of a Staff Sergeant. On a rotating basis, one trainee was selected to be the company Field First Sergeant. His stripes were of an actual First Sergeant. This was duty shared by all three other platoons.

In the real army these would be called "acting Jacks". A soldier would be given the stripes and the responsibilities without the actual promotion. This was done to see if the soldier could handle the elevated position before an actual promotion was finalized. Some made it; others had to turn in their stripes. The same applied to the trainees, more to test leadership potential and how the trainee dealt with his peers in a different position. In the upcoming weeks these positions would be rotated and shared many times over. There would be no explanations as to performance when they were "busted", and another took his place.

The new "sergeants" took their position and we were off for a long march. The Drill Sergeant and his assistant kept the cadence up and we began to learn the "Jodie" songs. Some trainees could not keep in step. The little guys had it the worst, in that their little legs seemed to be working overtime just to keep up. We got out on "the Grinder" (parade & exercise yard) and really looked bad as the orders were given that would change our direction of movement (such as column right, column left, to the rear march. (We were no way close to learning "Counter Column, March.) What made matters worse was that we could not always hear the DI clearly. Yes, we bumped into each other quite a bit during these first marching trials. After the platoon did a whole lot of pushups, we tried it all over again, and again. By the time we were marched back to the company area, we were a little better and we were starting to develop our arm muscles.

There was a lot of material to cover in Basic Training and only eight more weeks to master all the fine arts of soldiering. I do not recall the exact sequence of the training. It is much different today than it was in my day. It seemed that in a day or so, after we were "classroom" trained on the safety, disassembly and assembly and the cleaning of the M-14 automatic rifle, we were issued one. We were lined up beside the supply / arms room and the company armorer gave us a "weapons card" to sign. Whenever we were in possession of that weapon, the card would be placed in that weapon's slot in the rifle rack. He then issued us, one each automatic rifle, M-14. The armorer advised us to memorize the serial number of our weapon. We double-timed it back to our platoon barracks and stood next to our bunk. We were then given the instructions on how to properly clean our weapon. From that moment on it would be called a "weapon", not a "gun". The cadre sergeant emphasized this by grapping an M-14 from one trainee and stating, "This is my weapon... (Grabbing his gentiles), this is my gun... This is for killing (shaking the rifle) ... (rubbing his gentiles)...this is for fun." We never forgot the distinction!

The next order of business was to clean the weapon. As with the barracks, this rifle looked immaculate. With the DI close by, we began our first cleaning of our weapon. When I thought that it was "clean" I was to double time back to the armorer to turn in the weapon. As for just about every trainee, that afternoon, it took at least a couple of trips until the weapon was up to the high Army standards, as well as the company armorer's. The drill sergeant would spot check the weapons as well. I came to learn that by requesting the DI's inspection first, in spite of his cussing, it could save several trips back and forth to the arms room.

We finished the afternoon with a good round of unarmed close order drill. From then on, we carried our own M-14 everywhere we went. We would spend hours drilling with the rifle. At first, when doing a "To the Rear...March" or the "Counter Column...March", some trainee always got smacked in the head with someone else's rifle barrel.

As mentioned earlier, I do not recall the exact sequences of the training. With that said, there was a lot of drilling, mostly by now with the M-14. We were constantly doing PT (Physical Training). I thought that I was in good shape from my high school track team, but the Army found muscles that I did not know I had. When exercising in the hot sun, we were worked until the sweat just poured off. We would do the PT in a large field.

We grounded our equipment, pistol belt & canteen, fatigue blouse and fatigue cap and moved towards the "pit". The DI usually led the PT from an elevated "stage" As he began. He would call out the exercise; the trainees would repeat the exercise. Then He would say "I'll move to my right; you move to your left. I'll call the cadence you count the repetitions. "The assistant or another DI would meander through our ranks "encouraging" us to do more, do better and correcting any badly performed exercise. The "Daily Dozen" routine was our workout regimen. In addition to that we were taken on long runs, usually a mile in the beginning and two miles after we were past the half way mark. Sometimes PT was two times a day. Those who could not keep up physically, caught hell from the staff. Some just broke down and cried. A few were transferred to a "Special Training Company". (luckily, none from our platoon.) That either made or broke many trainees.

The "Daily Dozen" was developed in 1920 by Walter Camp for both the Army and Navy. Originally it was 12 exercises done in 15 minutes. We spent a lot more time than 15 minutes. Today the Army uses a different routine, although the "dozen" is used to maintain one's physical condition. The "Daily Dozen" consisted of four groups of three exercises each. They were designed for upper body strength, necessary in modern combat.

All Exercises Below are per Army FM 21-20

Conditioning Drill One: bend & reach, rear lunges, high jumper, rowers, squat benders, windmills, forward lunges, prone rows, bent leg body twists, and pushups.

Conditioning Drill Two: push-ups, sit-ups, and pull-ups. (Pull-ups were done at the monkey bars at the mess hall and at the main PT area.)

Conditioning Drill Three: power jumps, V-ups, the mountain climber, leg tucks and twists, and single leg push-ups.

The "run-dodge and jump" was added when we went to the main PT area. Sometimes we exercised near the company area, others we went to the main PT Test Area.

The running, both in the company area and on the road rounded out the exercise daily.

The other physical training included the strenuous guerilla and the grass drills, in which the unit was formed in a circle and the instructor was in the center calling out the various drills as the troops "power walked" around the circle until the next movement was called.

The Guerilla Drills Consisted of:

> The Shoulder Roll
> The Lunge Walk
> The Soldier's Carry (Fireman's Carry)

The Grass Drills Consisted of:

> The Bouncing Ball
> Supine Bicycle
> The Knee Bender
> Roll Left & Right
> The Swimmer
> The Bounce & Leap
> The Leg Spreader (It's not what one may think, we were all males.)
> The Forward Roll (Summersaults)
> Stationary Run (With four changes of direction on command)

When we were under arms with our M-14, we would often do the Rifle PT Drills.

The Rifle Drills Consisted of:

> The Fore-UP, Squat
> The Fore-Up, Behind the Back
> The Fore-Up, Bend Back
> (Bayonet training would come later in the training cycle.)

The physical conditioning was constant. It never ceased. There were many times we were pulled out in the middle of the night in our skivvies and combat boots to do grass drills at the whim of SGT Tarns. (He would often return to the barracks drunk.) In retrospect, when we graduated we all were in our physical prime. America's most dangerous weapon was and still is today, an 18-year-old just out of Basic Training. We felt ten feet tall and bullet proof.

The weather at Ft. Lewis during the summer alternated between rain, fog, overcast and sunny and hot. Many times, we would just get our ponchos on when it started raining, then it would stop raining and the sun beamed down on us. We were just damp enough that we "steamed" under the poncho. I often felt like steamed broccoli. But, we continued to train and adapt to the changing weather.

The next major segment of the training was BRM (Basic Rifle Marksmanship). This was stressed just as much as our physical training. It would take the combination of the two to make a decent soldier. We continued to break down and clean our weapons daily.

Next we would actually be firing the M-14. The company was transported out to the ranges via the "cattle-cars" out to the ranges. All of the company's weapons and ammunition were trucked out on a 2 ½ Ton Cargo truck. ("A Duce and a Half", or a "Twice and a Half")

We sat in the bleachers as the marksmanship instructor went over the range safety and the range rules. All marksmanship training was dictated by Army FM 3-22.9, c1. Safety was ever present, i.e. "All weapons will be pointed down range at all times. "There were safety regulations covering the corrective actions should a misfire occur, range movement and down range safety precautions. The range was controlled from a large tower where the range master could see all the firing positions as well as far down range. The range officer oversaw all activity on the range.

A large red wind sock blew in the wind, indicating that this range was "hot" (in use with live fire and gave us the sense of the wind direction. (There were safety NCOs who carried a large "safety paddle" who walked behind the firing order, observing everything. The safety paddle: One side was white, indicating safe conditions prevailed. On the other side of the paddle, it was red indicating an unsafe condition existed, at which time a "cease-fire" order was given from the control tower and all weapons would be cleared and checked by the safety personnel. Come rain or shine, we were out on the ranges during our Basic Rifle Marksmanship training. Many times, we "steamed", wearing the poncho in the firing position or in the foxhole when it rained.

We were to learn the basic characteristics of the M-14A1. It was developed to replace the Garand M-1 of WW II fame. It was issued to airborne units in 1959 and was later introduced to all units. The M-14 weighed 11.46lbs empty and was 46.5 inches in length. It fired a 7.62mm round from a 20-round magazine at a rate of 2800 ft. per second. This rifle had a sustained rate of fire of 750 rounds per minute. It was gas operated, air cooled, and hand held. Its effective range was 500 yards, although the round traveled much further. Only with specialized scopes and sights could it be effective for longer ranges. It is still used today as both a sniper weapon as well as for ceremonial purposes.

The basics of good marksmanship are basically as follows:

[Identify the target and distance, allow for terrain, tactical conditions, wind and weather conditions. When ready to fire:]

1. Maintain a steady position.
2. Proper aim (sight picture and aim point).
3. Proper breathing. (breathe in hold momentarily)
4. Steady trigger pull (squeeze, never jerk, do not anticipate the recoil).

Two trainees were assigned to a given firing position, one firer and his assistant or coach. The two would exchange roles and would rotate so that the coach fired next. First order of business with live ammunition was to "zero" our weapon. That is to adjust our weapon's sights. A three-shot group was fired at a 25 meter "zero" range bulls-eye target. From the shot group, the sights could be adjusted to that shooter. It could also tell if the basic marksmanship procedures were constant with that shooter. No two weapons had the same adjustments as it was adjusted for that weapon and that specific shooter. In many instants this was the first time the trainee ever fired a weapon. I was in this category, of sorts with this heavy weapon, other than my experience on the high school rifle team. Some trainees took several tries. Some simply could not shoot and the range instructors and / or the DI made sure they got "extra special training". Back then, there was no waiver for a "bolo" shooter. Some guys kept "recycling" BMT.

There was a "country" boy from the Kentucky hills who told the DI he could fire any weapon without zeroing. The DI halted the proceedings and let the boy demonstrate. This mountain man did just that. He fired one round and, studied where it had landed and adjusted his firing accordingly. He hit every target using "Kentucky Windage". Amazingly so, he did the same with a second random rifle. Needless this "Hill Billy" fired 39 out of 40, Expert. (He blamed the missed shot on a defective target.) That was not uncommon, in that the targets soon became so full of holes a bullet went through it without triggering the drop mechanism. We would note the puff of dirt behind the target to determine a hit or a miss.

In all we would spend about three weeks on the rifle range. We would fire with most of our field gear on, as well as a familiarization firing with the gas mask on for only a few rounds, as the optical inserts were not made nor issued yet. Those who had very limited sight without their glasses were removed from the range.

We then moved to the combat range where "pop-up" targets were set up at the various distances required for qualification. The distances of the targets, if I recall, were: 50, 75, 150, 175, 200, 250, 300, and 500 yards. From what I recall, we had time limits set for each firing sequence. There were 40 rounds total. Each set was given just the right amount of ammunition for that sequence, moving from prone, kneeling, sitting and unsupported standing. By the last week we were pretty good riflemen.

When it came to the qualification course, even the "bolos" (bad shooters) at least qualified as marksmen by now. To qualify on the M-14 the shooter had to hit 23-29 for Marksman, 30-35 for Sharpshooter, and 36-40 to fire Expert. Overall, our platoon (RA) had the highest scores in the battalion.

We approached the fourth week of Basic Training, commonly known back then as *"overload week"*, or **"Hell Week"** During this phase; all the physical, mental and psychological limits were tested. They really put it to us. I recall SGT Tarn coming into the barracks at some god-awful hour and rousting several trainees who did not do well during the training and having them "fall in" the shower room with their foot lockers ready for inspection and then turning on the showers. When it was all over, these trainees spent the rest of the night drying their clothes in the platoon's only dryer. He would also have us fall out at these awful hours for "grass drills". The inspections became more demanding. There was a lot of doubling of the PT routines.

It was in the midst of all this harassment that I received a "Dear John" letter from "Nancy". She dumped me, as she did not want to be with a soldier at that time. She had her college to think of and attend later in the fall. The "Anti-War" movement was at its height. I was devastated and felt betrayed. I took it very hard, but had to continue on with the Basic Training, the best that I could. This was not easy in that the *overload* week was quite demanding. A few other people that I was corresponding with stopped doing so as well. I felt alone and abandoned.

My best friend had enlisted a couple of weeks after I did and was going through his basic training nearby over nearby in the 2nd Battalion. We were able to meet secretly, as we were not to leave our company area because of the quarantine. We managed to remove our "maggot tags" and sneak over to the post donut and coffee shop and bring back the forbidden treats to our platoons on Sunday. We never got caught, luckily. It would have had bad consequences for us, had we gotten caught.

We continued on with our training, learning the skills needed to become soldiers. We were given extensive training in the following areas: NBC Training, (nuclear, biological and chemical) we survived "the gas chamber" with burning eyes and skin. That experience is one that one never forgets. Map reading was also taught, along with the actual land navigation course, both day light and as well as at night. We were trained on the grenade course and later were introduced to the new M-16 automatic rifle and later qualified on both the M-14 and the M-16.

The M-16 5.56 mm. (NATO round), was developed to replace the M-14. It began to be issued in 1963 and by 1969 was issued to all US forces. The M-16 is selective fired, semi-automatic and fully automatic fire. Sustained rate of fire was 700-950 rounds per minute. It is gas operated, air cooled and hand-held rifle. Problems surfaced in Vietnam, siting a failure to extract the spent cartridge. Cleaning was a constant task. It was fed by either a 20 or 30 round magazine. This weapon weighed 8.79lbs loaded, being much lighter that the M-14. It was 39.5 inches long with a 20in. barrel. Over 8 million were manufactured and is in use today worldwide. I actually preferred the M-14, as I qualified "Sharpshooter" with the M-14, but only "Marksman" with the M-16. Later in my military career, I would constantly fire "Expert" with the M-16.

I recall that SSG Zeek called us together one Sunday afternoon (July 20, 1969) and with a transistor radio, we heard the US astronauts landing on the moon. In a big way, I felt a very small part of that historic event, even though I was an Army private, merely a simple soldier.

We spent a lot of time on the bayonet course, (The spirit of the bayonet is to **Kill**!), pugil stick fighting and hand to hand combat and other vital skills. Our road marches were getting longer and longer, as our conditioning was in full force. At some point, we were introduced to bivouacs, with an overnight *"camping trip"*. Field sanitation was taught. Field first aid and basic medical aid was emphasized. We practiced fire and maneuver drills, mastered the "obstacle course".

We were given the basics of radio communication and communication security. It was also taught, the basics of the field PTT phone. (TA-312). We never stopped drilling under arms. Now we were looking really good, a lot more professional that at first. The weeks passed, and Basic Training was soon to be a thing of the past. We took our last PT test and scored very high. Our final exercise was a fire and maneuver drill and when we came off the course, our DI called us "soldier" for the first time.

At graduation, we were named *"platoon of the cycle"*, we are the **"Rock Platoon"**. We took up a collection and bought our DI a wrist watch at the PX. He was quite honored, in spite of all he put us through. Even today, I still thank SSG Zeek for skills that he taught us from Basic Training. I am sure that it kept a lot of us alive during our Vietnam tours.

Those of us who had been promoted wore the new stripes on our Khaki uniforms. We put on our weapons qualification badges. (We were authorized two marksmanship medals, as we qualified on both the M-14 and the M-16.). We then were given our first medal, The National Defense Medal. We stood tall and marched like the well-trained unit that we were on our graduation day parade. The "Rock Platoon" finally made it, we were soldiers now. The orders were read for our next assignments, we were off to our AIT (Advanced Individual Training) schools. I was lucky, in that

I had a brief leave granted, before heading off to Fort Monmouth, New Jersey for Signal School, Field General COMSEC repair course, 31S20. We then got our pay and travel money. We cleared post and were off on our way. Many in the company, mostly draftees, would simply go across post for Advanced Infantry Training. Most would be in Vietnam in the next few months. To this day, I do not know who made it home alive or not. I've wondered about this quite often over the years. Today, I was a US Soldier and proud of that fact.

CHAPTER ELEVEN

I took a bus over to the Seattle / Tacoma International Airport toting the heavy duffle bag with all of my issue. I had a couple of weeks leave and was soon on my way towards San Francisco. I was in uniform with my travel orders. The flight home was uneventful. It was only my second flight. The sensation and mystery of flight still amazed me, in that how this extremely heavy metal vehicle could even get off of the ground and fly like a small bird.

I could not but help to feel that people were staring at me. I wore my heavily starched Khaki summer uniform boasting my yellow "skeeter wings" (rank of a PV2, E-2), my two marksmanship badges and the National Defense medal. I decided to wear my overseas cap instead of the "saucer cap" (the garrison cap.) for the trip home. There were a lot of GIs on the flight. Some were returning from Vietnam and others, like me, were on their way elsewhere. Some civilians wished us well, others were not as kind. I was able to look out of the window and was amazed to see both the Pacific Ocean on one side of the aircraft and the Pacific Coast out of the other side.

I took a shuttle bus from the airport to downtown San Francisco and walked a few blocks to catch a city bus line home. I took the 31 Balboa bus across the city to 21st Avenue feeling very uncomfortably foreign in my own hometown. I got off at the 22nd Avenue bus stop and then walked a block and a half down the street to my home.

I finally reached home and was happy to have made it. My grandparents were almost in tears when they opened the front door and saw their soldier. It was a wonderful reunion with my old childhood home and all my memories of growing up in that house. I spent quite a long time telling my grandparents all about Army Basic Training. It definitely was not the Summer Camp that they had sent me to in those earlier years. A home cooked meal was greatly appreciated after nine weeks of "Army Chow". I recall sleeping for a very long time once I hit my own bed.

I spent quite a bit of time wandering all over the house and reminiscing. I went down to the basement and out the back door to the backyard of my childhood. It needed weeding and the trees and bushes needed pruning. These tasks would be accomplished before I left for Ft. Monmouth. There would also be many other tasks and chores that I would do for my grandparents before my leave was up.

I looked up all my neighborhood friends on my block. I got many strange looks as the doors were opened to greet me. They all seemed glad to see me, yet something was different. I had to phone most of my families, letting them know that I was home on leave. They all seemed glad to hear my voice and seemed very concerned and interested in my well-being. (Vietnam loomed in the near-future.)

It did not really register at the time, but not everybody, especially many of my classmates, were glad to see me. I went in uniform back to my high school to visit and also received mixed reactions to my visit. Overall it was a good experience, especially to see my old ROTC instructors again as well as many of my other teachers. They were proud of me and I felt as if I had joined their ranks as a soldier.

I could not help to stare at how pretty the girls were. My future wife, Scharlene had written me towards the end of basic, so I thought I'd give her a visit. Her father was a retired Army Medic (SP5, E-5) and her oldest brother was at West Point at the time. (I wound up re-kindling our romance, slowly and surely.)

I had called Nancy, my last girlfriend before I got her "Dear John" letter in Basic Training. We talked a while, but her mind was made up that this soldier would not have a place in her life at the present time. Ironically, she would later marry an Air Force enlisted man, a firefighter by specialty. Her father was a veteran of WW II and served with the 442nd, as did many of the fathers of my friends. He alone seemed proud of me. I guess after I learned of her child it was time for me to move on. Scharlene seemed to hold a flicker of a hope for my romantic ties. I would not hold my breath.

I spent a couple of days with my cousins (on my mother's side). That was probably the last time that I would ever see them. To this day, I have not had contact with them. My oldest cousin was in WW II, the Battle of the Bulge and did show some concern and caring for me. My three younger cousins were glad to see me but were still very much against the war. They all were living the upper-class life style in the suburban setting. I called my father's side of the family, but they did not seem to have the time for a visit. The real fact was that I was in the Army and a war that they opposed still raged on.

I continued to travel around the city, and perhaps took in the sights and sounds with a bit more interest than before. Who knows? This could be my last visit. The same held true of my house, my room and my neighborhood. I knew that I would be safe for a while and Vietnam seemed too distant to worry about at that time. I spent the rest of my leave simply enjoying life and my beloved city. Soon it was time to pack up and get on my way to Ft. Monmouth, N.J.

With all the good byes said, I headed out to the San Francisco International Airport. The transcontinental trip was very eye opening for me. I was in awe of how big this country was. I recall looking down at the mountains and was simply leaving me breathless. The Great Plains were just as amazing. There were the fields of grain spread out to the horizon. We flew over many farms and small towns. I saw huge circular fields of green that were being watered, as the irrigation sprinklers swept around and around. The clouds passed by the aircraft windows like cotton candy.

There were several other GIs on that flight as well. Some were just back from Vietnam. We spoke briefly as to where we were going, some here headed home, others would be headed to Germany to finish their tour. Others, like me were headed to AIT. The stewardess unofficially served us drinks which were greatly appreciated. It was a long flight and soon we began our decent into the Newark airport. My ears popped many more times as we dropped ever lowed towards the Jersey Soil.

I recall looking out of the plane's window and seeing a typical industrial skyline. It seemed to be surrounded in a haze of factory smoke. The city itself with a much more vivid skyline loomed in the distance. This was the "Garden State". Somehow from the air, one had to seek out the garden. I could see New York City off in the distance. I also felt that I would be descending into history as I was headed into New England. We were about to land at the Newark International Airport. I thought of my American History classes from high school. The aircraft landed at the Newark, N.J. International Airport, as a sense of anticipation flowed over me. I was about to enter the next phase of my life and my new military career.

New Jersey itself had a prominent place in American history. The colony was first settled by the Dutch calling it New Netherland and later by the Swedes, calling it New Sweden. The English took control of the area on June 24, 1664. It became one of the original Thirteen Colonies. New Jersey ratified its own constitution on July 2, 1776 just before the July 4, 1776 for the rest of the colonies. There was a clause that if the Colonies made peace and reunited with England, it would void its own constitution

The Battle of Monmouth was fought to a stalemate in June of 1778. The first Battle of Trenton was fought to an American victory. The Americans won later by defeating the British and the German mercenaries, known as the Hessians on 25 & 26 December and claimed victory on 3 January 1777. George Washington's famous "crossing of the Delaware" is depicted in the famous painting.

In 1804, New Jersey ended slavery, although indentured servants still were allowed. There was a lot more history there as, New Jersey fought in the Civil War on the side of the Union. I felt this as the New Jersey countryside along the turnpike whizzed past the bus window. I also could not but help to notice familiar businesses, such as Mc Donald's or Shell Gas. New Jersey seemed both foreign and familiar at the same time.

After a while the bus stopped at a small shelter and the bus driver informed me that Fort Monmouth was just on the other side of the road, the main gate, and my destination. I did not fully realize it at the time, but I would be travelling into history, in addition to what I felt upon my arrival in New Jersey and the East Coast.

Fort Monmouth, New Jersey: An Overview.

Today, (2018) Fort Monmouth is no longer an active US Army installation. It remains the heart and soul of the Signal Corps, although the Signal Center and School had been moved to Fort Gordon, Georgia in the 1970's. The Signal Corps Museum also went to Fort Gordon, with the stuffed "one-legged carrier pigeon", who had earned a Purple Heart from World War I. Carrier pigeon breeding and training at Ft. Monmouth ended in 1957. My new home would be finally closed as an active base in 2011.

This base was surrounded by several communities, to include Eatontown, Tinton Falls, and Oceanport. It was only about 5 miles from the Atlantic Ocean. The base, proper covered about 1,126 acres, or 4.56 square kilometers. It stretched from the Shrewsbury River on the East to Route 35 on the West. The base had all the support facilities, such as Medical support, dependent housing, PX and Commissary services, Chaplain Support and other moral and recreation support functions. Outside the main gates to the west was Naval Weapons Station Earle, (NADEARL), where many of the other support functions were provided by the Navy for the Marine students, to include a Navy "Brig". Overall, Ft. Monmouth was a small city unto itself.

Many government agencies and services also shared the facility, which included to name a few: US Army Material Command, Army Acquisition Command, Command & Control Communications, Electronic Research & Development, Intelligence, Surveillance, Chaplain School, NCO Training & Education, FBI, VA Clinic, etc. to name but a few. Also included was the 754th Explosive Ordnance Disposal unit, which provided EOD support throughout the New England Area. For a while, the West Point Preparatory School was also at Ft. Monmouth. Signal cadre from Ft. Monmouth also supported the communication / electronic training and support of all of the armed services, to include the Army Reserve and National Guard. This Signal support was nationwide in scope.

A small army of civilians supported the Signal School and these other government activities. Neighboring communities and businesses were enhanced and supported by this relatively small military base.

The property was gained in 1917 as Camp Vail. In 1919 it unofficially became the home of the Signal Corps. In 1924, it was re-named Fort Monmouth in honor of the Battle of Monmouth during the War of Independence. In 1928 the first radio equipped weather balloons were launched from there. The more permanent buildings were constructed as well. In 1938, the forerunner equipment of airborne RADAR was developed and tested. By 1948 the Signal Corps tested the forerunner of

TROPO, (Bouncing radio signals off of the Troposphere to compensate the curvature of the Earth.) Further tests were done bouncing radio signals off of the moon and receiving same signals back, which would prove a necessary technology for the Space Programs which followed. Satellite communication (SATCOM) was also developed there well into the 1960's.

This Army facility served and supported all wars and military operations from WWI through Vietnam until the its closure. Thousands of servicemen passed through the same gates that I was about to pass through as well. By June 21, 2010 all remnants of the Signal Center and Signal School were relocated to Ft. Gordon, Ga.

There I was at 17 years old and just about to venture on into the Signal world, which would remain with me to this very day. Many had gone before me, and as I felt at Ft. Lewis, I was a part of a tradition of military service that was as long as human history, not to mention that of the United States of America.

Signal School, Fort Monmouth, New Jersey 1969-1970

I shouldered my heavy duffle bag and crossed the road when traffic permitted. It was early evening when I arrived, and I was rather hungry, but low on funds. I walked over to the main gate and was halted by a couple of young MPs. One was a PFC and the other a Sergeant with ribbons on his chest from Vietnam. The two wore the Military Police armbands. Both looked sharp and professional. I felt lowly with my "naked dress uniform".

I showed them my orders and Army ID card then waited for permission to enter the U.S. Army Signal Center and School. All seemed to be in order. There was a Jeep parked off to the side of the guard shack and a bench where I was directed to sit for a while. One of the MPs told me to wait there on the bench for a while, as he had to take the Jeep and patrol his sector of the perimeter and upon his return, he would drive me over to the replacement company. I thanked him and asked if I could have a smoke. He agreed but added "…be sure to use the red "butt" can", which had been placed at the foot of the bench.

I was relieved, yet apprehensive of my near future in this strange land, 17 and in the Army. In one way, I felt freer than I ever had in the past. I also felt alone and away from home; yet I still felt proud to be sitting there in my sharp army dress green uniform with its single yellow stripe (PVT-E-2), US Army rank on my sleeves, a National Defense Medal centered on my left breast and my two Marksmanship badges, M-14 & M-16 rifles on the left breast pocket flap. I had calmed down a bit and enjoyed my smoke break. Another "trainee" joined us.

Soon the PFC returned with the Jeep and the Sergeant told him to take us over to the replacement company. I loaded up my duffle bag and climbed into the still-running Jeep. We "small talked" during the ride, such as where we came from etc. He asked me what school I was assigned to and I responded "31S20, crypto". He said that it was a good MOS and I would be studying in the "Cage". That had me worried. We passed modern buildings of what would soon become my battalion and brigade. He pointed out a large 3-story structure surrounded by barbed wire fences and plenty of spot lights around the perimeter. Armed guards would patrol the secure areas. He said non-descript manner, *That's the "Cage", secret stuff!* ".

We soon left the modern area and pulled up to an area of the old familiar 2-story WW II barracks. We pulled up to the orderly room of the replacement company. He helped me unload my bad and escorted me to the CQ, NCO (Charge of Quarters, Non-Commissioned Officer) who was sitting behind an old desk, with his feet propped up on that desk. He stood up as he saw the MP and me walk in. The MP simply said to the Sergeant, "Another "new bee" for you. "and the young PFC shook my hand and added" Welcome to Ft. Monmouth." I thanked him and pulled out my orders and handed them to the CQ.

He took my orders and offered me a seat and a cup of coffee. I declined the coffee, as I've never in my brief military career had a sergeant offer my anything but grief and pain. This was different. There were no Drill Instructors in sight and was informed that there were none on this post, except over at the "Special Training Company" and the stockade. I felt welcomed and relieved at this point. After he checked my orders and Army ID card he told his CQ runner (also a PV2) to take me to my barracks and told me to come back in an hour and I would be taken to one of the night mess halls (I did not know, but the Signal School ran 24 hours a day to meet the needs of the military) for dinner, if I was hungry. I was surely hungry by this point in time, as it had been a very long day. The runner advised me to only take out what I needed for a few days and a clean set of fatigues, as we would not need to set up a full wall locked display here at the replacement company. We would do all that when we got to our permanent company. I was assigned a bunk and I thanked the private for his help. I threw my duffle bag on the bunk. He then took me to the supply room where a very bored and tired Specialist 4 issued me a set of bedding, which I had to sign for. We returned to my barracks and I tossed my bedding on the bunk, thanked the young CQ runner, and went outside for a smoke. I was in!

Four of us were led to the jeep and the CQ runner told us that he was taking us to "chow", since we were the late arrivals. Since the Signal School operated 27 / 7, there were always a couple of "late night mess halls" open. We bounced along in the jeep and were dropped off at an old mess hall. We entered, signed for our meal and ate our meal. The small talk was basically about what school / course that we would be attending, and what MOS we would wind up with in the Army as well as where we might be stationed after completing our varied signal courses.

I was amazed that night, as well as later, on the wide variety of Signal specialties in the armed forces. They ranged from Avionics to the "Zulu Course", the Area Commo Chief, (MOS 31Z40) which I would become years later in my Reserve duty and assignment. Not only that, but the Army Signal School trained members of all of our armed forces, but foreign service members from nations around the free world as well. The largest number seemed to be Vietnamese. We would later be instructed who to salute and who not to salute of these foreign troops. It was quite confusing, even today.

After the meal and a smoke break, the Jeep appeared to take us back to the replacement company. We drove down a long tree-lined street, called "The Avenue of Memories", honoring past Signalmen who died in combat. Each tree had a small stone monument with a bronze plate inscribed with the name, rank and date of death in what theatre of operation in which he fell. We would later pass by this moving tribute many times during our stay at Ft. Monmouth. The jeep stopped at our company and we thanked the driver and we settled down for the rest of the night in our new and rather strange surroundings. Sleep came swiftly.

Slumber was rudely broken, as the KPs were rousted at some un-Godly time and their banging of the steel lockers accompanied their preparation for the kitchen detail. It was not too long after their departure that the lights were thrown on and the typical Army day began. (I must admit, that this awakening was not as harsh and hostile as it was in Basic Training. No Drill Sergeants were present.)

We were informed that there would be a formation in 45 minutes, and we were to be dressed, shaved, showered and ready for our march to the mess hall for breakfast. We complied, but it seemed that it was at a much slower pace that it was in Basic Training.

We complied and were marched off to a near-by mess hall for our first breakfast at Ft. Monmouth. I was pleased that they served the traditional "SOS" (Shit on a shingle, or also known as 'chipped beef on toast') we also had eggs to order, sides of bacon and / or sausage, good coffee, milk, cereal, toast, and fresh fruit. We even had much more than 5 minutes to eat, as was allotted in Basic Training. I could get used to this. This was going to be good being stationed here. We were being spoiled, or being prepared for something sinister?

After our meal, we were marched back to the replacement company and stood another formation headed by the permanent party cadre. The "first shirt "welcomed us to Ft. Monmouth and the "new" Signal Corps. He gave us a brief rundown on the "dos & don'ts" as well as a stern reminder of why we are here to become the futures Signalmen and the vital role we played in combat. Many lives would depend on how well we learned our various signal skills and the specialties we would master. A roll call was taken, when all were accounted for a senior sergeant took over from the First Sergeant and he would read off names and separated those men into small groups. They would either be assigned the additional duties of the day, of were to wait transportation to their permanent company and school assignment. The rest of us "New-Bees" were to be taken for "in processing" and orientation.

Most of the courses rotated about every two weeks or so. It all depended upon when we arrived as to how long we would remain at this replacement company. There could be several phases for any one given course. As usual, the Army standard of "hurry-up & wait" was still being upheld here. This process took most of the day and those of us who required security clearances had more to go through. We were given interim clearances by the end of the day of paperwork. It seemed to go rather quickly, and we even were marched off to an old theatre where we watched a couple of training films about security and SAEDA (or some alphabet initials) Subversion and Espionage Directed Against The Army. We were to be especially watchful of beautiful Russian and Chinese hooker / spies. It was also added after these 1950-style movies; that we should be aware of "Hippies" and college students who wanted to divert us from our primary military mission. (We looked at each other and shook our heads in disbelief at such statements.)

It gave us hope and yet fears in that the fate of the Free World could be compromised by our wrongful actions. We were to report any and all actions we noted to Army Intelligence and / or local authorities. I could not but wonder that this seemed rather extreme. (Hippies & college students were to be subversive to the United States? There were at least 10 colleges and universities in the New York, New Jersey area.)

We seemed to finish early that day and when taken back to the company area, were afforded to take advantage of a small PX nearby. It was actually an old WWII barracks where the first floor was converted to a retail store. They sold beer! That was all we needed to know, although it was forbidden back in the company. We stocked up on cigarettes, toiletries, "girlie" magazines and such.

While I was checking out at the check-out aisle, I noticed a display of brown paper bags stapled and the sign read "Grab Bags" I was curious. There was a lady and a couple of kids ahead of me and an older sergeant behind me in line. I was still wondering about those bags, so I began to pick them up one by one and shaking them to try to guess what was in the "Grab- Bag". After several attempts, I put one in my basket. That sergeant must have known that I was new, because he informed me in a loud voice, "Son, those are all the same. Those are Condoms in a plain paper bag, as not to offend the dependents! "All eyes were upon me as I checked out in extreme embarrassment. The lady shielded her children's eyes.

We managed to sneak a few six-packs back to the barracks and those who had been there a while advised us to be very careful of the "lifers". (Beer in the barracks was still forbidden) The other replacements also joined us in downing the beer. The cannon went off at 17:00 hrs. (5PM local) and "Retreat" was sounded by bugle call over post loud speakers. If outside, we were to turn and face the sound of the cannon and salute as the post flag was lowered. Even all motor traffic had to stop and do the same. We were in good spirits as we were later marched off to dinner.

After dinner we were allowed to use the company day room, watch TV, play pool and "foosball". There was plenty of reading material as well. This was going to be good duty. We got to know each other, even though we might not ever see each other again. We shared stories and photographs of girl friends and family. In later years, I often wondered if these young men made it home from Vietnam, and if they were sent there after Signal training.

I do not recall how long I was at the replacement company. It must not have been too long, as I only had one day of KP duty and did not go out to cut the officer's lawns or endless garbage and "police" calls as others did. I was soon assigned to my permanent training company:

Company "B", 1st. Training Battalion, 1st. Training Brigade, US Army Signal School.

We "New-Bees" parted from the replacement company and were transported off to our respective training companies. Once again there would be a much shorter process of checking in to the company, as we were already considered a part of the student troops of the Signal School. A cadre man led us downstairs to the supply room. We were issued bedding and assigned a bunk and locker. We were instructed once again of all the "rules", the "Dos & Don'ts".

We were issued a weapon and a scabbard with a bayonet. Both were kept in the arms room at all times. (I never saw that weapon, but a few times, months later when we were pulled out for "riot training" during many of the "anti-war" protests attempting to shut down several military installations.) We were issued a "pass card" to be used should we leave post. Yes, we were allowed to leave post when not in school or on duty. This was a well-earned bonus. We spent the remainder of the day stowing our uniforms and personal items in the locker and foot locker in the proper military order, per another training hand-out, such as we had seen in Basic Training. Actual training would begin on Monday. I looked forward to this new phase of my military career. I would remain at the Signal School from October 1969 until May of 1970.

We were billeted in a 60-man open bay, 4 men to a "cube", 2 bunks, 4 wall lockers, and an OD green field table as our desk. This was in a new cinderblock, 3 stories building, painted in a light "jail-house green". There were wide double doors entering each "Bay. Five platoons made up the company. These were the Co. HQ, Cadre personnel and 4 Student Platoons. Down each hallway there were the 2-man NCO rooms for both cadre and NCO students. The company orderly room and the mail room were in the center of this hallway. There was the large day room at the south end of the barracks, which also joined to the mess hall. The consolidated mess hall served two companies, A & B companies. Off in the near distance loomed "The Cage", the fenced & fortified secure training facility that was to be my home as a Crypto Guy / Student.

The other students greeted us and helped us get settled. We knew the basic lay out of the company and to our surprise there was a small PX and Canteen / Barber Shop just on the other side of the "A" Co. area. (Yes, that small Canteen and snack shop / grill served burgers & Beer!) There was a juke box in the canteen that played all the current and oldies" music.

I learned that most of "A" Co. was made up of US Marines. More about that bunch of "Jar-Heads" later. A couple would later become my class mates as their MOS was the same as mine, but with a different numeric / alpha designator in Marine nomenclature.

The new daily routine remained basically the same for me for the next seven months while stationed there at the Signal School. We were up by 0530hrs, SS&S'd (Shit, Shower & Shave), made up our rack, cleaned the bay and latrines. We then had breakfast and finished the tasks in the barracks. There was a morning formation when the First Sergeant gave us any needed information or orders. Promotion or disciplinary orders were read. The new duty roster was posted, mostly KP duty for the week. We were then formed up at "double-arm's interval and performed the traditional *"Police-Call"* of the company and surrounding area. (Assholes & Elbows, if it doesn't grow, pick it up!) We were then loaded up on the "cattle car" trailers and transported to our various schools.

By 0800 we were already in our place for the morning classes. We were given a five minuet "smoke break" about every hour or so. We were later rounded up and transported back to our respective company for lunch about 1130hrs. After lunch, we were transported back to our training area and remained in class until 1630hrs. Dinner was at 1730hrs and then we were free for the rest of the evening, unless we had additional duties to perform.

School was Monday through Friday and for the most part, the weekends were our own unless we had extra duty, or the company itself had "Post Duty" in which we were performing police calls or grounds keeping duties elsewhere on post, usually for only half a day. This only happened once while I was there since there were 25 other companies to draw this labor pool from.

A lot of our free time was spent studying or going to the large Enlisted Men's Club where the beer flowed freely at a nominal cost. Snacks were available as well. There was live entertainment and best of all civilian girls were allowed in. We danced to either live music or the blaring juke box. The whole place was loud and very smoke filled. These young ladies were quite welcome to us as a break from the all-male barracks life. Many young romances were born at the "EM Club" (One had to be careful, in that many dependent daughters snuck over to the club as well. All could drink and for a 17-year old, this was close to Heaven. At times it became wild and, I must admit, a few nights I staggered back to the barracks with by buddies. For many young troops, this experience was their first real "drunk". It was great, unless one threw up.

Sundays were rather lazy, and "church-call" was always offered and we were taken to the various chapels for those services, always Catholic or Protestant. A Jewish Chaplain was always available for our Jewish brothers. Naps were usually the order of the day after lunch. There was a washer / dryer in the barracks for our laundry, although most of our laundry was collected and done by the Quartermaster company once a week or so. The fatigue uniforms came back heavily starched and when putting on the new uniform, it was called "breaking starch" as we had to break free the sleeves and pant legs with a distinctive "tearing" sound. Linen was exchanged once a week at our supply room.

Seamstress services were provided to repair or to alter uniforms or to merely replace the buttons that the Quartermaster broke. Some of us preferred the small dry cleaner shop off post to do a much better job and specially to sew on our Signal School patch, worn on our left upper sleeve, centered and ½ inch from the shoulder. The lady, who owned this shop, was a "grandmotherly" type and really cared for all these young soldiers.

The course that I enlisted for first consisted of "basic electronics", which I excelled in. These non-secure phases were conducted to all in the electronic maintenance MOSs in the old WWII converted barracks. We learned the color code, which I already knew from Jr. High and how to solder. We wired a board of nails. This was old hat for me. We then were taught basic teletype repair, which was very, involved, the German inventor, Edward Kleinschmidt, spent his final years in the "loony bin". He went crazy.

The Kleinschmidt Corporation developed the basic machines in 1931. Some of the basic technology dates back to WW I. Since these first models were relatively light in weight, the military became quite interested in those machines. The company's biggest customer was the US Army Signal Corps in 1944. Both fixed station and tactical mobile units were sold to the military. In 1956 the Kleinschmidt Corporation merged with the Smith-Corona Corporation. By 1979 the Kleinschmidt Corporation branched off to the Marchant Calculating Machine Company. The teletype became obsolete as the thousands of mechanical parts which kept the teletypes running, were converted to a digital means of transmission.

We learned all of the non-secure equipment and repair skills during this initial phase of Crypto Equipment Repair. We were trained on the Kleinschmidt models: TT-4/FG, AN/FGC-25, TT-117/FG and the tape reperforator TT-179/FG. At this period of time, the electronic world was mostly all analog and solid state was just coming on line. A lot of the converters and radio equipment still had vacuum tubes.

We were also trained on basic wire operation, to include a small switchboard, the SB-22 and the field telephone, the TA-312. We would wire the room and transmit teletype and telephone signals around the classroom. Upon passing the Basic Electronic Phase, I was ready for the actual crypto phases at "The Cage". I now had a Secret Crypto Clearance.

I was later offered a part-time job in the cage as a janitor a few hours a week, which was great as I had extra spending cash each week. At that time a PV1 only made $97.50 a month and when I was promoted soon after my arrival to PFC. I made a whopping $134.50+/- a month. I still had a small allotment going to my grandparents each month. At that time, the military was paid once a month in cash.

On pay day, the 1st of each month, we lined up alphabetically by rank and the company commander paid us in cash. There was an armed guard behind the company commander. The commander himself wore a .45 Caliber M1911 pistol for extra protection. The Chaplain was always there with his hand out for his favorite charities and / or projects. We always gave a few dollars, just to keep in good graces with his boss.

Those of us, who had classes in "The Cage" were taken separately to the main entrance, lined up single file with our military ID card tucked under our chin. We entered, and a civilian guard verified that our face matched the ID card. Only then were we allowed to proceed to our classroom.

I cannot write of the specific content of this training, other that we trained to repair and operate the following machines: KW-7, (secure teletype), KL-7 (off-line encoding, similar to the famed Nazi Enigma crypto machine of WWII.), KY-8, KY-28, KY 38 (secure voice). We learned the basic operation, installation, trouble shooting and repair or the specific circuit boards and components.

I was enlisted in the full depot level of crypto maintenance, which was quite a long course. The needs of the Army had changed and because of Vietnam, more direct support personnel were needed. As with many of the Signal courses, each phase was getting harder to pass by raising the minimum passing score. Many of us were "phased out" and transferred to the direct level, which was easier and those of us who lasted longer in the depot level sailed through that course. I recall a couple of times; I was sent to the phase office for typing lyrics of Jefferson Airplane songs over the teletype as test tapes. Oh, well no sense of humor in "The Cage". Later when I phased down, I was transferred to "G" Company, 2nd Battalion, and my classes were held at night. I later graduated as a 31S20 in May of 1970. I came to learn that sleeping during the day and working at night was not an easy transition. (I would work many off shifts throughout my working life.)

I made many friends while at Ft. Monmouth. Sadly, there is only one man I was in contact with. Barry Smith, the Crazy Cajun. He was an old man; all of 21 at the time. He had worked for Louisiana Bell, and was lucky, as a draftee they sent him to the Dial Central Course, a very long school.

We would spend some wild pay-day week-ends up in New York City.

Those adventures were awesome. In 1969, the legal age in New York state was 18. A young man of 18 could go buy liquor and cigarettes in public then. Best of all, I now could go to the "titty" bars and other "adult" establishments. I was like a younger kid in a candy store. I was promoted to PFC, E-3 and celebrated my 18th birthday in November 1969.

It was always rather sad when a graduate received orders for Vietnam, as although we swore to keep in touch, often letters stopped. To this day, I do not know who made it home or not, just as it was from basic training. While I was training to be an Army Signalman, the world kept moving on. The top news headlines and events between October 1969 and December 1969 are listed in the appendix, timelines and notes.

On Oct. 15: The Moratorium to End the War in Vietnam erupts into demonstrations across the country. (Formal Signal training is suspended for the day. We trainees are pulled out of class for the day to receive riot control training, complete with gas masks, M-14 Rifles with fixed bayonets.

Training continues, and my Army life settles into a fairly normal routine. By now, Scharlene is about the only one outside of my immediate family who still is writing to me. Her letters are so sexy, that my friends would pick up my mail at Mail Call and deliver her scented envelopes to my bunk. Yes, I read some of the good parts to my friends.

We are informed that we would be granted a free leave for two weeks over the Christmas and New Year holidays. We could be on leave from 20 December 1969 until 02 January 1970. This leave would not be charged against out standard 30 days a year policy. My request was granted. We patiently waited for that first day of leave. I had two Marine buddies; one had a car, and one soldier friend. We all planned to share the expense to drive to Longview, Texas. The other Marine lived in San Diego, Ca. and we would get to Dallas, Tx. And catch a flight to California for the holidays. We were able to draw a small advance from the finance section

CHAPTER TWELVE

The Long and Winding Road Home and Out to See America: Christmas Leave 1969!

The sun rose at 07:53 EST, 20 December 1969 on the first day of our leave and the day of the Winter Solstice. It was early on this Saturday morning. The barracks were alive with activity. The usual Army duties continued, but the bulk of the troops were packing and loading up their cars for the holiday leave. Not everybody ate breakfast that morning in the mess hall.

I believe that the young Marine who had the car was named "Fink". The car was a Mercury Comet coup. It was *"souped"* up, had wide tires on the rear, and sported the "California Rake" (raised in the back, smaller tires in the front.) It was one cool ride. We filled the cooler with ice from the mess hall. We would wait to get the real beer on the outside. We loaded up the car.

All of us had to travel in uniform, as we were on leave orders. That was done so that if anything happened to us on our trip, it would be "in the line of duty" since we were on leave, but technically still considered "on duty". With the car loaded, we piled in, Marines in the front and we soldiers were in the back seat. We were ready and cleared for 'take-off'!

With a screech of his tires, we pulled out of "A" Company's parking lot and headed to Ft. Monmouth's Main Gate. The MPs waved us on through. As soon as we cleared the gate, we stopped at the nearby liquor store, bought plenty of beer and a bottle of bourbon. We all popped a cold beer, toasted our trip, the holidays, the US Marine Corps, and the US Army, Mom, Apple Pie and the American Flag. We were off and running.

Soon, Ft. Monmouth disappeared in the rear-view mirror. The stereo system was blasting away; we headed into the New Jersey traffic, heading towards the interstate. Texas or bust! (I thought "California, Here I Come" ... right back to where I started from!)

In 1969, all of the Interstate Highway System was not all connected, as it is today. The basic route roughly took us south on I-95, past Philly & DC and through Virginia, then heading west and south through the Appalachian Mountains. It was there that we wound up on some very small state and county roads, trying to find the interstate connectors. We would pass through Virginia, West Virginia, Kentucky, Tennessee, Arkansas and finally Texas.

This road trip proved to be quite a wake-up experience for me as far as my understanding of America went. The Christmas lights and decorations all over the landscape gave off a surreal aura to the whole setting and landscape. It seemed that the further south we went the two "red-necks" (the Marine driver and the other Marine) became more racist and "rebel" with each mile traveled southward. After several hours and many beers later, we passed the main urban centers of the eastern seaboard, past Washington DC and began to head into the mountains. America began to show me its dark side. This experience would remain with me for decades.

Somewhere outside of Roanoke Virginia, I recall an old faded roadside bill board with a picture of three hooded KKK Knights and the caption which read "If you are Black; don't let the sun set on your back. WELCOME TO ROANOKE." It was quite disturbing in addition; the driver swerved and tried to scare an old Black man who was riding a mule off of the road. Soon we were in the mountains on the back roads, as Fink knew a few "short-cuts "to get us back to the interstate. On this leg of the trip, I recalled being amazed as we passed huge colonial plantation mansions and just around the curve in the road, rusting tin sharecropper shacks. At one point, we stopped for gas and a bite to eat at a very run-down two pump gas station and grill on some wooded Appalachian "ridge-top". Old beat up rusting pickup trucks were parked nearby. There were rifles and shotguns in the gun racks of the rear windows. We got out of the car to stretch our legs and then headed in, as the other Marine pumped gas. We entered this small bar & grill / gas station "office".

Upon our rather awkward entrances, the place got silent. I looked around defensively. Now, I wore wire-rimmed glasses, as I do today. I never thought anything about it. One rather grizzled "mountain man" stood up; wiped beer foam from his grey beard and in a heavy accent asked me "Boy…is you a 'hippie'?" (Now mind you, all four of us are in uniform, two Marines, two Soldiers.) I braced myself for trouble and replied "No, Sir, I am a United States Soldier. These are my buddies; two US Marines and we are two United States Soldiers. We are on leave, headed home for the holidays. SIR!" The old guy looked me up and down and said, "Well you are wearing those 'hippie' glasses." I said something to the effect that my GI issue glasses got broken during combat training. That seemed to pacify the good ole boys. They accepted us and the obvious. We proceeded to pay for our gas and ordered our sandwiches and re-stocked the beer cooler. We paid up and left. I was quite relieved to be out of there and on the road again. The "red-necks in our group, began to laugh their butts off at that situation and of my awkwardness.

The rest of the trip seemed to become a combination of country back roads, state highway roads and in bursts, the new interstate system. We continued to talk about our high schools, girlfriends and hometowns. The beer flowed between "piss-stops" and often we simply had to relieve ourselves along the side of the road. I recall waving at the passing cars. Overall, we were having quite an adventure. The miles and the hours soon passed as we drove on into the night. We passed forgotten small towns and old farms. It was also getting much colder and there was a light snow falling. We all were getting hungry and decided to stop for dinner. A large neon sign lured us to stop. There was a bar & grill, live country music and dancing. It was a red-neck place of sorts. We pulled into the gravel parking lot and parked.

We dismounted the vehicle and headed in. Country music blasted the cold night air as we opened the door and entered. The inside air was heavily laden with cigarette smoke. A blue haze filled the room. At one end the band played country music and several couples were dancing on the small dance floor. Most of the tables were filled, as well as the long ornate bar.

We stopped at the "Please wait to be seated" sign. A cute country girl

/ waitress led us to our table. It was in the corner. "We are trapped", I thought. She handed us the menus and asked if we wanted a drink. "Beer all around!" we responded. All of us were in uniform and once again, we were not carded.

She left and soon after she disappeared, a very large young bruiser of a country boy in overalls with a 'John Deere' ball cap on his head came up to our table. This guy was missing a few teeth as well. He stood over six feet tall. There was tobacco spittle on his ragged beard of sorts. He looked me straight in the eyes and asked me "Are you boys' revenuers? "Now, I wondered to myself, are these people stupid or ignorant, or both? We all four are in military uniforms. (Two Marines, and two Soldiers.) I realized that I represented the greatest fighting force in the world, but this huge red-neck, behemoth of a man scared the piss out of me. I stood up. Bruiser inched closer. I replied "No sir, we are American GIs on Christmas leave, headed home for the holidays. Soon we will be in Vietnam and some of us may not make it home alive. I can prove it, SIR!" (I really wanted to say "Boy" but used my better judgments in this situation.) I was about to reach for my wallet to get my military ID out when, I swear I heard a round being chambered into some hidden weapon somewhere in the smoke-filled darkness. Big boy looked us over once again and said that we were OK. A few others nodded in agreement. I was relieved. The band played on. I think that as a sign of relief, I farted. The unseen weapons were placed on "safe".

The cute waitress returned with our beers and took our dinner orders. I don't recall exactly what that meal was. In fact, I was still quite on the defensive. We ate and continued to talk and joke around. I could not but help to think that my glasses must be spooking these red necks. We took our time and enjoyed the meal and the music. When we were done, the "Good ole Boy" returned to our table. This time he took out from behind his back a large Mason jar full of mountain moonshine and offered it to us. He went on to say, "Me and the boys wanted to thank you, support you and the war in Vietnam. Sorry for what happened earlier. We got to be careful, Y'all know? Merry Christmas!" he said as he handed us the Mason jar. Several others in the crowd raised their glasses in a toast to us. We nodded in response, paid our bill, noting that our bar tab was "O" d and we headed out to the car with our "Christmas gift". It was snowing heavier, but we had our anti-freeze.

The hot rod left that place in a spray of gravel, and we were once again on our way. Homeward bound and trucking! I was glad to be out of that place and still in one piece. All was good now as we sped along on into the cold December night in Dixie. We raced on, nipping on the moonshine and keeping warm, we were more than likely 'way over the legal limit and we prayed that no local yokel deputy would stop this racing Comet. The radio played some forgotten song at full blast. We were on a mission and had the orders to prove it. The two Marines up front took turns with the driving. The two of us here in the back seat, took turns napping and keeping an eye on the road as well as the driver. On into the night we raced on.

All I could think of was getting home safely for the holidays. I was also looking forward to seeing Scharlene once again and how I was going to act. Our guardian angels must have been watching over us on this adventurous trip. Booze, beer, and young bravado do not always mix on a cold snowy Dixie night in the mountains.

Like a band of gypsies, or perhaps, more accurately, a band of brothers, we drove on until the night faded into early dawn. The rising sun was to our back well to the East as the fingers of orange light raced westward.

We had been on the road for about 24 hours by now. We really had not slept much and the winter uniforms were getting rather ripe in that Comet, with the heater blasting to fend off the winter low temperatures. We were somewhere in Arkansas, headed towards Texarkana. By today's standards, with the present interstate highway system, it would be 1,381 miles, taking at normal highway speeds, an average of 21.25 hours. In 1969, before the connected interstate highway system, the same trip took much longer.

The landscapes slipped by me in an awesome blur. America was much larger and more fantastic than I ever imagined at 18 years especially with my coming from San Francisco. History made much more sense to me then; I was about to witness even more on this last leg of our trip.

It was still relatively early in the morning when we arrived in Texarkana, TX. We decided to stop for breakfast. I enjoyed a hearty meal and we all were refreshed for the last leg of our journey. Before we headed out to the highway, our Marine driver, Fink told us that we had to see something special.

He drove us to the center of town, where a small round flat monument was located in the concrete center of a traffic "roundabout". We stopped and got out of the car and walked to this monument. In a flash, it was obvious. All three state lines converged at this specific point and with a few movements of one's foot one could step in all three states in a couple of seconds: Texas, Louisiana and Arkansas. I danced about like a whirling dervish. I was amazed by this event, even to this day. Then, we sped off towards Longview, TX. It would be in Longview that this group would split up for the holidays. We survived a lot of beer and moonshine and avoided all the speed traps across 11 states. We had a good time, to say the least.

The other Marine was headed to San Diego, and I to San Francisco. The other two in our party were Texas boys, Fink in Longview, and the other marine nearby. They were home now and the two of us Californians would fly home from Dallas, Tx. To the West Coast. (My Grandmother had sent me money for the full trip, New Jersey to San Francisco and back. I pocketed the difference to pay in part for this road trip. Also, if I recall, the military paid us early, should we had been on leave orders. I had plenty of traveling money, still.)

Fink dropped me and my Marine buddy off at the Longview Continental Trailways bus line terminal. We then purchased our tickets to Dallas, Tx. We had some time to wait and after the usual "smoke break", we settled down to wait. We were sitting on a large, very hard wooden bench, one of many which were in the waiting room of the terminal. Soon, I had to take a piss.

I looked around to locate the restroom. I then noticed that there were four restrooms provided two women's, and two men's. How thoughtful of a bus line to do so. I was confused. I shrugged my shoulders and proceeded to one of the men's rooms. Continental Trailways must really care for their passengers' bathroom needs at this terminal.

An elderly Black man came out of one as I headed in to replace him. He abruptly stopped me and said in a grandfatherly voice, "Oh, no son, the white folks must use the other bathroom! ". He pointed to the men's room to the right. He also added that should we want a drink of water from the two drinking fountains, "…use the white one." With a wink he informed me that…"black marble was twice as expensive as white marble.". I suddenly realized that in spite of the passage of all the Civil Rights legislation, that local customs and traditions could not be changed from Washington. DC. Even though, I was only 18, many Black passengers referred to me as "Sir" or "Boss"; maybe it was the uniform that demanded their respect; or could it be my skin color. People in the South seemed to be much friendlier than out west or in New England, especially New Jersey or New York.

It was not too long after this revelation, that our Dallas-bound bus was announced for its departure. We gathered our duffle bags and headed towards the ramp where our bus was waiting. Our bags were checked, and boarding ticket was checked. We proceeded to get on board. As we climbed on the bus the driver reminded us to "…sit up front, and to ignore those dirty Hippies outside protesting the War. You white boys will sit up in front of "my" bus. Thank you, boys, for your service. "(Those simple words would echo decades later among us Vietnam Veterans.)

My young eyes were wide open as to the real life in America during this historic period of history. I came to realize that the following events and programs were not working in America at that point in time: The War in Southeast Asia, The Great Society of President Johnson, The War on Poverty, The War on Drugs, The nuclear standoff between the Soviet Union and the West, where thousands of nuclear warheads were targeted towards each other, but to name a few. My own experiences during this trip will leave a long-lasting impression on me.

Soon we were headed to Dallas and our final leg of this odyssey. We soon were fast asleep, as by now we were very tired and wired. The bus rolled along I-20. I woke up outside of Dallas, as I could tell by the highway signs. Not too much later, the bus driver announced our arrival at the Dallas Continental Trailways terminal. With the "hiss" of the air brakes, we gathered our belongings and departed the bus. Once again, the driver thanked us. We asked for a way to get to the airport and soon had bus tickets in our hands for the short shuttle ride to the airport. We were on our way to "Cali" and home. It was mid-Sunday afternoon. With the time difference, I should be home for dinner, California local time.

At the Dallas Love Field Airport, we departed company with a firm handshake and a manly hug as we headed to our different airline ticket counters and perhaps our survival of "the war". He was headed to San Diego and me, up to San Francisco both on different airlines. Other servicemen nodded, gave a "thumbs-up" or flashed the "Peace" sign in passing.

With my ticket in hand and over an hour to spare, I found the bar and tried my luck in ordering a stiff drink, it worked, and I reminded myself that I was in the patriotic state of Texas. I still could not shake the feeling that many eyes were upon this soldier. I had plenty of money left, as my grandmother had sent me funds for the complete round-trip from New Jersey. If, I recall, we were paid early if we were on leave orders for the holidays.

After a few drinks, one provided by an elderly couple across the lounge, I headed towards my departure gate. I do not recall which airline that I flew on but did get the military discount which gave me more money in my wallet. I was feeling no pain, as this would be my only fourth plane ride.

Not too much long later, the boarding process began, and a few kind people waved me ahead of them: I thanked them and entered the aircraft. We all settled in the plane and the stewardess gave us the in-flight safety briefing. Soon we were taxiing down the runway once disconnected from the tow-motor. At the ready point, the jet engines roared into life and we lunged forward when the pilot released the brakes. The acceleration and mounting "G" forces forced me back into my seat.

As if by magic, with a bump the airplane became airborne. We continued to climb and banked sharply, headed westward. As I looked out of the window, I could have sworn that Love Field was in downtown Dallas. I could have been mistaken though. It sure seemed that way. Texas soon dropped below us, and we reached the final cruising elevation. The "No Smoking" light was extinguished and the "Fasten Seatbelts" sigh was turned off. I was definitely homeward bound. It was late afternoon or early evening. After a few drinks again and a non-descript airline dinner, I fell into a well-earned sleep.

CHAPTER THIRTEEN

San Francisco, The City by The Bay and Where I left my Heart.

I was able to catch a couple of quick snoozes. I recall being awakened by a bit of turbulences. We were getting closer to the West Coast. I remained alert, looking out of the window at America passing underneath the aircraft. Once again, I was amazed at how vast the country is. The Sierra Nevada Mountains rose beneath us and the still snow-capped peaks shined in the afternoon light. It would not be long now, I thought.

After, what seemed like ages, I felt a few bumps and my ears popped as the plane began to descend. I could hear the hydraulics engage and could hear the air brakes pop up to slow the aircraft down. We began a steep banking move as we circled the San Francisco Bay area. It was a beautiful sight as we turned to make the approach to San Francisco International Airport. I could see the bridges and the bay almost in its entirety. That scene reminded me in reverse of my first flight to Ft. Lewis. We dropped relatively quickly, as I could now make out the traffic on the bridges and freeways below. My ears continued to "pop" as our altitude declined.

With the squeal of the brakes and the rush of the air brakes we were on the ground. The quick deceleration pushed us forward in our seats. There was a long taxi down the runway and turn around for the trip back to the terminal. Near the terminal, the aircraft shut down its engines and internal power as we docked at the terminal. I wished that the other passengers would hurry up and regain their carry-on luggage, as I was ready to leave the plane now. I grabbed my "AWOL Bag" from the overhead compartment and was ready to go home. When my turn came

I exited the plane, thanking the stewardesses. I was also very aware of the eyes that were upon me as I went through the terminal to baggage claim to get my duffle bag. I was still young and in uniform. I saw other service members, with the battle ribbons on their chests and thought, someday I'll have mine. But for now, I was home.

I got my duffle bag, shouldered it and went to the bus terminal for the shuttle ride into downtown San Francisco. It was about a 45-minute bus ride into the city during rush hour. I could not wait to get on home. I was debating whether or not to see Scharlene first, or my grandparents. I pondered this question all during the bus ride. I called her from a pay phone anyway.

I could see the city streets passing by as the bus headed to the downtown terminal. It all seemed so familiar, yet so foreign. I could not help but to notice all the changes, no matter how slight in every block, both on this trip as well as the entire route to my old neighborhood.

Soon, with the hiss of the airbrakes, the bus stopped in its designated gate and we left to go on our way.

I decided to see Scharlene first and to take the MUNI city bus to her place and save some taxi money. It was a short walk to the city bus stop. I was surprised to see that the bus fare had gone up to a quarter from 15 cents in my absence. I paid and was happily on my way to see Scharlene.

The #38 MUNI buses stopped at Geary and Laguna Streets. I was elated, and then I walked the couple of blocks up to Scharlene's family triplex. It was still painted green with white trim. It seemed a bit faded and the paint was peeling more since my last visit. I shouldered my duffle bag and headed up the stairs to her front door. I could hear their three small dogs barking even before I knocked on their glass front door.

She came down to let me in. When the door was opened, she gave me the most passionate hug and kiss that I think I ever had in my life from her. I almost fell over the railing, dropping my duffle bag on the porch. After what seemed like forever, we went upstairs to their home to meet the rest of the family.

Everyone was glad to see me again and that Scharlene and I seemed to have gotten back together again. As usual, the place was quite a mess, (housekeeping was not always a top priority.), and the dogs continued to bark and paw my legs. They had their Christmas tree up and decorated. The Christmas lights were turned on in my honor.

I was led to their living room and given a seat. I greeted her younger sister and brother as they joined us. Her parents came in and they were glad to see me and commented on how fit and trim I looked. (That good Army training, I guess.) I was offered a beer by her dad, Junior Martin, the retired Army Medic. He commented on my marksmanship badges and the conversation shifted to how well the Army was treating me. Scharlene sat next to me holding my sweating hand. I fielded many questions and answered their inquiries on my life since high school, the Army and the trip across the country. We must have talked for over an hour or so.

I was invited to stay for dinner, but I had to decline, explaining that I had not been home yet to be with my grandparents. The Martins offered me a rain check for dinner. I loved Scharlene's mother's (Yuriko) cooking. I had not had Japanese food since I left for the Army. Junior offered to drive me home.

I finished my beer and we loaded up the car. Junior proudly owned a 1963 Buick Skylark, blue and well worn. The interior smelled strongly of cigarette smoke, as he and his wife both smoked. (Later, all the kids smoked.). We headed west, out on Geary Street towards the Avenues. The Christmas decorations on the lamp posts flew by. The colorful Christmas lights shined on very brightly. It was starting to feel like Christmas.

Once again, I was amazed to see familiar buildings which had been painted since my departure, as well as the new constructions and re-modeling to many. It was both like meeting an old friend or meeting a new person for the first time. The city streets, buildings and land marks rushed by as we drove on. I actually was rather excited and anticipating seeing my grandparents again. It seemed like eons since I left, actually had been only about four months.

We turned left on 21st Avenue off of Geary Street. I was close now to home. Junior pulled up on our driveway and parked. I could see the Venetian blinds being opened as my grandmother peered out of the window to see who had come. Some of my neighbors also looked as this young, uniformed soldier stepped out into the sunlight. I waved and proceeded to get my luggage out of the trunk with Scharlene's younger brother, Willy's help. I offered the family to come up and meet my grandparents, but they declined, indicating that they were not properly dressed. I kissed Scharlene good-bye, gave her a big hug and headed up the stairs. The blue Buick pulled out of the driveway and left. I saw Scharlene looking back towards me out of the rear window of the Buick.

My grandmother, Jessie, opened the front door and greeted me, hugged and kissed me as if I was a returning hero of some sort. Perhaps in her eyes I was. I put down my luggage and went into the living room where my grandfather was seated in his old high-back chair, as if on a royal throne. A tall floor lamp was behind him to his left. There were the two small end tables on either side. Both had books and magazines piled on them. The table on his right boasted a small AM radio. He stood up and took a step towards me with his arm extended to give me a hand shake. I grabbed his hand and gave him a hearty hand shake. Then, what the hell, I gave him a powerful hug. He was a strong man for his advanced age but seemed impressed with my strength as well.

Jessie had put up a small Christmas tree on a large table in the window. It was decorated and lit. I could not help but to miss the large fresh trees and pine scents of the fresh trees and decorative branches decorated on the mantel of the past. The tree was always covered by the many boxes of ornaments. There were a couple of small boxes under the tree, perhaps from her sister and each other. I went over to my duffle bag and took out a box which was still in a plastic PX bag. I retied the bag, so they couldn't peek into it. I had bought a large Signal Corps coffee mug for my grandfather. I took out the second bag which contained a decorative New Jersey souvenir plate for my grandmother. I also got Catherine a small Texas souvenir glass. I had forgotten about her until we reached Texas.

He sat back down on his throne. I took a seat on the sofa on the end nearest to him. Jessie sat down in another chair on the other side of the room. The sun was slowly setting in the west and the December winter shadows began creeping down the street. We began to talk and catch up on what was happening in our lives. Both of them were very anti-military, yet I could sense that they were proud of this young soldier. I almost seemed to sense my father's presence with my mother in the room at that time. I guessed that they also were proud of me.

We must have chatted for about an hour, when Jessie excused herself to prepare our dinner. I could hardly wait to have a home-cooked meal after all those months of "Army chow". My grandfather and I continued to talk and reminisce over things in the past. Some of the things he related to me were those tales that I heard so many times throughout my life. A few were things that I never heard before from his life. I wondered if Jessie was listening as well. I could begin to smell the aroma of home cooking as I heard the banging and clanging of the pots and pans. When I heard the dishes being set, I knew that dinner would not be too long. Jessie set up a semi-formal table in the dining room on our large heavy round wooden table.

Before we sat down for our dinner, I had to take a thorough tour of the house, from the living room, all the way to the back bedrooms of the house. It seemed so foreign, yet so honestly familiar, like meeting an old friend after such a long separation. I took in all the smells and subtle differences in how various objects were rearranged throughout the house. I could not help but to reacquaint myself with some of the most common objects, such as a light switch or door knob. My old bed room seemed so inviting but would have to wait a few more hours for my reunion and a welcome good night sleep in my own space. It is said that once one leaves home, one can never really go back.

After a wonderful meal consisting of a salad, followed by a home cooked meat loaf, mashed potatoes, brown gravy, and buttered green beans followed by the apple pie ala-monde for desert we retreated back into the living room for coffee and conversation. I was full and very satisfied. We watched some television and I watched my eye lids begin to drop. I said my good-nights and I excused myself early (it was only about 22:00 hours, oops! 10:00 PM.) and went back to my room and got ready for bed. It was good to be home again.

I fell into a deep sleep in no time at all. I really must have been extremely tired. The California sun rose at 07:53. I slept on, as I slept about 12 hours, awakening at about 10:00 AM. I was wide awake, mostly due to the smell of fresh-brewed coffee, made on the gas stove with the old percolator, as had been done all my life. It was Monday morning. Christmas would be this Thursday.

My uniform was left strewn on a chair in my room from the previous evening in my haste to hop into my own bed. I properly hung up my uniform on a coat hanger and placed it over the top of the door. I fished

167

out a pair of old blue jeans and hastily put them on. I then got the rest of my clothing and headed straight to the bathroom and took a long needed hot shower. It seemed that thousands of miles washed away down the drain. I was reborn again.

I wandered into the kitchen and was offered a fresh cup of coffee by my grandmother. It smelled wonderful and tasted better than any Army coffee I have had to drink. We went into the living room to have our coffee. My grandfather sat there in his usual chair, reading and sipping on his coffee. We small talked for a bit and I was asked what my plans were for the day.

I wound up calling most all of the family and wishing them all a Merry Christmas and a Happy New Year. Once again, I felt mixed reactions to my greetings. "Peace on Earth" seemed to fall on deaf ears worldwide, not only here in San Francisco. (Whatever happened to: "Love Peace & Happiness"?)

Next, phone calls were in order to my friends on the block and from school. I later visited most the neighbors and childhood friends on 'the block' as well as in the area. I thought of Scharlene once again. I called her a few minutes later and accepted her invitation to come over for dinner. I really cared for her, but somehow 'love' had not really presented itself yet. It remained just below the surface, as I would find for sure later on this leave. Her mother was planning to prepare a Japanese dinner in my honor. I accepted immediately and then had to break the news to my grandparents that I would not be having dinner with them this evening.

Later, I walked down to Geary Street and paid a visit to the old bakery where I had worked in high school. Old Heinz Knopp was glad to see me as he gave me a bone-crushing hand shake in the back of the shop. The same sales ladies still worked there and were delighted to see me as well. I also stopped by to see the Chinese grocers in the two stores near the house. They too, were glad to see me and wondered where I had been all these months. I gave them the 'short' version. I extended my holiday greetings and wishes to all.

I continued to walk around the old neighborhood, seeing many things through my new eyes. I saw these things both as being the same, and somewhat different. The recently painted houses and minor alterations to the neighborhood were duly noted. I passed my good friend, Charlie

"Taco" Guerrero, working on one of his hot rods in his basement. It was a black, and "flamed" 1949 Ford, one of my favorite cars of all times. He stopped wrenching on his car, and we had a couple of beers (we both were under 21 at that time; it did not matter.) The beer went down quite smoothly. We reminisced about "the good old days". (Hell, today, those are the "good old days"!). I treasured these images and felt that they all could be different upon my next visit. The thought also crossed my mind that I may never live to see and experience all of this again, should I go to Vietnam.

Upon my return home, I realized that it was late. I had to get ready to go over to see Scharlene and have that wonderful Japanese home cooking. When I was ready, and just about ready to leave; my grandmother tried to talk me out of going. I refused and insisted that I go. It was important to me. I left, after saying good bye to my grandparents. I walked down the few blocks to Geary Street to catch the #38 Geary bus.

Once again, the bus ride was very meaningful to me, as I continued to observe the panorama of the city passing by, framed by the bus window frame. The sounds of the bus and the almost constant drone of the varied conversations of the passengers bombarded my ears. Foreign languages burst in and out of this new symphony, reminding me of the high-pitched cymbals.

When the rear doors opened to let the passengers off, the smells of the city wafted in. I smelled the spent diesel of the bus and the trucks passing by. Occasionally I recalled smelling the rich smells from the Boudin French Bakery on 6th Avenue & Geary. Other ethnic cooking smells snuck in as well. I could also sense the smell of stale cigarettes, in spite of smoking having been banned for years on the MUNI busses, trolley-buses, street cars and cable cars. People always managed to sneak a smoke in the rear of a crowded bus. Shortly after the bus crossed Fillmore Street, I pulled the cord to signal the driver that I wanted off at the next stop. I got off on Laguna Street, and walked the few blocks to "Schar's" flat.

I went up the stairs and knocked on her door. The dogs announced my arrival with their barking and scratching on the inside of the door. "Schar's" younger brother answered the door and simply said that his sister was still getting ready. We climbed up the interior stairs to the hall way. I was led to their living room and offered a seat. The television was on, but nobody seemed to be paying any attention to the day-time programming. Her sister, Jane Martin must be helping with either "Schar's" preparation or the dinner preparations. Junior went back to the kitchen and got us a beer. The small talk continued. We waited for the rest of the family to appear.

I noticed that the entire place seemed to be cleaner and more in order than it was on my last visit. The slight aroma of Pine-Sol settled in throughout the flat. The dining room table had been set in a "country" formal fashion, complete with two candles. Time passed for a while with conversations between Junior, Willy and me. Soon "Schar's" sister, Jane came in and sat on the floor "Indian style". She was full of questions, as usual. Yuriko poked her head in briefly and greeted me, but promptly retreated to the kitchen, which was in the rear of the flat, down the hall from us and returned to her cooking. The place smelled wonderful. I was anticipating "Schar's" grand entrance.

Without notice "Schar" entered the room, and my world just lit up. She had her long black hair done and put up. She wore a short skirt and a colorful top. In keeping with the fashion trends of the times, she wore a purple leather vest, complete with fringes. I was delighted at this wonderful sight that was before my eyes. I stood up and we approached each other. We hugged and kissed for what seemed like a life time. On the other hand, it wasn't really that long, since we were under the watchful eyes of her father, sister and brother. We sat next to each other on the couch. The conversations continued until the two girls were called in to the kitchen by their mother to help set the dinner out on the table.

At the dinner table, Junior offered a toast with the sake; we all raised the small sakes cup in unison. He toasted me and toasted for good luck for all. We began the dinner with sushi and "kon-kon" (a pickled Japanese salad.) We dined on tempura shrimp and sweet potatoes and beef teriyaki. A variety of Japanese vegetables were on the side. White rice was served in abundance as well. Japanese green tea was served with the wonderful meal. This was the most wonderful meal that I had had in ages. Needless to say, Yuriko insured that I was completely "stuffed". (That, I was.) We retreated to finish the large Sake Jar.

We retreated to the living room, as the girls cleared the table and put what little leftovers away. Yuriko announced that the dishes could wait and the whole family was together in the living room. We talked for a long time over the TV, which was on the game shows, that Junior and Yuriko always loved to watch. It was dark outside, and it was getting late, so I had to return home. Junior drove me home once again but did not come up with me to meet my grandparents.

The next couple of days were a blur of activity for me. The high school was on Christmas vacation, so I could not go back there to visit at this time. I spent a lot of time doing things around the house for my grandparents and the rest of the time with Scharlene.

At some point, I recall that the two of us were in her bedroom, on her bed, talking and in the course of the conversation, I somehow blurted out something like: "…how would you feel about becoming a soldier's wife?" Somehow that became my marriage proposal to her. (She confirmed that with her mother and father.) There was no one-knee proposal, no sky writing, no theatrics or drama; it was simple and to the point, although I somehow did not think of my ramblings as a marriage proposal. Yes, I guess, that I had committed myself. I felt happy, and at the same time very nervous. I would not tell my family until much later in a letter.

Christmas that year fell on a Thursday; it was damp and overcast in "The City". The sun rose at 07:55, above the clouds and fog. It was a quiet holiday. The neighborhood would come alive later in the morning when the kids would be out trying out their new bicycles and toys. We exchanged gifts in the morning. My grandfather had built a fire in the fireplace. With the glow of the fire and the decorated tree, Christmas seemed special this year.

My grandmother was a flurry of activity, preparing the dinner. Her sister, Catherine Walker, (More on her later in this writing.) also came by to celebrate the holiday and help her sister. I helped where I could, mostly lifting and moving things also opening jars and cans. Once everything was set and cooking she would venture out of the kitchen to join us. A wonderful aroma filled the entire house with a variety of scents. The fireplace added the smell of burning wood to the pine smell of the Christmas tree. The kitchen smells completed the picture of a traditional Christmas.

The Taylors (Cousins: Glenhall Jr. wife, Pat, daughter Susan, oldest son, "Glennie", youngest son "Jamie", and adopted son James came by later in the afternoon. After all the holiday greetings, hugs and kisses, we all settled down in the living room. (Unknown to me, this would be the very last year that I would see all the Taylor family together.)

The room was quite crowded and a few of the dining room chairs had to be brought into the room to accommodate everybody. Wine and ginger ale were passed around. (No, in that house, one had to be 21 to have an alcoholic beverage, in spite of the fact that I was 18 and in the Army.) I, once again was bombarded with questions about my Army life and my travels. My oldest cousin, Glenhall Jr. was an Army veteran of the Battle of the Bulge. He still carried the metal from his wounds in his back. He seemed quite interested in how the Army had changed since his days, as well as how many things remained the same. The conversations went from the family updates to my cousin's wife, Pat going on a misinformed rant against the Vietnam War. I merely defended the war as being proper and defended my role as a soldier. (Oh hell, this would become commonplace in the next few decades.)

They all stayed for my grandmother's traditional Christmas dinner, ham, (more on the ham later in this writing.) with all the trimmings. We feasted on with buttered green beans, mashed potatoes and gravy, corn and a salad. There was always the choice from three pies (apple, pumpkin and mince.) for desert. Later on, after an hour or so of conversation, coffee and desert were served. A very happy and well-fed family departed, and we finished cleaning up. It was getting late and all of us were quite tired. Christmas had been a very long day. It was almost midnight when I drifted off to sleep in my own bed and room.

The next few days and that weekend of the 27th & 28th, were time spent between Scharlene and my family. There were a few breaks with my friends on the block and from high school. I got a lot done around the house for my grandparents. The back yard and basement had been cleaned up and trash removed to the city dump. I made many minor repairs around the house, under my grandfather's supervision and instruction. He was not above grabbing a hammer or wrench and getting right into the project and getting his hands dirty, even at his age. I know he enjoyed it.

That Monday, Junior and the family had planned a trip to the Presidio of San Francisco to go shopping at the PX and commissary and had asked if I wanted to go. I accepted, and they would pick me up in a couple of hours. I promptly asked my grandmother and her sister if they needed any groceries. They drew me up a list.

We made the trip to the Presidio and did the shopping. After unloading and putting the groceries away at "Schar's" place, we proceeded over to my house and brought the groceries upstairs. "Schar" helped me and I introduced her to my family. They eyed her with curiosity, since "Schar" was ½ Japanese. I would hear more about this later.

Both Jessie and Catherine really appreciated the few groceries and extras that I bought for them. They saved a good deal on the purchases. In those days, before Wal-Mart and the 'big-box' stores, the military PX and commissaries really saved the shopper a lot of money. The only 'catch' was that one had to be active duty, retired or reservist / national guardsman on active duty to enter the buildings. The posted, armed M.P.s insured that.

The next two days, the 30th and the 31st were pretty much spent the same way. I got rid of a lot of my "childhood things" and did some more around the house for my grandparents. In the afternoon of the 30th Junior, Yuriko and "Schar" took me to a discount jewelry and appliance store on Mission Street. We picked out an inexpensive wedding set and Yuriko put it on her account. I would (and did.) pay the Martins back monthly at a rate I could afford on my Army salary. (I thought to myself: 'You are really hooked this time, Bunkie.')

I had already purchased my return airline ticket when I was in Texas and was able to book a seat on an early flight back to Newark, surprisingly on New Year's Day. I made all the "farewell" visits and phone calls that had to be made. I re-packed my duffle bag and AWOL bag on the afternoon of the 31st. I was all set for the return trip and back to Army life once again.

My grandparents and I stayed up to toast in 1970. We watched 'Dick Clark's Rockin' New Year' from Times Square, New York. (It was a small milestone; in that they normally would have watched the 'Guy Lombardo and The Royal Canadians' New Year's Show. I went to bed about 01:00. (1:00AM for you civilians) The alarm was set, as it would be an early day for me. Junior, Yuriko and "Schar" would be taking be to the airport in the morning. (My grandparents still did not know that I was engaged.) We would say our "good-byes" in the morning with my "taxi" outside blowing his horn.

With the Peter, Paul & Mary hit song "Leaving on a Jet Plane", playing on the radio, "Schar" tearing up, I was off. We made it to the San Francisco International Airport with lots of time to spare. (TSA and the three-hour pre-departure checks had not been put in place yet.). We all went to the proper departure gate; I checked in and waited over coffee with my "new family" for my flight to board. I was in my dress greens and, once again, felt that all eyes were upon me. (The real fact is that 95% of the people in public never notice you.)

Soon, it was time for me to leave, as the plane began to be boarded. I said my "good-byes". "Schar" hugged and kissed me for a long time with tears rolling down her sweet cheeks.

It was hard for me to leave, but "duty called" and I was a soldier. I would not be back home until May 1970.

The flight back was uneventful. I was getting accustomed to flying now, as this would be my 5th flight. I was still amazed, but the "awesomeness" of flight was not as powerful as that first actual flight. The only thing that bothered me was the older stewardess, actually 'carded' me on this flight, I was only 18. I could not drink on the plane for this flight. That fact would "bug" me until I turned 21 in 1972, after 4 years in the Army, and a Vietnam tour behind me.

I made it back to Ft. Monmouth in the early evening and checked into my company. I was on time and was in good shape with all my leave status. I would have to wait until Friday, 2 January to get a beer at the small PX and Canteen grill near our barracks. I would also get a haircut, at the small barber shop next to the PX. I had to be all "stract" for Monday. Classes would not begin until 5 January. We would spend the weekend performing a full GI Party in the barracks. Monday came 'way too quickly and we were back in the Army routine. I sure missed home.

CHAPTER FOURTEEN

1970: AND THE THINGS CAME AND WENT

The year 1970 would prove itself to be a monumental year in my life as well as the entire world in general. It is said that history repeats itself and that we must learn from the past to understand and live for today.

It did not take too long for me to settle back into the Signal School routine and to keep up with all the Army "stuff". The day still began 'way too early. During the morning formations, the snow and the wind still froze this California boy to the bone, in spite of the 'long-johns', gloves, army wool scarf, fur-lined Korea winter hat (with ear flaps and 2 position visor) field jacket or heavy army wool overcoat.

As the winter progressed, so did the snow drifts which were at window the height of the first floor of the 3-story barracks building. The full unopened beer cans that were dropped out of the windows when an NCO entered the bay, were quickly covered up, buried in the snow until the spring thaw. (Hopefully they were saved during the morning "police call".)

One cold and snowing Saturday morning, I happened to look out of one of the windows facing "A" Company, (which housed the Marines), to see a young Marine sitting outside on a boatswain's chair seeming to be chipping away at the side of the barracks. A few of us ventured outside to the common between the buildings. A small crowd had assembled to watch this strange spectacle. It turned out that this poor young Marine had gotten extremely drunk Friday night and had vomited out the window. His barf froze almost immediately on the outside of the barracks. To teach him a lesson, and to keep good relations between the US Army and the

US Marine Corps; the Marine sergeant rigged up the chair and had that kid clean up his mess. Needless to say, none of us soldiers would ever puke out of our windows that winter.

We saw many classes graduate and attentively listened to the graduates read their new re-assignment orders. Some of the top students would remain there at Ft. Monmouth, receive instructor training and become a part of the school cadre. Many would receive leave and then off for Vietnam training and then off to the war. The lucky ones got orders for Europe, Germany mostly. Some others got assignments to the various divisions stationed here in CONUS (Continental United States.) One poor guy got Iceland and his buddy got Alaska. I also have heard of signalmen being sent to Antarctica. I still had my mind made up that I would go directly to Vietnam when my time was up.

One guy from our crypto course got the perfect assignment. He would be on "civilian status" (new wardrobe provided by Uncle Sam,) to the US Embassy, Vatican City, Italy. I then realized that every US embassy around the world had secure teletype lines as well as secure voice protection. (AUTOSEVOCOM; Automatic Secure Voice Communication.). We provided those technicians.

As I mentioned briefly earlier in this writing, that I had enlisted for the full depot level crypto repair course, which was a much longer school. As fate would have it, the Army's needs changed almost daily due to the Vietnam War. In many of the longer signal courses, the standards were raised; higher test and performance scores were needed to pass a given phase. In some instances, the low scoring student was phased out and, in some cases, transferred to an entirely different course. This happened to me and a couple of other men from my course.

About half way through my long course I "phased-out" and was reassigned to the shorter version of my specialty, the direct support maintenance position, same equipment's, but geared to providing rapid repair and or replacement support to the line units.

I was transferred to "G" Company, 2nd Bn. across the parade field from my original company. That course was taught in "the cage" on the "graveyard shift". This was not going to be good at all. I reported in to the new company and got my bunk assignment, and after a briefing, moved in.

We actually did quite well academically in the scaled-down version of our specialty, having been trained in depth on the same equipment. It was rather rough going to school at midnight. Not only did we suffer, trying to sleep through all of the normal "daytime" noise of a busy Army post. The routine barracks cleaning and other duties still had to be done. It was no wonder why so many students would "nod" off during the class. A sharp reprimand, an eraser thrown at them, or "be quiet, we'll wake them *after our break."*

What often happened was that we tended to sleep in two shifts, morning and then perhaps for a few hours later in the day. Believe me, sometimes, we would not even stop for breakfast at the company mess hall. If we were not careful we would miss the dinner meal at our company and have to hope that we would be able to make the "all night" mess hall. If all failed, we could always go to the PX canteen, lunch and a few beers. I guess that in retrospect, I was preparing for work in my later years, in which, over time, I've worked all three shifts.

The training continued, and we were feeling quite adapt and ready to charge into battle with our tools, meters and codes to do battle with the forces of evil. To be young, 18, ten feet tall and bullet-proof, once again, would be a gift from Heaven. These opinions and beliefs would be challenged later. We drove on, with "Mom, apple pie, and the American flag "dancing in our young heads. More and more of our classmates were being sent to Vietnam. I continued on every day and night in the hope that my Signal training and expertise will save many American lives in the future.

The days and weeks seemed to pass at a different, but faster pace. Scharlene's letters kept me both aroused and hopeful for our future. My grandmother's letters made me think, also that I had abandoned them. I finally broke down and told them that I was engaged to be married to Scharlene. They did not seem very happy but wished us well and that we would "talk" when I got home. Yet in spite of all, they all loved me, and I had to give back somehow.

Our wandering around New England and its history, and the EM Club occupied my free time; those experiences made all seem worthwhile. We developed the attitude that we would live only once, for today, and the Devil may take the rest. We felt indestructible. For those nights, (afternoons for us night owls.) the beer and booze got us through.

I finished the 31S20 crypto course sometime in April 1970 and graduated with my MOS and was up for reassignment to my first permanent duty station. I drew an assignment to Germany. I was relieved for the time and my family, including Scharlene, were all elated. I would have leave and be paid for travel, in the wrong direction. They would only pay for the trip: Ft. Monmouth to Ft. Dix, both in New Jersey. (Bummer.) I was still a Private First Class, and somehow felt cheated, in that others were being promoted ahead of me. I drew a "free" leave and cleared post and headed with my trusty duffle bag and AWOL bag to Newark and the airport for my flight home, once again. I am truly becoming a "frequent Flyer" by now.

The flight back to San Francisco was, for the most part uneventful. The same strange feelings and thoughts of being stared at or commented about still ran through my head. I wore my dress greens, once again, proud to be a soldier. The sensation and experience of flight still had me in awe and wonder. I did manage to have a stranger buy me a drink at the airport in San Francisco. It was a beautiful spring afternoon upon my arrival in "The City". It would stay this nice for my two weeks of leave.

This time, I went straight home to see my grandparents first. They were extremely glad to see me and that I had received orders stationing me in Germany. My high school good friend, Bill Garrett, had gone to Vietnam first out of his AIT training and then to Germany after his Vietnam tour. He loved Germany, especially the beer and the ladies. I was looking forward to this new phase of my military adventures. After all the hugs and kisses from my folks, we sat down for a while and I brought them up to date on my Army experiences and told them what I could about my German assignment, which was not much, other than I would be processed through the replacement battalion in Frankfort. I had no idea where I would be stationed after that. I then called Scharlene and I would see her that evening.

I made my customary phone calls to my friends, only finding that I was unable to contact many of them. I went out into the neighborhood and found many of my friends were not home. I guess that most had jobs now and were at work at this time. The parents of my friends all said that they would let their child know that I had stopped by and for them to give me a call. Later only a couple of guys called me back. I guess my circle of friends was getting smaller, now that I was in the Army and about to go overseas. Come to think of it I also had mixed results from my family as well. This pattern would continue until I had no one, only ½ of my family.

I changed into my civilian clothes and informed my grandparents that I would be going over to see Scharlene and perhaps we would go out to dinner so don't plan for me to be home for dinner. I walked down to Geary Street and, once again caught the #38 bus for the cross-town ride to Laguna Street and "Schar's" place in Japan Town.

As it was in previous homecomings, I had a "rubber neck" from looking at all of the small changes in the neighborhoods that the bus passed through. I do believe that we went to a small Italian / Pizza restaurant near "Schar's" place. It was quite a contrast to the "east-coast" pizza that New Jersey had to offer. These old "Mom & Pop" places were always the best, especially if there were no gangsters or mobsters dining in the back. It seemed that many of the New Jersey pizza & sub joints had "mob" connections or were fronts for money laundering and other illegal activities. We enjoyed our "west-coast" pizza, feeling free from being killed in the cross-fire of a "mob" hit. (Gangsters always seemed to get killed when eating Italian food, seated at a red and white checkered table cloth setting.)

We wandered throughout the Union Street district, mostly window shopping at the unique antique and art galleries walking hand-in-hand and arm-in arm. We were the picture post-card of "young love". I tended to prefer the modern "chrome look" and some of the Scandinavian designed pieces instead of the "old" stuff. In some ways I thought that she was looking in the store windows for "nesting' material.

We returned to her neighborhood, "Japan Town" and strolled through the new mall and continued to window shop as well as going in the shops that were still open. Many of these new shops closed late. Many people were still out and about on this warm evening. Much of the crowds were tourists and Japanese businessmen, who were staying at the new and modern Miyako Hotel, at the east end of the mall. I walked her home and we talked for a while more. I left rather late and caught the bus home.

The balance of my leave was spent split between my home and Scharlene's. I got a lot done around the house for my grandparents. We also got groceries for them at the commissary at the Presidio. I really never knew of their financial status, evidenced by their frugality and hesitation for my college expenses. They wanted me to go to college and seemed to be glad that when I finished my military obligation, I would have the GI Bill to go to school on. I felt as if I was the "good" grandson.

I introduced Scharlene to my grandparents and it seemed a warm welcome on the surface; yet I felt their approval was at a distance. (As I was told that in as many words, later after our marriage, "…that I had married below my station in life.") It was very British Colonial. My great Aunt Catherine expressed it that plainly and was disappointed that I did not become an Army officer. At best, I would later become an NCO.

Each time that I came home on leave, I would see and reflect upon my home, family and city through different eyes and mind-set. Some things seemed to never change, yet others were in constant flux and change. In any way a city as diverse and vibrant as San Francisco always has something to offer the keen observer. My San Francisco proved to do just that and has done so ever since those precious times as a small child with my mother. This leave proved my point.

This leave would be my last before going overseas to Germany. The last few days sailed past in what seemed like "fast-forward mode". Soon I was packing up the old duffle bag and getting all my last visits in order. It was summer time and the weather made me feel rather happy, yet sad in having to leave. I never got the German weather reports; and as these San Francisco spring / early summer days passed by, I could only think of a cold panorama of European Christmas cards.

All the travel plans had been made. I was to fly out of San Francisco International Airport to Newark, New Jersey and then catch a bus to Ft. Dix and the overseas replacement battalion. I went to the Presidio and got my pay. I was all set for the next morning with my departure. Scharlene's father offered to drive me to the airport, as it was a Sunday flight. I think he did so in order that Scharlene and I have a little more time together. I spent the rest of my time at home, as I would be seeing "Schar" in the morning. It was a sleepless night in anticipation of both leaving home and the uncertainties of an overseas assignment. All of the good-byes had been said. I was all packed and ready to go.

In the morning I was up and ready early. After a quick breakfast, (coffee) and prolonged good-byes with my grandparents, I was out of the front door as Junior was waiting in the driveway for me. Scharlene was sitting in the back seat of his Buick. Her brother, Willy, rode "shot-gun" in the front. I threw my duffle bag and "AWOL" bag in the trunk. We pulled out into the street. I watched my neighborhood pass by in the rearview mirror as well as the buildings and land marks pass by as I peered out of the side windows. It was still early on this San Francisco Sunday morning. The church bells had not even begun to ring.

The streets were deserted, but a few cars and the "early-morning" people walking on the streets. The paper boys were out delivering the Sunday papers, just as I had a few years earlier. We passed my old bakery on Geary Street and I recalled those other early mornings working there and the smells of the fresh pastries. We crossed about half of the city and got on US 101 and headed south towards the airport. The freeway also did not have much traffic on it. The morning sun was just creeping up over the Oakland hills. Pink and orange clouds blanketed the sky and framed the rising sun.

The Sunday traffic on US Highway 101 was very light. There were mostly delivery trucks and semi-tractor trailers on the road making their rounds. Most of the automobile traffic seemed to be either out for an early Sunday drive, or perhaps headed to the airport, just as we were. Once again, I could not help but to see the passing sights and landmarks as we drew closer to the airport.

Junior turned the old Buick onto the off-ramp that took us to the departing airline ramps. I unloaded my baggage. He left to park the car and Scharlene and I went to the baggage check point. I checked my duffle bag but kept my AWOL bag for my only carry-on luggage. We went back out to the ramp and we were soon met by Scharlene's father and brother. I was dressed in my summer khakis and felt as if I had a thousand eyes upon me. (That was not the real case.)

We all then went to the proper departing flight waiting area. "Schar" and Willy went to get us all a cup of coffee. It was not long until we all were enjoying our last cup of coffee together. The conversation was light, but there was an underlining sense of sadness on "Schar's" and mine, not knowing how long it will be until we are together again.

Soon the call came over the PA system that the boarding had begun. As others checked in we said our final good-byes. It was a long embrace and kiss. I could see tears welling up in her eyes. My time to board came and I broke away from her embrace, handed the clerk my ticket and boarding pass. I then waved and entered the tunnel to board the aircraft. Not long after, I was in my seat on board as the aircraft was towed out on the tarmac for its final preparations to take off.

Out of the window, I could see the terminal fade into the distance as the plane taxied down the runway. I was pressed into my seat as the jets exploded into a burst of power and acceleration. With a couple of bumps, we were airborne. Newark, Ft. Dix, and Germany, here I come.

CHAPTER FIFTEEN

Fort Dix, Here I come !

Today (2018), Fort Dix is the common name for the Army Support Activity, presently located at Joint Base McGuire-Dix-Lakehurst. (Of Hindenburg fame.) It is about 16 miles southeast of Trenton New Jersey. It had an area of 10.389 square miles. In 1970 there were 26,290 persons included in that census. (Contrast: 2010, 7,716)

Fort Dix was first established in 1917 as Camp Dix, named after Major General John Adams Dix, who remembered for being a veteran and military officer of the War of 1812 and the Civil War. Dix was also a US Senator, Secretary of the Treasury and later a Governor of New York.

The facility, as Camp Dix and later Fort Dix has had a long history from WWI until 2015 for training and mobilizing troops for the many theatres, wars and conflicts as well as supporting the readiness of the combined armed forces. Fort Dix ended its active duty training mission (primarily BCT & AIT) in 1991. It remains today (2017) as a training site for all components of the armed services. It served both as a mobilization as well as a de-mobilization and discharge point. On March 8, 1939 its name was officially changed to "Fort Dix". It continued throughout WWII to train and deploy troops and units, primarily for the European Theatre.

Fort Dix became a Basic Combat Training center on July 13, 1947 and home to the 9th Infantry Division. Later in 1954 the 9th was moved out and the base became home to the 69th Infantry Division until its de-activation in 1956. Basic training continued there throughout the Vietnam War. A mock Vietnamese village was constructed to train troops for that conflict with realism. The facility continued to train troops for all the conflicts throughout its re-alignment in 2015.

On June 5th, 1969 (just before my high school graduation and enlistment) there was a riot in the post stockade of about 250 prisoners (mostly for AWOL charges.). They were protesting both unsanitary living conditions as well as the Vietnam War. The uprising was soon put down by the military.

The revolutionary group, The Weather Underground, in 1970 planned to explode a fragmentary / nail bomb at the main NCO club during a dance. The plot was foiled when the bomb exploded unexpectedly in Greenwich Village, New York. Three of the plotters were killed as a result.

During this same period, the Federal Department of Corrections maintained a low security installation for male prisoners. The facility is still in operation and in 2009 it housed 4,310 prisoners.

The famous bronze statue of the charging infantryman (Follow Me, I am The Infantry.) was the design of two enlisted men in 1957. Specialist 4 Steven Goodman and Private First-Class Stuart Scherr made a small clay sculpture in their spare time. Their model was noticed by a public relations officer and the idea and model were presented to the Post Commander. The idea was accepted and the two enlisted men (both illustrators in the army as well as industrial arts students.) made the statue out of Bondo. Later, with private funding, the statue was cast in bronze and placed on a marble base. It is sometimes known as "The Ultimate Weapon" I would be headed to a very interesting place for sure.

Just as it was before, as I traveled in my Army uniform, I could not help but to feel as if everybody was looking at me. I settled into my seat and prepared myself for the long flight to Newark, NJ. This time the airline stewardess checked my ID card for my age. (Drat!) No alcohol for this trooper on this flight. The airplane banked, and I saw the San Francisco bay area's fade into the California Central Valley. The plane continued to climb to its proper cruising altitude. The clouds hid the Sierra Nevada Mountains. Soon we were over Nevada, continuing eastward.

Once we leveled off and the eastward journey began, I was able to strike up a brief conversation with the older passenger sitting next to me. He was in the Korean War in the Air Force, so we had some in common. I told him what specialty I had and that I was headed to Germany after

Ft. Dix. We swapped "war" stories and surprisingly not a lot had really changed regarding military life since Korea. He told me that he had spent most of the Korean War in Japan but did spend a little time in Korea towards the end of the conflict. (Little did I know that I also would spend some time in Japan in route to Vietnam later this year?) He snuck me a "double whisky".)

The cloud cover disappeared from under the plane, as we flew over the Great Plaines. I could see clearly the cultivated farmlands which stretched all the way to the horizon. Some of the fields were plowed and planted in straight unending rows. I could also see the countless round circles which the irrigation fed. The panorama was a mixture of vivid greens and gold. Small towns passed below us and looked like small model train sets. The interstate highway systems could be seen, although they were not all connected as I had learned due to my Christmas trip home.

We were served the typical airline meal, although not a five-star affair, but was welcomed by me, as I did not eat too much before this flight. Somewhere over the Great Plaines, we hit some turbulence. The aircraft rose and fell as the meal was served. As fate would have it, there was a side of green peas which did not stay in place and were difficult to eat. I made it through the meal and the green pea episode. I had a quick smoke after the meal and soon dozed off for a nap.

A couple of hours later I felt my ears "pop" and felt the aircraft begin to descend. It was ever so slight as we approached the Newark Airport. With a few more bumps we began a steeped decent. The "Fasten Seat Belt" sign and the "No Smoking" signs all came on. The captain came over the PA system and announced our approach to Newark. He also gave us a weather report for the New Jersey area.

Before long, I could see the towns and the Newark suburbs we continued the downward decent. Roads and cars became very visible and I had the sensation of being over a huge model train lay-out. The ground raced up to meet us.

Not long after we made our touchdown with the whining of the air brakes and the squeaking of the plane's tires with a couple more bumps we were solidly on the ground. The plane taxied towards the terminal. "Welcome to Newark" boasted the sign on the terminal. We soon docked at the assigned terminal. We felt the plane's internal power being shut off as the airport's power was attached to the plane. The doors were opened, and the deplaning process began. Before I knew it, I was off the plane and headed towards the baggage claim area.

It did not take me too long to walk to the baggage claim area. I was carrying my AWOL bag and had my baggage claim ticket in hand. I had to wait a while for the baggage to be regurgitated from the bowels of the airport. I got my duffle bag and headed to the bus terminal. I purchased a ticket for the bus that would take me to Ft. Dix. After a little wait, the bus pulled in and the passengers got off who needed the airport. A few GIs nodded their greeting to me as we passed each other. I got on the bus found a good window seat and settled in for the trip to Ft. Dix.

It is 63 miles from Newark to Ft. Dix, NJ. The bus went south on the new Jersey Turnpike. (Later it was combined with Interstate 95.) We passed several small towns and villages along the route. There were patches of green, I guess giving New Jersey the name "Garden State". It was quite a contrast to the rather dark and industrial appearance of Newark. We rolled along until we reached the junction of Hwy. 68 and then on to the 680 loops. We passed through Liberty after a brief stop. It then was on to the main gates of Fort Dix. The whole trip took about an hour and a half, considering that the bus was a local and made many stops along the way.

It was early evening when I arrived. I showed the MPs on duty my orders and I asked where to find the replacement battalion. The MPs directed me to a taxi stand and there I caught a cab to the replacement battalion. Soon I was at the orderly room of the battalion HQ. I once again showed my orders. I was taken (damn. I am in the Army, waiting to go overseas, and you bastards want me to pay for a cab? …guess AWOL is worst.)

to my company. I was processed in and was issued my bedding. I had missed the regular mess hall hours, so I walked to a nearby snack bar and got my dinner. I was lucky, in that, being that it was Sunday; the snack bar would close early. I was glad to have eaten.

Other soldiers came in after me and once we were settled, we watched TV, played pool, and Foosball in the day room. These barracks were like the old ones at Ft. Lewis, World War II vintage and almost identical, two stories, wooden and quite used. I soon retired for the evening, as I was very tired. It had been a very long day for me. I lay down and was almost oblivious to the noise in the barracks. It did not take too long until I was sound asleep.

As usual in the Army, a deep sleep was broken at 0600 with the flash of the lights being turned on and the CQ sergeant awakening the troops. Previously, about 0500, I was awakened by the CQ runner waking up the KPs. Off in the distance we could hear the basic trainees shouting their "Jodie" songs as they were marched or ran through the morning routine. Ft. Lewis resounded in my mind. I was so glad that I made it through all of that.

It would be almost the same routine as in basic training; that being SS&S get dressed in OD green fatigues, clean the barracks and then chow time. We were formed up and a roll call was taken. (It seemed a few troops had not checked in as of this formation.) We were then marched to a very large consolidated mess hall. It looked like a huge barn or aircraft hangar. There must have been several hundred troops being fed.

After chow we were marched back to our company area. We finished cleaning the barracks and policing up around the buildings. At 0800 we were formed up again and the first sergeant took roll call again. He was a rather fat Latin master sergeant who kept reminding us to "...work in togetherness..." The First Sergeant had the acting platoon sergeants inspect their troops. Those needing haircuts were weeded out, held back and were at the barber shop when it opened. After the roll call, he proceeded to call out names. Some were to pack up their belongings and told that they were manifested on a flight and told where to form up to wait for transportation. Next, he would call out more names and each group would be assigned to a specific detail. Some duties included, but not limited to be guard duty, grounds keeping, garbage pick-up, painting, motor stables on the replacement battalion's vehicles, and I guess whatever else was needed to keep Ft. Dix operating. He also called out the names of the KPs for the next day. The KPs were given a board to hang on the foot of their buck for the early wake-up call. The most senior ranking man in each group was assigned to be the detail NCOIC. Then off we went for our given assignments. Some were marched to their duty station, others like myself, were loaded on the back of an old "deuce and a half" cargo truck.

I had been issued a painted helmet liner, a pistol belt with a canteen, a box of "C" rations and a baseball bat. I at first had no idea what I was to do, play baseball? I was not so lucky. I eventually was taken out in the Ft. Dix boondocks to a very large open field. I was ordered off of the truck next to on old battered 20-foot sea container. The buck sergeant informed me that I was to guard this container. It was a paint storage facility of sorts. A camp stool was provided for me to sit on. Should anybody ask for paint, they were to sign for the same on a clip board which hung just inside of the door. I studied my surroundings as the truck pulled away with a huge puff of diesel smoke. I could not see anything to paint out there. Not too far away was a lone water spigot, just poking up out of the ground with nothing around it. I was to walk around periodically patrolling this portion of a barren field. I guess that I was keeping America safe, preventing the "commies" from stealing Uncle Sam's paint. It was going to be a long, hot, and boring day for this warrior. He gave me the "key" and sped off.????

The morning sun crept up in the New Jersey sky. Wispy clouds dotted the sky. The sun was quite warm, and it was going to get warmer on this clear spring day. I had to laugh as I "patrolled" this sector of Ft. Dix. I did not see any VC, Russian, or any other "enemy", for that matter, not any other person. Soon I was lulled into an almost trance-like state as the crickets and other insects began their symphonies. I began to talk to myself and in the process, must have solved all of the world's problems and sang every song that I knew the words to. Yes, it surely was going to be a very long and boring day, but our paint was safe. Uncle Sam must have spent thousands on me by this point in time, only for me to be guarding a stash of paint.

About noon, I ate my wonderful "C" ration lunch and drank some warm water from the water line in the middle of nowhere. At some point in the afternoon a jeep pulled up and the sergeant of the guard checked on me and the status of my charge. All was in order and I guess that he was pleased that the "commies" had not invaded to capture our paint.

Around 16:30 (4:30 PM) I heard the distinctive sound of a "deuce and a half" army cargo truck coming down the road. Several troops were seated in the back. The driver informed me that I was relieved and to "lock" up the container and hop into the back of the truck. I complied and was glad that this assignment was over. Nobody even came to get any paint all day long. It was my first real military assignment and cold-war duty since graduating from the Signal School. I was both relieved, yet in a strange way proud to have contributed to our nation's security and safety.

Fort Dix seemed to be quite green and flat. The barracks and other buildings were all of the traditional WWII vintage as was common nationwide. We passed several basic training companies as we motored back to our barracks area. There were exchanges between the soldiers riding in the back of the truck and the trainees. We did portray a sense of superiority, as we were about to go overseas, while those poor bastards were still in Basic Training.

Upon our return to the company area, we were off-loaded and had time to clean up before chow. At 17:00 (5:00 PM) we heard the report of the post cannon which signaled retreat, the end of the work day as well as the lowering of the post flag. We stood at attention and saluted the unseen flag, much as we would do throughout our military tenure nation-wide. Soon we were formed up and marched to the consolidated mess hall for dinner. I do not recall what I had for that meal, but it was hot and plentiful. It was much appreciated after the "C" rat lunch.

After all of the company had eaten, we were once again formed up and marched back to our company area. For the rest of the evening, we were on our own, watching TV or playing pool or Foosball in the day room. Some of us went to the small PX and snack bar to either purchase needed items or perhaps enjoy a cold beer. We relaxed and enjoyed the rest of the evening. Taps were played over the PA system and lights out was at 23:00 (11:00 PM). My first real day in the regular army had come to an end. America would be safe for another day. I soon fell into a deep sleep.

The routine at the Replacement Battalion did not change much. Many troops would leave, new ones would come in. The details were assigned and alternated daily. I do not recall my other assignments, although I caught KP duty once. I was rousted at 0500 three days later. I was marched with five others over to the large consolidated mess hall. The rather large Black mess sergeant collected all of our ID cards first thing. (That must have been done to prevent any of us escaping. It was mandatory that every service person have their military ID on their person at all times.)

I pulled the position of "clipper-room-man". That was a very messy duty. It entailed knocking off uneaten food from the metal trays into a large in-place garbage disposal, rinsing off the tray and loading the wash rack. My helper would separate the cups, glasses and silverware and load their respective washing racks. All were fed into an ancient industrial dishwasher. The others cleared the dishwasher and drying rack and resupplied the serving line with clean dish wares.

The work was at a very fast pace in order to keep up with the ever-moving chow line. It was very hot and steamy in the rather confined space. My freshly starched and pressed fatigues looked like a soggy dish rag by the end of the shift, which ended about 20:00 (8:00 PM). My highly shined boots would need extra care after being exposed to the wet environment and food spills. We served all three meals, yet there were two shifts of cooks. I do not know how many troops we fed all together, but it was easily over a thousand.

It would not be an evening of entertainment for me. We did not have the regular Quartermaster laundry service, so we would wash our dirty things, iron and put them away in our baggage. The combat boots took an extra effort to restore their high gloss finish that was expected.

On that Thursday, my name was called along with about 25 other soldiers. We were manifested for a flight that afternoon. We avoided the work details that day and got our things in order. All was re-packed, and we were ready to roll. We were formed up and marched over to a small dispensary where the medics gave us our up-dated shots and those required for Europe. When all was completed, we were once again marched back to our company area to wait further instructions. Yes, "Hurry-Up & Wait" had not died in the Army.

Our orders were handed out and were to be kept with us at all times. One copy was to be on our person and the balance with our baggage which we would need upon arrival in Germany. All of us were confined to the company area and day room to wait for our final movement to our transport over to Mc Guire Air Force Base and our flight to Frankfort, Germany.

It was late that morning that we were finally formed were loaded onto an Army OD 45 passenger bus. Other troops were already on board. When all the luggage and bodies were accounted for, we were off to Mc Guire Air Force Base. It was a short trip over to the air base, only about three miles or so. We were off-loaded to a passenger waiting area. Roll calls were taken, both as we got off of the bus, as well as our arrival at the terminal. No one had "bugged-out" yet. I got up and looked out of the large windows and saw all sorts of military aircraft on the tarmac. A couple of civilian charter airliners were already docked near our terminal. I was hoping that we would fly on one of those instead of the sad grey Air Force cargo planes.

We milled around the immediate passenger area. More troops were arriving, and I guessed that we all would make up one plane-load. At some point, the entire group was assembled, and roll calls were once again taken. It was a short march to one of the civilian planes (thank God) and we were loaded for the flight. It was some off-the-wall airline, such as Frontier, Alaska or perhaps Flying Tiger. By noon, we were airborne and east-bound. (actually northeast) The innocent thrills of flight were becoming quite routine for me by this time. I still was amused, though.

CHAPTER SIXTEEN

We would be flying to Germany in a government-chartered civilian airplane instead of an Air Force cargo plane. The stewardesses were older, but still quite pretty. It was much better to have a female serving the meals than a pimple-faced airman. We flew to Loring AFB, (Bangor) Maine. It was 938.17 miles away, so the "hop" flight only took a couple of hours, with approach and departure times. Loring AFB is where we re-fueled for the Trans-Atlantic flight.

Lunch or dinner was served somewhere over the ocean. Conversations soon quieted down as we were well into the flight and I guess, all were rather tired by this time. It is 3628 miles from Bangor (Loring AFB) to Rammstein AFB in Germany. The average flight time is 10 hours and 35 minutes. We settled in for the flight. There was not much to see over the Atlantic Ocean. The worst parts of this government-chartered flights were that there was no smoking, or liquor served. I noticed many of the "old" sergeants nipped occasionally from their pocket flasks. Many of us took advantage of that fact and the flight time to catch up on sleep. There would be a lot ahead of us. I dozed off for a couple of hours.

It was a very uneventful flight. We experienced only a few bumps of turbulence as we approached the Irish Coast, but otherwise, it was quiet. The next hour, my ears popped and that meant that our altitude dropped. Yes, we began our decent over Germany in preparation to land. As we dropped, the German countryside rose up to meet us. Soon, I could make out clearly the towns, villages and farms below us. Once again it appeared that I was the master of a huge HO model train panorama. With the whine of the air brakes, squeal of the tires, a few bumps and a rapid deceleration, we were on the ground and taxing towards the Ramstein terminal.

GERMANY:

After landing, a senior sergeant and a couple of enlisted men appeared at the open door of the aircraft and promptly took control of our group. As usual as we disembarked our name was checked off of a passenger manifest list. We all made it and we had not lost anybody over the Atlantic Ocean. Thank God. We were herded to the baggage check area and we claimed our baggage. With little fan-fare, but with military precision, we were formed up and marched to a waiting army bus. Soon the bus was winding its way through the Frankfurt evening rush hour, headed towards the replacement battalion. To the surprise of many of us, a young soldier peered out of the bus window and announced to us in a very loud and alarmed voice: "..._damn, I have not seen so many foreign cars in one place in my entire life!_ My neighbor and I looked at each other in amazement. I thought and said to my neighbor: "I thought that we and this bus are the foreigners." (And that we were), we were now in Germany. It was evening time.

In 1970, there were two Germanys, the east (communist) and the -west (free, capitalist, us, the 'good guys'). The proper name for West Germany is _die Bundesrepublik Deuchland_, or BPR. On the opposite side, East Germany was called: _die Demokratish Republik auf Deutschland,_ or DDR. East Germany was under the military and social control of the Soviet Union and the Eastern Block. For all practical purposes, West Germany was a lot freer, but still "occupied" by the United States, Great Britain and NATO and its member states. That was the reason that I was on this army bus in Frankfurt to the replacement battalion to find out where I was to defend the free western nations, Germany, Mom, apple pie and the American flag.

As the bus drove the few miles to the replacement battalion, it often stopped and moved ahead slowly with the evening traffic. I could not help but to think back to my World History classes. My mind raced at light speed, as the bus worked its way through the traffic. I recalled my history lessons.

Like every nation and peoples of the world, the Germans of today can share in its pre-history with the rest of humanity. The discovery of the Mauer mandible in 1907 revealed the very early human presence in the area some 600,000 years ago. (In 1995 three wooden hunting spears were discovered in a coal mine in Schoningen, dating some 380,000 years old.)

In the Neander Valley the Neanderthal man's remains were unearthed in 1856. Those fossils are estimated to be 40,000 years old. Other relics are also to be found throughout Germany to include weapons, flutes, small figurines, and decorative items of clothing and simple nature jewelry.

The ethnic composition of today's Germans actually can be traced to many sources. Migrations to this area came from many directions. During the Nordic Bronze Age, throughout the pre-Roman Iron Age tribes came from the northern Scandinavian regions, the eastern Slavic and Baltic regions, as well as from the Middle Eastern areas now Iran. This is also to include the migration of the Celtic tribes throughout Europe. It was also noted migrations that from the west included the Gaul's of what is now France. It goes to say that the modern German shares quite a mixed background and the 100% pure German Aryan is very rare. (Much to the Third Reich's disappointment, I would think.)

Thousands of years passed, and the tribes moved all over Europe and some settled in small villages throughout Germany. The Germany that we know of in modern times can say be traced to the 1st century AD. The Roman Legions waged very long campaigns into the area of what is southern Germany. The Caesars called this region *Germania*. This was the area north of the upper Danube and east of the Rhine River. This Roman expansion was basically halted in 9 AD when the Cherusci chieftain Arminius (Roman name.) defeated a large Roman army at the battle of the Teutoberg Forest. (The Teutonic Knights trace their roots to that time and battle.)

By 100 AD, Imperial Rome solidified her holdings and many Germanic peoples remained in the Roman controlled areas and intermarried with the Romans. The areas north and east remained out of Rome's control. The dividing line became known as *Limes Germania*. Later the Romans occupied what is today: Austria, Baden-Württemberg, southern Bavaria, the southern Hess, Saarland and the Rhineland. These became the Roman provinces of Noricum, Rhaetia, and Germania. The other provinces in the west were: *Germania Inferior,* (its capital was situated at what is now Cologne, *(Colonia Claudia Ara Agrippinensium).* The rest of the area became known to the Romans as *Germania Superior).* The provincial capital was named *Mogontiacum.* (The modern city of Mainz takes its name from the Latin in a shortened version).

By the 3rd Century AD, the Roman Empire was beginning to be on its decline. To Rome's alarm, eight powerful Germanic tribes emerged from the west. These were known as: the Alamanni, (today, the French word for Germany is Allemande.), the Franks (French), the Bavarii, (Bavarians.), the Chatti, the Saxons, the Frisii, the Sicambri, and the Thuringii. In 260 AD the Roman lines were broken, and these tribes continued their movement unopposed.

Seven of the major German tribes all saw the end of the Roman Empire. These fierce tribes included the following: the Visigoths, the Ostrogoths, the Vandals, (vandalism), the Burgundians, the Lombards, the Saxons, and the Franks.

Christianity came to Germany after Emperor Constantine (306 AD-337AD) converted to the new religion in the 4th century AD and declared Christianity the official religion of the empire. Christian evangelical monks and priests began to spread the scripture and Christ's teaching throughout the land. (Many met gruesome deaths at the hands of the locals.) Christian structures were built in the region one of the first of these was the *Aula Palatina of Trier.* Many people converted, either in public, or in private to Christianity during these years.

The Roman Empire was at its height in 117 AD. Due to many factors, the Roman Empire began its decline from that date on. The Huns begin to challenge and occupy many parts of *Germania.* The Germanic tribes continued to challenge the Roman frontier settlements between 117AD until the final collapse of the empire in 476 AD. In that year, the Vandal chieftain, Odoacer, invades Rome proper. Odoacer dethrones the last Roman Emperor, Romulus and sacks and burns Rome itself. The Empire is split, and the period of migration sees the Germanic tribes move in the areas that now are Germany proper.

Germany evolved into many duchies and feudal estates. This continued with little changes until consolidation created East Francia in the mid-9th century AD. Eventually the Franks gained control and consolidated many of these small duchies and subjugated the people to their rule. To the north the areas were consolidated to become *Brandenburg (later North March,) (Prussia), Lusatia, Billung Marsh.* In the south these 'marches" became *Carniola, Styria and the March of Austria.* Other areas became under the rule of the Merovingians and the Franks.

In the year 962 Otto I became the first emperor of the Germanic region of the Holy Roman Empire. By the high middle ages, the stronger dukes, barons and various local chieftains gained so much power and wealth that the empire lost its power. The year 1648 marked the end of the Holy Roman Empire. Germany then was divided into larger independent states such as Prussia, Bavaria and Saxony. Protestantism, with Luther, spread throughout Europe and challenged the rule and doctrine of the Holy Roman Catholic Church.

Soon after the French Revolution and the Napoleonic Wars (1803-1815) feudalism across Europe gave way to more liberalization and nationalism, which clashed with each other. The Industrial Revolution was transforming the face of the world. The failed revolution of 1848 forced people to seek other means of their livelihoods and the work force looked quite different than a hundred years earlier. In Germany, as the rest of the industrialized world, people flocked from the farms to the cities seeking employment.

German universities grew and became renowned world-wide. Students flocked to these centers of learning from around the world. The sciences, engineering, medicine, music and the arts all flourished.

The Unification of Germany was achieved under the strict leadership of the Prussian Chancellor, Otto von Bismarck in 1871. That same year the German Empire was created. (This solved the *Kliendeutsche Losung* (Germany without Austria) problem or the *Grosbdeutche Losung* (the greater Germany with Austria). The new *Reichstag* was an elected legislative body but had limited powers in the imperial system. Germany became a world power as she joined other European nations in a global colonization process. The varied colonies stretched from Africa to the Pacific islands.

By the turn of the century, Germany had become the dominant power in Europe. Her industrialization proceeded at a blistering pace. By 1900 Germany became a naval power as her industrial might surpassed even that of Great Britain. This led to power struggles on the European continent.

The *"War to End All Wars"* (World War I) was about to erupt in Europe and change the world forever.

{As the bus got closer to the replacement battalion, I became quite aware that the next years of the German history were within the lifetimes of my parents and grandparents. I was also aware that I was a "post-war" baby or "Baby Boomer". The bus driver, a young PFC, navigated the Frankfurt traffic with great skill.}

The roots of the First World War were formed prior to 1914. Kaiser Wilheim II adopted policies, both foreign and domestic that edged the continent closer to conflict. Germany's imperialistic expansion and industrial power threatened the status quo among all of the other European powers. The Kaiser's personal and diplomatic belligerence did not endear other national leaders at the time.

In June 1914, Franz Ferdinand the Austrian Archduke was gunned down by a Serbian national in Sarajevo. The Archduke was heir to the Austro-Hungarian throne. Rather than a measured response to the assassination, the Kaiser gave the Austrians his approval to invade Serbia. If Serbia's allies and/or if the Russians intervened, Germany would act as well.

The actual war began on 28 July 1914. On 1 & 3 August, Germany declared war on France and Russia. Great Britain soon entered into the war. Overall, 15 Allied nations combined to face 4 Central Power nations in the conflict.

Germany initiated the *Schlieffen Plan*, a long-standing strategy to invade France through neutral Belgium, avoiding the French defenses and the *Maginot Line*. The plan was successful only briefly. Paris was not taken in a month as the Germans had hoped. The war evolved into stalemated trench warfare. The Western Front then stretched from the Swiss border to the North Sea along a 450-mile-long network of trenches, minefields and barbed wire emplacement. Following the Battle of the Marne; the Western Front became a stalemated and costly campaign for both sides.

In late 1914, the Ottoman Empire was brought into the war. The war now stretched all the way into Mesopotamia, also enveloping the entire Middle East and Egypt. The British suffered heavily during the Gallipoli Campaign. British successes on the Arabian Peninsula were the result of

Lawrence of Arabia unifying the various tribes as a single force to defeat the Turks.

The Germans soon faced the Russians on the Eastern Front. Forces were mobilized to meet the Russian's advance into East Prussia. The war on two fronts would drag on for four more years. A naval blockade was implemented along the north shores and food was declared contraband by the Allies. German world trade almost vanished. The German high command demanded "total war and victory" at all costs. (This would haunt Germany in the second war.) Germany managed to hold her own on the two fronts, suffering heavy losses; but as time passed, the civilian population suffered under the strict rationing and food shortages. Many resources were diverted to the war effort instead for providing for the civilian population producing the materials of war.

By the year 1916, two years of war began to take its heavy toll. The civilian government of Bethmann-Hollweg was most indecisive and very ineffective. As both the chancellor and the Reichstag proved to be weak and ineffective, the High General Staff took over more and more of the civilian governing. This period became known as *The Silent Dictatorship*. Generals Paul von Hindenburg and Erich Ludendorff soon took over most of the governing decisions.

The new junta introduced the *Hindenburg Program*, which sought to double the war production and relocated agricultural workers to the cities and the war industries. In July of 1917 as conditions worsened, the Reichstag called for a peace proposal. This forced the resignation of Chancellor Bethmann-Hollweg. Puppets of the High General Command replaced him. The two revolutions in Russia were: The February Revolution, which over-threw the Tsarist Romanoff throne and the feudal system and The October Revolution which overthrew the liberal Provisional Government bringing the Bolsheviks into power in Russia. These events gave the High General Command hopes for victory in the East. The Reichstag's bid for peace was defeated and did not alter the pace of the war. The military high command assumed even more governing powers.

General Ludendorff forced through his plan of unrestricted submarine warfare. This decision would bring the United States into the war. In early April of 1917, the United States, angered by the attacks on its ships in the Atlantic, declared war on 6 April 1916. The United Stated also declared war on the other three Central Powers. General Pershing led the American Expeditionary Forces for over two years, greatly aiding the Allied victory.

The United Stated mobilized over 4 million military personnel, and sent them into the European Theatre, thus suffering 110,000 combat deaths, which 43,000 were attributed to the influenza epidemic. Europe mobilized over 9 million military personnel and over 7 million civilians for the war effort. Overall over 70 million people were directly affected by the war.

After the October Revolution, in November 1917, Russia pulled out of the war. The war dragged on with heavy losses on both sides, both military and civilian causalities. The war was basically fought to a costly stalemate. The "shooting war" officially ended with The Armistice on the 11th Hour, on the 11th month 1918. (Today's 'Veterans Day' used to be called Armistice Day.)

The war was very costly, both financially as well as in human losses. It is estimated that over 12 Million were killed as a result of combat and disease. Over 20 million were wounded in the war. "Shell Shock" became a new medical diagnosis. (This evolved in the 1980s to become PTSD.) The artificial prosthesis industry grew from a cottage industry to a profitable formal industry. In monetary terms, the war cost the Allies over $125.6 Trillion. It cost the Central Powers over $60.6 Trillion. (These were in 1914-1918 dollars.)

The official diplomatic end of the war was detailed in the Treaty of Versailles, sanctioned by the League of Nations, 21 Oct. 1919. Once again, the map of Europe was redrawn, and the seeds of the next conflict were already in place. Germany was to disarm and pay repartitions to the Allies to the tune (in today's dollars of $442 Billion.). The oversea colonies were all but re-distributed to the Allied powers. German territories and lands were greatly re-shaped as the European map was re-drawn. This year saw the beginning of the Weimar Republic and a new constitution for the country. The legacy of the failed republic left the nation in debt, high unemployment as well as three-digit inflation rates which grew daily. In 1914 the exchange rate was 4DM to $1.00. By 1923 the exchange rate became an unbelievable 4.2 trillion DM to $1.00. People were said to go shopping with their cash in wheelbarrows. The economy collapses under hyperinflation and worsening social conditions.

These factors left the German nation broke, depressed and greatly weakened militarily and economically. Germany was charged with starting the war and the population could not but feel a sense of national guilt. The terms of the treaty wove the threads for German discontent and later nationalism and the rise of the military once again during the 1930s.

In 1923 Adolph Hitler, later the Furhrer, becomes the leader of the National Socialist German Workers' Party, (NAZI) and leads an abortive coup in a Munich beer hall. He is tried and given a five-year sentence. While in prison, Hitler writes *Mein Kampf (*My Struggle*)*. He outlines his vision of a new Germany and his racial hatred of the Jews, which he blames, along with the communists for all of Germany's troubles. When Germany defaulted on the war debt, France and Belgium send troops to occupy the Ruhr. This feeds nationalism and the demand for a renewed national purpose to rise above the present conditions. This gives rise to the "brown shirts", the SA.

Hitler's rise to power would take volumes to explore, but in this brief manuscript, it would suffice to say that Hitler used force and brutal means to achieve his ends when legal means failed in his opinion. He calls for a *Pan-Germanic* nationalism and for expanded *Lebensraum (*living space*)* to the East.

In the 1928 national election, the Nazis remained a fringe radical political party. They polled only 810,000 votes or about only 2.5% of the votes. They slowly gained ground, membership and political power. In contrast, by the September election of 1930, they commanded 6.5 million votes or 18.3%. The NAZI party expanded their seats in the Reichstag from only 12 seats to 107 seats, making them the second largest party in Germany.

With the "crash" of the American stock markets in 1929; banks recalled money from the European banks and cancelled the numerous loans which had made it possible for Germany to pay off her war debts. By emergency decrees, taxes were raised, and massive spending cuts put even more Germans out of work. Bankruptcies and failed businesses worsened the situation. The German banks came under direct government control in 1932.The rest of the world also falls into the Great Depression.

Unemployment in Germany reaches over 6 million. On 1 June 1932, Chancellor Bruning is replaced by Franz von Papen. His cabinet had very little support, so he is forced to get the Nazi's support. He does so by repealing the ban on the SA, or the Brown Shirts. The streets soon erupt into riots as the SA and the communists clash in the streets. These 400 street riots produce 82 deaths. Papen calls for new elections to be held in July. He was hoping to be able to isolate Hitler.

Later, on 30 January 1933, President Paul von Hindenburg appointed Adolph Hitler as the Chancellor of Germany. This event was celebrated by a torchlight vigil. The next year saw Hitler and the NAZI Party consolidate their power. The Nazis claim over 37% of the votes. On 27 February 1933, arsonists torched the *Reichstag* building. The NAZIs blamed the communists and the Jews for the crime. President Hindenburg, under NAZI pressure, declared a "state of emergency" and suspended civil freedoms and liberties.

Later in the early part of the year, Germany begins to re-arm itself in defiance of the Versailles treaty. Later the Jewish exclusion Act prohibits Jews from holding civil servant jobs and other employment, further complicating the civil and political climate in the country. The Nuremburg Laws strip all Jews of German citizenship. Many flee, yet most cannot escape, since they cannot prove their citizenship.

In 1935, Germany re-arms in full force and conscription is re-instated for all German males, 18-45 years of age. The world seems too involved in the Great Depression to notice, and weary of war, nations do not want to challenge Germany. Germany also promotes "glider clubs", which later had trained pilots for service in the *Luftwaffe*. Boy scouts later became the core of the *Wehrmacht*. Enrollment in the Hitler Youth grows, often pitting children against their parents in the new NAZI social order.

It was in 1938 that Germany annexed Austria and the Sudetenland, against the 1919 treaty. Hitler maintained that ethnic Germans were being abused. Germany continued unchallenged. Kristallnacht, (Night of Broken Glass), raged on in many cities across Germany, and saw the wide spread destruction of Jewish property, businesses, and synagogues, continued to promote Hitler's policies against the Jewish German population.

The road to war in Europe for a second time was being paved a long time before the first shot was fired. In Hitler's mind the conquest of Poland would give Germany his promise of *Lebensraum* (Living Space.) and would be cleared of the *inferior races*. (These were: The Poles, Slavs, Jews, Gypsies and anyone else who opposed the German superiority and authority.)

Meanwhile talks between Great Britain, France and other European nations and Hitler's diplomats stalled and reached no agreements to stop the German demands for her expansion. On 16 March the Wehrmacht rolls into the remainder of Czechoslovakia and Bohemia and Moravia are declared German Protectorates. This move goes unopposed by the other European powers.

To neutralize a potential threat from the Soviet Union, Hitler drafts and signs a non-aggression pact with his ideological enemy on 23 August 1939. In secret talks, Poland is to be divided between Nazi Germany and the Soviet Union. Shortly after noon on 31 August 1939, Hitler orders the invasion of Poland to begin at 04:45, 1 September. Britain and France persuade the Polish government to postpone their general military and civilian mobilization to oppose Germany.

That move proved fruitless as the Wehrmacht rolled over the border and into Poland. This swift armored invasion and aerial bombardment became Hitler's legacy of the *Blitz Krieg,* or "Lightning War". Sadly, because there was no time for Poland's mobilization, horse cavalry often challenged the armored Panzer units, ending in the Poles massacre. Hitler was immediately on a propaganda blitz alleging Polish atrocities against the ethnic Germans in the region. These events marked the beginning of World War II.

The war would rage on until 1945, leaving most of Europe in ruins and worse social conditions than after the First World War. Hitler commits suicide in his underground bunker with his wife Eva Baum. Germany is divided into Occupational Zones, leaving the Soviets and her Eastern Bloc allies facing the Western nations during the Cold War, thus the underlining reason for my being stationed in Germany in the first place. The war was very costly in both monetary and human terms.

It is estimated that the war cost the world $160 Trillion and suffered the loss of 80 million lives of which 25 million were military deaths alone. The monetary costs did not reflect the costs of rebuilding all that was destroyed or heavily damaged throughout the world.

Nazi atrocities are brought to the world's attention and many Germans are tried during the Nuremburg War Tribunals. Many are imprisoned, and some are executed. Many escapes to South America. Only a few are returned to stand trial and face justice. German guilt is just below the surface among the population.

I will present a brief history of the war later in this writing as it is reflected by my German contacts and my interaction with veterans of that war, many who were still serving on active duty at the time of my enlistments.

The Army bus pulled into the building's courtyard of the replacement battalion in Frankfurt. It was housed in a very large multi-level stone fortress. There was a large central courtyard and the bus had to pass through a "Sally-Port" entrance to the large court yard / parade field. It was a very dark and foreboding structure. We were told later that it was the SS and perhaps the Gestapo headquarters during the war. There were cells in the basement levels which had very heavy steel doors that were welded shut after the Allied occupation, thus leaving us with a very dark feeling, thinking of what tortures and executions that must have taken place below our feet. In the upper attic areas, officers' quarters were built. It was rumored that a SS officer had brought his girlfriend up there to his room and when she learned the truth of what was happening in this building, she committed suicide in his room. The door was nailed shut later. None of the present cadre was billeted in those upper levels to this date.

As usual, we were formed up and another roll call was taken. The billeting assignments came next and we picked up and signed for our bedding. Once we had moved in to our assigned areas, we were instructed as to where the mess hall was and given a general lay out of the compound. We were restricted to the compound. Out of the large windows, we could see the night lights of the city. Out of our latrine window, we could see the vast Frankfurt railroad terminal and freight rail yards. I was impressed at the much-worn hardwood floors in this old building and could not help but to wonder how many soldiers, both NAZI and American had walked over these floors. Since we could not leave the compound, many of us retired early that night, as it had been a very long day. We were now officially in Germany and instantly had become a part of the NATO forces facing the Soviets and the Eastern Bloc. That fact weighed heavy on my 18-year old mind that night.

I recalled my first real "social shock" when in the next morning I took out my electric shaver (a high school graduation present) only to find out that the European electrical grid ran on 220 Volts instead of the 120 Volts that I was accustomed to. The sockets only took the round European plugs. I had to borrow a razor from one of the other replacements. I was later able to get the proper shaving supplies from the small PX.

The bulk of our time was spent "processing in". It seemed another round of paperwork, lines and a lot of "hurry-up & wait". The Army in this way was the same worldwide. Overall it went rather quickly and after a couple of days we were lined up and given our new orders and broken down into the various travel groups depending on where we were to be stationed in the country.

CHAPTER SEVENTEEN

KAISERSLAUTERN: School & Social Introduction

About six of us (all Signal Corps troops) were assigned to attend the Multi-Channel Radio School of the 11th Signal Battalion, 32nd AADCOM (Anti-Aircraft Defense Command.) in Kaiserslautern. We would be temporarily assigned to the HQ 11th Sig. Bn. A young "buck" sergeant from the school met us and soon we were taken to the train station for the brief trip to "K" town as it was called in Army jargon. We were on our way. The 11th Signal Battalion got its final designation on 21 November 1967 and maintained its connection with the 32nd AADCOM. The main companies were located in Kaiserslautern (HQ & Co. "A".), Wurzburg, (Co. "B") and Co. "C" Munich. Co. "A" supported the 94th Arty. Group, "B" Co. 69th Artillery. Group and Co. "C" supported the 10th Artillery. Group. Each unit had 3rd echelon maintenance capabilities. The signal sites and radio relay facilities covered over 20 sites throughout the area. There were both fixed and mobile assets throughout the command.

The 32nd itself can trace its lineage back to 1918 when it was known as the 32nd Coastal Artillery Group, stationed in Key West, Florida. The unit later was reactivated and saw action in the Philippines Campaign in 1942. Once again, I could feel the sense of history each time I was assigned to a specific unit and in a small way joined a "long line" of soldiers and veterans.

We arrived at Kaiserslautern that afternoon. The ride on the electric train, the Bahn Hauf, was great. German school girls wanted to "practice their English" on us. "What the hell!" We flirted with them under the watchful eye of the young Sergeant. We did not give a *damn!* He was 'way too young and too lower in rank to affect us. Besides, he did not even wear a combat patch on his right shoulder. It was a short trip to the kaserne, once again, on an OD Army bus. Nearby, were the Panzer Kaserne and the Army Depot. Not too far in the other direction was the US Army Hospital, Landstuhl. (Where even today, causalities from Iraq and Afghanistan are stabilized and returned to the US. Also, where Junior Martin had served as an Army Medic years earlier.)

Upon our arrival at the Kapaun Kaserne (Barracks), we were processed in and shown to our barracks. It was a three-story structure that once billeted Hitler's finest. The latrines and some of the front had the opaque class cinder block type walls. The hardwood floors were well worn as soldiers utilized these billets for decades; the bunk beds were all placed in the same "head to toe" configuration. The wood was worn where thousands of feet had jumped out of bed over the years. Friend and once foe had carried out their various duties on this very compound. It left a weird feeling that I would experience many times during my two tours of duty in Germany.

The Multi-Channel Radio School would train us to become tactical multi-channel radio operators and mechanics. We would learn the basic 12 channel systems and radio interface. The main radio sets were the terminal, AN-TRC-117, Repeater AN-TRC 110, Cable Interface AN-TCC-61 (Cable & System Multiplexers). We also would be trained on the power generating equipment, primarily the PU-618/M, twin 5kw trailer mounted sets, 120/240V.

AN-TRC-117

- Truck Mounted: 2 ½ Ton Cargo Truck, with Shelter. S-330 / TRC-117 or the modified shelter, S-280 / G.
- Frequency: 600-999 Mhz. and 1.35-1.843 Ghz. w/plugs.
- 12 Channels, Voice, Data (Teletype, 2 or 4 pair).
- Set Configuration: 2 stacks of radios, AN/GRC-50, Multiplexers MD-352, TD-202 Radio Modem, TD-202 TD-204, Multiplexers, cable driver, CV-1548 Signal Converter and Antennae Set AB-577

50 Foot mast, (extensions were available for higher heights, to clear forest canopies.)

- and AT-903 wide band microwave horn.
- TA-312 Field Phone.
- LS-147 Intercom.
- Voltage Regulator 45-amp, 120 VAC, CN-514.
- Dummy Load / watt meter ME-189.
- Twin 5,000 K Generators, trailer mounted.
- Mounted weight, approx... 5,000 lbs.

AN-TRC-110

- The relay set was basically the same as the AN-TRC-117, with the major exception that it consisted of three stacks of AN-GRC / 50 radio sets and did not have the multiplexing capability. One stack received the signal from the AN-GRC / 117 and transmitted on the other stack either to another relay or a terminal.
- The antennae horn system consisted of two horns mounted on a "T" base. One horn picked up the receive signal and the other transmitted forward to next radio set.

These troops would operate in a tactical environment and were quite mobile, since the "systems" were mounted on the back of an army "deuce & and a ½" cargo truck, which also towed its own power source, a trailer mounted twin 5K gas powered generator set.

The young "buck" promised us that if we did well and passed this course, we would be awarded the MOS of 31M20 and there would be quick promotions in our future. We bought the entire promotion story, since we already have had another signal MOSs.

The 32nd AADCOM's main weapon system was the MIM-23 "Hawk" missile system. The "Hawk began its military service in late 1959. It was replacing the aging MIM-14 "Nike Hercules" anti-aircraft missile systems. (These "Hawk" batteries would later, in 1994. Be replaced by the MIM-104 "Patriot".) The "Hawk" never saw actual US combat duty, although Israeli forces have used this system. (The USMC kept their "Hawks" until

2002.) These were either replaced and / or augmented by infantry men's FIM-92 "Stinger" shoulder fired weapon.

The "Hawk" was primarily mounted on an armored chassis and the other radar and guidance units were also very mobile. The site was powered by two 60K generators. The crew of the launcher system was also armed with heavy machine guns for their ground defense.

THE MIM-23 "HAWK" MISSILE

- <u>Type:</u>   Surface-to-air.
- <u>Place of Origin:</u>   United States.
- <u>In Service:</u>   August 1960.
- <u>Manufacturer:</u>   Raytheon Corporation, Inc.
- <u>Unit Cost:</u> $250,000 / per missile.
- <u>Launcher / Fire Unit Cost:</u> $15,000,000 per fire unit.
- <u>Battery Cost:</u> $30,000,000 per Battery.
- <u>Weight:</u>   1,290 lbs.
- <u>Length:</u>   16 feet, 8 inches.
- <u>Diameter:</u>   14.5 inches.
- <u>Warhead:</u>   119 pounds / blast, fragmentation war head.

- <u>Engine:</u>   Solid fuel rocket propelled engine.
- <u>Wing Span:</u>   3 feet, 11 inches.
- <u>Effective Range:</u>   + /- 45-50 miles.
- <u>Flight Ceiling:</u>   65,000 feet.
- <u>Speed:</u>   Mach 2.4 > (approx. 1,900 miles per hour)
- <u>Guidance System:</u>   Semi active radar homing system.
  AN/MQP-55 CWAR and AN/MPQ-50 PAR

The other weapon systems that we would support would be the Vulcan Chaparral anti-aircraft defense batteries of the 32nd Anti-Aircraft Defense

Command. The first battalion was deployed to Germany in 1969; a year before I arrived in Germany. This was the basic defense against low flying aircraft. The Vulcan Chaparral system had two mobile units. These were the M-163 self-propelled gun system. It consisted of a single gun with 6 rotating barrels capable of firing 10, 30, 60, 100 round bursts or 1000 (max of 3,000, then a barrel change was needed.) rounds per minute continuous fire. The detection and guidance system were the AN/MPQ- 49 radar system. The weapon platform was mounted on the tracked armored vehicle chassis. A crew of four operated one single unit. The system weighed 12.3 tons yet was highly mobile.

The sister unit was the M-72 Chaparral, which was outfitted with surface to air missiles, the AIM-9 which was similar to the Navy's Sidewinder air to air missile. These were also deployed in 1969. It turned out that the 11th Signal Battalion was to support 6 battalions of various air defense units.

Between these two mobile systems, the lower defense umbrella was covered, as well as both being capable of direct ground support. Just as these anti-aircraft batteries were mobile, so were the supporting signal units. When the Vulcan units went to the field, so did the supporting units go to the field. Both the AA and Signal worked as a rapid deployment team, should Soviet and Eastern Bloc nations challenge NATO air space. Needless to say, we spent a lot of time in the field as the super powers continued to play a deadly and dangerous game of "cat & mouse".

Scharlene's father, Junior, was a medic at the nearby Landstuhl Army Hospital in the late 1950s. Elvis Presley was one of his patients. ("Schar" never forgave her father for not getting any autographs.) Elvis demanded no special treatment and only wanted to serve as an "average 'Joe". He was discharged honorably as a sergeant, having had become a "tank" commander.

We arrived at the school's orderly room at Puluslaski Kaserne, and the Multi-Channel Radio School at the HQ Company, 11th Signal Battalion. Once again it seemed like there was a mountain of paperwork, *damn, if the Army does not know where I am by now, God help them.*) But we were in and had the time off before classes started on Monday.

There was a small PX / Snack Bar nearby and once we were settled in we went for a cold beer. The small PX snack bar offered a German beer on tap, which I ordered and finished with a great relish. Needless to say, by the time we all returned to our barracks after dark, we all were quite "lit", young and not accustomed to the stiff German beers. I do believe that our barracks once belonged to the NAZI German Army during the war. The glass tinted mason blocks seemed to give it away. There was a soda machine which dispenses both German and American sodas.

The school routine was very simple, in that we really did not have all of the strict routine and "B.S." that the other troops went through each day. Reveille was at 0600.We were Signal "students", and "special". There were always the barracks details, clean-up, polish and police call as would continue everywhere throughout our army tours. (The BS would come later for me.) We formed up at 0:7:30 and went to our signal classes; 0800-17:00 (8:00 AM to 5:00 PM for you civilians), then dinner and free time.

The basic course comprised of: basic electronics (again), radio theory & propagation, specific equipment, radio alignment, proper radio procedures, signal security, operator maintenance, power generation, multiplex theory and operation, cable operation and cable interface. Antennae erection and construction would also be included as we were taught about those erections. (All jokes later, please.)

We also had to sit through SAEADA (Subversion, And Espionage, and Against Department of the Army) briefings to warn us of enemy agents spying and espionage activity. A lot of these warnings revolved around pretty women and hookers. (That got our interests.) The curriculum also included basic small unit defense, since communication assets were a very high priority on an enemy's list to disrupt command and control. We also were instructed in many aspects of our tactical venerability, defense and offence. We were going to challenge the Soviet Block; we were all under 25 years of age.

"Free Time" for an American young soldier could have had very bad and / or interesting consequences. We finally got a chance to explore "K" town, and man, what an experience that would prove to be. Four of us headed to downtown Kaiserslautern for fun and adventure. We were to be harshly exposed to European culture and discipline. We were young and inexperienced, and innocent. Many troops had not ventured too far from their home towns, now they were in a foreign country with very different languages, customs and social norms.

We wandered around in the town and, at least how I was impressed with the contrasts between the Medieval and Modern structures. Down one small side "strassa ", we observed all of the centuries' history down one street. We were informed that "Ze butcher" und his families have been there for 400 years: "Ze cobblers also for 300 years, Ze tailor und his family only 100 years, and on and on down the street, each shop clearly placed on a timeline. We Americans, as a nation are young. On one occasion, I had to look up, as the overhanging windows and balconies once were used to throw trash and other "waste" out onto the street. (Gave "shit-faced" a new meaning.)

I recall that it was mind-blowing, in that I could walk down one "strassa" and be in today, yet turn a corner, be in Medieval Europe. (I was hoping that garbage and human waste would not be thrown down on top of me.) It was weird that these ancient buildings now have electricity and indoor plumbing. I was still overwhelmed by the sense of history, where so many other feet had walked these streets.

Later on, in my German tour of duty; I had the same most eerie feeling when I stood on an ancient Roman aqueduct. How many Imperial Legions had crossed this same place where I stood. I also thought of General George Patton as he had the same feelings in North Africa.

It was a warm autumn day and we decided to stop and grab a bite to eat and enjoy a cold German beer. We found a small "schnell imbass" (fast food / snack bar) which had both an indoor seating area and, of course the traditional outside delivery window. We must have stood out like a sore thumb; in that we all had GI haircuts and wore the army "low-quarter" shoes. We received a very warm welcome in broken English, and we placed our orders ant took up a large table in the back. Shortly our meals were delivered to our table. Of course, we ordered a pitcher of *good beer.*

It was not too long after settling in that three young female German college students came up to us and asked if they could join us and *practice their English with us. Of course, they could!* This was too good to be true. They boldly asked if we could buy them a bottle of strawberry wine. We stumbled over each other to comply with the request. (This is going to end up very well for us, so we thought.)

The young ladies spoke in very good English, although not up on the trendy American and army slang. The beer and the wine flowed. We finished our meals, yet the ladies wanted to stay and enjoy another bottle of wine. Oh, this is going to turn out very well. After a most enjoyable time, nature called, and I had to excuse myself. While I was relieving me, an old weathered German man looked over to me and began to speak in rapid German. I agreed with most of what he was saying, merely to be polite. He kept saying something like "fook 'em…" I tried to answer by saying "…kaserne?" He kept on and he was pointing in some direction. I thought, perhaps he was a taxi driver and was asking how we were getting back to our base. Then I said by the "autobus". He broke into a hysterical laughter and left the bathroom. As I was washing up I could hear everybody in the small restaurant laughing madly. My friends were angry with me and the girls were gone, leaving their partial wine glasses behind. I had no idea what had just occurred. Soon another young German male student informed me that I had told the old man that we were going to *fuck* the girls on the bus on our way back to the kaserne. Needless to say, we left in a hurry. I must have turned beet red at that point. I finished the rest of the week end on base.

The classes and the "hands on" training continued, and we were getting pretty good at setting up and aligning the radio and multiplex systems. The time passed quickly and soon another week end was upon us. My pals had forgiven me for my social *faux pas* and we decided to go into town again and try our luck, but this time we were going to go see a movie. Soon on Saturday morning we all were off and on to our next adventure. Of course, we stopped for beer first.

We had located a small movie theatre and thought we would check it out. It was not any movie that we were familiar with. It was a Japanese samurai movie. A little blood and guts in Germany seemed in order at the time. The action was intense, although the dialog was in Japanese with German sub-titles. We had no idea what was being said and we could not read German. It seemed that when the audience laughed, we had no idea why. When we laughed, the Germans turned towards us and gave the "hush" sign with scowls on their faces. We were definitely out of place, strangers in a strange land. We decided to leave before the movie ended, much to the audience's delight.

After walking about town, checking out the stores (and women) we decided in that warm afternoon to get some more German beer. As we soon learned, it was not the same as PX beer or American beer in general. The alcohol content was probably more on the order of what we would classify as "ale, or stout beer". Soon quite a way down the *strassa* we found an outside table at a small *guest Haus*. We sat down and ordered our pitcher of *bier*. A cool breeze blew down the strassa. Life was good.

After quite a bit of time we had finished a couple of pitchers of beer and decided to "explore some more". We were really impressed with this whole German experience, both modern and medieval, somehow; perhaps the NAZI stereotype was wrong. Soon the beer had taken its course and all four of us really had to "take a leak". We were now somewhat familiar with the basics and recognized a sign for the public rest rooms, below the street level. It took us a long flight of stairs to get to the underground rest room. In we marched.

To our horror: There was a huge room with no urinals mounted. There was a trough running around three of the walls. We were not quite sure what to do. We just stood there until a German pushed pass us and pissed on the wall. Oh, well I guess that is what we do. So we followed his lead and watered the walls. He left with a puzzled look and muttered something in German, perhaps thinking that we were a bunch of faggots looking for a "pick-up".

That was definitely not the case for these horny heterosexual young GIs. As we were finishing, one of our pals, a young black kid noticed the air ventilation shaft pointed up towards the street, which had a grated cover over it at street level. He practically crawled up that shaft and he announced in a loud voice "...these bitches do not wear any panties! "That did it. All of us were peering up into that air shaft. Yes, he was correct, not all European women wear panties, nor do they shave their pubic region. Our fascination was broken by a loud blast from a police / D.I. type whistle.

We turned to see a uniformed attendant (cop / SS, Gestapo: he had on a high-pitched military style cap. We didn't know what he was.) This man was yelling in harsh loud German words and waving his hands about like a madman. Needless to say, we left in a rapid manner, as he was on a telephone shouting. We "double timed" it out of there. I guess he was calling the *Polizai*, police.

On the street, we caught our breath and left the area and headed to the bus-stop that we knew would take us back to the *kaserne*. Soon we were back to our base and had experienced another adventure in paradise. Later, we would laugh at all this and slowly get acclimated to European, and especially German customs and social norms. In many ways, we young American troops are not as "world-wise" as we thought that we would be. There would be more awakenings and adventures during our tours in Germany.

On one weekend we planned to catch a train to Paris, but before we had even left the compound, we were informed that we were to be restricted to base due to Soviet air activity along the border. (We were attached to the Air Defense Command, by being assigned to the 11th Signal Battalion's radio school.) I have yet to make it to Paris and reconnect with my French roots.

It was not long after that we finished the month-long course and graduated with the new MOS of 31M20. It took a day or so for our orders to come down from the higher headquarters. The class was split up and we all headed to different assignments throughout the command. I was assigned to Company "B", 11th Signal Battalion, 32nd Army Air Defense Command. Wurzburg.

Wurzburg lays about 200km east towards the "border", and equidistance to Frankfurt and Nuremberg about 75 miles each direction. I was given my orders, travel instructions and collected my small travel pay. Once again shouldering my duffle bag, I was off.

It amazed me as to why the Army had this young soldier travel alone in a foreign country. As it turned out, the travel instructions were easy to follow, and the German Bahn Hauf rail system was so efficient.

Wurzburg proper had a population of over 124,000. The city traces its history to the Celts in the 4th & 5th centuries. Later the city was inhabited by a Frankish majority during the 6th & 7th centuries. In later centuries, the area was dominated by various Barons and feudal lords. The French at various times occupied the area. (That was why I could speak French & English and was able to get around, since I knew no German to speak of.) The University of Wurzburg was founded in 1402 and the city also became a Rabbinical Academic Center until the Jewish massacres in the 1600s.

The American and British soldiers stationed in the area were treated at times with distain, because in the last days of WW II, the Royal Air

Force destroyed or damaged 90% of the city with a massive bombing raid by their Lancaster Bombers. The city was occupied by the American 12th Armored Division and the 42nd Infantry Division. Various other U.S. units were stationed there as both the Occupational Force as well the NATO Cold War Defense forces. I've had many a beer with the soldiers of the BOAR (British Occupational Army of the Rhine). The 3rd Infantry Division (Mech / Light) arrived earlier in 1970 before me from Ft. Hood, Texas.

It was a rather short and quick trip on these swift electric trains. Upon my arrival at the Wurzburg depot, I noticed an Army courtesy station. The MP there pointed me to a bus stop where I was informed that an army bus would be by to take me to my unit. There were several other GIs also there and greeted me warmly and informed me that my new company was within a short walk from the bus stop.

WÜRZBURG & THE SIGNAL GOPHUR (Go-for)

The 3rd Infantry Division traces its history in Europe to WW I & WW II, and the Cold War. The 3rd Infantry Division was the main Army unit stationed with us at Wurzburg. The units there included:

Leighton Barracks

- HHC, 3rd Infantry Division Mech. / Light.
- 3rd Adjutant Company.
- 3rd Finance Company.
- 3rd Military Police Company.
- 3rd Quartermaster Company.
- 123rd Signal Battalion.

Emery Barracks

- 35th Supply & Transport Battalion.
- Co. "B", 11th Signal Battalion (Home)

I arrived at Emery Barracks compound, Wurzburg. After a short walk from the bus stop, I found my new unit. It was clearly marked with a big sign (Co. "B', 11th Sig. Bn., complete with the Commanding Officer's name, along with his First Sergeant's name.) I have now forgotten both names as of this writing. This was in front of an old NAZI-looking barracks. The building had been recently painted and boasted the NAZI tell-tale glass cinder block trim at the entrance and on the second floor. It was early afternoon when I dropped my duffle bag in front of the company clerk's desk in the orderly room of Company "B".

The young SP4 checked my orders did some typing and shuffled some more paperwork. I had officially been assigned to this unit. I was told to have a seat and when the First Sergeant was available, he would have a word with me. I moved my luggage and took a seat. I waited a little while and was escorted into the "Top's" office.

The First Sergeant was the typical senior NCO, starched fatigues, "high & tight" haircut, and he was smoking a fat cigar. He introduced himself and made no bones about him, being the First Sergeant. He informed me that he was having a good day and offered me a chance to "smoke" with him. I did not know what to do, as this was not very "army-like". On his second offering, I pulled out a cigarette, lit it and began to smoke it. Next to my chair was the standard army brass ashtray stand, complete with the PX amber glass ash tray. The small talk was basically where I was from (California always gets some snide remarks and a reference to "hippies" and "fags", I ignored it as usual.) and he asked of my Army training.

The First Sergeant went into his solo lecture on the usual *army stuff*: He runs a "tight ship" (…in the Army?), the equipment is to be maintained in a *combat ready condition, at all times,* he expected his troops to be in the same condition, and we were the best unit in the command. He expected very high standards of his troops. He then went over all the *do's and don'ts* of the unit. When he was done, he got up to see if the commander was in. Since the Captain was not in and available for me to meet him, I was excused. The company clerk was right there in the doorway, as if by magic, when the First Sergeant barked "EXCUSED"!

The company clerk took me to my bunk and new room on the second floor. I dropped my things and he had me follow him to the supply room to draw and sign for my bedding. We returned to my room and deposited said bedding. I was informed to have my bunk (top) made up before dinner and have my things stored properly in my wall locker. I spent the next hour or two making up my bunk and stowing my uniforms and personal items in the wall locker, by the same chart that I've seen throughout the Army. When I was finished, I returned to the orderly room to see what else was expected of me. I knew from experience, that to be left alone unsupervised was not too good. It was too easy for a young soldier to get into trouble. I had already spotted the small EM / NCO club up on a small hill down and across the street from the company.

The company clerk thanked me for returning and that he had forgotten to give me my specific duty assignment. To my surprise, I was assigned to the 3rd squad, HQ Platoon, Motor Pool Section. I reminded the clerk that I have two vital signal specialties and I believed that a mistake had been made assigning me to the Motor Pool. I was promptly informed that no mistake had been made and I would have to speak to my section sergeant and platoon sergeant over this matter. The clerk handed me a slip of paper which clearly showed my assignment and who the sergeants that I would be working for. I still had some time to kill before the company would return from work. I snuck over to the club for a cold one.

I was back in my room for a very short period of time, when a cacophony of noise and voices filled the barracks. My roommates came in a burst of noise, paused and noted that I must be the FNG (*Fucking New Guy*). They all greeted me warmly and introduced themselves. There were two white guys and one black guy. They all seemed friendly enough and asked me if I knew where everything was. I answered that I did. The mess hall was down the street and the "club" was on the hill. That was all I really needed to know. They all laughed at that statement and informed me where the small PX was.

We all left for *chow* at 1700 hours and after the canon blast and the flag was lowered from some unseen flagpole.

After dinner we went to the club and had a few beers and got to know each other better. One guy, a bit older than I, had served a tour in Korea up along the DMZ. He was wearing a patch on his right shoulder, which was reserved for one's combat unit. When I asked about this, he informed me that there were only a small few units in Korea that could claim "combat status".

It was still relatively early in the evening when we returned to our barracks.

217

Once back in our four-man room, a transistor radio came out of one guy's wall locker and with the volume turned up we were "rocking". I had just enough of a "beer buzz" not to care about the volume and was enjoying the music and the new-found comradeship. Out of nowhere, the black guy produced an oval shaped pipe and a "baggie" a quarter filled with hashish. The smoke-in was on. The pipe was passed around and soon I was feeling quite "stoned". This was a most different high, unlike any I had experienced in San Francisco. I was informed that we were smoking Lebanon's finest "hash" and more was due in over the upcoming pay day weekend. I soon learned that I could not keep up smoking with these guys.

A slight smoky haze filled the upper part of the room. Other troops came and went in and out of our room. I was introduced to several other soldiers. No one seemed to notice or care about the strong smell and the smoke. They teased me for being such a light weight. They went on to say that for a "hippie" I was not up to the stoner standards. I laughed it off and crawled up to my upper bunk and laid down. With the music rocking along and the smoke, I soon drifted off to sleep. I had no Idea what time the party ended. I recall that after smoking "hash", I had the most vivid dreams.

We were up early, with the sunlight slowly creeping in and the banging on the door from the CQ runner. The whole barracks fell into a rhythm as the troops did their *(Shit, Shower & Shave!)* and their other morning building maintenance tasks. We all had specific tasks to complete before we could go to breakfast each morning. By the end of the meal, I had been introduced to so many guys, that if there was a "spot-quiz", I'd surely fail. I seemed to have been accepted by most.

The morning formation was at 0700. The First Sergeant would receive the roll call from the platoon sergeants. He would read any announcements and sometimes a short intelligence report on what the "Reds" were doing. Any details were announced and those assigned to them would be taken out of the formation and would report to the First Sergeant after the work call had taken place. I had already met my section chief, an older (maybe late 20s or so.) slender black staff sergeant. He seemed glad to have me in the section.

A small 20-man army bus was parked down the street and all 15 of us got on board when the morning formation was over. The company's main motor pool was on the other side of Wurzburg, for reasons that I never knew why. There were only a few vehicles kept in our company area. I always enjoyed the short trip across town in the early morning.

School children were on their ways to school and the streets seemed to be filled with bicycles as people headed to work. Some people would wave to us as we passed them. Others would flash us the "V" peace sign or the universal "one finger" salute. I thought we were still occupying their country 25 years after "The War", strange. German city workers would be out working on the streets. At 10:00 they got a beer break, which I thought was noble. All of the older German men that I met always emphasized that they fought "…on the Eastern Front…" we knew different.

Today we still have military units stationed in Germany 70 years after the war. In 1970, we had over 74,000 stationed in Germany. This total roughly broke down to 59,000 Army and 15,000 Air Force personnel. This does not include dependents, Navy or Marine personnel. Today (2017) there are about 68,000 assigned to the European Command. Over 300,000 military personnel are stationed overseas out of a total active force of about 2,500,000. This does not count reserve and National Guard assets. Reserve and Guard units frequently deployed either directly to combat or sent to Europe to replace those units deploying from Europe.

We passed through the city of Wurzburg and I was amazed by the contrasts that I saw. The architecture ranged from ancient to ultra-modern. The medieval cathedrals soared skyward in the early morning sunlight. The morning "rush hour", Euro Style was in full swing as we headed to our motor pool.

Soon we arrived at our compound and motor pool at 0800 sharp. A gruff-looking SFC (Sergeant First Class) greeted us as we dismounted the bus. There was an informal formation as he told the team leaders (usually a "buck" sergeant or a SP5 Specialist 5th class.) The Staff Sergeant seemed to be the "second in command". I was given a "buddy" to work with me and show me the ropes. Up to this time I had never worked on *any* military vehicle. This was going to be interesting for sure.

My first real duty was "spot painting" the various vehicles. I was given a stiff wire brush and a putty knife and was instructed to scrape off the rust and then paint in abstract patterns to break up the outline of the rusted spot. The trucks at that time were not camouflaged, yet there were always

219

many shades of OD green paint. The color palate ranged from almost a tan to a deep forest green. The paint cans were still labeled: "Paint, Olive Drab Green" and a number. There was a long row of vehicles for me to do, ranging from the M-151A1 ¼ ton "Jeep", M-35A ¾ ton "weapons carrier / utility truck", up to the M-35A1, 2 ½ Ton Cargo trucks, the "Deuce and a Half". Most of the "deuces" had communication shelters mounted on the back and were cabled down to the truck bed. I was instructed not to paint any of the shelters, because the shelters required a different special paint designed to deflect radar and infra-red heat detecting equipment. So off I went wire brush, putty knife, paint can, and paint brush in hand to defend the *Free World!*

My "buddy" stood by as I started on a "jeep". He pointed a few spots to be painted. Those that I pointed out to him did not seem 'that' bad, but he said to paint them anyway. The basic rule seemed to be "if in doubt" dab it! "Always look busy!" he said. After a few minutes he left and encouraged me to do a good job, as an inspection was coming up soon. I must have cost Uncle Sam several clutches, as I was learning to drive those military vehicles. I never got an actual military license until returned from Vietnam.

At 1000hrs, my "instructor" returned to inform me that we had a 15-minute break and there was coffee and do-nuts in the garage / shop building. These were a long series of shops with service bays for even the largest of out trucks. There was a step-down service cement pit so the vehicles could be serviced from underneath. All of the windows were painted black. I was told that they were kept that way since WW II when the NAZIs followed strict light discipline at night when working on their trucks.

I was ready for this break because by then I was on my third jeep and my hands and wrists were getting sore. We enjoyed the coffee, do-nuts and cigarettes outside in the warm morning sun. Other troops introduced themselves to me and I seemed to feel welcome. When the break was over we all returned to our assignments. My "buddy" followed me and gave me a "thumbs-up" on my work so for and reminded me to: "… keep busy, take my time, don't rush, make it last."

A few minutes later the staff sergeant came by to check on me and inspect my work. In the standard sergeant fashion, he found a few "missed" spots, but other-wise seemed to be satisfied with my progress.

At noon, we loaded back into the bus and were transported back to the main company area and mess hall for lunch. It was then that I noticed the beer machine in the back of the mess hall. When I asked about that, I was told that we could have two beers at a meal. Oh, I think that I am going to enjoy this, so I did. After the meal we were loaded back on the bus for the trip back across town to our motor pool. The lunch break took about an hour and a half. The afternoon was easy, in that we were full, and the pace seemed to slow down a bit. There was another break at 1500hrs. The exception with this break was that there was coffee in the motor shop, if we wanted, but rather we took our break mostly right there in our work area. This time several other guys came over to where I was. After a bit of small talk, a "hash" pipe was lit and passed around covertly. I was not feeling any pain and I guessed that they trusted me and decided that I was not a "narc" or CID (Army's Criminal Investigation Detachment). We shut down and cleaned up about 1630hrs and once again were bussed back to the company for dinner at 1700hrs.

After dinner, some guys changed into their "civvies" and headed to town or were picked up by either other friends or their girlfriends. The rest of us either went over to the club or hung around in the day room for an evening of TV, pool, or "foosball". Some others read of wrote home. By late in the evening, I could have sworn that the barracks seemed to have a slight combined smell of cigarettes, beer, after shave, laundry smells, and hashish.

After about a week or so of pretty much the same routine, except now I was doing a lot more in the motor pool that just spot painting. I was becoming a "go-for" first class. When I mentioned to the sergeants that I was not working in my signal MOSs, they seemed not to care and I was told to just be patient, as there were a lot of men working outside of their primary MOSs. This was confirmed when I learned that even a cook had a signal specialty.

On that pay day, I was amazed that my roommates were the biggest drug dealers in the company. A shoe box-sized package arrived for one of my roommates. It was a huge block of Lebanon's finest hashish. They got to work that evening dividing that block of "hash" into small baggies or envelopes for distribution within the company and out to the numerous remote signal sites. The beer flowed, and the hash was smoked. Later I dropped acid (LSD) and was quite entertained by the "naked girlies" dancing off of my calendar, which was taped to my wall locker. The experience was like nothing I've ever experienced.

The room pulsated, and images blended into fantastic colors and sound became both vibrant as well as distant. The drug distribution continued well into the early hours of the morning. I could not keep up with my friends and was soon in my bunk, fast asleep. This "dope was the best! ".

I woke up in the morning, recalling the evening and most of all the most vivid dreams that I had ever dreamt. My roommates were all asleep and the room was quite left in disarray.

The "lava" light was left on and the hot wax continued to change shape diffuse its light throughout our small room. Being that it was Saturday on a pay-day week end, I decided to get lunch at the small PX snack bar. The rest of the week end was rather uneventful, other than the constant knocks on our door.

I went to the larger club on the other side of the kaserne where a live band was playing. I liked the larger enlisted /NCO club, in that young German women could come in unescorted. On a few occasions we would have these ladies at our table, and we would share a few dances, drink and just enjoy the evening with female company. It seeded that these German girls enjoyed Cognac & Coke as well as strawberry wine. Some more permanent relationships developed from these evenings. I was engaged and felt rather guilty for enjoying myself as such, and as much. I even had a few dates with these local beauties.

The weeks went by and I noticed that during some morning formations, one or two troops were absent. The "grape vine" had it that CID had busted them for drugs. This sent a chill down my spine knowing that my room was the hub of the drug traffic in our company. New replacements would arrive and were under constant scrutiny as I was at first until it was determined that they were not "narcs". I continued to ask my chain of command why I was not being utilized in either of my signal specialties. The answers varied. Sometimes it was a simple "wait" and be patient. Other times were that I was waiting for a slot to open up. At other times it was blamed on the "levies" as troops were reassigned to

Vietnam. Some units went as a whole, while other "levies" merely singled out individual soldiers. This process messed up the PLL (Prescribed Load List, of personnel & equipment.) I was also reminded of the *small print* at the bottom of my enlistment papers that I would be guaranteed my school, yet all else was by the *needs of the service*. With that in mind, I was basically a signalman / infantryman working in the signal company's motor pool. My "1049" (disposition form and my request for a transfer) were being denied. I was not promoted as "promised" at the Radio Relay School in Kaiserslautern; I was still a PFC (Private First Class, E-3). I was becoming rather disappointed in my whole lot.

{Years later, I learned that President Nixon was playing a numbers game with the American public. He would announce that, let's say, 5,000 troops were to be pulled out of Vietnam and at the same time, 1,000 trained troops would be transferred from Germany to Vietnam. Overall it appeared that we were rapidly reducing our troop levels in Vietnam. I became concerned, in that signal was considered a critical specialty.}

The weeks turned into months and the routine was the same duty wise. I was still in the motor pool and I saw no way out. I did get out more and me and a few friends would go into Wurzburg proper. I enjoyed eating in the German restaurants and the German night life in general. I even got to know a young German lady and took her out to dinner at a place that was off the main "GI" path. I was well received by her peers and the German public as well away from the "GI" traffic.

There was a festival in town that dated back to Medieval times. I recall that it was called "Killicrankey" (Spelling?). It was a combination of a wine festival, Mardi-Gras and Halloween. The basic celebration was the summer wine harvest but got wild like the other two holidays. A person would wear a mask or disguise and was allowed to engage in *"sinful"* activities which often included sex. The church allowed this as long as the next Sunday everybody went to church, repented and left a generous donation in the collection plate. I guess that they did have a sense of humor in those olden medieval times. It was during this festival that I was introduced to *"Forty Mark Park"*. (At that time the exchange rate was 3.50DM to the US $, so 40 DM was about $12.00)

A couple of my friends talked me into experiencing the pleasures of the festival and especially "Forty Mark Park". It was another pay day week end and I had some extra cash. The "park" was on the river bank and was surrounded by trees on three sides. It was just a large open area, a parking lot. There was a makeshift entry gate and a taxi stand with several cabs waiting. We paid our cab fare and walked past a couple of "security guards" into the "park". On three sides cars were parked and beautiful women were often sitting in their cars with the doors open or were sitting on the hoods of their Mercedes Benz's. Many were hiking their skirts or bearing their breasts to the crowd. Men, "GIs", as well as German civilians, were wandering about checking out the women. Every once in a while, the man would get in and the car would be driven to another secluded spot. It was clear to me that this was an open-aired brothel.

The German laws allowed prostitution in certain areas such as this. We seldom saw the street walker types often. The hookers were licensed, similar to a cab driver. She displayed her document on the sun visor complete with her picture. They all were medically cleared of any diseases and if diagnosed as such, they were barred from working until cleared again. There were very stiff penalties for offenders. The customer was given her card, somewhat like a movie ticket stub. We were told to hold on to her "receipt" for 30 days, should any problems arise health-wise. This stub would be shown to a doctor or medic and the girl could be identified and was shut down until medically cleared again. Other "blue" laws were very liberal, if non-existent. Sex clubs abounded in town as well. Pornography was wide open, yet extremely monitored for "kiddie-porn" and some very extreme practices.

I was speechless to say the least. My friends instructed me to pick out the girl I wanted and "have fun". We would meet at the gate and take a taxi back into town. I was an 18-year-old kid in a "nookie" store. I finally made my choice rather timidly and off I went with a beautiful young dark-haired lady. Her eyes were most beautiful, and she sported a body that was quite fit and proportioned. Off we went into the shadows.

Her English was not all that great as she rattled off her menu of sexual delights, but I guess we understood each other quite well. For a few more DM, I agreed to an *Around the World*. This consisted of a "blow-job" which would end with straight sex. I was more than ready and excited. The whole act could not have taken very long for any of us, in that when she dressed and drove me back to the gate, my friends were waiting for me. With sheepish, *"shit-eating grins"* on our faces we caught a cab back to town, feeling quite satisfied and manly. After several bar hops, we decided to head back to our company. We kept a watchful eye out for the MPs and the "courtesy patrol". No pain was felt by these troopers.

The rest of the weekend went very well. We returned to our barracks late that evening and made it just under curfew. Upon my arrival to my room, it was quite obvious, the smell of hashish purveyed. Over all this time, I still wondered why there were not more arrests and / or why the command did not do more. Their lack of concern seemed to be able to be broken rather quickly from directives from the higher commands. (In later years, it was Nixon's *"War on Drugs".)* I still feared my signal status and that of my "Secret" security clearance. I also was not working my MOSs.

I really enjoyed my "off-duty" time, yet our unit was constantly being alerted to "the field". My explorations of Germany were very limited, yet very wondrous. These 'tours' often had comical conclusions. Yet, in other situations the history and the various "vibes" really affected me. I recall in one of our outings, stepping on an ancient Roman aqueduct, and getting an electric flash feeling and vision that I had been here in the Legions. The other older strassa in the city left me with the same feelings, yet not as strong as the "Roman" ones. (Perhaps I was a soldier in past lives that I was just now acknowledging.)

The weeks and months marched on and to put simply; I was concerned about the drug traffic and my involvement, even as only by association. My working in the motor pool without any real responsibilities coupled with my not working my *"Critical signal MOSs"* really began to wear on me. The majority of the staff, the officers and senior NCOs were so laid back it was amazing. (I can understand that, in that they were not in combat.). Yet some soldiers were arrested and sent to the infamous Mannheim Military Stockade. I made my last attempts to get out. Lastly, I went to the unit "Career Counselor" for his advice. I choose the Vietnam option, in that Uncle Sam would pay my travel to the West Coast

I informed my commanding officer that I was leaving and was very upset over all the above. (He seemed to know about the drugs yet wanted to maintain his troop strength.) The captain then told me, point blank, my only way out was to dessert or re-enlist. Desertion was not even in my vocabulary. This was in late July. I returned to the "Career Counselor's" office.

On August 3rd. 1970, I re-enlisted for three more years, taking a "short". A "short" re-enlistment meant that one was discharged from his / her original enlistment. Then one was reenlisted and re- contracted for the terms of the new contract. My only option that I agreed on was Vietnam, because I was guaranteed non-charged 30-day leave, plus the bonus of $1,000. I then signed and began my out-processing from Emery Barracks and the 11th. The process took only a couple of days, in which I was promoted to: Specialist 4th Class, E-4. It was rather odd that the Army promoted me in the specialties that I have yet to work in. I then began my out-processing of Emery Kaserne and was headed for my new career and life.

My orders were cut for my travel home, leave status and assignment to the RVN Training Company and course at Ft. Lewis, WA. I had my re-enlistment papers and instructions to Rheine Main Airport for a commercial flight to Newark, NJ. I then took the train to Frankfurt and the airport.

Upon my arrival at the airport a few hours later, I gave my travel orders to the Military Travel Liaison Desk. A few minutes later the clerk informed me that I was "bumped" off of the flight was re-booked on the next Newark bound for flight tomorrow. My boarding pass was cancelled and a new one was issued. It was a government paid ticket. Upon my arrival in Newark, I would arrange my own transportation to San Francisco. I would be flying "stand-by". I would be spending the night in the terminal. I was able to catch a few beers and dinner in the airport facilities. I wandered about a bit and then went to the waiting area at the gate of my flight. It was going to be a long night.

I secured my duffle bag to a bench and used my "AWOL" bag as a pillow and settled in for the night. There was very little sleep to be had in that this was a very busy international airport. Many US service men were in the terminal, either arriving or leaving. A few joined me in the waiting area. One guy was going to Ft. Dix to be discharged, another was being transferred stateside, and a couple, as I was, were on their way to Vietnam.

We finally made it through the night, only catching "cat-naps", no real sleep. We seemed to keep a watchful eye on each other and our baggage.

When the time came, the duffle bags were checked in, leaving us only with our "carry-on" luggage. We straightened up and cleaned up the best we could and after a quick snack, we were to be boarding in about an hour. It seemed to take forever, but finally we were on board the aircraft and were taxiing down the runway, stateside bound.

CHAPTER EIGHTEEN

"Homeward Bound"

When the plane reached its cruising altitude, we were served the lunch meal. As tradition would have it, green peas were served along with the turbulence. There would be no booze for me on this trip, as I was only 18 and I was traveling courtesy of Uncle Sam.

The flight was, for the most part uneventful. There was the polite small talk with the civilian passengers next to me. I was tired both from the long sleepless night in Frankfurt and the meal. I must have slept for most of the flight. I awoke just before our decent into Bangor Maine for the routine re-fueling and maintenance checks. The last leg of the flight would take us to the Newark, International Airport. It would be about an hour flight, as it was only 393 air miles, not counting departure and arrival flight patterns. I remained awake for this last portion of the flight.

The decent and landing a couple of hours later brought me to arrange the rest of my travel arrangements. I found the cheapest fare home. I would fly to Chicago and then catch another plane to San Francisco. It would be "the red-eye express". Jet lag was planning on catching up with me, especially with all the time zones I will have passed through on this trip from Europe.

I made it across the huge expanse of O'Hare International Airport to my boarding area for the flight a few hours later. Once again, I noticed many service members all over the airport and as before everybody was either going or coming from somewhere. There were those who were returning from Vietnam, as the ribbons on their chests testified to. Others, like me were probably on their way over to Vietnam. Yet, many others were probably in route to some military installation to be discharged. I still had three years to go. I surely hoped that I had made the right decision by re-enlisting. I settled in for the wait, looking forward to my leave and seeing "Schar" and the family again. It seemed like it had been a long time, yet in reality it had been only 3 months.

I killed some more time by wandering around, yet never ventured too far from the waiting area and my baggage. After about an hour or so a few more servicemen joined I and we exchanged the usual military "war" stories, even though this group had not yet seen combat, all of us were headed to *"the war"*. A couple of guys were merely being reassigned to duty stations on the West Coast. One guy was headed to the Oakland Army Base to be discharged. It seemed that the rest of this group was headed home for leave, then off to the war. We kept an eye on each other and our luggage. Soldiers traveling in uniform meant to the criminal element that they were on orders and more than likely had a lot of cash on them. Soon we began the boarding process after checking in our duffle bags. We were all split up as far as seating on the plane. The flight was not fully booked; there were a lot of empty seats. It would be a four-hour flight covering 1844 air miles. (That is not counting the departure and arrival flight patterns.)

Before long the roar of the jet engines and the rapid acceleration forced me back into my seat as we taxied down the runway and off into the wild night sky yonder. As usual, when we reached our cruising altitude, the Captain turned off the *seat belt & no smoking signs*. I lit a cigarette and settled back in my seat. (Oh, yes, we could smoke on domestic continental flights back then.)

A while later, the cute stewardess came by and asked me if I would like a drink. The small serving cart was filled with the various liquors and mixers. I paid the $1.00 and thought that was per "airline" bottle drink. She just winked at me and informed me that the rest was on her, in that they had to turn in all the unused bottles of booze at the end of the flight. It was the only time in my young life that I could drink all night on a buck. I learned later that she made the same deal with all of us "GIs" on this flight. This was going to be a good flight for many reasons for me. I had all three seats to myself and had a window eye view of the blackened

Mid-West. Small patches or blobs of light marked our passage over the many small towns and villages of the Great Plains.

I was able to get up every once in a while, to stretch my legs and walk up and down the cabin. I exchanged pleasantries with a few of the other civilian passengers. The rest seemed to be totally indifferent and oblivious to this group of servicemen and their ultimate destinations. There was still that awkward feeling that people were watching us and talking behind our backs about the war. Even to this day, I often wonder about the thousands of service members that I have come in contact with, either directly or indirectly as to their fates and where their lives may have gone. I wonder how many of these young people never made it home alive. This is the soldier's lament.

Quite a while later, as the airplane began to climb; I felt the difference of the air pressure, in my ears, which told me that we were climbing over the Sierra Nevada Mountains. The expanse of Nevada dessert remained almost totally black in the night sky. Soon, the difference in the cabin pressure and my ears told me that we had begun to descend from the mountains. I was much attuned to the aircraft's turns and leveling flight. We were approaching San Francisco across the Central Valley of California.

The "buzz" from the liquor left me quite excited and looking forward to my landing and my future. As we descended, I felt the anticipation of being with "Schar" and my family and friends. With each turn and banking of the aircraft, we were on our final approach; the familiar outline of my San Francisco Bay was outlined in twinkling lights out of my window. Which a "whoosh" and with the Captain's announcement "Extinguish all smoking devices, fasten your seat belts; and be sure that the tray is returned to its original position and your seat is in the upright position. We are on our final approach to San Francisco International Airport. Thank you for flying with us. We hope to see you in the future." (He then read off all the weather conditions, time, and a warm welcome to San Francisco.) I loved his care, and consideration, and corporate welcome on the behalf of his airline. We touched down with a few *bumps* and made our way to the terminal. I was excited; and I was **home** once again. San Francisco never looked any better.

By now, I knew the routine. I'd catch the shuttle to downtown S.F. and either caught the bus, locally or catch a cab. I was also in a quandary as to who to go to first, my grandparents or "Schar". I choose "Schar". I headed on towards my destinations. I choose a cab to take me to "Schar's' place. They were expecting me. As was "Schar" when she soon came down to greet me, even before I exited the cab. The August lows in temperature here in San Francisco reminded me of the contrast to where I was headed eventually.

So, in a while, I had all of my luggage and a cab to "Schar's" place. I still was amazed by the historical buildings, and those that I remembered, land marks that all passed me by. Soon, I was at Geary & Laguna, actually at "Schar's" front door. I paid the "cabbie" and climbed up her stairs and pressed her once again, even closer and tighter. The dogs came down to meet us as well. It was all as I remembered it, the deteriorating look of the building and its interior, and the smell of cooking and of the dogs. I called my grandparents and told them I was delayed and would not be home for dinner, but I was on my way. Yes, I had lied, but I think they knew where I would stop first. It was very late, or was it early morning? We spent our intimate time together and I was to actually go home when it got lighter outside. The smell of her, coupled with the incense left me intoxicated.

Marriage, True Love and The War

We had a lengthy conversation about marriage. Yes, I loved her dearly, at times the only one kept my spirits up, being in the Army. I thought it best to wait to see if I would come home alive from the war. She was quite convincing; in that we should wed as soon as possible. I did have thoughts in a negative manner, that she was only after my *"bennies"*, should I become a possible KIA. I stalled as long as I could over the next week or so over this situation. Her parents were asking the same question.

The second week on leave, we decided to go to Reno Nevada to get married. I thought since I was in the Army and over 18, I could get married without guardian's signature. I was under the impression that there would be no problem. With her parent's permission, we packed a couple of small bags, packed a bottle of champagne and bought our Greyhound tickets. When I told my grandparents, they went ballistic. They wished me well when they calmed down. The next morning, we were on the *"hound"*, headed towards Reno. We were like a couple of naughty school kids. We giggled and talked of our future for most of the trip. I was not in uniform, since this was not an "official trip" related to my reassignment. I did need my leave orders on me at all times. The other passengers on the Greyhound must have known that I was a GI, short hair and all. In those days most, young men wore their hair long. There was that ever-present feeling of people staring and commenting.

Upon our arrival in the "Biggest Little City in the World", we got a motel room with no problem. We went to city hall and showed the marriage license clerk our IDs and blood tests. The clerk then asked me where I was stationed and where was my commanding officers signature on the permission slip. I informed him that I was "in-transit" to Vietnam and did not have a permanent C.O. The clerk calmly said to me "Well, son, you are going to need an active duty officer to vouch and sign for you. We cannot allow you to get married; you are under 21 years of age. Your bride is 19; she can get married on her own." I then asked, "Well sir, where can I find an active duty officer?" He told me to wait a while he made some phone calls. A few other clerks came out to see what was happening and a crowd was slowly forming. He thought that he could find some officer from the recruiting command. He came back to inform me that all the officers were not available, and I would have to go out to the Naval bombing range out in the middle of Nevada. There was also the Nevada Test & Training Range; Nellis Air Force Base near Las Vegas or Area 51 (I could never get access into anyway.) **I was floored and embarrassed.** We sheepishly returned to our room. We began to weigh our options. I could not help to think; "Someday we'll laugh over all this."

After much deliberation, Schar had to tell her parents and made the embarrassing phone call, revealing our innocence and misinformation. (Of course, we had separate rooms she told her mother. (To this day, her parents knew that we consummated our pending marriage a bit early.) I called my folks and broke the news to them. They were quite taken aback and told me to come home immediately. We went out to dinner and ate quite well with all the discount coupons that were left in the room for us. I really felt badly about the whole situation. I was in the Army, headed to Vietnam, but cannot legally drink, gamble here in Reno, or sign a contract, hell I could not even vote. I could sacrifice myself for the country; I could make war, not wedded love.

All was not lost; we still had the "bubbly" on ice. Without going into graphic details, we showered and drank to our future. We made love all night and were rather innocent and perhaps clumsy in the procedures. It was the most memorable night of my young life. We pledged ourselves to each other and drifted off to an exhausted sleep. We later got dressed and explored Reno in the early hours of the morning. I played a couple of slot machines and won a few bucks in change. That was a good omen. We left in a hurry, as had we been caught, we would have to forfeit the winnings. We had an early breakfast and returned to our room and packed up for the long trip home.

We headed over to the Greyhound terminal and had our tickets re-issued for San Francisco on the return trip. We caught the next available bus which would put us home for dinner. It was rather quiet on this trip, but we were very much in love and were going to get married. There was a lot to our story that we would have to go over for our families and friends.

We made it home and our reception at "Schar's" place was rather cool. Her mother, Yuriko, merely looked me straight in the eyes and called me **"BAKA"! (That is the Japanese word for 'stupid & without honor'.)** I felt bad. Her sister and brother thought that our elopement was *"cool"*. I called my grandparents, and to say the least, they also were not very pleased.

That Monday and following week were flurries of activity for all of us. Schar looked for a wedding dress and eventually found a used one at a good price, which her mother bought for us. I contacted the Army at the Presidio's Chaplain's office and told them that I wanted to be married at the post chapel. Before I could (since I was under age) we would have to attend a "few" classes by the Chaplain explaining marriage and our status as a married military couple. We agreed to this and eventually the date of 20 September 1970 was clear both for the Chaplain and the post chapel. We were to be married on Sunday, 20 September 1970. We took the classes presented by the Chaplain and he seemed to agree that we were mature enough for marriage and knew "the birds & bees". He did question why we wanted to be wed *before* Vietnam. (It was **love**, we replied.) He seemed to see that in our eyes and actions. He continued to sign our paperwork.

We called all of our friends that we could and sent out invitations to all that we could. My family did not respond, other that Jessie, my grandmother, since I lived there. Despite the fact that all of my immediate family had met Schar, not attend later on 20 Sept 1970. Just about all of our high school crowd did not even "RSVP" on such short notice. Finally, about 30 attended our wedding.

When we went to my former employer, Heinz Knopp at his bakery and ordered our wedding cake, his wife was glad to see me and quite surprised to see us, especially in that we were getting married and I was soon to be shipped out to Vietnam. She went into the back and brought her husband out to see us. As usual, he was dressed in his baker's whites with his apron covered in flour and frosting stains. He told me not to worry as I attempted to pay for the cake; it was on "the house" as a wedding gift. As usual I left his artistic talents to his own. He wished us well and we parted after his steel vise handshake grip. I did not see that cake until the reception, as another in the family picked it up. It was a very beautiful work of art, a three-tier white wedding cake, decorated very elaborately.

I had to get a Notary to my grandfather's house, so he could sign the required documents allowing me to get married, since I was under 21. (Yet, I was about to go to war overseas and in a foreign land, risking my life for these rights.)

That Friday, before the wedding on the 20th, we had to pick up our marriage license at city hall. We were greatly distracted that day, and since none of her family was home, we took advantage of the situation and forgot about time. Somewhere about 3:00 PM, I said with many explicative, "We got to get to city hall, or this whole thing is off until Monday! ". Panic set in as we waited for the Yellow Cab to arrive. The ticks of the clock echoed in my head. When the cab finally arrived, we poured in. I waved a $20.00 and told the driver to get us to city hall ASAP!. That was all the encouragement that he needed. Off we sped. I was hanging out of the window, shouting at the opposing traffic. I must have seemed like a mounted cavalier headed into battle. (I was.) We screeched in front of city hall and I gave the driver the $20.00 for a $5.00 fare. We made it at about 4:00.

That past week seemed to be a blur. My time was divided between the two "houses". It was rather uncomfortable for me. Although my grandparents were not thrilled with both my decisions to enlist in the Army and to get married so young, they seemed to see our love at a distant.

I spent a lot of time photographing my neighborhood and backyard, the house and all I could in "The City" (These photos as well as those of Vietnam would be lost in later years.) The evening news kept reporting on the war in South East Asia in a *"matter of fact format"* which angered me as the causality reports poured in. I often thought that someday in the near future, I would be one of those "KIA" numbers. We even had a 'full dress rehearsal' and the party was treated to a dinner.

The wedding day arrived, way too soon for me. Schar was sequestered. My "best Man", Jeffery Mori, fortified me with a lot of liquor. We were in a very festive mood. He drove me to the Presidio Chapel. We waited in a back room. Another "shot" was in order when I heard the organ play the 'wedding march'. Jeff encouraged me the best that he could yet had a devilish smile on his face as we exited the door. I was a pile of nerves and my mind was travelling at 'light-speed'. As Jackie Gleason said in each of his shows, "A w a y… we go…!"

I stepped into the chapel. Near the alter, I awaited my bride. Junior walked her up the aisle to recorded music. In the very back of the chapel, two ladies walked in. (Oh, shit two of my "Ex" girlfriends.) I was shaking as the marriage ceremony was about to start, yet these girls came in and sat at the back of the chapel.

My knees were shaking, like a leaf in the wind. I looked over to my future 'father-in-law' for assurance. He was in worst condition than I was. The Chaplain began his wedding sermon. I do believe that in God's house, the angels smiled upon our future, which would last 34 years.

The family noticed the "crashers" and kindly asked them to leave, they did so without incident.

The ceremony went on without hitch. We both said, "I do" and we meant it. (Young love is eternal!)

We exited the chapel under the usual rain of rice. (Today that is taboo, due to the birds ingesting raw rice.) In Asian cultures the 'spreading of rice', indicates wealth and good fortune. We were loaded into the Martin's Buick for the trip to Oakland Ca. (We had the markings, "Just Married", string of empty cans trailing the car, courtesy of family and friends.) Off to Oakland we went! Jeff's Bourbon and Sake had me feeling no pain. He would join us later in Oakland.

After the reception and other festivities, I was quite drunk; I was the 'happy fool', drunk and groom in uniform. Her brother, Jim took us to a

'Motel 'for our "honeymoon", paid for with unlimited room service. The "desk" must have seen all of these "soldier marriages" in their time.

There in Oakland Hilton, near the airport, we ate our dinner, with a lot of seafood, and I later fell asleep. The oysters worked, I was soon awake and ready to consummate our marriage, which I did multiple of times. We awoke to 'housekeeping 'rattling our door, we had overslept in bliss. She called her family to pick us up. Soon, we were back at Schar's place. The whole family was grinning, ear to ear.

The next day we went out to the mall a few blocks away in Japan town and window shopped for many things that we would need in our married life. We ate lunch at the Chinese restaurant, Fay Ling located on the covered bridge connecting the two buildings of the mall. Somehow, when "shopping" with one's new bride, my perspectives changed being married now and having more responsibilities than I did when single. We picked up some Oriental groceries at the "Asian Super Market" on Post Street across from the mall and went home to Schar's place. Yuriko prepared a wonderful Japanese dinner for us.

We spent the next few days at my grandparent's home, my childhood home and in the old neighborhood. We visited friends and were wished well, along with the owners of the local neighborhood businesses.

We spent a few days once again helping my grandparents around the house, finishing some last-minute projects. Schar took over the cooking, relieving Jessie from that duty. My grandfather had been retired now several years now and I could see the difference in the two of them, although being still very active and mentally alert. They approved and praised Schar with every meal that was prepared. They teased Schar, in that when I came home again, she would have to put a few ponds on my slender (but buff) frame.

Our time was getting rather short, in that I was to report to Ft. Lewis by October 5th of that year, a Monday, for RVN (Republic of Vietnam) jungle & unconventional warfare training.

The newly married couple took advantage of every moment that we still had together. That time was filled with both gladness and sadness. The evening news reminded me of my destination and that I was expendable.

We finished out that week and said all of our good-byes and farewells. I was all packed and ready to ship by that Sunday when Junior and the family took me to the San Francisco International Airport for my flight to Seattle. I checked in for my flight and the time to depart seemed to arrive in a "fast-forward" mode. Our good-byes were said, and I boarded the plane with Schar's tears on my Army uniform. Too soon I was airborne and on my way to Ft. Lewis and the next chapter in my life. The San Francisco Bay Area soon faded out of my sight and I was headed to Fort Lewis once again.

CHAPTER NINETEEN

PREPARATIONS FOR WAR, FT. LEWIS, WASHINGTON

We landed with the usual sensations for me and I made my way to the Military Movement desk and got my instructions for my transportation to Ft. Lewis. The usual feelings were still with me as I crossed the terminal to catch my bus that the whole civilian world was staring at me and commenting in low voices after seeing all these young service members scurrying about the airport. I had time to kill before my departure and tried to buy a beer at the nearby bar, but, in spite of the uniform, I was carded and denied the brew. I felt betrayed at that point in that I was young, in the Army, now married, and soon I would be in the "Nam".

As I arrived at the bus stop, I noticed many young soldiers, also headed to Ft. Lewis for the same training. Others were headed to Ft. Lewis for their final discharge or ETS. (Expiration of Term of Service.) They wished us well, as many wore their combat patch on the right sleeve of their uniform. We all got to talk to each other and compared our military experiences. My right sleeve was bare, and I still wore the orange & yellow patch of the 32nd Air Defense Command in Germany. About 10 of us were headed to Ft. Lewis for RVN training.

We boarded the Greyhound bus for the trip to the main gate of Ft. Lewis. Although it is actually about 33 direct miles from the airport, 9.1 miles south of Tacoma, WA. It took over an hour and ½ with all the local bus stops. Soon, we arrived at Ft. Lewis's main gate, which was an old stone gate with its old cannons protecting the base. The bus dropped us off at the initial reception station, where we were checked in and would wait for a shuttle bus to take us to the RVN training company. The "old post", North Fort was on the other side of I-5. That was where basic training was still being conducted.

I was quite surprised when the shuttle bus dropped us off at a modern, newer barracks building. It was on the main post and was nothing like those old WWII wooden barracks of my basic training days. It was late on that Sunday afternoon, and we were ahead of that "NLT" (no later than") date on our orders. There was a quick check-in and we were issued our bedding and told where the mess hall was. It was within walking distance. There was a small PX and snack bar near by which we would frequent later that week. They were closed now. We made up our racks (bunks) and stored our baggage. We went to dinner about an hour later. It was quite a decent meal by Army standards that evening. It was either that we were quite hungry, or the Army was fattening us up before the kill. We entertained ourselves before lights out in the day room and television, pool, and foosball. Many of us retired early, exhausted from our travels.

RVN (Republic of Vietnam) TRAINING

Prior to being deployed to Vietnam, all Army troops underwent a week's training to prepare for their tour in Vietnam.

The purpose of this training was to:

- Physical re-conditioning.
- "Introduction to Vietnam" (other than what the evening news provided)
- Qualify on the M-16 rifle.
- Principles of Unconventional Warfare.
- Basic jungle survival techniques.
- Brief tactical training.
- Field first aid refresher.
- Communications.
- Map reading refresher training.

- NBC Training (Nuclear, Biological & Chemical.) {as if this applied in Vietnam,}
- Lastly, the ever-popular simulated tactical raid on a simulated Vietnamese village to include:

1. Fire & maneuver techniques.
2. Security.
3. Search and seize techniques.
4. Handling of civilians.
5. Capture and handling of enemy combative personnel.
6. Intelligence gathering and reporting.

(All this would be invaluable training to combat support and rear echelon troops.)

The rest of our time spent in the RVN Training Company would include all the administrative functions, to include the writing of our last will and testament (difficult for this 18-year-old to fully comprehend). We would also go to the main post supply warehouse and be issued our new "warm weather" (Jungle Fatigues) fatigue uniforms.

The Training Company

The company was comprised of four platoons of approximately 50 men each and led by the senior replacement NCO. The company did not go through the training company unit, but rather was divided up by the above training or function. These trainee / replacements were mostly young of about my age or a bit older (21!). There were also several older soldiers and career NCOs, all much older that I.

The company's cadre included its own commanding officer, first sergeant and several tactical and training NCOs. In the field, each training site had their own set of cadres from the overall Training Command which also were responsible for overseeing the Basic Training Brigades.

As mentioned earlier, we were billeted in the newer three-story barracks with four open bays of approximately 50 men each. The bay was then divided into two bunks, 4-man cubicles with 4 wall lockers for those troops. It was very similar to the newer barracks at Ft. Monmouth.

The first floor included the orderly room, CO's office, a TV room, day room, and a classroom. Down in the basement was the arms room and supply room and any additional storage space. The mess hall was modern and served two companies very professionally and proficiently.

The daily routine began early, at 0530, We performed our daily constitution, SSS (shit, shower & shave.). The barracks was cleaned, our racks made up, the shower & latrine GI'd, and overall prepared the barracks for the daily inspection. The uniform of the day was: fatigues, standard or jungle, depending if the jungle fatigues has been issued yet. We had a pistol belt with canteen and rolled up poncho. The summer / fall weather at Fort Lewis was alternatively hot and dry, or wet and downpouring. We were prepared.

We went over to the mess hall to eat on our own when our tasks were completed and had breakfast until about 0630. We finished the barracks detail and enjoyed some free time until the morning PT formation at 0700.

There was about an hour of PT, (Physical Training.). We did the "daily dozen" exercises and our two-mile run, most of us who had been out of Basic Training or AIT for a while really dreaded this routine. Some of us had a short tour somewhere that did not really promote a rigorous PT program. Some of us really felt this morning routine and began the training day rather sore. After a week of this, we began to feel more in shape.

At 0800 sharp, the First Sergeant called for the second morning formation work/ training call. Several army buses were already standing by to take us to our training. The platoon sergeants reported to the "Top" as to the personnel status present or on sick call. Then the first sergeant announced the training assignments by platoon. The training was split up in that while one platoon was on the rifle range, another would be going through the "village", and so forth each going to the assigned required training or administrative function. Each platoon had its own bus assigned and when the First Sergeant dismissed the company, we were promptly loaded onto the bus and were driven to the training site for the day.

THE TRAINING

M-16:

1. Safety and range procedures.
2. Technical data on the weapon.
3. Firing positions.
4. Familiarization on the weapon.
5. Cleaning and maintenance of the weapon.
6. Clearing of the weapon and quick action, in case of a jam. (most reassuring)
7. Zeroing of the weapon on the range.
8. Qualification on the 500-yard range.

TACTICAL TRAINING

This phase usually took two days.

- Basic fire and maneuver in which the squads were run through a course of cover and open fire zones.
- Low crawl and attack positions.
- Cover & concealment.
- Camouflage.
- Light Discipline.
- Noise Discipline.

Review of:

- Field First Aid.
- Map Reading.
- NBC training.
- Communications: CEOI (Communication Electronic Operating Instruction.) Basic radio procedures.
- Land navigation.
- Bayonet training. (Heaven help us if this is needed.)

"THE VILLAGE"

This phase of the RVN training came the closest to what we would expect in Vietnam if we were in the field. A typical Vietnamese village was re-created in almost exact detail from its gates to the various "hooches" (local huts.). There was a central well and pens for the domestic animals. Chickens ran wild all over the training area. The village was manned by both male and female troops, some acted as civilians, others in the traditional black pajamas, acting as the VC (Viet Cong.). The village was in a rather dense forest area to simulate a typical Vietnamese jungle setting. Training evaluators and the Tactical NCOs would monitor the exercise.

The arriving platoon would be dropped off a distance from the training site and divided into two squads. The two squads to begin the course were instructed on how to tactfully approach the village as well as maintaining its own security all around. On the closest approach to the village, the squad in the lead, or point, would approach, enter and secure the site. The second security squad would separate the villagers and search them thoroughly (Especially the females, who often carried concealed weapons. We were warned not to search too intimately the females.) Should there be no defensive fire, the village was searched, often resulting in the taking of VC POWs. Sometimes with a fight and perhaps causalities on both sides. Sometimes the hostile fire would come from outside the perimeter of the compound and we would have to directly engage the enemy or call for artillery or a good air-strike. All items of intelligence importance would be gathered and reported.

When it was determined by the squad leaders that the village was secure, they would announce to the evaluators of same. Sometimes there was a surprise, a missed booby trap, a well-hidden enemy, or missed weapons, ammo, documents or any missed intelligence assets.

The squads were evaluated and critiqued. The next two squads would then begin their challenge on the course. Time permitting in the training day, the squads were re-mixed and sent through the course for a second time banking on what was learned during the previous training sessions.

We returned from this exercise dirty and tired but feeling like real soldiers and warriors. It was in a strange way very gratifying as well as giving a sense of dread and doom. I often thought during this period, "… next week at this time, I shall be in Vietnam."

We were always treated to a hearty meal upon our return to the company area and we took advantage of our off-duty time for relaxation, writing home, television watching (always watching the news and what was the latest from Vietnam.), There was always the nearby PX canteen and cold beer and traditional fast food and the grill treats. Sleep after training often came swift and deep. The company was pretty much down for the night by 2300.

FINAL PREPARATION AND DEPARTURE

Most of the rest of the training was either rather brief or covered by some of the Army's most boring training films. Other aspects were additionally covered by some boring lectures by some NCO who may or may not have even been "in-country". I looked for their combat unit patch, worn on the right sleeve of the uniform. Some were, and others were not combat veterans. Oh, well that is the Army.

We were fitted and issued our new jungle fatigues (US ARMY & LAST NAME tags sown in place.), and jungle boots, canvas and leather with steel re-enforced sole plate. (Protection from the dreaded "punji" stakes, in some cases.) Any additional administrative actions were completed. Finance records were also updated, so we would get paid, complete with $75.00 / per month combat pay upon our arrival "in-country".

There was also the intensive medical preparation which included a brief physical exam (if still breathing the soldier was 'good-to-go'!) Then there was the very long series of inoculations which even included "the black plague" anti-virus. That shot was administrated near the arm bone, leaving that arm quite sore. Our blood type was verified, just in case!

The last thing, once all the above training and administrative functions were completed and we were to return to the company area, was a brief sermon and blessings by the Chaplin. "We all felt wanted, he was a good Holy Man; The fate of your country was in your young hands." (Thank you, Eric Burdon & The Animals, "Sky Pilot".) We were all bussed back to the training company area and the other platoons came in from their training at various times after our arrival. We had the week-end off,

"Thank You, Uncle Sugar! "We cleaned up, both the weapons and our bodies, and later went to chow. This phase was over, now it was only a matter of time. I now pondered what my fate would be, crawling closer to the realities of war and, perhaps my own death.

LAST WEEK-END IN "THE WORLD" (GI slang for The States.)

We had the time off until early that Monday morning when there would be a muster formation and the orders read. We would be assigned to a travel stick with the most senior NCO in our platoon as our troop movement leader.

That week-end was spent relaxing, catching up on correspondence, TV watching, last trips to the small PX, phone calls home (A special bank of phones was set up near the company area for our last calls home.) All troops in this training unit were restricted to the immediate area. (The Army wanted to be sure nobody went AWOL or headed off to Canada, to the North.)

The Army let us sleep in, but breakfast was still served on its regular schedule. Many choose not to eat breakfast. We still were responsible for the barracks cleaning and maintenance; but we were not under a stricter time table. Just if the place looked good, we were not bothered too much by the cadre, who was very scarce, being the week-end.

Some of us spent time at the PX canteen and lots of cold beer and treats off of the grill. It was also some of our last chances to see "round-eyed women" (American, as opposed to Oriental which would be common place soon.) Others passed the time shooting pool, playing foosball or playing cards. There were a few who played chess, checkers or dominoes in the day room.

Saturday afternoon proved to be very interesting for me. The Dick Clark's American Bandstand came on the TV at the same time one of the cadre members offered porno films for a small fee and cold beer for a dollar. It surprised me that many of the guys preferred to watch young teen-aged girls dance on the Bandstand instead of the skin-flicks. They would later wander in and take part in the porn and beer. Ah, yes "round-eyed" porn and American Bandstand, what a combination.

Later that afternoon a young newsboy came in to refill the newspaper rack. He handed out free papers if asked, "…save your money, this paper is on me." he said. There was also in the dayroom a coin stamping machine that would stamp your name or message on a silver coin with a cut out star in the middle and a four-leaf clover in the center wishing one 'good luck'. (We would really need that!) That newsboy also knew how to by-pass the coin slot and gave out free good luck coins, minus our specific stamping. (I to this day have two of those good luck coins on my key chain. Those good luck coins have gotten me this far despite their being very worn and smooth as well as rather bent from wear and tear over all these years.

The overall mood varied from being very triumphant after finishing the training to a bit of a depressed and gloomy feeling, knowing that Vietnam was in all our futures. A few almost had that "Death Row" state of mind, knowing that Vietnam was drawing closer. We heard of suicides in the past, but no one in our cycle went to that extreme to prevent going to "The 'Nam". Most of us took it all in stride and lived for the moment and let our fate and destiny take its course. We enjoyed all the Saturday sports and evening programming presented on TV.

The next day, Sunday seemed slow and rather peaceful. A lot of us slept in. There were two church calls, Catholic and Protestant services in the morning. It felt strange for me, as I had joined a Buddhist Church last the previous year. I guess I better touch all spiritual bases before our departure to war. I went to both services, just to be sure.

The Jewish rabbi came by and blessed us all, Jewish or not. He was on call for the Jewish troops all day. Those injections of religion really made us think very seriously of our spiritual well-being. A few troops accepted Christ at that time.

If I recalled the mess sergeant prepared a good steak dinner with all of the trimmings, it was sort of our "Last Supper". We ate well and went to bed much later, full of steak and beer. Some could not sleep, tossing and turning or wandering the halls and day room. I slept well and was ready when the lights came on at 0500.

We were up early and got the barracks looking tall, clean and "spit-shined' for the next batch of Vietnam-bound trainees. We turned in our bedding in the supply room downstairs along with our field equipment. Then it was off to chow, and any last minuet packing. We were all dressed in our newly issued jungle fatigues, many still smelling of "warehouse".

At 0700 sharp, the morning formation was called by the First Sergeant. A muster roll call was taken, all were present and accounted for. The platoon sergeants received their movement roster. We were then put "at-ease" and the cadre Commanding Officer, (A young captain, maybe 24 years old give or take, wearing no combat unit patch.) addressed the company and reminded us of our upcoming mission for the country and the free world. He wished us all well and a safe combat tour. I could not but help to think of the irony that the CO responsible for training troops headed to combat, never experiences one hostile moment himself. I also thought of a couple of the enlisted cadre who also had no patch on their right shoulder. Before too long, the busses pulled in behind with a smell of spent diesel and the "whoosh" of their air brakes, they waited for us. Soon we were loaded up, duffle bags and luggage stored in the compartments under the bus. After seating down, the troop movement NCO took another head count. After a few minutes, we were on our way to SEA-TAC. (Seattle-Tacoma Airport) I recall taking in all the greenness of Washington's beauty and the snowcapped mountains in the far distance.

We were at Sea-Tac within the hour and after unloading the busses, we gathered and put our duffle bags and luggage. We were herded through the terminal among the stares of the civilian travelers. To a waiting area which seemed to be all government. It seemed that all the chartered military flights were secluded from the main civilian terminal and waiting area. After a roll call, once again, we had to wait. Yes "…hurry-up and wait…" seemed to be the order of the day

CHAPTER TWENTY

After about an hour or so, the boarding process began, our luggage was being fed into the belly of the jumbo jet. I noticed that we were to be flying on an Alaskan Airliner. That aircraft had a very large image of a parka-dressed native Alaskan covering the entire tail of that plane. It seemed rather ironic that a plane from the frozen Artic would be flying us to our "tropical paradise"

Soon we were all on board and the aircraft was towed out to the runway, awaiting its turn to take off. The stewardesses gave the usual safety briefing and "water-ditching" procedures, as we would be flying over the vast Pacific Ocean. We were advised that in a few hours, we would be fueling in Anchorage, Alaska, home of this airline. We settled in and waited for the take-off.

Overall, the trip covered over 7,249 miles, should a direct flight path be taken. That direct flight today would take over 19 ½ hours, non-stop. With stops, such as our flight would take could take as long as 37 hours. (It actually took us over 28 hours of actual flight time, not counting hold-over time on the ground.)

Soon with a great roar, and the press of the "G" forces which pressed us to our seat backs we were accelerating down the run-way. With a few bumps the aircraft lifted airborne. With a large collective sigh, we were on the first leg of our journey; we were on our way to Alaska and Vietnam, all on the same day. The actual flight time was three hours and an additional thirty or forty-five minutes for approach and landing times.

The flight plan took us west, out over the Pacific Ocean traveling "North to Alaska". (Thank you, Johnny Horton, but this was not the Gold

Rush.). Outside, we could see at times, the western coast of Canada way off in the distance out of one side of the aircraft, and nothing but clouds and ocean on the opposite side of the plane. There was a lot of talking among the troops, sharing their life stories and expressing concerns about our futures. After an hour or two it all seemed to settle into a dull murmur as we raced forward. We could hear the hydraulics and the gears being activated as the aircraft adjusted its flight.

Soon with the same noises and bumps of the aircraft, we began our decent down towards Anchorage. It was rather dark outside, as it was the "evening" there, before the Alaskan "night" in November. It was snowing and we all were dressed in thin "warm weather fatigues" (Jungle Fatigues) After several minutes, the aircraft gently touched down. It was snowing outside.

The aircraft slowly made it near the terminal. We sat about 100 yards on the tarmac, just outside of the terminal. The airline mobile stairs were brought up to the plane and the doors were opened. We were met by the Air Force ground crew members, all dressed in fur lined parkas. We felt the cold invade the warm cabin. We then were instructed to "Double Time" (Run) to the terminal door, which was lit for us in the darkened area in the snow. It was cold! We were then led to a large waiting area and told in no misunderstood words: "Do not leave this area!". There we sat, once again hurried and were waiting. The aircraft was de-iced, and re-fueled and any other maintenance tasks were done that were needed to get us across the Pacific Pond.

After an hour or more, we were called to and instructed to once again "Double-Time" in back to the waiting aircraft. It was cold outside, and the snow was steadily falling. The parka-ed airmen stood by, waving us on to the waiting "bird". After much shuffling and confusion, we found our seats, buckled in and were ready for take-off. The heat was turned on and we began to feel better after the cold Alaskan greeting. The plane was towed out a way, clear of the terminal. The tow motor tractor disconnected, and the plane started its jets and we taxied towards the runway take off ramp. With the usual acceleration and the roar of the jet engines; we were pushed back in our seats as the plane jumped into the dark, snowy Alaskan twilight. Next stop, Yokota Air Base, Japan.

THE FLIGHT TO JAPAN: (Crossing the Pacific Ocean)

It was a smooth accent to our cruising altitude, 30,000 or so feet over the Pacific Ocean. We would be airborne for over 18 ½ hours, plus approach time. We basically took a south-western flight path, following the Aleutian Islands then turning south. It was still dark outside and remained so, as we raced towards the International Date Line and the next day. A meal was served by the cute stewardesses. As usual, during my limited flight history, upon seeing the green peas, I knew that we would be hitting some turbulence before the little green vegetables could make it to my mouth. It came to pass somewhere over the Pacific Ocean, we hit some disturbances before dinner was over. One could say: "…we pea-ed on ourselves.". We finished our meal and the trays were removed to the galley area. We settled in for the long flight.

The conversations continued for quite a while, but after a couple of hours the passengers all seemed tired and slowly began to drift off to sleep. It had been a long day for all of us. I recall that upon looking out of the window, I could see the plane's wing and the marker light was slowly rising and falling. I immediately thought that the wing was going to fall off and we were doomed, even before we got to Vietnam. When I flagged down a stewardess and relayed my concerns about our safety; she laughed and told me that that was normal, there was nothing to be concerned about. In fact, if the aircraft did not flex a bit, we then would be in trouble. I felt a lot better then. We continued along our flight path. The flight would take over eighteen and one half hours plus approach time. Before dozing off into a deep sleep, I peered out of the window into the darkness and could see very small beams of light, of which I was informed that those tiny lights on the ocean were in fact huge ships. I was impressed.

I probably only dozed off for a couple of hours or so. There was still murmured conversations and the occasional laughs among the troops in the cabin. The night was rather foreboding and on occasions it seemed endless. Endless darkness was not a good thought to have, considering where we were headed. Several hours had passed when the Captain came over the PA system and announced that we would soon be crossing the International Date Line as we headed ever more westward towards Japan.

"The Date Line":   This global marker originally was observed strictly along the 180th Meridian, separating, let's say, Sunday in the eastern half of the world and Monday on the western half of the world. Over the years this imaginary line changed its shape to accommodate trade and the growing world travel. Time had to be easy to understand. Since most of the Date Line covered the ocean area, it was modified to suite the people in what land it passed through.

For example, the land masses on the western side experience time zones which are 10-12 hours more than Greenwich Mean Time. ("Zulu Time Zone or The World's Universal Time", in other words the entire world has the same time, regardless if it is physically night or day.), used in communication and air travel all over the world. For example, Hawaii is 10 hours behind Greenwich Mean Time, while New Zealand is 12 hours ahead of Greenwich Mean time. Alaska and Russia are on either side of the Date Line. The line passes equidistance between the two Diomede Islands. "Little Diomede Island" belongs to the United States, while the "Big Diomede Island belongs to Russia. They both are 1.5 KM from the line. The line swings around the territory of Kiribati, almost to the 150th Meridian. In a simple way, when one travels west, one gains a day, while in reverse, going east, one loses a day. (I would relive the same, time wise, upon my return from Vietnam about a year later. In either case I suffered "jet-lag" and time displacement, in either direction of travel. Sometime later, I had to clarify all this time in the world in my own mind. The following clarified most of my confusion.

{*"Greenwich Mean Time":* Greenwich Mean Time (GMT) is the mean solar time at the Royal Observatory in Greenwich, England. For practical purposes in runs along the 0 Meridian Line.

Today it is counted at midnight because the sun's passing over this meridian at noon can vary 15 minutes due to the elliptical orbit of the Earth. In the comm center, all traffic is recorded in GMT, or "Zulu" time, as described above. World-wide time zones are therefore measured by being either plus or minus the accepted GMT, which doddered from local solar time. Ships and aircraft (some railway systems) kept two-time pieces, GMT and local solar time. Today atomic clocks keep more accurate time recording. Some countries also use GMT as their standard time.

The following countries use GMT as their standard time. (plus, one hour in the summer).

- United Kingdom
- Republic of Ireland (Irish Standard Time, GMT in the winter.)
- Portugal (with the exception of the Azores Islands.)
- Morocco
- Western Sahara

Territories:

- Canary Islands (Spain)
- Faroe Islands

Countries that use GMT as their standard time:

- Iceland
- Burkina Faso
- The Gambia
- Ghana
- Guinea
- Guinea-Bissau
- Ivory Coast
- Liberia
- Mali
- Mauritania
- Senegal
- Sierra Leone
- Togo
- Saint Helena, Ascension and Tristan Da Cunha (to UK)

Countries that use GMT + one hour:

- Most of France
- Monaco
- Andorra
- Belgium

- Netherlands
- Luxembourg}

Yokota Air Base:

Our flight continued on its schedule and another meal was served, we were close to Japan's northern most islands. After the meal trays were cleared, we could see faint lights all along the coast. Much later we began our decent towards Tokyo and Yokota Air Base.

With my ears "popping" and my ears clearing we soon were on our approach to Yokota Air Base and our final landing approach. Out of the window the ground and the lights seemed to race up to meet our airplane. With several bumps and the "whoosh" of the air brakes we began to slow down as the mechanical brakes were pumped along with the squealing of the tires on the tarmac run-way. We had landed safely, and the aircraft slowly moved towards the terminal and docked. The on-board systems were shut off and the plane was connected to the airport's power system. The doors were opened to the Japanese night. It was comfortably warm in the fall night.

There would be a crew change as the plane was re-fueled and safety checked for the last leg of our journey. We would stop on Guam and then on to Vietnam, Cahn Rahm Bay.

We were led off of the plane and after thanking the cute stewardesses (many troops gave them a hug and a kiss before departing the plane.) and we were guided towards a waiting area. The air crew would be changed, and we would have different cute stewardesses to hug & kiss, The terminal was very busy at that early morning time. We were restricted to our immediate area. There were several small shops and souvenir stands in the waiting area. Some of us took advantage and bought a few small souvenirs.

I picked up a small pamphlet and learned a little about the Yokota Air Base. The base was originally constructed in 1940 for the Imperial Japanese Army. It remained in service until the end of the war. It supported Japan's war effort and was also considered a vital asset, should the Allies be forced to invade Japan. It was never bombed during the massive allied bombing raids elsewhere in Japan. The entire base remained intact when the Allied Occupational Forces took over Japan in August of 1945. It soon became an American Air Force Base which housed both tactical fighter and bomber groups as well as a supply and personnel transportation hub for the Pacific and East Asia areas of operation. The base kept its traditional name, Yokota Air Base. The base itself covers about 7.07 square miles and has about 11,000 military personnel and dependents on base. The Japanese economy bustles around the base. It is a very busy area around the clock 24 hours with both military and civilian activity.

After a couple of hours, we were assembled, and another muster roll call was taken, nobody had escaped. Once again, we were loaded back onto the plane for the next leg of the trip, taking us to the Island of Guam, landing at Andersen Air Base.

We settled in for the next leg of our journey with the usual pattern of anticipation, curiosity and boredom. It is approximately 1,619 air miles between Japan and Guam and the flight will take over 3 hours, not counting take-off and landing approach times. We were on our way to Guam and Vietnam.

THE ISLAND OF GUAM:

It was many years later, when I was in college, that I really learned so much about Guam that I would have liked to have known then. I also researched much later facts about Andersen Air Base, where we would be landing. Both research projects proved to be very valuable to me.

Guam is an unincorporated and organized territory of the United States of America in Micronesia located in the Western Pacific Ocean. Guam is approximately 212 square miles in area. The highest point on the island is Mount Lamlam (1,332 ft.) Its natural born citizens are US citizens. It is 30 miles long and about 4 to 12 miles wide in various areas. It enjoys a tropical climate year-round.

The capital is Hagatna and its largest city is Dededo. Other major cities include: Yiga, Agana, Barrigada and Santa Rita in the south. The official languages are English and the native tongue, Chamorro. Ethnically Guam is made up of: 37.3% Chamorro, 26.3%, Filipino, 9.4% Multiracial, 7.1% White, and 19.9% all other racial and ethnic groups. The economy is basically tourism and the presence of the US military. The historical populations: 1910 11,806; 1940 22,290 (about 10% were killed by the

Japanese during WW II) and finally 84,996 then in 1970. Today's population (2018) is over 162,000.

The first Europeans visited the island in 1521. Guam was colonized by Spain in 1668. It remained under Spanish rule (Spain's rule was very harsh.), until The Spanish-American War in which the United States captured the island, 21 June 1898. Spain officially ceded the island to the US under the Treaty of Paris of 1898 on 10 Dec 1898, where it remains under the American control today.

After the Japanese raid on Pearl Harbor, 7 Dec 1941, Guam was invaded and taken over by the Japanese on 11 Dec 1941. The Japanese occupation was very brutal, and many were executed for supporting the US. The island was liberated by American forces on 21 July 1944. (Liberation Day). Guam remained a vital base and staging area during the rest of the second world war. It saw the B-29 Super-Fortresses take off to bomb Japan in the closing months of the war. Today, it remains a vital base of operations for American forces in the Pacific region.

As we would experience, Guam was a vital staging base for supporting the war in Vietnam, both logistically and tactically. Andersen Airbase is the main base on the northern portion of the island. The Navy and Coast Guard also have facilities on the island. There are also both military and civilian communication facilities scattered throughout the island.

ANDERSEN AIR BASE:

Andersen Air base is located approximately 4 miles northeast of the city of Yigo near Agafo Gumas on the US territory of Guam. It is placed under the command of the Joint Military Region, Marianas. It is a vital base of operations in the Pacific and East Asia. It has recently been named a target of North Korea and its nuclear & ICBM program, being of a great concern to its citizens, the President, and the US military.

Andersen Air Base was established in 1944 as North Field and later named after Brigadier General James Roy Andersen (1904-1945). General Andersen graduated from the US Military Academy in 1926 and obtained his wings at Kelly Field in Texas in 1936. He served in the Pacific theatre and was killed in the crash of a B-24 Liberator on a flight between Kwajalein and Johnston Island on 26 Feb 1945.

During the Korean War, 1950 the base supported the various bomber units which would operate over South Korea in support of the ground effort there. Fighter units supported and protected these bombers. The same was true all during the Vietnam War which also saw the base supporting the KC-135 Stratotankers which refueled aircraft operating over North & South Vietnam. The base also was vital in supporting the evacuation of Saigon and South Vietnamese personnel with the fall of Saigon in 1975. Personnel at Andersen received over 40,000 refugees and overall processed over an additional 109,000 during the long migration out of Southeast Asia after the war.

One of the most interesting units to fly out of this base during the Vietnam War, besides to actual combat aircraft, was the 54th Weather Reconnaissance Squadron, flying WC-130 modified aircraft. These were "storm chasers" and flew directly into the tropical typhoons and gained vital information for both military and civilian weather agencies. This unit also "seeded" the clouds over the Ho Chi Minh Trail in order to bring monsoon rain to flood the enemy's supply trail. During these missions, the 54th also provided additional intelligence information to our military. They flew between Guam and Udorn, Royal Thai Air Base in Thailand. The 54th was finally de-activated in September 1987 and flew into Air Force history.

Today, Andersen Air Base is under the command of the 11th Air Force and the Pacific Command. It is garrisoned today by the 36th Wing (USAF). It is the most important air base west of Hawaii. It still supports both tactical and logistical units.

MAJOR UNITS ASSIGNED

- 314th Bombardment Wing: 16 Jan 1945-15 May 1946
- 19th Bombardment Group: 16 Jan 1945-1 Jun 1953
- 29th Bombardment Group: 17 Jan 1945-20 May 1946
- 39th Bombardment Group: 18 Feb 1945-17 Nov 1945

- 5th Bombardment   14 Jan 1955-12 Apr 1955
  Wing:
- 99th Bombardment   29 Jan 1955-25 Apr 1956
  Wing:
- 303rd Bombardment   12 July 1956-4 Oct 1956
  Wing:
- 41st Fighter-Interceptor 5 Aug 1956-8 Mar 1960
  Squadron:
- 330th Bombardment   18 Feb1945-17 Nov 1945
  Group:
- 19th Refueling Group: 20 Dec 1947-Aug 1948
  (North Base)
- North Guam AFB   15 May 1946-24 Aug 1948   Re-designated:
  Command: 605th
                                                     Airlift Support
                                                     Squadron 8 Jan
                                                     1966
- 19th Bombardment   10 Aug 1948-1 Jun 1953   Re-designated:
  Wing: 734th
                                                     Air Mobility
                                                     Squadron 1 Jun
                                                     1992-Present
                                                     (2018)
- 54th Strategic   21 Feb 1951-18 Mat 1960
  Reconnaissance
  Squadron:
- 6319th Air Base Wing: 1 Jun 1953-1 Apr 1955
- 3rd Air Division: 18 Jun 1954-1 Apr 1970
- 92nd Bombardment   16 Oct 1954-12 Jan 1955
  Wing:
- 509th Bombardment   10 July 1954-8 Oct 1954
  Wing:

- 6th Bombardment Wing: 14 Jan 1955-12 Apr 1955   Re-designated: 36th Wing: 12 Apr 2006-Present (2018)

- 3960th Air Base Wing: 1 Apr 1955-1 Apr 1970
- 320th Bombardment Wing: 5 Oct 1956-11 Jan 1957
- 327th Air Division: 1 Jul 1957-8 Mar 1960
- 605th Military Airlift Support Squadron: 27 Dec 1965
- 4133 Bombardment Wing (Provisional):   1 Feb 1966-1 July 1970
- 43rd Strategic (Later Bombardment) Wing: 1 Apr 1970-30 Sept 1990
- 633 Air Base Wing: 1 Oct 1989-1 Oct 1994
- Helicopter Sea Combat Squadron 25:   3 Feb 1984-Present (2018)

CHAPTER TWENTY ONE

NEXT STOP: VIETNAM (What in the Hell are we fighting for? Thank you Country Joe & The Fish)

The trip continued on schedule and we were closer to Vietnam with every mile traveled. We were now traveling into a new day and time as we flew ever westward into our "tomorrow" having crossed The International Date Line. The muffled conversations continued. The troops dozed on and off. We were very tired by this point as it had been a very long day and so much had happened, but this flight never seemed to end. Another meal was served, and I could not help but to think; "Is this our last supper?" Thoughts of the unknown and the approaching war zone kept moving in and out of my thoughts and being. I also could not stop thinking of home and family, as well as my new bride. Would she become a young widow in the near future? My mind kept these thoughts active as I tried to keep a very positive mindset as we flew ever closer to Cam Ranh Bay, Republic of Vietnam. The cute stewardesses would periodically check on us. (I am sure that they had done this flight many times and were used to our concerns about our futures.) In addition to my thoughts, those ladies must also be wondering about our combined fates as well. I looked out of the window and the ocean was bather in the early morning sunlight.

After several hours, I felt the plane bank and adjust its flight. It seemed that we were slowly descending. The Vietnamese Coast was off in the horizon ahead and below us. We could see the various ships off the coast, both military and civilian as well as in the harbor. A while later as we broke through a cloud bank, there it was Vietnam. We continued on a downward path. My ears kept "popping" as the air pressure changed. With another great drop and a banking turn, we began our final landing approach to the airfield. It would not be very long now until we would touch down and we were "In Country" at last.

With the screams of the air brakes, we dropped down on the tarmac. The mechanical brakes squealed. After a few bumps and lurches, we were firmly on the ground and continuing to slow down. We then taxied under our own power to the waiting terminal area. The pilot slowed down the jet engines just enough to keep all the onboard systems going. We stopped quite a distance from the actual terminal building. We later learned that the charter aircraft remained "hot", as they were not to stay on the ground very long. It would remain on the ground only long enough to have us disembark and be reloaded with troops who were headed home, back to the "World" (The USA). They had finished their tour and were just minutes into ours.

The boarding stairs were placed against the aircraft. We began our exit. When the cabin door was opened, the stifling tropical heat immediately came into the cabin and all of our nice cool air disappeared. It was hotter than hell! The humidity was at 100%! Sweat broke out right away as we stepped out. I immediately thought, "It is going to be a long hot year.". It seemed that each service man hugged and kissed the stewardesses before they exited the plane. We were ordered to "Hurry Up" and double time to the waiting army buses. We were informed that our luggage would be behind us and it would be available at the Replacement Battalion. The few officers that traveled with us were quickly separated from our main body and taken to their separate Officers Quarters.

Once I was firmly on the ground, I noticed off in the distance the choppers and gunships firing off in the distances, seeming to be strafing the mountains and hills that surrounded the base and immediate areas outside the base perimeter. The reports of the field artillery from a nearby firebase echoed off the surrounding mountains. Small arms fire could be heard in the distance.

Soon fighter / bombers flew low over head to add napalm to the fire.

The reality of finally being in Vietnam set in a very serious way. When the busses were all filled, and our seats were taken, we sat back for the short trip to the Replacement Battalion on the other side of the huge base. We passed tactical aircraft parked in their protective revetments. Air crews were at work preparing some of the birds for their next missions. A couple of fighter jets roared off the runway passing us and took to flight on another combat mission.

CAM RANH BAY: Khanh Hoa Province, Republic of Vietnam, October 1970

I was headed to this strange sounding place that was only a dot on a map of a foreign land. All I really knew was that it was a very big base in Vietnam and critical to the war effort at that time. Most of what follows, I learned many years later as a result of this writing.

The base of Cam Ranh Bay was a major US base, constructed in 1965 as the war escalated. It became a major logistics port and supported deep water naval and logistical operations. The airfield supported both military and civilian flights in and out of the country. Units from all the US military had units there until the later base closure. The base opened in 1965 and was in operation until the US stood down in 1972 when it closed.

The major Air Force units during the war were:

- 12th Tactical Fighter Wing, (deployed from Mc Dill AFB in Florida.)
- Airlift Command
- 483rd Tactical Airlift Wing
- 43rd Tactical Fighter Squadron (F-4C Phantom II)
- 557th Tactical Fighter Squadron
- 558th Tactical Fighter Squadron
- 559th Tactical Fighter Squadron
- 391st Tactical Fighter Squadron
- 315th Air Division (C-130E, C-130A, [flare ships] C-123,), a detachment of the 6485th Operational Squadron (C-118 Liftmasters.)
- 903rd Aeromedical Evacuation Squadron
- 360th, 361st, 362nd Tactical Electronic Warfare Squadrons
- 20th & 90th Special Operations Squadrons

- 14th Aerial Port Squadron
- Royal Australian Air Force, No. 35 Squadron, assigned to the 834th Air Division
- Numerous VNAF units (Vietnamese Air Force) [A-1 Skyraiders, F-5s A-37s]
- At its peak, the facility supported 27,000 aircraft movements per month.

In addition to the above Air Force units the other branches had their various support units.

- US Army: Cam Ranh Bay Support Command.
- 63rd US Army Regimental Support Command.
- 22nd Replacement Battalion.
- 507th Replacement Company.
- 54th Signal Battalion (Corps. Area).
- US Army: 510th Signal Company (1st Signal Brigade).
- US Army: 6th Convalescent Hospital.
- US Army: 266th Chemical Platoon.
- "C" Battery, 94th Artillery Battalion.
- US Army: Various Attack Helicopter units rotated in and out of the facility.
- US Army: Various Engineer Units.
- US Army: Various Supply & Transportation Units.
- US Army: A Detachment of Special Forces.
- US Navy: Many of the "Swift Boats" (River Patrol Boats, PBRs) passed in and out of the base facility and naval support activities.
- Naval Communications Station.
- US Navy & Marine Support Command.
- US Merchant Marine Support Units.

In 1979 after the US was completely out of Vietnam, the Soviets leased the facility from the Vietnamese government, rent and lease free for 25 years. The Soviets used the deep-water port and air facilities. They also maintained signal and communication facilities, to include their Electronic and Intelligence monitoring units. The Soviets expanded the port facilities which could support their nuclear submarines. Cam Ranh became the largest Soviet facility outside of the Warsaw Pact. This base provided the Soviet Navy with its much-needed warm water port.

The Soviet Air Force stationed Mig-23 fighters, Tupolev Tu-16 Tankers, Tupolev Tu-95 Long Range Bombers, and Tupolev Tu-142 Maritime Reconnaissance Aircraft. In 1989 the Soviets withdrew their Mig-23s and Tu-16s and halved their personnel strength from a high of 5,000+ to 2,500. On 17 Oct 2004, the Soviets withdrew all but their aero-refueling personnel and the, Il-78s Tankers (used to refuel the Soviet Tu-95 Long Range Bombers). They left leaving only their diplomatic (intelligence??) personnel in Vietnam. In later years the Vietnamese allowed India to share the facility with its military personnel.

Today, 2018, Cam Ranh Bay is a major tourist attraction and transportation hub for both air and maritime traffic. Many new economic and commercial activities surround the old base. The Vietnamese are expanding its international airport to accommodate the increased demand for these activities.

THE REPO-DEPOT

Shortly, we were getting off of the busses at the 22nd Replacement Battalion and formed up in another company formation. A muster roll call was taken. All of us were present and accounted for. Nobody had gone AWOL or had died during our long trip from Sea-Tac. A senior sergeant welcomed us to The Republic of Vietnam and to the Replacement Battalion. He drew our attention to the "pissers". A sign proclaimed: **_"PLACE USED BEER HERE!"._** These facilities were located all over the base. It basically was an impromptu urinal consisting of a sand filled 55-gallon drum with a square hole cut into the top and half buried in the ground at a 45º degree angle, surrounded by a 3 sided canvas privacy wall. Should any of us have to go, now was the time to do so. Soon there were several lines waiting to use these facilities. The sergeant reminded us that we would be busy until chow time.

A couple of "Deuce and a Half" trucks, carrying our luggage, pulled up after the empty busses had left. A detail was formed to unload our duffle bags and luggage. The unloading crew was soon drenched in sweat as they unloaded the trucks in this tropical heat. They laid out our luggage in what looked like a company formation of duffle bags.

The sergeant continued his introductory speech. When he had finished we were filed out of the formation and sent to pick up our luggage and return to "his" formation. It looked like a "Chinese Fire Drill" (Vietnamese?) as the troops searched for and picked up their duffle bags and luggage and quickly returned to their place in the original formation. When this "cluster" was over, we were marched over to a couple of empty barracks.

This would be home for a while, the 507th Replacement Company. We were then given our billeting assignments. We then went to the company supply room and drew and signed for our bedding. A couple of junior cadre men oversaw our making up our bunks and storing our duffle bags and luggage in the old metal lockers.

When these tasks were completed, we were advised that we were free until chow time. The mess hall was pointed out to us, as well as a small EM club down the road. Needless to say, many of us made a bee-line to the club. That first beer was a small piece of heaven after all the heat and constant dust. We stayed for a couple of beers and then headed back to the company area and waited for chow call. After dinner we returned to the company area.

Some of the troops went over to the day room to watch TV and relax. Most of us were too tired to do much else. Many of us simply laid down on the newly made-up bunk and tried to catch a nap. The heat was unbearable to most all of us "newbies". Even the "cold" water in the showers was hot. Thank God that the water cooler in the barracks produced ice cold water, as we were instructed during the introductory briefing to keep ourselves well hydrated in this tropical weather. Several hours later, the sun set in the west and the temperature slowly fell. It still was *hot!!* The drone of the UH-1 "Hueys" and the "Cobra" Gunships echoed all night long. (Even to this day, as I write this, I still look skyward to the sound of a helicopter.). The roar of the various jet aircraft never ended. The first few hours "in-country", soon slipped into darkness and a sound sleep, and a broken sleep at best, as our ears got accustomed to all these new sounds. Home was far away in a different galaxy!

As tradition would have it, the Army got us up 'way too early'. The sun was just trying to rise, and the heat was just turned on. We performed all the usual morning tasks. Those being: SSS (Shit, Shower & Shave) straightened up the barracks. (Not to the Basic Training Standard, to say the least.) Then it was a short walk to the mess hall where we enjoyed our first Vietnam Army breakfast. The air was filled with a whole new cacophony of sounds. The nose was treated to the smell of spent diesel fuel and spent aviation fuel. It was a wonderful mixture to all these "Newbee" noses. The tropical sun was up, and it was already getting hot. The nighttime dew began to steam. I knew that after 1700hrs, there would be a cold beer waiting for me at the small EM Club down the road.

Overall, we were not there in the Replacement Battalion for very long. It was but a few days total The daily routine was just about the same every day. There were the usual army things to do first thing in the morning. The First Sergeant would hold his morning formation and roll call was taken. He would then call out troops for the various details needed in the unit.

There would be several formations throughout the day in which men were called out to move out as their orders came down for their new unit assignments. As the new units of assignment were read off, I could not help but to think of all these young men who were headed to the various combat units. I often wonder, even today what their fates were. It also dawned on me, that even though I held two Signal MOSs, I was still in the Army and could always be re-assigned to wherever the Army needed a warm body. I did feel a bit of apprehension as those names were called out and I was worried that perhaps I could wind up a "grunt" (infantryman) somewhere in the jungle. We all served "by the needs of the service" and could be sent anywhere. Daily we saw the newer replacements arrive along as well as with those of us departing to the various units and locations throughout South Vietnam's theatre of operations.

I do recall that it was on the morning of my third day in country that my name was called out along with a farm boy from one of the Dakotas. We were temporality to be assigned to the 90th Replacement Battalion, Long Binh, RVN. We were given our orders and a time to meet our transportation to the airfield. In all there were about twenty-five of us that were headed to Long Binh.

We turned in our bedding and gathered up our things and once again shouldered out duffle bag when we were called later that morning for our ride over to the airfield. We were loosely formed up on the side of the flight line and another head count was taken. That airfield was a very busy place in the morning sun. Military aircraft seemed to be like the bees around the hive, many departing, and many returning. We were given a break in place and were allowed a smoke break. We were far enough off of the actual flight line where we could be afforded this last luxury before meeting our aircraft. It was getting hotter that morning!

When the time came for us to head towards an awaiting C-130 (cargo aircraft) we "double-timed" it to the plane, struggling under the weight of our duffle bags. The plane was waiting for is, with its props slowly idling. We boarded the bird from the cargo ramp in the rear. The prop-wash bathed us in the smell of spent aviation fuel. It was very hot in the troop bay as we strapped in. The cargo ramp was raised and soon the C-130 was taxiing towards its place on the take-off runway. With the roar of its prop engines we were soon speeding down the runway. After a couple of bumps, the plane lifted skyward and slowly lumbered ever higher towards its flight altitude. Cam Ranh Bay seemed to fall below us as we climbed higher. Long Binh and Saigon here we come!

CHAPTER TWENTY TWO

Saigon, HERE WE COME!

The flight between Cam Ranh Bay and Saigon (Ho Chi Minh City today, in 2018), was 241 Miles / 388 Km. Our flight would be landing at Tan Son Nhut Airbase. We just sat back in the straps and waited. After a while, I realized that the soldier next to me was the same guy from the Repo-Depot. We soon got to know each other, and unknown to us at that time that we would become "hooch-mates" and do our tour together. As the conversation continued, it became known that we had the exact same MOS, and were headed to the same place, another "repo-depot" at Long Binh until the Army figured out where we would finally be stationed, in the near future. His name was Pat Cobban, from the Dakotas. We were the same rank, SP4, E-4.

Outside, I could see the landscape go by so green and so far, down. To this day, one of my fondest images of Vietnam was from the air. (Later, out of Can Tho, I would serve as a Special Air Courier.) The land was so green, and I came to realize that "green" came in hundreds of shades. It ranged from almost extremely dark OD (olive drab) green to a very pale pastel green. We passed over muddy brown rivers and canals. We bounced along, as the aircraft caught up-drafts of the warm tropical air. It was very hot in the troop / cargo belly of the C-130.

We passed the time, mostly in a friendly conversation. Pat was several years older than my 18 years. I was reminded that the "old men" in the army were only 25years-old or younger, that was not counting the much older career men, officers and senior enlisted NCOs. Soon we knew all the basics of our lives up to this flight.

It was a bit unnerving to see combat aircraft pass next to us with a "whoosh" of a jet wash, or to be flying either below or above our plane. In a way, I later guessed, that it was a good thing to have air cover during our flight. The jet fighters would pass so close to us that our aircraft bounced in the jet-wash. All this and the heat reminded us that we were in Vietnam and that there was a war going on all around us. It was a very sobering thought for these young soldiers.

A couple of hours later we were approaching Tan Son Nhut Airbase, just outside of Saigon. With the usual plea of the airbrakes and the "popping" of the ears, we touched down on the runway as the mechanical brakes protested the abrupt landing. The plane slowly taxied towards the terminal but maintained her engines at a slow idle at a safe distance. This is known to aviators as a "hot touch-down". We then unbuckled and grabbed our duffle bags and about 25 of us "double-timed" it to the terminal. Those service members remaining on the C-130 would be off to another airfield, somewhere else in Vietnam. We wished them luck as we departed the plane.

TAN SON NHUT AIRBASE

It would be many years later that I would learn some of the base's history. The actual airfield was established in the 1920s by the French during the Colonial Period of, then French-Indochina. During the Japanese Imperial expansion in the area during World War II, the air wing of the Imperial Japanese Army expanded the base and used it until the end of the war. It was later returned to French control until their departure after Dien Bien Phu in 1954. The base was then turned over to the South Vietnamese Air Force (VNAF)

The American expansion in Vietnam forced the expansion and modernization due to the war effort in 1966. The base quickly became a tactical, personnel and logistical hub for the US's III & IV Corps areas of operation. The facilities were turned over to The South Vietnamese in 1972 as the US was standing down its effort in South Vietnam. The facility also supported civilian international air traffic at the time and today is an International Airport.

The following US Air Force units were stationed and operated from the base during the Vietnam War with honor and distinction.

- 505th Tactical Air Control Group.
- 619th Tactical Squadron.
- 620th Tactical Squadron.
- 621st Tactical Squadron.
- 481st Tactical Fighter Squadron.
- 416th Tactical Fighter Squadron.
- 315th Air Commando Wing.
- The Supporting Maintenance Units for the above units.
- Personnel Support Squadron.
- Base & Terminal Operation Command.
- Various Communication Squadrons.
- Various Air & Ground Intelligence Units.
- Various VNAF units until the fall of Saigon in 1975 when the People's Airforce of Vietnam inherited the base and all of the other bases and all the equipment left behind.
- The US Army & US Navy maintained liaison detachments.

Soon an Army bus picked us up for the short 12.4-mile trip to the huge base at Long Binh. The bus passed through a section of Saigon with its clogged streets, noise and smells that we had not experienced yet. The bus driver advised us not to open the windows as he had the AC on full blast, yet some of the stench seeped in. The Saigon streets were a mixture of countless humanity and traffic patterns that defied logic. Little Vespas and small Hondas and any other small motorcycle that made it to Vietnam. People were often stacked three a piece on these small bikes. Pedi-cabs darted in and out of this sea of confusion. Our bus seemed to cut a wide swath through this mad-house, as the Vietnamese seemed to know to avoid those "dinky-dau" (crazy) army drivers. Nobody was killed on this trip. The bus finally was waved on through the main gate on the Long Binh Base.

LONG BINH COMBINED BASE, VIETNAM

Long Binh Base was a vast base and was called home to many distinguished units over the course of the war. I only recently learned much more of the history of this facility and of the units assigned there. The sense of history and my connection to the Army really became apparent even then, but more so as of this writing.

The Long Binh Army Units that were there or had served there over the years were as follows:

1. The base was constructed by various Army Engineer units well as civilian contractors (Pacific Architects and Engineers, PAE) in 1967. Expansion continued during our brief stay there.

2. HHC MACV (Military Assistance Command, Vietnam) {some elements HQ'd in Saigon to include the Defense Attaché Office (DAO)
    *   United States Army Vietnam (USARV).
    *   I Field Force.
    *   II Field Force.
    *   XXIV Corps.
    *   III Marine Amphibious Force (III MAF).
    *   Naval Forces, Vietnam (NAVFORV).
    *   Seventh Air Force (7AF).
    *   5th Special Forces Group.
    *   Civil Operations and Revolutionary Development (CORDS).
    *   Field Advisory Element, MACV.

3. HHC USARV (US Army, Vietnam) Consisting of the following commands:
    *   1st Logistics Command.
    *   1st Aviation Brigade.
    *   1st Signal Brigade.
    *   18th Military Police Brigade.
    *   34th General Support Group.
    *   44th Medical Brigade.

- 93rd Evacuation Hospital.
- 24th Evacuation Hospital.
- 525th Military Intelligence Group.
- US Army Security Agency Group.
- US Army Engineer Command (Provisional)
- US Army Headquarters Area Command (USAHAC)

4. HHC 1st Signal Brigade. (At its peak strength, the brigade consisted of 21,000 men and covered most all Vietnam and Southeast Asia)

5. HHC 2nd Signal Group. (III Corps & later included IV Corps)

6. 160th Signal Group:
   1. 4oth Signal Battalion.
   2. 44th Signal Battalion.
   3. 60th Signal Battalion.
   4. 69th Signal Battalion.

7. II Field Force
8. 199th Light Infantry Brigade
9. A Fully Manned Dental Detachment and Clinic.
10. 266th Supply & Service Battalion (with various supporting transportation companies.

At its peak strength, the Long Binh complex had over 60,000 troops stationed there in 1969. That was just before our arrival at which time, some units were being reduced in strength or had stood down the year we arrived.

We were taken over to the 90th Replacement Battalion. No sooner after a roll call was taken, Pat Cobban, myself and about 6 other signalmen were separated from the rest of the troops and were pulled over to the side for a break. We were informed that another bus would be by soon and we all were headed to the HHC 2nd Signal Group. The other troops were processed in and would be assigned to units there on Long Binh or in the outlying areas. After some paper-work at the HHC 1st Signal Brigade; a clerk checked our new orders and we were to be taken to the HHC 2nd Signal Group not too far away on the huge base.

We were given a break and soon a bus arrived to take us to our new unit of assignment. I saw what must have been a football sized fenced-n area, containing what seemed like thousands of urinals. The vastness of this base was amazing. I thought: "Toilets for Freedom! Perhaps we can 'piss off' the Viet Cong". All of us would eventually be assigned to the various units of the 2nd Signal Group.

Units of the Second Signal Group:

- 36th Signal Battalion.
- 39th Signal Battalion.
- 40th Signal Battalion.
- 41st Signal Battalion.
- 44th Signal Battalion.
- 52nd Signal Battalion.
- 54th Signal Battalion.
- 69th Signal Battalion.
- 86th Signal Battalion.
- 972nd Signal Battalion.

Note: There were 7 Signal Groups assigned to the 1st Signal Brigade, covering Southeast Asia at that time. Over 20,000 signalmen at the 1st Signal Brigade's peak strength.

(The 2nd arrived in Vietnam on 3 June 1966 and its AO (area of operation) was later adjusted to include parts of the Mekong Delta, IV Corps.)

Once again, we drew our bedding and would spend the night there before our next assignment and move scheduled for the next morning. All of this group were signalmen and were all very new in-country, not sure what the Army had in store for us. There must have been a collective sigh of relief at this point that at least we were headed to a Signal Unit and not the Infantry.

We settled in to our new barracks and later went to chow. We met many of the permanent party troops and tried to get as much information that we could from them in this new country. One thing that stuck in my mind was they all seemed to inject into the conversation as to how "short" (how much time they had left in-country). There was no nearby EM club available to us because we were pretty much restricted to the company area. Needless to say, the cadre troops were most willing to sell us "newbees" an overpriced beer. Some of us took advantage of the day room, others simply "crashed". All of us were tired by this time. It was an early evening for most.

The evening passed quickly, but sleep was interrupted by the heat and the constant sounds of trucks and heavy equipment. The air traffic to and from the Tam Son Nhut was a constant distraction. I could not but to think that sleep would be difficult in Vietnam. This place is a very busy, hot and noisy.

In the morning we packed it up and turned in our bedding after breakfast. During the morning formation, the First Sergeant informed us that Pat & I were part of a small group that would be sent to temporary duty at the small airfield at Ben Cat (Lai Khe). We would be serving as the airfield's security force, perimeter guard duty as well as interior revetment guards. This would become our first taste of combat, in spite of being in country less than a week. I could not but help to think that we are too new for such an assignment, but I guess the tradition of "baptism by fire" continues.

BEN CAT / LAI KAE:

Ben Cat is located about 20 km / 12 miles north of Thu Da u Mot, along Highway 13 to the northeast of Saigon in the AO of the US III Corps. It was the garrison town for the ARVN 5th Division throughout the 1960s & 1970s. Lai Khe was the home some elements US 1st Infantry @ Ben Cat, Division from October 1967 until January 1970. (We were surprised upon our arrival that there was not an infantry division around us; we would be on our own. In fact, the assault helicopter company and the Thai Army Fire Base were all the actual combat units we had, perhaps other than half a dozen signalmen and other non-combat types, only being in-country less than a week or so.

Units based at Lai Khe during the war included:

- 2nd Surgical Hospital,1968-March 1970.
- 2nd Battalion,5th Cavalry, April 1969-December 1969.
- 5th Battalion, 7th Cavalry, April 1969-December 1969.
- 11th Armored Cavalry Regiment, February 1969.
- 6th Battalion, 15th Artillery, May 1967-July 1968.
- 18th Surgical Hospital, 1967-February 1968.
- 2nd Battalion, 33rd Artillery, July 1967-April 1970.
- 173rd Assault Helicopter Company, 1966-March 1972.
- 554th Engineer Battalion, October 1960-1971.
- 1st Signal Brigade HHC's Flight Detachment.
- The ARVNs kept a few units in the immediate area.
- The Royal Thai Army maintained an artillery firebase nearby.
- The Royal Thai Army also deployed an infantry platoon and an armored APC-113 detachment.
- The Royal Australian Army maintained a Signal Detachment, 10th Signal Detachment.

Today, the People's Army of Vietnam maintains a garrison there as well as maintaining part of the airfield. The surrounding area has returned to farmland and civilian housing. As with most all of Vietnam it has been rebuilt and modernized. The same goes for most of Vietnam, veterans today would not recognize those places that they were in their youth.

CHAPTER TWENTY THREE

GUARD DUTY, AND THE REAL INTRODUCTION TO WAR: *THE FIRST CASUALTY OF WAR IS INNOSENCE.*

It was a short trip by truck from Long Binh to Ben Cat. The two troops who sat near the tail gate of the "deuce and ½" were given M-16s. The assistant driver also had his M-16 and the driver packed a .45, M-1911 semi-automatic pistol. A M-79 Grenade launcher hung by its strap off of the cab's canvas roof's support rib.

The canvas cargo cover had been removed. The sun beat down on us. We all sat on the wooden troop benches. It was hot, but the breeze felt good as the truck sped along. The Vietnamese were busy traveling this road and doing their best to avoid these crazy GIs. The huts, road-side vending stands, and the merchants whizzed past us. I could see that they were selling mostly American products and beer & sodas. They also sold many items that were issued by the Army. The surrounding area was very green (Just as we were.) On the open road, the driver did not spare the accelerator pedal. The truck bounced in and out of several pot-holes along the way.

Some of the smells were the same as in Saigon, spent diesel, spent aviation fuel, kerosene, charcoal, incense, and of course, the rotting garbage along the side of the road. It seemed that a new smell was introduced to us that could only be described as a musky, damp, plant and mildew fragrance. We passed several military vehicles, both US & Vietnamese and the faint smell of marijuana wafted past us in the heat and dust.

Soon we slowed down and stopped at the main gate of Ben Cat and were waved on through by the guard. "More fucking newbees! ", we heard him say as we went on through the gate. The place was well maintained, and we saw the Vietnamese civilians mowing the grass, pulling police calls (trash pick-up.) and doing many of the routine things that were usually left to the soldiers.

We were let off in a small clearing near the orderly room and were greeted in formation by the guard detachment First Sergeant. He welcomed us to Ben Cat and proceeded to brief us of why we were here and the importance of the war. He also said something that both stuck with me, even today. I would pass his saying on to my troops years later while I was in the Army Reserve and later when I was a platoon sergeant and then First Sergeant. The First Sergeant said:

"The night-time is your friend. Darkness is your cover. You are a light fighter, a night fighter. You will become a heart breaker and a widow-maker. He who controls the night rules the battlefield!". He went on to say, "Signal guides the battle!". I respected his wisdom.

It was a short march to our barracks, two single story "hooches". After we drew our bedding and our TA-50 gear (pistol belt, steel helmet / with liner, canteen, ammo pouches, poncho, back-pack and settled in, we were shown where the arms room and the mess hall were. Soon after we were enjoying our lunch.

Upon returning to the company area, we were advised that we would be ready, weapons drawn from the arms room for the guard mount where we and the weapons would be inspected by the sergeant of the guard.

It was also mentioned that we would be free until then. Those needing haircuts were told to do so before the guard mount. There was also a small EM club that opened at lunch time. They sold beer; we were hot, that beer was cold, so most of us went over for a cold one. (or many) I had a couple and returned to the company area.

I was able to get a few hours' sleep that afternoon and got up, showered and got ready for the guard mount and what would prove to be quite a different night for me. As I was finishing up a young soldier, a SP4 (Specialist 4th Class, E-4) burst into the "hooch" and shouted out loud, "I got a haircut AND a blow-job!!" We all looked at each other in total disbelief. We had the young man sit down and explain this to us. I have never heard these two words used in the same sentence in the Army; or anywhere else for that matter. We were all very interested to hear what this young man had to say.

The young troop went on to tell his wonderful story. "Well I knew that I needed a haircut and went over to the barbershop. While I was waiting, a cute young Vietnamese girl came over and asked me if I would like a steam bath and massage in addition to my 'number-one chop- chop'. Hell, how can I refuse such a beautiful girl? I agreed and was led into the changing room and handed a clean crisp towel. When I was ready, she returned, took me by the hand and led me to the steam room. It was hot and filled with steam so thick it was hard to see who else was in there with me. There were a couple of other guys in there and must have recognized me as an FNG (Fucking New Guy.) and asked me if this was my first time in a "steam and cream",… "'steam and cream'?" I asked. Well those two guys laughed at my feeble response of 'affirmative'. They told me that I was in for a surprise. One by one they were led out by young Vietnamese girls and I could hear them first in the shower next door. A bit later I heard the sound of flesh being pounded. Muffled sounds came in the room. "He said without skipping a beat. The rest of us looked at each other in amazement.

"Go on!"; one PFC demanded, "…what about the blow-job?". "Hold on"! The Specialist said. He then continued his story. "That chick returned and led me to the shower room. I showered. Hell, she even washed my back. She then helped me dry off. Shit! I was getting a hard-on by then. I was led to the massage room and told to lie on my belly. My ass was covered by the towel as she began to massage me toes to head after a good sprinkling of baby powder. Her touch was deep into the muscles and was really relieving my sore muscles. I felt great and thought I was in Heaven."

"Damn-it dude what about the damn blow-job?", another troop sounded off. "I'm getting to that part, hold your horses, man." The Specialist continued: "She worked my legs, back, chest and arms. Then she told me to flip over on my back. She continued to massage my front. By now, I had a full hard-on. When she was finished, she stood there with her hands on her hips, admiring either my body or her work. Then out of the blue, she leaned over and whispered something in my ear. I could not understand her, but I had to agree. The next thing I recall, the towel was yanked off of me and she was yanking on my pecker. With one hand whacking me off, she undid her thin blouse baring two of the cutest small boobs that I have ever seen. In a very stern voice, she told me 'NO CAN TOUCH…!'. I nodded that I understood."

"Then what happened? "another guy yelled out. The Specialist then said "What the hell do you assholes think happened? She began at first licking my dick and balls, then all of a sudden began very quickly blowing me real hard. When I was just about to cum she reached under the massage table and produced a small paper 'Dixie' cup. She finished me off, taking my load all in her mouth. Just as fast, when I was finished, she spit out all of my warm load, rebuttoned her blouse and wiped me off. Then very professionally I was led to the dressing room. When I was dressed, I went out to the actual barber shop and got my hair cut. After the haircut, I went to the Papa-san at the cash register and paid him.". "How much?" a couple of guys yelled out. We all were surprised at the answer: *$5.00 !!!*

Everybody was not the same, after hearing that story. That "lucky guy" we thought! All us looked at each other with a "shit-eating grin" on our faces but did not say a word until two of us were in a bunker later that evening. Then, although we did not say so, we all thought that we would need a haircut tomorrow. We then finished preparing for the 'guard mount".

Guard Mount & First Tour of Duty

We ate dinner early because we were *special*. Guard mount was held at 1700hrs. (5PM). We then went over to the arms room and drew our weapons. In Vietnam, this guard mount was not the same that I had stood before both in Germany and in the States. (They were serious here.) There we stood tall, all "spit & polished" One young troop was too intoxified to go on guard duty and so was sent back to the barracks. Later he got an Article 15! (Non-Judicial Punishment), usually a fine and extra duty or restrictions.) At most he could be reduced in rank. We learned later that he was only fined. He got off easy.

Other than one troop being relieved of guard duty, all went well. The weapons were clean (that was extra duty for us, in that I learned later that Vietnamese civilian labor cleaned all of our weapons after we turned them in at the end of the guard duty tour.) We were in good clean, proper uniforms. Then there was a briefing on what to do and what to expect while on the perimeter, and the interior security detail. We were loaded on a 2 ½ Ton "Deuce" truck and taken to our guard post bunker. There were two men per bunker and there were ten bunkers on our side of the perimeter. The other units covered the balance of the perimeter.

The sun was just hovering above the horizon and the weather remained quite hot. The insects had not gone to bed yet and were creating quite a cacophony of noise. The mosquitoes were hungry, and we became their dinner buffet very quickly. The dust from the passing vehicles was stirred up to add to our misery so early in this shift. If we wanted a box of "C" rations, we could sign for one.

After unloading a lot of ammunition cases and securing our weapons, the M-60, M-79 and a couple of cases of hand held and fired lamination flares we were finally able to sit back and wait. I surveyed my new kingdom, all seemed well at this point in time and the natives were too quiet.

Being the good signalman that I was, I wanted to know if the field phone (TA-312) in the bunker worked. I cranked the handle and my call was answered by the TOC (Tactical Operations Center). Commo in both directions was "5x5" ('Loud & clear, excellent send and receive voice signals.) The perimeter field phone line was what was called a "hot loop. That meant that it was separate from the rest of the phone lined on base should we lose that base system during an attack. Ours rang each bunker and the TOC. We could reach the entire perimeter defenses. Good!

I surveyed the rest of the bunker. The base of the wall was made with 55-gallon drums, filled with sand standing up. The outside of the bunker was all double layered sand bags. There was a wooden shelf centered on the bunker on which the M-60 machine gun was mounted. It was loaded, with the safety on. The whole bunker was covered with galvanized / corrugated metal, covered with sand bags. Behind us a few yards, was the perimeter service dirt road.

Out in front of the bunker was a screen, similar to those used in a baseball practice batting cage. It was an RPG (Rocket Propelled Grenade) screen. It was a few yards in front of our bunker, covering the whole front and part of the sides of the bunker. It was about 15 ft. tall. The idea was that if Charlie (VC) fired his RPG round at our emplacement, this screen would detonate the round before it hit us in the bunker. Hopefully we would not be wounded or killed. I put a lot of faith in those American screen manufacturers. (I was not too sure if his second round would be that foiled.) Further ahead of the RPG screen was a single sand bag on which we would place a Claymore Mine. We would run the wires from the bunker to the Claymore Mine. When that was completed, we were ready for action. In the morning we would retrieve our mine, being sure that Charlie had not turned it around during the night. This was a typical move by the enemy, should he come across one facing his route of approach.

The Claymore Mine: M-18 Anti-Personnel Infantry Weapon.

The kit consisted of the M-18A1 mine, M-57 firing device ("the clacker "), finally M-4 electric blasting cap. M-7 Carrying Bag, M-40 Circuit tester. When deployed the Claymore had a killing range of 55 to110 yards, launching ball-bearing sized metal projectiles (3.2mm.) at a 60-degree fan shaped arc. It is a command detonated device, manually and visually sighted. (peep sight) Field expediency can deploy the device by a trip-wire or a timer (seldom deployed)

This awesome weapon can be used in both defensive and offensive applications. It was developed by a Scotsman, Norman Macleod and was named after the famous Scottish battle sword. This weapon was developed between 1952 & 1960 when it went into military service. It was introduced in Vietnam in 1966.

[Specifications:

- Unit Cost: $119 (in 1993).
- Manufactured by Mohawk Electric.
- Weight: 3.5 lbs.
- Length: 8.5 in.
- Width: 1.5 in.
- Caliber: 1/8 in. / 3.2mm. (700 per loaded unit set into an epoxy resin compound.)
- Velocity: 3,995 feet per second.
- Effective Range: 55 yd.
- Maximum Firing Range: 270 yd.
- Filling: C-4 Plastic Explosive (24 oz.).

- Detonation Mechanism: Blasting Cap assembly M-4.
- NOTE: The front of the weapon has an embossed warning: **FACE TOWARDS ENEMY! & Beware of back-blast** (15 Meters)]

It was still light out as the sun slowly sank in the west. The two of us got as comfortable as we could and passed the time in conversation. The shadows grew as the daylight faded with the setting sun. It was still very hot and there was very little breeze in the early evening. The "skeeters" were having a feast. To this day, I am convinced that mosquitoes used army-issued repellant as their cocktail mix. We figured out the shifts. It was reasoned that the two of us would stay up until 2200hrs. (10PM) then one of us would sleep while the other remained on guard duty. We would take 2 hour shifts throughout the night. The two of us would be up at shift change. Should either of us notice anything "out there", we would wake the other guard until the situation was either clear of taken care of.

Once it was dark, we were surprised and rather startled when from behind us the dog handler and his huge German Shepard snuck up on us. We did not think to look behind us until then. (A good lesson learned here.)

The young sergeant introduced us to himself and his dog, "Killer". The dog handler told us that he would be out in front of the perimeter barbed wires with "Killer". He went on informing us that should we hear the dog barking, do not fire right away unless we had a distinct enemy target in our sights. Should he release the dog, Charlie was in or near the wire. "I will drop to the ground should the shooting begin.", said the handler.

He then had the dog sniff each of us and identified us (We were the good guys.) They both then bid us a good night and proceeded on to the next bunker to repeat this process. I was very impressed at how that dog kept it all straight.

I found it completely amazing that this dog knew the good guys from the bad guys, since this dog was attack & kill trained. It further amazed me in that all of the guards on this side of the perimeter were new guys and would only be here a short time. These "newbees" rotated in and out every week. That dog kept all of our scents straight. (Thankfully) The flight line was somewhat busy at night and added the "scent" of spent aviation fuel to the night air.

With a jolt, I was brought back to reality. Off in the distance a large "Boom" echoed in the night air a few seconds later the night sky was lit up in the distance. It was the Royal Thai Army's artillery firebase firing night illumination rounds. They were the next compound over. After the flares died down we heard several more "Booms". That meant that they were firing real artillery rounds at the enemy. This pattern would continue on all night. It took a while to get used to. (REMEMBER: Boom…Swish is OK: Swish…Boom…take cover!)

Then there was a series of smaller "Pops" and the smaller illumination flares were being launched by the perimeter guards. Those flares really lit up the night along the perimeter. We did not have to ask permission to use these flare launchers. That gave us the opportunity for some "4th of July fun in October. Overall it would be better to use these flares should, we suspect any enemy activity along our line. We had to step out to the side of the RPG screen, so we did not blow the flare back on ourselves and get badly burned in the process. It was also a great distraction when fighting the heavy eye lids and the nodding head during the "wee" hours of the night and very early morning.

It was about 2300hrs (11PM) when a Jeep pulled up behind us and stopped. It was the sergeant of the guard and his driver. He walked up to our bunker. We challenged him with the sign; he responded with the correct counter-sign. We allowed him up and to the bunker. His driver remained in the Jeep with the "black-out" lights on, engine running. The sergeant praised us for challenging him. He made a quick check of our weapons and how we were doing on this post. He informed us that all was quiet and for us to get our canteen cup out and go to the Jeep for coffee & fresh Danish pastries. We were glad to have the hot coffee, as the night temperature was falling. I noticed that he had no patch on his right shoulder, like us it meant that he was not a combat veteran yet or assigned to a specific unit. He was a "Newbee" like us. (We learned later that he was a "Shake & Bake Sergeant", That meant that all he had to do was complete BCT (Basic Combat Training), his AIT (Advanced Individual Training) and the NCO (Non-Commissioned Officer) Academy. That translated to about six months in the Army and he was a "buck" sergeant. (There will be more on this young sergeant later on.)

The night and early hours of the tropical day passed by without much happening, other what I noted before. We were getting used to this and in a strange and twisted way wanted something to happen, so we could shoot our weapons. Yes, we had more than enough to do "Charlie" a Juliet, Oscar, Bravo (job).

Before long, our shift was over, and the truck came by to pick us up. We re-loaded onto the truck all the ammo and weapons. The day shift guards relieved us. It struck me as very strange that the day guards were all the veterans and the night shift guards were all the FNGs. Would not the base and airfield be more vulnerable at night? Somehow it did not make any sense; oh well, military intelligence at its best. The weapons were all accounted for as they were turned in at the arms room.

We were relieved for the day and went to breakfast. As for this meal, the guards ate last, as everybody else had already eaten and were headed to their duty stations. (*Guards are Special!*)

Guard Duty: FIRST ENGAGEMENT

We would be off until our next guard mount. Most of us went over to the Barber Shop when it opened later in the morning. Haircuts were not the only thing on our minds. When we were all properly trimmed, showered & bathed and satisfied with the *full-service* barber shop, it was time to try to get some sleep. The activity on the base continued on, with all of its noise, ignoring our need for sleep. On top of this the hooch-maids scurried about cleaning our quarters, polishing our boots, ironing our uniforms and any laundry, if needed. We had to pay a modest fee in advance of their services. (Another $5 for the week.)

After a while, we were tired and tried to get some decent sleep, but it was not easy due to the heat, bugs, noise to include the constant chattering of the hired help. There was still talk of the first night on guard duty and our experiences at the barber shop. ("steam & cream"). It reminded me that at one time General Westmoreland wanted to have the brothels moved onto the American bases in order that they could provide a safe place, secure and monitored by health officials. That plan seemed to create more of a fuss back home than the war itself.

Before I knew it, we were up getting ready for the guard mount. We ate dinner and stood guard mount on time. This time, we all were present and in good form. Nobody over-did it at the club. Most of us were too tired to have done so anyway today, sleep seemed more important than beer.

After being dropped off at the bunker, we made the commo check, arranged our weapons and ammo. When all was in order, we just kicked back and waited for the tropical sun to set in the west. I must admit that those sunsets in Vietnam were really beautiful, in spite of the ugliness of war raging below here on Earth.

The hours soon passed without anything out of the ordinary for us and the whole line. We were able this time to stick pretty much to our nap schedule. We kept a keen eye out for any trouble as during the briefing at the guard mount, Army intelligence had reported small enemy units were known (I guess that they would be "small units", as they were made up of small Asian men.) to be operating in our AO.

The hours dragged by and I found myself fighting the heavy eyelids again. The coffee served earlier had worn off. It must have been about 0300 (3 AM) when I was startled by the sound of small arms fire from the other side of the base. It only lasted a little while. I was also aware that "Charlie" would often merely fire harassment fire at our bases merely to create disruption and spook the guards. I woke my partner and we both waited and watched.

Out in front of our position, the ground fog created eerie shadows and shapes. I rang down the TOC on the field phone and asked what was happening. I was instructed to "hold fire" and wait for further orders. "It was nothing to worry about, stay alert!", came the reply from the TOC. The shadows in the mist danced about as we strained our eyes to determine if the enemy was actually out in front of us. We were also aware that our enemy was noted to make "human-wave" frontal assaults on the American positions. I estimated that about an hour had passed since the first sounds were heard.

All of a sudden M-16 fire erupted from our side and our perimeter bunkers. Soon, it seemed that several more guards had joined in the firing. At that time, I suspected something was happening that we should respond to. I could have sworn to have seen myself small slender figures were approaching our lines and then disappearing in the mist and darkness. The field phone was madly ringing up and down the line. I grabbed several flares and told my partner to be ready on the M-60. From the airfield a "Bright Eyes" (A converted Bell UH-1 "Huey" helicopter light ship, equipped with a very powerful search light in front and capable of the crew dropping additional illumination flares on the area below them.) quickly flew overhead and began his search of the perimeter. Behind him a Cobra Gun Ship hovered also searching for the enemy.

I exited the bunker and stepped off to the side to clear the RPG screen. I launched a couple of flares but still could not see anything distinctive out in front of us. I readied my weapon and took it off of "safe". My partner finally answered the phone and yelled "Cease Fire". This was repeated up and down the line, The gun fire seemed to end as abruptly as it had begun. There was gun smoke rising from down at the other end of our line.

The phone rang again after I returned into the bunked and I answered it. It was the sergeant of the guard asking if we had fired. I told him negative. He went on cussing the guards for firing without asking for "fire permission", as there could have been friendly forces out there that we could have hit and caused "friendly fire causalities". He was pissed. A while later the officer of the guard followed up with a phone call asking a lot of questions trying to determine what caused the violation of fire discipline. With both the officer and the sergeant of the guard all pissed off, I figured that we would hear about in the morning after our shift was over. (That we would!)

When it was time, we stood down, and we were loaded up on the "twice and a half" and instead of us being dropped off at the mess hall, we were taken to the company area where we were greeted by a very angry First Sergeant. We stood in formation when all of our guard detail was present.

We were highly reprimanded, cussed-out, yelled at in the harshest sergeant style for violating the fire-discipline order, rules of engagement and above all not recognizing our targets. We were to call TOC, the sergeant of the guard, and the officer of the guard, if need be should we have any concerns or questions. *"DO I MAKE MYSELF CLEAR? Any QUESTIONS?"* bellowed the First Sergeant. (Nobody dared to ask anything.) He went on in closing: "Anybody found violating these instructions will be in *deep kimchee!* "(trouble) We were dismissed to turn in our weapons and ammo. It struck me that was not wise for the 1SG to have yelled angrily at us, as we were very heavily armed, tired and pissed off. We then left for breakfast, only having to face the pissed off cooks and

KPs for having delayed their closing down the chow line and cleaning up the mess hall in preparation for the next meal. Because of our misconduct, we put the mess operation off of its time schedule. (Pox be upon us, we "Newbees!")

We went about our business for the rest of the morning. That afternoon, just before guard duty, the First Sergeant assembled all of us and advised us that we had killed over a dozen Communist Party card-carrying monkeys in the previous engagement. They must have been NLF (National Liberation Front) or perhaps just part-time VC (Viet Cong). I thought to myself: "...he has got to be shitting us;,,, he can't be *that* serious."

Every morning, a Jeep with a trailer drove all around the perimeter both as a security precaution as well as a "body retrieval" detail, should we have hit anything during our guard tour of duty. A couple of the monkey bodies would be sent to an Army Veterinarian Detachment to be checked for rabies and any other diseases.

We learned that during the cover of darkness, these humanoid primates would sneak in and raid the mess hall edible garbage before it could be picked up during the day. That would fully explain why a jumpy guard would mistake these figures for approaching VC in the mist and ground fog. We were strictly warned to be sure of our targets before firing and to call for fire permission before firing.

"Top" (First Shirt, First Sergeant.) further reminded us on how much of the tax-payers money was wasted that night between all the wasted ammunition and the cost of dispatching the two "choppers. We also disturbed the eco-system by killing all those monkeys, regardless of their political affiliations.

We finished getting ready for the guard mount, went over to the mess hall, ate dinner and later stood guard mount. I could not but help to think that we would be ready for tonight's duty and that we would not make the same mistakes, monkey business.

It was with no doubt that this evening, we would be alert and ready for action. The routine, by now was almost second nature. We were becoming more acclimated and were sleeping a bit longer than on our first nights and days in-country.

The next couple of nights passed without any incident to speak of. The

Thais kept up their barrage and light, the few aircraft that were active came and went. We did not give it a second thought. All else seemed to pass all too slowly and about 0300hrs, the field phone rang, and an excited guard hollered, **"GOOKS in the wire"**, (Asians / VC) gave his post number and the general location of his sighting. He was further down the line from our position. I woke up my bunker mate. We immediately went on "full-alert". We loaded our weapons and took them off of "safe". Time passed as if it was switched to "slow motion". He called again and said something to the effect that he had lost his visual contact with the "gooks". By now the TOC had been alerted. The ground fog and mist whisked by. Eerie shadows played games with us.

The sergeant of the guard had the only night-vision goggles on the line and he was soon at the bunker that had reported the "gooks". The sergeant then surveyed the perimeter with the night-vision goggles and ordered us to hold fire, "...as there are women out there!". Another position then came on the phone and reported the same and he requested "...permission to fire!" The minutes passed like hours.

That *"shake and bake wanna- be sergeant* "continued to have us hold our fire. The phone line was still open, and we heard one guard say: "Fuck this, I'm getting the officer of the guard from the TOC. He should be out here now. This sergeant is crazy, and he is going to get us all killed at this rate.". The adrenaline rate was peaking, beads of sweat appeared and were not credited to the tropical heat. Many troops were cussing out the sergeant and threatening to "frag" or shoot him for refusing the request to fire. By this time, several guards had seen the figures in question. They were a lot closer that when first reported. They then seemed to disappear.

In what seemed like hours, (although it was only a few minutes) the phone rang once again: The OIC (officer in charge) must have seen the enemy women by now in the perimeter in the night vision scope. "This is Lieutenant Walker, the officer of the guard. BY MY COMMAND, **OPEN FIRE!"**. He then gave the general direction to fire at. Just like the Fourth of July the entire line opened fire. Both M-60s and the M-16s all joined in concert. I heard a couple of "bloops" from the M-79s. We created a deadly rain of lead.

The flight crews were alerted by the TOC and by all of our gunfire. Above the gun fire we could hear the unmistakably "Huey" chopper sounds. "Bright Eyes" was in the lead as the "Cobra" hoovered to the rear. Just as "Bright Eyes" approached over our position, the field phones screamed "***CEASE FIRE, CEASE FIRE!***". Just as quickly as the gunfire started, all became quiet as the choppers advanced forward over our perimeter line. The only sound was the drone of the chopper's blades. Even the insects decided to be quiet.

"Bright Eyes" continued searching the entire area on both sides of the wires (the wire line was about 200 yards ahead of us.). After about a ½ hour or so, "Bright Eyes" turned off her powerful search-light; the choppers returned to the airfield. Soon, we got the call from the TOC that all was clear, stand down, and continue our mission (which was 'guard duty'). Before hanging up an officer at the TOC simply said, **"Well Done Men!"** That made me feel like a real soldier and in a way finally a part of the war effort. The smoke cloud which was created by all our gunfire slowly dissipated, but the smell of cordite and sulphur remained in the area as a reminder of our combat actions.

We learned much later that the "Shake & Bake" sergeant was taken over to the Red Cross tent for his own protection since there were so many death threats levied against him by now. To this day, I do not know if he was merely transferred, sent home or discharged for being "unfit for military service".

The rest of our tour went without any new developments or situations. The whole line must have been talking about the action. We policed up all our brass. I do not think that any of the guards slept for the balance of the shift. Soon afterwards, we cleaned our weapons, turned them in along with the unused ammo, ate breakfast and returned to our billets. From our area we saw the Jeep Detail (Security & body retrieval.) off in the distance, near the wire-line. A few of us stayed up and met the Jeep as it came in from its trip around the perimeter.

Loaded in the trailer were 5 bodies, dressed in black pajamas. They were a bloody mess and a couple distinctly had limbs missing. These human carcasses looked like hamburger meat. Blood sloshed about in the trailer. From the torn uniforms, it was quite apparent that these five were female. I would never forget that sight and often had nightmares over that. Their unexploded satchel bags were carefully set in the rear of the Jeep. The bags would be turned over to the EOD (Explosive Ordnance Disposal) detachment. It was confirmed that the "Newbees" had killed an all-female sapper team whose mission it was to mine and destroy our aircraft and any GIs who were in the area.

The First Sergeant paid us a visit that afternoon and congratulated us on our action and "body count". Our team had become the talk of the base, especially at the EM club where we hoisted a few beers in victory.

JOINT OPERATION:

On one of our nights on guard duty, Pat & I were assigned to be the "interior security detail". That meant that we were to patrol the revetments and check all the grounded aircraft. Two 12-gauge riot shotguns were issued to each of us, along with a M-1911 .45 Cal. Pistol. The choice of this combination of weapons was to minimize aircraft damage should we have to fire. It all seemed to make sense. It was *recommended* that in walking our rounds, we use a different route each pass. This tactic was meant to confuse any enemy who may be watching us. The element of surprise was to be ours.

Darkness came quickly, and we were ready. I thought to myself: "This ought to be different." (…and so, it became.) So, off we went wandering around the revetments and checking all the aircraft for any tampering also being aware that trip wires could be placed about the aircraft to set off an explosive device.

I carried an army-issued flashlight (90 degrees type, with red night lens installed, OD green body.) Pat carried a much bigger "floodlight". We were cautioned not to use the big light, unless it was absolutely required for the safety of the aircraft and us. It was also advised not to use the lights at all, as that would give away our position.

After a few hours of this mindless wandering and several coffee-stops in the guard's break room, upon exiting the break room, I noticed a quick movement at the end of one of the sandbag walls of the revetments. I quietly alerted my buddy.

We immediately moved forward, each of us taking one row of the revetments. Shotguns off "safe", loaded and ready. The blood and adrenalin were pumping madly. When we got to the bunker in question, I saw a slender person tampering with a compartment on the helicopter which was open. The faint glow of a flashlight was seen peering from the inside of the compartment in question. I went to the firing position and challenged this person in the shadows with the sign challenge word. Pat was covering be from behind. When the figure answered with the correct counter-sign, I lowered my weapon and asked who he was and why he was out at this aircraft at this ungodly hour. The Thai artillery kept launching the lumination rounds lighting up the tropical night sky.

He said that he was the avionics repairman and he was authorized to be out there working on the aircraft. He handed me his army ID card, as was proper protocol. He went on to explain that since it was cooler at night, it was easier to work on the gear, especially since it had cooled down by this hour. His M-35 ¾ ton utility truck was parked around the corner.

We told him that we were new, and nobody had told us that he would even be out here. I said, "You were lucky that we did not shoot you. We have not been in town very long." That made for a good laugh and relieved the tension.

The repairman finished up and secured the aircraft. He then picked up his tool box and invited us over to the truck. "Do you guys smoke?" he asked as he threw his tool box in the cab. We said yes, and I showed him my pack of cigarettes. "Oh, hell no! Have you tried something from Uncle Ho's victory garden yet?" he said without skipping a beat as he produced an extremely thin "pinhead" joint. Pat and I looked at each other in disbelief. "Wanna smoke?" he said, taking a long drag on this tiny joint. The joint was handed to us. We both took a good hit.

I asked how the three of us could even feel anything from such a small joint. I was used to much larger "bomber" joints from my Haight-Ashbury days in San Francisco. The avionics man simply replied, "Just wait, it'll kick your ass. They call it Thai-sticks. Some call it 'Boo' because it sneaks up on you.". Then without any warning. He packed up his gear and drove off of the flight line. Pat and I looked at each other, shrugged our shoulders and proceeded on our rounds.

Time seemed to slow down, and it seemed like we were walking in pudding. Pat was now carrying his shotgun by its sling, not very military. I realized that I was very stoned. The lumination rounds danced across the sky, leaving a string of "tracers" in their wake. I was impressed and very amused. It seemed that Pat was equally stoned. We enjoyed the light show for a while.

Now a mild panic set in. We were both stoned, on guard duty in a combat zone. I reminded Pat that the sergeant of the guard had not been by to check on us for a while now. We rushed over to the break room and the two of us got a large cup of coffee and got some breath mints out of the nearby candy machine. That should fool them.

By now, we were beginning to straighten up. We could not but to comment on how powerful the local weed was. MAN ! The two of us continued walking our post. The light show had returned to normal to us by now. We rounded one bunker and almost walked into the sergeant of the guard. (That scared the shit out of me. I thought it was "Charlie".) This was a new sergeant and was smart enough to have parked his Jeep and walked over to check on us. I could not but to think "He knows that we are stoned.". I was worried for the rest of the night over this.

NOTE:

(I learned much later that most all of the weed that the GIs smoked had been laced with heroin.

The enemy's tactic was if they couldn't kill them on the battlefield, to return the GIs home with an addiction. This was later confirmed by military intelligence.)

When our shift was over, and we stood down, I was expecting the sergeant to have words with us. That never happened, and we were safe. We both seemed to be grinning over this all day. We returned to our regular routine.

The rest of the week passed without any action on our part. We did hear of an incident on one of our last nights. The incident occurred at the NCO club. At some time during the night and the drinking, an American insulted the Thai King.

That was it, the Thais all rose to get an apology from the offending soldier. Soon both sides were on their feet and a fight was just about to happen, when a young Thai private jumped in front on the Americans and produced a hand grenade. There was dead silence for a few seconds. The Thai began shouting and demanding an apology. The only weapons that the Americans had were their beer bottles. The club manager slowly approached the embittered sides and tried to reason with both sides.

A few minutes later the MPs arrived with drawn weapons and a Thai Army officer. Both sides stood down, in light of the MP's drawn weapons. The offending GI was forced to apologize and the young Thai private replaced the pin in the grenade and handed it over to his officer. As the two sides were ordered out of the club and while departing, it was heard that the Thai officer really was dressing down the young Thai for disrupting the comraderies of the two nation's armed forces joined in a common cause and enemy. The offending American sergeant was given a written reprimand for the same reason as the Thai.

On our last day we got up, packed up, cleaned up, picked up and turned in our equipment and bedding. By lunch time we were waiting for orders and transportation. In some cases, the units came to pick up their replacements, in other cases the replacements were given their travel orders and met their transportation.

My buddy, Pat and I were given our orders and taken to the shuttle bus stop which would take us through Saigon (Ho Chi Minh City, today.) and on to Tan Son Nhut to report to the troop "movement" station to be manifested on an aircraft to our new unit assignment in a place called "Can Tho". We would be flying to Binh Thuy Airfield and then we were to contact our unit to pick us up. We had no idea where we were going and what awaited us in the near future.

CHAPTER TWENTY FOUR

SAIGON AND BEYOND

This all seemed very odd to us. Here were two unescorted "newbees" on an army bus passing through a very foreign city, no idea where we were going. It had occurred to us that we could simply get off the bus at any time and either spend a few days in Saigon or simply disappear. We thought against those ideas, in that it was getting towards the end of the month and we did not have a lot of money left until pay-day. (Remember: Back then the military paid once a month on the 1st, in cash.). As tempting as it sounded, we decided against a vacation in Saigon and remained on the bus. Besides, there were too many military headquarters and a whole lot of MPs in the area. It was best that we remain on the bus and get off at Tan Son Nhut as ordered.

At the "troop movement" desk, our orders were verified, and it was confirmed that we would first be assigned to the USASTRATCOM (United States Army Strategic Communication Command) detachment, HQ Co. 52nd Signal Battalion, at the Can Tho Army Airfield. We checked the large map nearby and we learned that we would be located in the Mekong Delta region of Vietnam and IV Corps. We would be joining one of the seven signal battalions of the 2nd Signal Group, IV Corps, 1st Signal Brigade.

{1st SIGNAL BRIGADE:

The brigade was first established on 1 April 1966 as the Strategic Communications Command Signal Brigade, Southeast Asia in Saigon,

293

RVN. On 16 October 1967 the unit was re-designated 1st Signal Brigade and reassigned to Long Binh. The new unit was comprised of several communication units and assets belonging to USASTRATCOM (United States Army Strategic Communications Command). By early 1966, the brigade was manned by 12,000 signal troops and supporting personnel. At the height of the war the brigade boasted over 23,000 troops, making it the largest brigade in the military. (It actually over-manned a typical Army division.)

It covered Southeast Asia from Thailand to the DMZ in the northern part of South Vietnam. Over 300 signal sites were manned by the brigade's personnel. The 1st Signal Brigade's AO covered over 60,000 square miles of territory.

The unit's mission was to provide the theatre communication needs, consisting of:

- Courier Service.
- Long & Local Cable Construction.
- Land Line Telephone Service.
- Wire & Cable Maintenance Support.
- Teletype & Tape Relay Service.
- Radio-Teletype Mobile Support.
- Radio-Wire Interface Support.
- Cryptographic Support Service.
- Radio Relay Service.
- Microwave Service.
- Photographic Support.
- Tropographic Transmission.
- Satellite Service. (First time in a combat theatre.)
- Electronic Maintenance Support.
- Field Communication & Signal Training School.
- Aviation Support of all Communication Systems.

The brigade needed air support, due to the vast area that it was responsible for. In 1966 and 1967 the brigade acquired 15 aircraft by the end of January 1967. Later the brigade got an additional 6 U-1A Otter fixed wing aircraft. The original UH-1B helicopters were swapped out for the newer UH-1D, in order to provide greater lift capacity. Later on, the brigade would have 45 aircraft, to include: 9 twin-engine fixed wing aircraft, 12 light Observation helicopters, and finally 24 Utility Helicopters.

During the 1968 TET Offensive, signalmen had to rely upon their infantry training to defend and repel enemy attacks on communication assets. In many locations throughout the war the signalmen were on their own with no combat units nearby to defend and support these remote sites.

In the later years of this war in the Mekong Delta, signal units were on their own since by that time there were no US divisions south of Saigon. (That was the situation that we experienced.) At the end of the war, in 1972 the brigade had been reduced to only 1,300 men. Many units became MACV Signal Companies.

The South Vietnamese Army's Signal Corps took over many of the communication sites and assets. Effective 7 November 1972 the brigade's colors were folded, and the unit was transferred to South Korea, where it still serves proudly under the command of the 8th US Army.

The brigade was awarded 3 Meritorious Unit Commendations and its colors boast 15 Battle streamers. The 1st Signal Brigade lost 193 men during its mission in the war. Those signalmen who were attached or on TDY (Temporary Duty) were not counted in this total.

The 1st Signal Brigade has lived up to three Signal Corps mottos: "Signal, First in Last Out." (At least one signalman had to report the two major events, and another to take the photographs.) "Signal Leads the Course of the Battle." And "Signal Keeps the Shooters Shooting!".}

We were directed to the proper gate and were to wait until called to board our aircraft. The whole terminal was a very busy place, with the military personnel from all branches and allied nations as well as civilians, all hurrying about with very determined looks on their faces. Beads of sweat dripped off just about everybody's face. The hot air in the terminal was pushed about by huge overhead fans. We settled in and waited patiently for our flight. There was not much else to do besides "people watch" and read ancient magazines. (Guns & Ammo seemed appropriate, right at home here.)

When our time came to board the plane, an airman directed us to the door and our plane awaited us on the tarmac. We jogged over to the aircraft with our baggage and boarded. There was about 20 of us manifested for this flight. To my great surprise, what awaited us was an old aging C-47. Many of these "birds" were converted to become gunships. They carried 4 mini-guns, had grenade launchers and flare capability. They affectionally became known as "**PUFF, THE MAGIC DRAGON**" **or "SPOOKY".** The enemy dreaded and feared seeing these warbirds approaching overhead. They must have realized that: *"Beaucoup Hurt!"* was on their way.

This aircraft had US Army markings and sported a camouflage paint job. This aircraft was of WW II vintage and affectionately was called, "The Flying Boxcar". This was really reassuring, considering where we were and how old this plane seemed. This plane was noted for dropping troops and supplies all over the globe during the Second World War. At this point in time, I thought a small prayer might be in order. I silently said one for the group as we boarded this aging workhorse.

All of us quickly strapped in the troop benches along the sides of the plane. An army crew-chief came back from the cockpit, and informed us that there would several stops, as this was both a supply and courier run, stopping at several points around the Delta. I reminded him that me and my friend needed to get off at a place called Binh Thuy. "No sweat, I'll let you know when it is time to get off.". (I thought suddenly of the WW II paratroopers leaping from this plane. We were not issued parachutes!)

We were given (and signed for.) a small bag lunch, consisting of a bologna sandwich, potato chips a cookie of some sort and a small fruit drink. It would be a long time until Pat& I would eat again. The crew chief informed us to save our trash, as it would be collected later. He did not want a messy bird nor risk any FOD (Foreign Object Damage) should any trash slip outside of the aircraft to do some damage to ours or other aircraft on the runway.

All of a sudden, the propeller engines roared to life and we began to slowly taxi out to the take-off runway. The plane began to speed forward. All I could feel was being pushed sideways in my seat as the plane made a couple of bumps and magically was lifted skyward as the engines raced at full-throttle.

From out of the window, I could see the clouds dropping on by below us. I could see military aircraft off in the distant skies. Once again, the landscape was bathed in countless shades of green, with muddy brown rivers and streams flowing madly out to the sea to our east.

It was early afternoon by now as we made our way around the Delta. At each stop a few troops got off and small supplies were off-loaded. The courier delivered his "mail" accordingly. (I did not know it at that time, but I would be doing the same thing months later as a Special Air Courier.) The aircraft bounced up and down as we hit up-drafts due to the rising hot air from the land and rivers below.

The flight continues on, making several stops. Each time that the door was opened, and troops, supplies and "the mail" were off-loaded, the tropical heat was sucked in, adding to our discomfort. The crew chief came back and told us that we would get off next. There were only about six of us left from the original 20 or so troops that had started this trip with us. The flight continued on. Pat and I were getting rather nervous as what was to be next for us. All this had been quite an adventure so far. It was about 1500hrs. (3:00PM) when we finally touched down at our destination, Binh Thuy Airbase. {I would learn much about the base during this writing.}

CHAPTER TWENTY FIVE

Binh Thuy Air Base:
Binh Thuy Naval Facilities:

Binh Thuy Air Base was constructed in mid-1963, when MACV (Military Assistance Command Vietnam) required a better airfield to support its war effort in the Mekong Delta. The airfield was expanded to have a 6,000 ft. runway and also support heavier aircraft and night tactical operations in the area.

HIGHLIGHTS:

USAF

- 8 May 1965 the 22nd Tactical Air Support Squadron with O-1 Bird Dogs & Cessna O-2A and B Super Skymasters, were established on the base. (505th Tactical Control Group under the command of 22nd Air Division at Tan Son Nhut.)
- In June 1965, the base became the forward operating base for the AC-47 "Spooky" gunships of the "E" Flight of the 4th Air Commando Squadron.
- On 15 September of the same year, Detachment 10, 38th Aerospace Rescue & Recovery Squadron assigned 2 HH-43F helicopters to support the base operations.

- An enemy mortar attack was stopped by the massive fire of the "Spooky" gunships on 20 February 1966 and again on 8 July 1966.
- On 14 October 1967 after the activation of the 14th Air commando Squadron at Nha Trang Air Base, the AC-47s of "E" Flight were replaced by 5 AC-47s of the "D" Flight of the 14th.
- During the 1968 "TET" Offensive by the enemy, the base was attacked by rocket and mortar fire. A ground attack was later launched, but repelled by "Spooky", the USAD Security Police Squadron. There were many enemy losses, but none to the US and Vietnamese forces.
- 26 June 1969 all of the AC-47s of "D" Flight were transferred to Nha Trang Air Base.
- On 20 December 1969, Detachment 10, 38th Aerospace & Recovery Squadron was disbanded.
- The 22nd Tactical Air Support Squadron left and was reassigned to Bien Hoa Air Base.
- In February 1970 as a part of Nixon's "Vietnamization Program"; the USAF began to turn over assets and control of Binh Thuy to the 4th VNAF Air Division. It would be completed by the end of the year, leaving only a few airmen to support the continuing supply and joint missions. The US Navy would continue its operations with its river patrol boats and Light Attack Squadron 4, (VAL-4)
- *(In retrospect: Binh Thuy would be Vietnamese operationally during my tour.)*

US NAVY USE:

- On 19 April 1969, the Light Attack Squadron $ (VAL-4) began its combat operations. They flew close air support missions in support of the Mobile Riverine Force, operating in the Mekong Delta. Their missions included air patrol, overhead air cover, scramble alert as well as artillery and gunfire spotting and direction. VAL-4 flew its last combat mission on 31 March 1972 and was disbanded on 10 April 1972.

- The Navy moved its operations from Can Tho to Binh Thuy in July of 1967.
- The facilities at Binh Thuy were expanded to accommodate the Naval operations of the 10 boat River Division 51. They supported the US Navy Seals / "Other Special Operation Forces & Mercenaries.)
- Binh Thuy supported the Navy Seabees and Army Engineers who were expanding and improving the facility at Can Tho, 1966-1969.
- In 1969 major components of Helicopter Attack (light), Squadron 3 "The Seawolves" and Attack Squadron 4, "The Black Ponies" were established at Binh Thuy.
- Operation Sealords-1969-1972. This program was a part of Vietnamization in which the US trained VNAV (Vietnamese Navy) personnel and slowly began to turn over naval assets to the Vietnamese.
- The Navy ceased operations in Binh Thuy in April 1972.]

We were directed to the small terminal building, duffle bags on our shoulders, we walked over to the terminal. It was hot outside. Upon entering the terminal, there was a slight relief, in that there was some air-conditioning in the waiting area and there were huge overhead fans slowly mixing up the air.

We went up to the desk where two American airmen were kicked back in the office chairs. With a "grunt" one got up and came up to the desk and asked if he "Could help us?"

I thought to myself: "Dumb question, two army "newbees", carrying duffle bags, wet from sweat, on an Air Force base, in a passenger terminal, in a foreign land, dazed and confused…

YES! …he could most certainly help us.". I gave him our orders and explained that we were assigned to HHC 52nd Signal Battalion, Can Tho. Other service members, both American and Vietnamese darted to and fro, knowing what they were doing and going. We surely did not.

The airman replied:" Oh, Can Tho is about 5 miles south of here." Pat and I looked at each other in disbelief. I thought to myself: "They are not going to make us walk there, are they in this heat? ". I quickly came out of my thoughts and asked if the airman: "…would be so kind as to call the unit for our transportation.".". He reluctantly picked up a phone and called for us. After what seemed like a long conversation, the airman turned to us and said "OK, they'll pick you guys up in a while." Pat & I moved over to some seats and just kicked back, with our feet on our duffle bags. (Where were our red carpet and brass band and the welcoming committee?) There we sat, periodically checking our watches. A while later, I think that we must have dozed off for a much-needed "power-nap".

Just before 1630hrs. I woke up to check the time. Damn! I woke Pat up. I went over to the airmen and, demanded that they keep calling our unit, as it was getting late. The airman advised us that they were off duty in a half hour. "Don't worry!" he added, the VNAF guys stay until 1800hrs. "Great!" I thought. In a half hour, the English-speaking airmen are off duty, leaving us under the watchful eyes of our allies who probably do not speak a lick of English and will be off duty in another hour. They will be closing the passenger terminal at that time. WONDERFUL!

The airman came over again and advised us that he got ahold of our unit and they would be sending a truck to pick us up as soon as they could. "Hell, that's what we were told a couple of hours ago!" I said to the airman, who just shrugged his shoulders and returned to his office chair. The other airman seemed to be picking up and filing paperwork. He then swept and mopped the area. The senior airman then got up and handed Pat & me two boxes of "C" rations, should we get hungry. This is really not going to be a good introduction to our new unit.

The sun was setting, and the Vietnamese airmen began their cleaning of the terminal. They smiled and nodded at us. One flashed the universal "Peace" sign as he continued to mop the floor. This was not looking good. Promptly at 1800hrs., we were politely escorted to the doors as they began shutting down the terminal. Once we were outside, they locked the doors. The shadows grew as evening was upon us and the mosquitoes were on the prowl for new blood, us. The smell of spent aviation fuel and spent diesel fuel mixed with the charcoal and kerosene smells floated in our direction and frustration. "cell Phones were not even in a thought.

We had no phone out here; no means of communication; we had no idea what kind of vehicle was headed our way and we had no idea if anybody was even going to show up. If the VC decided to attack the Combined Passenger Terminal, we had no weapons to defend ourselves. To make matters worse, we had no water. There was a water faucet on the side of the building, but we were leery about drinking it, not knowing which army purified it. We both took turns peeing on the side of the building. What a mess that we were in. There we sat waiting.

It was pretty dark by now, about 2000hrs. (8:00PM) when a rather old and noisy army ¾ Ton Weapons Carrier truck pulled up it a cloud of dust. A sergeant got out on the passenger side front seat and asked who we were and if we were replacements for the 52nd. Sig. Bn. I was tired and rather pissed off by now.

I said" Sarge, who in the hell do you think we are in American uniforms, carrying duffle bags sitting outside a locked air passenger terminal at this hour? We have been waiting for a ride since we landed at 1500hrs." "Well sorry for your wait, we had no idea that you guys were even coming today.", the sergeant said with an apologetic tone in his voice as he handed us a couple of M-16 rifles complete with 2 full magazine and a fully loaded bandolier of ammo. "Hop on board and sit on the rear seat near the tailgate, keep the weapons on "safe" for now. We have over 5 miles to go at night in 'Indian Country'. Keep your eyes open." Said the sarge in a much more serious tone. Pat looked at me with a look of complete disbelief and frustration. We waited over 5 hours for this??

With the squeal of the tires and leaving a cloud of chocking dust, we sped off towards the main gate. We stopped, and the Aps (Air Police, or "APES".) checked our vehicle. We had to show our orders. We turned out of the gate, made a right turn and headed towards Can Tho. The air was filled again with a potpourri of exotic and sickening smells. We navigated through a sea of Vespas, Hondas, pedicabs, and pedestrian traffic. On into the night we headed forward into the darkness, rifles at the ready.

CHAPTER TWENTY SIX

HOME: HHC 52nd Signal Battalion, Can Tho, RVN 1970:

Macarthur's "Misguided Children"

There we sat on the rear of the truck, one leg hanging over the tailgate, hands firmly on the M-16 and our heads on a swivel, not knowing what to expect. We finally got to a break in the local traffic and the driver shifted gears and we were speeding towards our destination. Soon we were halted by the MPs at the main gate of the Eakin Compound, aka, Can Tho Army Airfield. The dust swirled around the truck. We stood down, rendering our weapons safe. The MPs waved us through after a quick check of the truck and, of course, our orders. We had arrived safely in Can Tho. We then were driven to the orderly room of our new company. The air traffic control tower was only a few yards away. There was still air traffic that night.

CAN THO, RVN. 1970

Can Tho is the largest city in the Mekong Delta region of Vietnam. (Today's population in the Can Tho Metropolitan area is over 1 Million, plus.) Oddly enough, its sister city is Riverside California. It is also known as the "second capital", "southern capital "and "The Capital of the West". People in the area speak with Vietnam's version of a "southern accent". It is in the heart of a vast rice and agricultural area.

The Delta itself was one of the main objectives of the enemy forces during the Vietnam War (Second Indo-China War.), as this area was the "rice bowl of Vietnam". It is also a transportation hub for air, ground and water traffic. Can Tho lies on the left bank of the Hau Giang River. It is also a religious and historical center for the nation. Today it is a tourist attraction and many veterans include Can Tho and the Delta as an important part of their honor tour.

Can Tho was established first as Tran Giang in 1739. Previously it was under the Khmer (Cambodian) rule. It was later under the control of Lord Nguyen who promoted expansion and settlement. Just as it was at our arrival, the area has seen many wars and battles over its history. In 1867, the French gained its colonial control of the area. When the French left in 1954, the Americans began to become deeply involved in the new war, pitting locals and "communist" forces of the VC and NVA.

The administrative districts are:

Urban Districts:

- Binh Thuy
- Cai Rang
- Ninh Kieu
- O Mon
- Thot Not

Rural Districts:

- Co Do
- Phong Dien
- Thoi Lai
- Vin Thanh

Soon we were at the company orderly room and the CQ (Charge of Quarters) sergeant took copies of our orders and welcomed us to HHC 52nd Signal Battalion, Can Tho, RVN. The 52nd Signal Battalion is known as "MacArthur's Own" because of its noted service during World War II. Many signalmen remained in the Philippines after the retreat and joined the guerrillas to report back to Australia the Japanese troop movements and ship traffic. The battalion's motto is ***"WE TRANSMIT!"*** I could not but help to think that I was joining a very distinguished unit. Pride welled up in me upon learning those things about the 52nd.

We then signed into the unit. The CQ had his runner take us to draw our bedding and then over to the barracks. It was about 81 degrees F at this time of the night. The humidity was at about 85%.

Pat and I got lucky, in that there was an open "cube" (a makeshift room constructed of plywood and scrap lumber.) in the barracks with two open bunks. This was because the previous residents left for home, (DEROS: Date Expected Return from Overseas.)

The two of us were very tired as we temporarily stored our gear. The other troops welcomed us and over a couple of cold beers we got acquainted with small talk. We were asked what our MOSs were and were informed that we would be working in one of the two communications centers. There was one Comm. Center here on the airfield and one "downtown" Can Tho, at the IV Corps HQ Compound (Trai Lei Loi, near the soccer field and the French National Cemetery.). All seemed to be happy that these two FNGs showed up. These two FNGs were exhausted and I recall, we were both fast asleep before 2300hrs. I did not even change out of my uniform. I just took off my boots and jungle fatigue blouse and "died".

It was up early, once again and the usual barracks duties. (which were not much, since the "ma-ma sans did it all.) We were greeted by more troops as we walked to the mess hall. After a good breakfast we were ready. At the morning formation the First Sergeant called me and pat out and were told to report to the orderly room after the formation. We met the "hooch maids" and for a small fee, payable in cigarettes of PX items. For three cartons of Salem cigarettes (At the time, PX price per carton was $3.50.), I got the full service, laundry, boot shines and a spotless living space to boot. Nga, the mama-san, told me "Guarantee top sergeant be happy, all clean. Boots, uniform, all numba ONE!"

There would be more processing in both here at the airfield and up at the actual battalion headquarters in Binh Thuy. We were taken by Jeep back up to Binh Thuy and over to the HQ. There was more paperwork to complete to include a mountain of forms to fill out for our TOP SECRET, CRYPTO security clearance. We were further welcomed aboard to include greetings from the Sergeant Major. After several stops at the various administrative stations; we had plenty of time to kill before lunch. After eating lunch in Binh Thuy, (We paid a quarter, MPC for table service.) we were taken back to the airfield where there was even more in-processing to be completed, such as the postal locator, arms room, supply room and the motor pool. (Oh no, I thought, not Germany all over again.)

We learned that we both would be working right here on the airfield at the Comm. Center. I was impressed by all the air traffic, for what I thought was a small airfield. After we were all processed in we had quite a bit of time to kill before chow. All the important places were located and duly noted: The PX, the post office, the mess hall, the latrines (next to our barracks), the pizza stand (in Vietnam?), the ice cream stand (in Vietnam?) but most important of all was the EM club.

We met many who worked the night shift. I learned that we would work 12 hours on and 12 hours off, not including guard duty which was about every 5 days or so. The guard got ½ a shift off and then worked the second half of his shift. On pay day the shifts reversed, the day became the night and visa-versa. This usually translated to a 48 hour "jet lag" of sorts as well as a time to party.

As much as possible, we might be allotted one day off a week, but this was not always possible, depending on troop strength and the work load. The messages must go through! After dinner we were invited by several guys to go over to the EM club. I surely not about to turn down the invite in spite of a dwindling cash flow. We went over to the club and those first cold beers just slid down.

The next morning, Pat and myself were taken over to the Comm Center by our fellow signalmen who worked in the facility. We were told to wait outside the door. Entrance to the facility was done by an electronic key-pad locking mechanism. We were informed that the Comm. Center NCOIC (Non-Commissioned Officer In Charge) would have to sign us in daily until we got either an interim Top-Secret Clearance or the actual Top-Secret Clearance itself, which would take a month or less., SSG Chasse, is still a friend in contact, Facebook, 2019.

Our NCOIC came out, greeted us, and welcomed is to the Can Tho Army Airfield's Communications. Center. As required, he signed us in and gave us the "nickel tour". The place was quite noisy as many teletypes were pounding out their messages, as other messages were being "poked" on off-line machines. That is, the originating messages were being prepared by the teletype and tape punching machine and reader. There was a lot of activity this early in the morning. He showed us the maintenance shop, which was in the back of the Comm. Center separate from the main floor. He then turned us over to the SP5 (Specialist 5th Class), who was the maintenance chief who was in charge of the repairmen for the two Comm. Centers.

In the back room there were the stacks of the KW-7 crypto machines (tactical) and the two KW-26 crypto machines (fixed station). There was a small patch panel, where the equipment and circuits were routed or could be re-routed to other lines. (If I recalled there were 10 separate dedicated teletype circuits.) There was a sturdy Federal safe, where the codes, data cards for the KW-26s, and the classified "KAGS" (maintenance manuals for the crypto equipment).

There was a long work bench that had a KW-7 and a teletype machine set up in a mock circuit, where the repairman could insert equipment to be tested. There were hand tools, test meters and an oscilloscope. There was a couple of teletype-repair tool boxes available and in use.

There was a small book shelf that had the technical manuals for all the non-classified equipment. It seemed that when we were not working directly on a piece of classified gear, there was always a teletype to be repaired. It was also noted that on a regular basis, the teletype machines would be taken out of service for routine cleaning and preventative maintenance.

Overall, I was impressed at how thorough the Comm. Center was manned, equipped and run. Over on one side was the "ways and means" clerk's desk and chart board. His job was to statistically monitor the speed and accuracy of the message handling time. It was also noted on how long it took outside units to pick up their messages. There were a couple of circuits that had an automatic tape reader that would check the "header" (routing instructions) for accuracy. If it was not letter perfect, the tape would stop and not be transmitted until the corrections were made. This process then created what was known as the "reject rate". This data was also part of the ways and means clerk's duties. The service clerk would prepare and send "service messages" to the distant stations to advise that they needed to re-send a message that might have been received "garbled" (unreadable) or any corrections to messages. The message preparation section would actually prepare the messages by teletype & tape for transmission and file copy.

The log clerk would document the time that an originating message was delivered to the Comm. Center for preparation ("poking", off line.) and transmission. He would also track inbound messages from time of receipt to time of delivery to the addressee unit. There also was a pigeon-hole mail slot cabinet where all the local units had their own "mail box".

In the far corner of the Comm. Center, there was a weapons rack which held our M-16s, M-79s and M-1911 .45 Ca. pistols A locked foot locker kept the ammunition and thermite grenades, should we have to destroy the classified machines and documents in case a ground attack forced the abandonment of the Comm. Center. (Frightening thought; coupled with the urban legend that the teletype operators would kill all the crypto men in such a situation, so we would not fall into enemy hands and tortured for the "top secret" information and disclose how our crypto gear worked.)

Next to the weapons rack, the NCOIC of the Courier Section had his desk. He oversaw the dispatching of the couriers, both motor / ground and the Special Air Couriers. There were about six men assigned to these duties. Two routine air missions were run daily around the various Delta sites. One ran "clockwise" around the delta and the other ran in the "counter-clockwise" direction. In this manner, every site got at least two courier deliveries a day. Any special deliveries were made as needed or dependent on the high priority or for a special for "eyes-only" document. The guy in charge of this section was some young be-spectacled "buck sergeant". He was good at what he did. I forget his name today. (I did not know it at this time, but I also would become a Special Air Courier myself in the future.)

There was an M-35 ¾ ton truck assigned to the Comm. Center. This truck was used daily to transport the crew to the downtown site and pick up the crew relieved of the daily duty at the Can Tho Comm. Center. It was also used to transport equipment to and from the Comm. Centers. We would be responsible for the operator's maintenance on the truck.

We later met the warrant officer, CW-3 Jacques, who was the crypto officer and OIC (officer -in- charge) of the Comm. Center. His office was just outside the Comm. Center door. He gave us the basic overall picture of the operation and really emphasized the fact that a couple of the circuits had a high priority and had a 15-minute restoration time. That meant that we had to fix the problem or get the system re-routed. We had to maintain an accurate log on each circuit and document all that was being done to restore communications. This was known as the "outage report" which would be reported to BATCON (Battalion Control) and up to SYSCON (System Control). Eventually these reports would end up at the HQ 1st Signal Brigade and beyond to USAPAC (US Army Pacific). Somewhere after those 15 minutes, colonels were getting concerned and / or out of bed when these systems went down.

We would also be responsible for the twice daily changing of the codes on the "patch-block" on the KW-7s and the card-code reader on the KW-26s. This process was known as "HJ" time, the changing of the codes. It was important that these be done correctly in order that the two crypto machines could be in sync and timed to each other for accurate communications.

Soon we were answering trouble calls from the comm center floor. It was usually minor things like checking the motor speeds of the teletypes with the 60CPS tuning fork. Other times it was a blown fuse or something simple.

When not actually on the floor, there was always the equipment on the test bench to check out. We always kept a back-up teletype and a KW-7 on hand, ready to go or to replace in a moment's notice out on the floor. We kept all in good working order. It was also a good idea to have the KW-7 code blocks coded to the next code period or "radio-day" (HJ hour). We checked each other's work just to make sure the codes were set right.

Overall, the first day went very well, no major circuit outages occurred on our watch. We got to meet all the teletype operators, (MOS 72B20, or "tape apes".) The maintenance section was well manned that day. We would spend the next week up here at this Comm. Center for a thorough orientation. The next week we would spend some time "downtown" at the IV Corps Can Tho Comm. Center. in the Trai Lei Loi Compound. This was located in the An Phu area of Can Tho. The various sergeants and officers were watching as to how good we were. Me & pat were "Aces",

The next day we visited the "downtown" facility which was on a joint US & Vietnamese compound of the IV Corps HQ. It was also about a 5-mile motor trip from the airfield. The actual Comm. Center was much smaller and cramped. The maintenance section was housed in about a typical office "cubicle" sized area in the back of the center. The overall operation of the "center" was identical to that at the airfield, only smaller and with less circuits, but very important, very high priority in nature. Some of these circuits were tactical.

One of the memories of the Trai Le Loi Comm. Center was the lizards. Now, these were not your "run of the mill" reptiles. These were the *"Fuck You ! Lizards"*. They were named as such because at night and in the "wee" hours of the morning these lizards would get on the metal roof of the Comm. Center and warm their cold-blooded bodies from the heat rising off of the warm metal. The horny males would inflate a pouch on the front of their neck (quite colorful) and with the expelling air try to woo a female with a very distinctive sound that sounded as if they were saying < *F...U...C...K ----Y...O...U !*>.

JANAP-128 Format:

All messages were prepared according to the JANAP-128 publication for military teletype traffic. The format differed from the civilian versions.

EXAMPLE:

JANAP-128 Format Element	Message Contents	End of Line Functions (EOL)
Header:	RTTUZYUW RUEBABA 1081400-UUUU- RUKKLAA	(2CR, 1LF)
Transmission Instructions:	ZNR UUUUU	(2CR,1LF)
Precedence; Date-time Group; message instructions:	R 181230Z APR 81	(2CR,LF)

Originator:	FM AFSC ANDREWS AFB MD	(2CR, LF)
Action Addressee(s)	TO ELMENDORF AFB ALASKA	(2CR,1LF)
Separation:	BT	(2CR,1LF)
Classification:	UNCLAS (TEXT)	(2CR,1LF)
	1. This is a test of this teletype circuit.	(2CR,1LF)
	2. Respond NLT 0800Z 19 APR 81	(2CR,1LF)
Separation:	BT	
EOM (validation number)	#1234	(2CR,1LF)
End of message Functions:	(2CR,8LF) NNNN	(12 LTRS)

The message would appear as follows:

RTTUZYUW RUEBABA1234
1081400-UUUU-RUKKLAA
ZRR UUUU
R 181230Z APR 81
FM AFSC ANDREWS AFB MD
TO ELMENDORF AFB ALASKA
BT
UNCLAS
   1.   This is a test of this teletype circuit.
   2.   Respond NLT 0800Z 19 APR 81.

BTT
#1234
NNNN

1. NOTES: Every military unit, government agency, and government contractor have its own routing indicator: RUEBABA, RUKKLAA. **Thousands of addresses.** We had a "New York Phone book for all of these governmental / contractor addresses.
2. Transmission & Receipt times are in "Zulu" Time (Greenwich Mean Time).
3. Classifications go from Unclassified, For Official Use Only, Confidential, Secret, Top Secret, (Above Top Secret)
4. EOL: functions are typed to avoid line run-ons.
5. BTT: (Back To Traffic)
6. Validation Number: Originating station log number.
7. NNNN: (Nothing follows)
8. 12 Letter functions: Insures that receiving teletype is ready in the letter case for next message.

When all was running fine and there was no equipment to work on, many maintenance men would begin to learn JANAP-128 and would learn how to process and prepare messages when time and priority were not critical. (At the time I did not know it, but years later when I was in the Army Reserve, I actually became the Comm. Center NCOIC, 72B30 / 72E30.)

GUARD DUTY, CAN THO ARMY AIRFIELD

After a couple of weeks of regular duty, I was up for guard duty. I was working at the airfield and overall there were no major problems with the communications, and we got a lot accomplished on the maintenance back-log and readied quite a lot of gear to be ready to go back on line. I even got a chance to "poke" up a couple of messages off line.

I was released from the comm center duty a bit early to get ready for guard mount. I ate early and later drew my weapon and stood guard mount. I was very surprised when we were briefed on the "rules of engagement" for our sector of the airfield perimeter. It went something like this:

- Always report to the TOC any unusual incidents. One man is to be awake and aware at all times.

- Never fire unless permission was granted from the TOC, sergeant or officer of the guard.
- The first position was on the main road and was armed with an M-60 machine gun. "Do not fire unless your section is being breeched. There are Vietnamese civilians living on the other side of the road and you may kill a lot of innocents." (Huh?)
- The next position, a guard tower & bunker position which overlooked a Vietnamese national cemetery. We were advised that often families would remain grave side after sun down, when they are supposed to leave the cemetery. Many do not. "Contact the TOC and they will notify the Vietnamese MPs to escort the families out of the cemetery. Fire only with permission or to defend yourself immediately." (The enemy would often hold the family hostage and use their cover to launch RPGs onto the airfield or fire harassing fire our way.) (WTF?)
- The next position was also a tower / bunker position and it overlooked the fenced and barbwire encircled compound. It was the "Choi-Hoi" prisoner camp. "These are the enemy who surrendered peacefully (??) and now are being re-educated and are willing to help our cause and either fight on our side or become 'Kit Carson Scouts'. (These "Scouts" were to lead our forces to their camps or trails.) Do not shoot them. Try to halt them and contact the TOC. Let the Vietnamese MPs re-capture them. (This is getting weird.)
- The third position also consisted of a tower / bunker configuration. It overlooked the "hard-core" POW camp. (The purple pajamas.) "These guys are the really bad-asses of the enemy. Contact the TOC should you see an escape attempt. Try to halt them, and only shoot to defend yourself. Let the Vietnamese re-capture them," (Do not shoot the 'bad-asses'?)
- The last position faced one side of the airfield. This was a "free-fire". That meant any activity out there after sun-down were fair targets. "Contact the TOC before opening fire. Remember that 'way over there' is the Michelin Rubber Company's rubber plantation. It was overseen by a Frenchman. We have to pay for all damaged rubber trees." (Now, I thought: kill the enemy, save the rubber trees?)

Now that was really confusing, but in later years it seemed to me to sum up the whole controversy over the war. Killing for peace is like fucking for chastity. So, there we were.

We loaded our weapons and boxes of ammo onto the truck. Each position was manned by two soldiers. Upon arriving at our position, we unloaded our ammo boxes and weapons, to include the M-60 machine gun. One troop climbed up the ladder from the bunker to the tower. At the top was a rope and pully set-up which was used to haul up the ammo and M-60. It was quite a bit of work hauling everything up to the tower. When done, we sat back and watched the sunset and the approach of darkness. I recalled what I was told at Ben Cat about the darkness and the night.

The tower was wood-framed it had a metal roof, a shelf for the M-60, sandbags all around, and a heavy steel plate to cover the trap door into the tower. This plate was to cover the hatch and protect the machine gunner from being shot from the bunker as he stood on the plate. Most of the time we just left the steel plate off. That way we could hear and see the sergeant of the guard climbing up the ladder to check on us.

From the height of the tower, we could see the village, the road, the cemetery, the two POW camps, all the barracks, buildings on the base, and the airfield runway. Off in the distance we could see the lumination rounds light up one side of the river from an ARVIN fire-base. We really had a 360-degree fields of fire. From time to time, we would be able to see the various aircraft take off or land on their night missions from our airfield. There always seemed to be air traffic during the night.

The lower bunker was constructed of sand-filled 55-gallon drums surrounded with sand bags. There were gun ports on three sides. The front gun port took up most of the front giving the sentries a 180-degree field of fire. The door was directly to the rear. Overall it was quite a rugged construction, a lot safer that a grunt's fox hole.

Most of the time guard duty was uneventful and rather boring. The bugs seldom gave us any peace, as they enjoyed their cocktails made from our sweat and army-issued bug repellant. We would sometimes sneak a few beers up in the ammo cans and a transistor radio, kept at a low volume and hidden, for our entertainment. It helped us pass the hours and helped to keep us awake. The arrival of the sergeant of the guard always meant a quick inspection and hot coffee.

Over the course of many months, there were a few incidents that broke up the routine and monotony of guard duty. A few times we took some harassing fire, that only kept us on high alert all the rest of the night. On another occasion, a single RPG exploded near our position throwing a lot of mud our way and I caught a couple of hot metal shrapnel fragments on my arm. (My battle scars. !)

One night, we got a call from the TOC that there was a POW on the loose. The TOC could not advise if he was a Choi-Hoi or a bas-ass, purple pajamas. We were ordered to send one man down to check our line, the wire and our surroundings.

I lost the coin toss, loaded my weapon, fixed my bayonet and climbed down to investigate the situation. To say that I was not scared would be a big lie. I poked about and even held my rifle and bayonet at the ready position and made a few jabs, just to make sure nobody was in the grass or the dark out in front of me. I carried out my instructions very cautiously and rather nervously. When our sector was clear, I returned to the tower and reported that we were all clear at our position. (What a relief.)

Before we were off duty, the First Sergeant stopped by and surveyed our section. He commented that "Charlie" must have stopped by and had a couple of beers. Pat and I looked at each other, expecting the worst. "Top" found two empty beer cans in the drainage ditch. I thought that we were in "deep Kim chi" (trouble). Drinking on duty could wind up in a court martial and a stay at LBJ (Ling Binh Jail, the stockade for Vietnam). He seemed OK, and did not say any more, other that "…police up those empties.". I volunteered to go retrieve the offending cans in the muck and mud. That was my second big relief for the day.

MY VIETNAM TOUR CONTINUES:

I celebrated my 19th birthday there in Can Tho at the EM club the day after Thanksgiving. (Now known as "Black Friday" for retail sales.) All the troops enjoyed the traditional turkey dinner & all trimmings the day before. A hot meal in Vietnam was a slice of Heaven, after so many "C" Rat meals. Those army cooks were in their finest hour. I would not have guard duty for a while, as more replacements had arrived.

By this time, I had pretty much had gotten used to the routine and often would be taken downtown to the "other" Comm. Center. At the first of December, on pay-day, we rotated and became the night shift. That took some getting used to and was different. The good point of working the night shift was there was a whole lot less teletype traffic and usually fewer "trouble calls". But at night should a circuit go down, all hell would break loose because it was thought that we were most at risk of attack at night and the tactical circuits had to be maintained at all costs.

Sometimes we would receive a telephone call that a given circuit was down or one of the "tape apes" would run in to tell us. There could be "negative contact" at the distant end, messages were coming in garbled and unreadable, too many errors and many other problems. Troubles were checked quickly for the obvious. The protocol was for us to put the circuit in a "loop-back", that is at the patch panel, we would send a test tape to ourselves. Should that be bad, the problem was "in house". We would then locate the problem or switch the equipment to an alternative routing. The next step was to trouble shoot the system by having a "loop-back" put on the circuit at our "patch", or the local cable control. Then we would have our multi-channel radiomen check our signal to see its quality and if it is being transmitted ok. These tests would go in reverse at the distant end.

At each step in this communication we could know where exactly the problem is. The distant end would then do the same. The problem would be isolated, and the correct steps would be taken to restore communication. Sometimes this process would take a long time, other times it could be written off as "operator head space". (operator error). We were always under the pressure of the 15-minute rule.

Afterwards an "outage report" would be prepared, detailing each step that was done to fix the problem. Once the communication was restored, the original problem could be tracked down and corrected. The challenge was not to make one's own station look bad, if the circuit outage was at our end.

I once had an outage on a circuit at the airfield that was actually due to a Sigma relay which was on the line side before the signal left the station. We were able to adjust the relays on a tester, but in this case the wiring at the panel was bad. The outage lasted over 48 hours at I remained on duty trying to resolve the issue. It was finally corrected by having a government contractor remove and re-wire the panel. This resulted in many other systems being re-evaluated and / or re-wired.

Time passed by ever so slowly, as we checked each day off of our "short-timer's calendar". Big events on many days was mail call bringing letters or packages from home. There was such a mixture, boredom and sheer adrenalin overload. There was always the diversion downtown in Ben Xe Moi (the bus stop). Can Tho's Vietnamese bar and "red-light district.

THE BURN PIT:

Near the end of each Comm. Center shift, all undistributed paper (except file copies) had to be burned. This included: notes, mis-typed drafts, garbled messages, documents that had come due for destruction, and any other waste paper, to include idle "doodling". At the Eakin Compound, the area was between the Comm Center and the Army Veterinary Medicine Detachment's building. It was an open area about the size of a basketball court.

There were two 55-gallon drums which were cut in half and hinged so they could be easily opened. There was a latch slide to secure the two halves when the drum was rotated on a spit mechanism. On the upper half, a small door was also cut and hinged with a latch mechanism also to allow the entire assembly to be rotated. They sat on their own cement pad.

Each "burn barrel" was equipped with its own set of accessories: a rake, a long fireplace poker, a fire extinguisher (Just in case the burn got out of hand.), a push-broom and a pair of welding gloves to allow the "burn-master" to handle the drum when its red-hot. There was a regular garden hose nearby. There also was another open area before the first strands of barbed concertina wire. Out of this area a pit was dug to receive the ashes once they were completely burned. After the "ashes were scattered" they were watered down to prevent and ashes or scraps from escaping. (It was a direct order that all paper surfaces were to be completely burned and the ashes stirred up so not a single scrap could be re-constructed by the enemy.) The "burn pit" at the "downtown" Comm. Center was similar, excluding the running water and the concrete pads. The "burn barrels were all the same for both centers.

The routine was the same each shift. The waste paper would be taken out in secure courier bags. The total to be burned could fill two regulation duffel bags, plus or minus, depending on the shift's traffic volume. Two men were on this detail. One man was an armed guard with an M-16 Rifle and a magazine of ammo. The armed guard provided security and was there just in case the enemy wanted to steal our scrap paper. (There could be data of an intelligence asset before its destruction.

It was not a bad detail when one was on the night shift because it was a lot cooler at night. During the day, on the other hand, it was a real bitch during the heat of the tropical day. But, in both cases in was a relief from the fast pace in the Comm. Center, besides it was a hell of a lot better than the popular "Shit Burning Detail".

One night, I got this detail, strapped on my .45 M-1911 pistol and went out with the mail bags and my armed guard. This young man was rather large and had played football in high school. He was a "good-old boy" from somewhere on the ridges or down in the "hollers" of the Appalachian Mountains. He was just a simple farm boy stuck in this war with me.

As usual, I filled the barrels to the max, douched them with gasoline, threw in the match and jumped back", *and with a "Whoosh",* both barrels were ablaze. We settled back for the burn; I was periodically adding more paper or stoking the flames. We would be out here for a while, so my buddy, "Bubba" took off his steel pot and leaned back against a wood and wire chain link cage, just a way from the Vet hut. He lit a cigarette and we continued the small talk, as I kept the trash ablaze. Soon, I let the flames die down and re-loaded the barrels. All was quiet, except for the drone of the insects and frogs. An occasional aircraft flew over us. It was a peaceful, starlit night. There was not very much moonlight.

After a while of silence out of nowhere, the night was pierced by a sound that I had never heard before. It did not quite make it to a yell or a scream but sounded like a gurgled: "…AH. AH,OOOO HA, HA,…. OOOO, ah…shit…". Was Sasquatch here in Vietnam? I looked over at a trembling "Bubba", he just was waving his left hand at me, as he dropped his weapon (,,,a Cardinal sin in the military.) He was as pale as a ghost for a weathered farm boy. His lips were moving, but no words were being emitted, just guttural sounds and moans. I noticed that he must have wet his pants. I unholstered my .45 M-1911 pistol and slowly approached him. I was in shock at what I saw.

There on his right shoulder was a small black withered hand, firmly clutching this terrified farm boy on. "Bubba" was still shaking. I lowered my pistol and began to laugh at the sight in front of me. One of the monkeys then began to laugh and howl along with me. My poor friend thought for sure that the VC had him and was about to slit his throat. The monkey released his death grip and bounded up in the cage to his perch.

My poor friend was mortified, embarrassed and was still shaking from fear. I gave him time to calm down as I reloaded the burn barrels. He nervously smoked a cigarette. We were almost done by now. After he calmed down and was able to speak coherently, "Bubba" made me swear not to tell a soul about what just had happened. I had to both laugh and agree to his plea. I kept my promises for a few years after leaving "the Nam". We finished our job on time. A few dying embers in the pit winked back at us.

BEN XE MOI

(The New Bus Stop)

Ben Xe Moi was the local bar and "red-light" district. An army of Pedi-cycles and small motorized "rickshaws" always waited outside of the airfield's compound gates for customers needing a ride "downtown". Prostitution was legal but there were always risks to be aware of. Back then, AIDS was not heard of, so the only sexual problems could be too much booze or a variety of STDs (sexually transmitted diseases).

There were also the two most frightening 'urban legends": the "black syphilis", where the victim would spend the rest of his life on an isolated island, never being allowed to return to the States, because there was no known cure for the "black syph", and the hookers who inserted razor blades into their vaginas to slice up an unsuspecting penis. There was always the risk of bodily harm or death, should the VC be in town on any given evening or a GI partaking in an (unauthorized) overnight "sleep-over" with a hooker.(A couple of GIs were brutally murdered and dismembered in previous years during Tet (the lunar new year) when they remained in town. Their "girlfriend" was savagely beaten or killed in a most grotesque manner.

319

We were cautioned to be aware of the "cowboys", young teens or kids who would slit a GI's pocket with a razor blade and take his money or wallet or simply outnumber a lone GI, overpower him and roll him. Further warnings were not to lose one's money to the bar-girls who would show a GI a lot of affection and attention in exchange for the GI buying over-priced "Saigon Tea". It was also warned not to over-pay the hookers for their services. That also applied to the girls who worked in the "steam & creams". *"Never go to Ben Xe Moi alone, always use the 'buddy system"!*

I must admit that I have taken my pleasures there. It was always a treat for me seeing these young and beautiful Asian girls. Their jet-black hair, petite build and small boobs drove me nuts. I preferred that they did not dye their hair blond or use too much make-up. Let their natural beauty stand by itself. I have always had a propensity for Oriental women and women with Latin or darker features. Since I grew up in such diversified neighborhoods in San Francisco, I was naturally attracted to these girls. The Vietnamese bar girls and hookers all tried to be up to date with "hip" fashion and speech. It seemed to me that the current trends "back in the world" suffered a time-lag in foreign countries. That is to say, American pop culture that was already obsolete in the states was the rage overseas. Even the local bands were mostly behind the times as far as the top 40 was concerned.

Usually a group of us would head downtown, around pay day. The routine was just about the same each time. Sometimes it would be a trip to the local "steam & creams" and finish up with a blow-job and / or sex right there in the "massage studio". For a few dollars more, we could get a private room. We would venture through a few bars, drinking beer and girl watching. Should one of us want to go "upstairs" with a young girl; the rest of us would remain in the bar as "security". When he was done, either another of us took a girl upstairs as well. If not, we would head out to find the next bar and "girlfriend".

In this district there were many shops, to include a custom tailor shop (Everybody had bought a fine suit made there and hand stitched.) One could buy just about anything one could imagine, for a price. There a black market flourished, where PX items, to include small appliances could be sold or exchanged for "other services". We would often use cigarette cartons in exchange for quick cash or "favors". (I once spent most of a weekend with a young lady for a carton of Salem cigarettes and a stick of deodorant. She bought the beer !).

There were the Indian money changers who ran a thriving business. We could exchange the GI MPC (Military Payment Script) for Vietnamese piasters at a higher rate that the American Express desk on post. They would also exchange American "greenbacks" for either MPC or the piasters at a rate of 2 to 1 ! For example, $5.00 greenbacks would fetch $10.00 MPC. This practice was highly illegal and could be punished under the UCMJ. (Uniform Code of Military Justice). I learned later that the American legal tender would eventually find its way onto the world monetary market where the enemy could buy arms. It was used sparingly by this soldier only as a means of getting rid of Christmas or birthday cash sent from the States since it was also illegal even to have greenbacks in one's possession. They had to be exchanged at the American Express desk at the PX.

There was thriving drug trade in Ben Xe Moi that was actually controlled by the VC. It was learned later that the powerful local marijuana was deliberately laced with heroine, China White, over 95% pure. It was called "skag" and was sold in a small glass vial. It was either snorted, smoked or "shot-up" with a needle. Many GIs who only smoked weed came home with a drug habit. Ironically the best place to get weed and smoke was in the apartments next to the American Military Police apartment and station. Many people involved were American civilian contractors such as Air America (the CIA's 'air force" and drug "mule") and the various Pacific Architects & Engineers (PA & E) contractors.

Many of the units had "their" bar and although we patronized many bars, some bars were almost exclusively frequented by a given unit or military branch, (army, navy or air force). Every once in a while there would be intra-service brawls that the MPs would have to intervene. "Our bar", The Snoopy Bar was owned by a Vietnamese signal warrant officer, that we knew and his wife. It was such a good relationship that the owners extended us a limited line of credit to be paid promptly on pay day. Once, when a group of South Vietnamese soldiers took over the bar and gave us a bad time, the "brawl royal" was on. The joint patrol of US & Vietnamese MPs had to break up the fight. Luckily, none of us were arrested. We helped to pay for some of the damages. That warrant officer partied with us before TET sharing with us his "Tiger Bone Wine", a rice gin. (Just as powerful as Tequila.)

It is now that I look back at these events and people that I feel a bit nostalgic and wonder how these events played themselves out over the years. I must confess that on my many adventures down in Ben Xe Moi, I took a fancy to an "older" woman in the bar, or perhaps she took her fancy to me, in that she must have heard me trying to speak French to the bar staff. Her name was Mai.

She was well built and quite attractive to me, considering that she was well into her forties at the time. Mai had been educated by the French and studied in Paris before the exodus of the French colonists after Dien Bien Phu in 1954.

Although I never took her upstairs for sex, we managed to make out quite well between "Saigon Teas". What stuck with me in her was that she was a master linguist of the French language and loved to hear me butcher the language, which allowed her to be constantly correcting me. Her husband who was an ARVIN officer, had been killed a couple of years earlier. Because her command of the French language was no longer in demand, economics forced her into the bars to support her family. It was not love, but it grew into a strong attraction.

It goes to say, that many a young GI lost his "cherry" and perhaps compromised some of his morals and gave up a lot of money and innocence in Ben Xe Moi.

CHAPTER TWENTY SEVEN

CONVOY DUTY:

Being *"Young and dumb, and full of cum"*, and *"ten feet tall and bullet-proof"*, I volunteered one morning at formation when the First Sergeant called for volunteers for *"... a little road-trip up to Saigon"*. That sounded like fun, so I said yes. The mission was to take a lot of equipment which needed major repair work up to Long Binh depot and return with lumber, teletype paper and tape, and a lot of other supplies needed by the battalion. It sounded like a lot of fun. Besides it would provide a needed break from the routine here in Can Tho.

The First Sergeant took my name down and thanked me and all of the other "volunteers" for doing so. We would be ready to roll out the next morning. All the sections affected then modified their work schedules to make up for those leaving on this convoy. All together there would be about 25 troops on the convoy and 10 vehicles.

The break-down of the convoy would be as follows:

1. Commander's Jeep, w/radio: driver, assistant driver / radio operator and the convoy commander.
2. Six 2 ½ Ton 6x6 cargo trucks, driver, assistant driver, security man riding in the rear.
3. One 5 Ton wrecker, Driver and assistant driver. (recovery crew, mechanics both).

4. Rear "chase" Jeep w/radio / as rear guard, driver and assistant driver / radio operator.

Armament:

- Convoy Commander: .45 Cal M-1911 Semi-Automatic Pistol.
- All Drivers, assistant drivers, truck security man, wrecker crew: M-16 Automatic Rifles.
- The truck security men also carried an M-79 40mm. Grenade Launcher (Thumper)
- The two #3 & #4 Cargo Trucks carried an M-60 Machine Gun each.
- The "chase" / rear guard Jeep also had an additional M-79.
- There were plenty of ammunition boxes loaded for each vehicle.
- Every man was also issued a heavy and bulky "flak jacket" (It was constructed of four heavy steel plates, laced on the sides and fastened in the front. Most troops on convoy, usually either sat on it or stood on it for protection from land mines.)

NEEDLESS-TO-SAY: We were well-armed and prepared to fight to protect the convoy.

After a good army breakfast, the convoy was assembled, all operator maintenance was performed on each vehicle and additional fuel cans were loaded on each vehicle. All the weapons and ammunition were checked and re-checked. The radios were checked and a "radio-check" was performed. Commo was 5x5 (perfect). All the returning equipment was loaded onto the trucks to be turned in for depot maintenance in Long Binh. We were issued 2 boxes of "C" Rations each. We were ready, waiting the order to "move out".

At the given hour of departure, 10 military vehicles of the 52nd Signal Battalion roared out of the main gate of Eakin Compound and headed north towards Saigon. We left in a cloud of diesel exhaust and delta dust. The MPs and the locals waved us on.

It was early in the morning. The sun was up, and it already was getting hot. We would basically take Highway 1 north, passing through Vinh

Long, My Tho, Long Xuyen, Tan An, and passing on through Saigon and then on to Long Binh. We had to cross the river by navy barge at Long Xuyen. It was roughly 105 miles from Long Xuyen to Saigon

To our horror, crazy scooter drivers darted in and out of our convoy, often cutting in between our trucks. The driver laid on the horn with no avail. "These people are crazy!" I said out loud. All the familiar, yet foreign smells were accented as the temperature climbed ever so much higher.

The locals either ignored us or waved to us with the "peace-sign", or was it the "bird"? People were everywhere going about their business. I wondered if their "business" was killing Americans. My head was on a continual swivel, taking in all the sights and sounds and being constantly reminded that we were in *their* country. I kept reminding myself why we were there in the first place. (I also began to question my "gung-ho" streak in volunteering this time.)

The convoy was halted near Long Xyuen and we queued up in line for the large "ferry", an old Navy flat motorized barge. A couple of US sailors operated the large cargo barge. This was because "Charlie" has managed to blow up every single bridge that the US and the ARVN Engineers had built across the river. We could still see the rusting skeletons of the bridges and all the twisted steel girders. There were guard shacks on either side manned by both ARVNS and American MPs. While we were waiting, I saw a Navy PBR (Patrol Boat, River) speed by, maneuvering around the anti-mine barriers placed in the river to prevent any mines or explosives from being floated towards the bridge sites. (They never worked in the past; "Charlie" merely took the land route and blew up the bridge.)

Since tactical convoys had priority, we had quite a long wait for our turn in crossing the river. Meanwhile scores of children swarmed the convoy, begging for food, money or cigarettes.

My truck driver looked up at me from the cab and said, "Hey, watch this!" He took a single can of our rations and heaved it a long way, away from the trucks. The children scampered in-mass to retrieve the cherished can of, whatever. This game was repeated by several of the troops all up and down the row of trucks, gaining a rather sick sense of humor by refusing to give the kids a can opener. (I was amused, but also knew that those cans of rations would be opened by any means and enjoyed at some point in the future.)

After the mob of kids seemed to be satisfied, or bored with our game, they merely fell back in the shade and sat down to watch us or continue their games with each other. A while later a few young women (girls) approached the trucks and with sheepish grins, bared their tiny tits and announced: "Boo-Coo numba one 'boom-boom'. Luv GI long time ! ". (THE BEST FUCK, I CAN FUCK FOR A LONG TIME) Yes, the sex trade seemed to follow us GIs everywhere. We had to decline for a couple of reasons: #1. We did not know when we would proceed and # 2. Sex was often used as a diversion to allow another person to mine or booby-trap the vehicle or bunker. We had to keep yelling and waving our rifles saying to the ebb and flow of the crowd: "DEE-DEE MAU !" (leave).

There we sat feeling like sitting ducks. It got rather quiet and I could see parts of the river as it snaked around our location. The quiet was broken be a strange noise that to my ears, did not belong in a combat zone at all. I told the driver and assistant driver of the sound. They both stood up on the truck's bench seat for a better look. We all could see a good stretch of the river. That sound grew louder and closer. I said, "Damn, that sounds like a dragster !" All of us could not believe our ears. The two seemed to agree with me. The driver said, "Shit, that sounds like a Chrysler Blown Hemi Engine for sure. In a blink of an eye, on the river, appeared, moving at a crazy speed was a custom "drag" ski boat, shining and sparkling in the tropical sun, sporting a red candy-apple metal flake custom paint job. It had a huge "blown" racing engine. ("Hemi" or not, we could not really tell at our distance. It still sounded beautiful.) Behind that ski boat were two half naked Vietnamese girls **water skiing**! They moved at a dizzying speed. Aboard the boat were several men and women, just partying away as if it was New Year's Eve, 1999. We could not believe our senses at this surreal display. The boat and "crew" turned and disappeared around the bend in the river. MAN ! I've seen it all.

We later learned that these were highly paid American government contractors and Air America pilots, who by the appearance of things were making 'way too much money' at our taxpayer's expense in the middle of a damn war, no less. We all shook our heads, shrugged our shoulders and continued to wait for our order to "move out". "What a strange war, 'Master Jack'.", I thought to myself.

Soon, the diesel engines roared back into life and we were moving forward to be loaded onto the navy barge. A sailor directed each truck to its allotted space on the deck of the barge. When the barge was fully loaded, we braced for "take-off". With a huge cloud of black, stinking, exhaust soot and smoke, the marine engines burst into life. Slowly we moved forward, crossing the river. One American MP came by and advised us to be watchful of anything floating towards us in the water. That put the adrenalin on fast flow and our heads on a swivel. The heavy-ladened barge slowly inched towards the far river bank. The river gently rocked the barge with a soothing rhythm.

Finally, after what seemed like the good part of an hour, we were at the distant bank and our convoy was being off-loaded from the barge, and on to dry land once again. Onward we moved, Saigon bound.

After a while, the driver looked up at me and told me to be on the alert, as we were in "Indian Country", hostile areas. (That was re-assuring.) A couple of choppers flew by us and they both dipped their skids in salute to us. I waved back in acknowledgement.

A few military vehicles, both American and Vietnamese, passed us in the opposite direction, headed south, moving at a high rate of speed. We exchanged hand signs and salutes. After a while on the road I seemed to become electrified and alert. My gut told me that there was something up ahead going on.

After a few miles up the road, a MP Jeep was parked on the road, partially blocking our lane. We slowed down to a crawl. The young MP halted the convoy and told us to dismount, and take up a defensive stance around the convoy, leaving the drivers behind the wheel, engines still idling.

The Convoy Commander, a young SFC (Sergeant First-Class, E-7) came down the line directing the troops to various positions on both sides of the road defensively. I had seen this guy before up at our battalion headquarters, he was one of the personnel "clerks". We complied, but still wondered what was going on.

Out of nowhere, a gun truck (A heavily armored and converted "deuce and ½" cargo truck, sporting a "mini-gun". The "mini-gun" was the primary armament of the Cobra Gun-Ship. The gun-truck was painted black and sported in flaming yellow custom letters on the side armor plate which protected the cargo / gun bay. *GUN RUNNER*. That announced to the world in that bold yellow paint, *"…we mean business"*. That mean machine came racing up the road traveling at a lightning speed in the empty oncoming lane. He stopped a few hundred yards up the road from us and pulled off the road. He took up his firing position.

Soon we could see his awesome volume of fire, as his mini-gun "whirred" and spit out its message of death and destruction. This massive display of fire was met by the choppers who also were joining in on the fire-fight. The fire was so massive, the recoil actually rocked the heavy truck off to its side, leaning but not tipping over. I was really impressed and seemed relieved when all the commotion suddenly stopped. A little while later we were ordered to remount and slowly the trucks moved forward.

As we passed the gun-truck, I could still see wisps of gun smoke surrounding that "death truck". We waved to the crew and noticed a huge pile of the spent brass casings from the mini-gun's massive fire. The choppers soon departed and went on to other battles. I was glad to have these guys on our side and could not but help to wonder how any living thing could survive such a display of sheer firepower.

Off in the distance across huge open fields of rice paddies, the edge of the jungle seemed to be smoking, perhaps 500+ yards out. We were about at the half-way point of our trip. So far, it has been interesting, to say the least, a massive display of firepower and water skiing all on the same day. I was so relieved that I farted signaling a massive salute. No one noticed over the roar of the diesel engines.

There would not be too much else to report on this leg of the trip, other than being on an adrenalin high and our heads on full swivel. I still found it amazing in how many shades of the color "green" there were. The landscape whizzed by with all those shades of green. It was in the early afternoon and the heat of the day was upon us. The traffic on this road was very light. at this time. I guess that Rudyard Kipling was right in writing, "Only mad dogs and Englishmen (American soldiers?) go out in the mid-day sun."

Soon, we were navigating the crowded Saigon streets on our way to Long Binh. I believe that at one point we passed through Cholon, the ethnic Chinese district of Saigon. Just as before, those streets were noisy, crowded and fragrant. It was a relief to have made it this far. In just a bit, we were being waved through the main gates of the huge base by the MPs.

I was glad that the lead Jeep and the convoy commander knew where to go. We pulled up and parked in single file off the street in a clearing near the 52nd's HQ's company orderly room. We were welcomed and given our instructions.

The trucks that carried the electronic gear, were sent over to the electronic depot maintenance facility and unloaded the equipment to be repaired. In exchange, the newly repaired equipment was picked up. Once the paperwork was completed, those trucks and gear returned to our convoy line. The other four trucks were sent over to another part of the base. Three trucks picked up lumber and plywood, and the other was loaded with cases of teletype paper and teletype tape. With space left behind the truck's cab, the gunner arranged the load, so he had plenty of room to operate. The loads were secured and tarped to protect against any sudden rain storms.

We were shown where we would be billeted, but there were not enough bunks open for all of us. Several of us were ordered (I volunteered again.) and others choose to remain as armed guards on the trucks. It would be a nice warm night with no rain in the weather forecast. Sleeping outdoors seemed to be a nice break. We worked out our shifts for that detail. We were given a long break before chow.

After dinner, we hung around and spent some time in the cool day room watching TV, playing 8-Ball, and Foosballs. Our "war stories" from our trip amused the other soldiers. These REMFs (**R**ear **E**chelon **M**other-**F**uckers) really did not know how easy they had it. We enjoyed ice cold beer provided by them, even though it was over-priced compared to our club prices down in Can Tho. It really did not matter, since the EM / NCO clubs were too far away on this big base. We would surely get lost.

Those of us who would spend the night with the trucks were issued an air mattress and a sleeping bag for the night. I was very tired and somewhat fatigued from all the excitement and heat of the day. I crashed early and slept very well considering the rather Spartan quarters.

We were all awakened early, SS & S'd, got ready and went to breakfast down the road at a large consolidated mess hall. The sun was beginning to peek over the horizon. Another hot day was getting ready for us. After breakfast and a break, we returned to the trucks and performed our daily "motor-stables" for the trip back to Can Tho. The weapons and the cargo were re-checked as well. We were ready to go, and by 0900 our convoy was headed off post southbound to the Delta.

CONVOY DUTY: THE RETURN TRIP TO CAN THO:

There we were once again, weaving through the crowded streets of Saigon, passing Cholon (the ethnic Chinese district of Saigon) and Phu Lam (This is where the 1st Sig Bde. Maintained a huge facility: The Phu Lam Tape Relay Station. (That was where two of our teletype circuits went.). At one time that relay processed 1 & ½ million messages in one month. After a while and a lot of horn blowing, rapid braking and cussing in several different languages, we were clearing the Saigon city limits and headed south on Highway 1. The sun was getting higher and hotter in the tropical sky this morning.

The traffic was light at this time of the day as we put Saigon further behind us. There were always the constant air traffic above of both tactical and support aircraft. The local huts and small hamlets whizzed by us and once again the color green was ever present in my eyes and awareness. Overall, the first half of this trip was uneventful. As we approached Long Xuyen, I noticed more ARVN vehicles passing around us headed towards the ferry.

It was not too much longer when a large convoy passed us near the ferry. We slowly pulled up and took our cue in line for the crossing. I guessed since it was a "tactical" convoy they would have priority. But upon a closer look, that was not quite the whole story. There were women in the trucks along with heavily armed ARVN troops. To say the least, once halted they seemed to be continuing to party. They waved liquor bottles and tossed empty beer cans over the sides of the trucks.

The lead Jeep of the ARVN convoy pulled out of line and the Vietnamese officer began to wave his trucks on ahead of us. I noticed that he was waving his pistol like a traffic paddle. His troops obeyed and soon their line was slowly moving towards the ferry assembly point. Something did not feel right.

Our young convoy commander, the SFC took offence to the Vietnamese officer's actions. He jumped over to confront "our allies". I could not hear them, but there was definitely an argument taking place in two different broken languages. The Vietnamese trucks stopped moving forward at this time. Our sergeant ordered his driver forward. Two Jeeps were now completely blocking the road along with the ARVN trucks which were in various stages of pulling forward and out of line.

Our commander continued to argue with the officer. The Vietnamese officer yelled something at his troops and in the blink of an eye, the ARVN troops locked and loaded their weapons and pointed them our way. Our convoy commander then did the same, ordering us to do the same. We complied and in no time there was a deadly "Mexican Stand-Off" there in the Mekong Delta of Vietnam among "Allies". I could not but help to think that I was going to be killed in Vietnam by "our allies" over plywood and teletype paper. The silence was deadly as both armies faced each other in a fierce game of "saving face". Who would back down and cross the river first?

A bit later, an angry ARVN jumped off of his truck, and now is waving a hand grenade and probably cussing us out in his native tongue. I could hear the safeties being switched to "fire" from our M-16s. This is not good and could get worse.

Soon, after what seemed like a couple of eons, I saw a US Army MP Jeep approaching towards us and our "stand-off". His red light was flashing as he raced towards us, sometimes going down the center of the road, and others racing off road. He pulled up in a cloud of dust right up on the two arguing convoy commanders. Riding along with our two MPs were two Vietnamese MPs. (In this sector, luckily, the MP units worked together in a "buddy" plan.). All the policemen dismounted their vehicle. One Vietnamese and one GI went over to the ARVN officer, while the other two pulled our sergeant to the side. The one ARVN MP pulled out his .45 and began to give the young ARVN troop orders to "...put the pin back in the grenade ! ...lay it on the ground and step away !". The grenadier yelled something back at the MP and in a split second threw the grenade over and behind us. We all took cover as the grenade landed in a small stream next to the road some ways behind us. The grenade exploded, throwing muck and mud all over us. Luckily, nobody on either side was injured. After many tense minutes, all of us, both sides, were then ordered to stand down. (I think many of us needed a change of skivvies.)

Not long afterwards, I saw the ARVIN convoy moving forward once again. I guess, in spite of the party atmosphere that was demonstrated by the ARVNs, it was determined to be a tactical convoy. One of the American MPs explained to us that this unit, a part of the 9th ARVN Division, was returning from a victorious engagement with the enemy. I thought to myself, "…it's a good thing that they are on our side and that we were *almost* their second victory."

After a long time, we were moved forward and began to take our places onto the barge.

We settled on the barge and with a burst of diesel soot and smoke the barge jumped into life and then slowly lumbered forward like some prehistoric river monster. The sun was still dominating the afternoon sky and it was still very hot. I could feel a slight sunburn on my shoulders and arms but knew that if I sought medical attention, there would be an Article 15 in my future. I would have to wait until we were "back home" in Can Tho. We rolled on with no further excitement. I felt my heart returning to a normal rhythm.

Our convoy pulled on through the main gate of Eakin Compound, Can Tho Army Airfield. We all were safe, and our cargo was also safe. The loads were divided between what remained here at the airfield and what was to be transloaded and sent up to Binh Thuy. When all was done, we cleaned up and headed to chow. It was good to be back in familiar surroundings, safe and sound. Later, we would hoist a few at the "club".

CHAPTER TWENTY EIGHT

SPECIAL AIR COURIER.

I guess that after a while of a pretty fixed routine between the two Comm. Centers, I got somewhat bored. For the most part the maintenance section kept all the commo gear in top working order. When something did go wrong, it was usually minor and was repaired rather quickly. On the few occasions when there were major outages, we responded with a professional "zest" and challenge. I rather enjoyed those pressured times.

For reasons unknown at the time, the sergeant who was in charge of the courier section began to talk to me about joining his team. This seemed to me a wonderful opportunity to get out of the noise, pressure, and the fast pace of the Comm. Center. It also would give me the chance to "see the country". There was also the element of adventure and danger that appealed to my 19-year-old machoism. I agreed, and he would let the First Sergeant know of my decision. They would be in touch. I had a huge grin on my face and a sense of adventure flowed over me.

I was surprised in how fast my request was approved. I was attached to the HQ MACV, IV Corps from the 1st Sig. Bde for this assignment. (HQ DMAC IV Corps and Team 96, if I recall correctly.) I did not feel badly, in my decision because we had plenty of repairmen to keep the messages flowing. A day later, at the morning formation, "Top" let me know that I was released from the maintenance section and transferred to the Courier Section. That morning, I was officially a "courier". The section chief welcomed me, and we spent most of the morning going over the paperwork that was entailed in delivering "hard copy" messages. Later when he was certain that I understood the courier protocol, he proceeded to brief me on the routine. I was then taken over to the airfield terminal and was introduced to the air operations crew as the FNG of the Special Air Courier Section.

There were two fixed courier runs routed around the Mekong Delta. Basically, each flying in opposite directions, clock-wise and counter clockwise around the Delta. In this manner each site or team would / could receive two deliveries per day. We would deliver to the main sites and outposts around the Delta, to include, but not limited to: My Tho, Tan An, Ben Tre, Tra Vinh, Tay Ninh, Cau Long, Long Xuyen, Soc Trang, Rach Gia, Bac Lieu, Ca Mau, Ha Tien, Chau Doc, and sometimes, Vung Tao, Long Binh or Bien Hoa. Most of the time there was a given flight pattern, other times an odd stop would be in place or one deleted. There would also be those "non-routine" deliveries dictated by the priority of the message, and the tactical situation on the ground at the time.

The courier would pick up his orders as to which route he would be flying that day and any special instructions for the addressees and the handling of that message. We would be advised if we were to be on a *"special mission".* That was usually apparent when three of us reported at the same time. (2 routine & 1 "special".) We always got the "SITREP" (Situation Report.), tactical, flight and weather for that flight day.

All the couriers were handed their orders, which in turn would be given to the air operations personnel at the terminal. This determined which "bird" we would be taking and manifested on as a "non-permanent" crew member. We then drew our weapons from the arms locker with our ammunition. I always went "heavily armed", drawing the following: M-1911 .45 Cal. Pistol, M-16 automatic rifle, and sometimes the M-79, 40 mm. grenade launcher, if I was on a "special mission". The air crews always loved to see me on board, as I was "extra firepower". We always carried at least three grenades. (A Thermite Grenade, should we have to destroy our mail, a HE-"Frag" for protection and a colorful smoke grenade whose color was changed daily to indicate that a courier was on board in the event our aircraft was shot down.)

The couriers would report early in the morning to the air operations section there at the terminal. For the two-routine flights, we mainly flew in one of a variety of fixed wing aircraft. (C-47 & C-119 "the Boxcars",

DHC-4, "Caribou", UV-18A Twin "Otter "De Havilland (twin engine) & U-1A "Otter" (single engine). The "special missions" were usually flown in a chopper. (Huey, UH-1A or maybe the "beast", CH-47A, "Chinook").

My first few missions were very thrilling; in that I was on board a smaller fixed wing aircraft. These flights were always a thrill as we bounced around a lot due to the wind, weather and updrafts. The one thing that really intrigued me was, once again "the color green". From the air, it was ever more evident of the vastness of the different shades of green that were possible. We also flew over areas that were "carpet-bombed" by the B-52s. These areas looked like a relief map of the lunar surface. At times these bomb craters filled with water from the Monsoon rains. The shocking thing was that the water in these craters were of different colors. It made me wonder what other chemicals were used besides our favorite, *"Agent Orange"*.

When I looked down I was also amazed by the endless maze of canals, small streams and creeks as well as the branches of the tributaries of the mighty Mekong River. There were always the presence of the sampans and small boats up and down these waterways. When we were low enough, I could see the tiny people in these crafts and wondered when they were going to uncover their weapons and fire on us, as we were unarmed aircraft. The only weapons were on board that we were carrying.

There were endless patches of green rice paddies, covering most of the ground areas below. I also wondered who was going to look up at us and open fire. As I learned earlier on; in this war, it is difficult to tell the good guys from the bad guys. What also struck my young self was how much life, human, animal and plant was thriving down below in this war. I could see the Navy PBRs patrolling up and down the waterways as well as the military vehicles on the various roads. We flew over many small villages and hamlets. I also thought if we were somebody's target. We were at such an altitude that most small arms fire could reach us, perhaps not accurately, but still could do some damage to the aircraft. At our altitude, it was hard to tell who was down there, friend or foe.

Other military aircraft were always present, both above and below us. Some signaled us by a "wing salute" (dipping the plane's wings up and down in passing.) or a sharp change in flight. At times they flew by so close that I could see the pilots' "thumbs up" or "V" peace sign gestures. There were times that due to the tactical situation, I could see the gun-ships or the jet fighters strafing or bombing a given location off in the distances. Our aircraft often made wide turns to get out of any possible stray rounds from either side. Even on the ground, I was not really concerned about the bullet with my name on it, as there was only one of those. It was all the others that I worried about, those being: *"Occupant", "Resident", "To Whom It May Concern", or "Current Resident", and all others sent my way via "Special Delivery" or "General delivery".*

For most of the tour on this assignment all went well, the classified "mail" got through safely and was delivered. I could not but to feel that my small efforts helped shorten this war in some strange way. Sometimes I would receive messages or other correspondence to be returned to Can Tho for their final distribution and actions. After a while, this assignment seemed to me to lose its thrill and settled into a routine, flying each route alternatively. I got to see almost the entire Mekong River Delta region in a manner that the tourists of today could not. I made a few friends along the way, the flight crews and the other personnel on the ground that I delivered to regularly. In our brief conversations, I learned a little bit of the progress of this war and shared my experiences as well.

After I was on this assignment about a month or so and was flying in the small single engine "Otter" aircraft with a couple of other troops, when I had a major "reality-check". We were flying over the most southern part of the region near Rach Gia when I heard several metallic "pings" and felt vibrations echo throughout the airplane. There were several shudders as the plane bounced a couple of times and then banked sharply. The pilot was making a sharp evasive maneuver. We braced ourselves and mentally prepared for the worse. I looked out of the small window to check. I saw no smoke or flames; the engine was heard just humming along as if nothing had happened. I knew that something had happened, but I did not know exactly what. I released a nervous fart and grabbed the side of the seat.

The pilot came over the inter-com and announced that we had taken some small arms fire, but all was well, and we were not experiencing any problems. When we landed there at the tip of Vietnam at Rach Gia, we all got out of the plane to check out the damage. To our surprise, there were several bullet holes on the rear stabilizer and rudder. The flight crew assured the rest of us that there was no real concern for worry. I thought to myself: "...*Damn !*, I was in an aircraft that took small arms fire while I was riding inside." This could have been a lot worse. Thank God, we all are OK and will continue the mission.". That we did, allowing my pulse and blood pressure to return to acceptable levels. This would give me a few things to tell later on.

Later that evening, I went over to the EM club with a few of my Comm. Center buddies and told of my adventure and felt good to have been able to tell my "war story" over a few drinks.

CHAPTER TWENTY NINE

R&R. (Rest & Relaxation)

{Or in GI slang: I&I In-toxification and Intercourse.}

Back then in 1971 a service person could take his or her R&R either "in-country" at China Beach (Bac My An), in Saigon, or at Vung Tau. Vung Tau was mostly used for earned R&R "in-country" for other than the main R&R. (decorations, promotions, meritorious service, etc., or at the commander's discretion. This sea resort was located 80 miles southeast of Saigon. It was also the home of the Royal Australian Army and American support units. Vung Tau was (and still is) a "Party Town".) Most of the Vietnamese "boat people" fled from there in later years.

For "out of Country R&R there were minimum requirements for time served "in-country". These were as follows:

- Australia (Sydney, Melbourne, or Brisbane)   10 Months
- Bangkok   03 Months
- Tokyo   06 ½ Months
- Hong Kong   03 Months
- Manila   03 Months
- Hawaii   06 Months (Most favored for married couples.)
- Singapore   03 Months

- Taipei   03 Months
- Penang   06 Months (From 1 July 1969 onwards.)

It was a bit overdue, but my time came up for my well-earned R&R. In 1971 I was married less than one year when I was eligible for R&R. It was in April of that year when I decided to go to Hawaii with Scharlene for a real honeymoon and R&R.

We saved up what we could for two months when I knew of my eligible date. When the time drew near, we booked Schar's flight from Oakland, California to Honolulu, Hawaii. My flight was courtesy of "Uncle Sugar", Saigon, RVN to Honolulu, USA! We both wrote about all our plans for sight-seeing tours of the islands. We both were quite excited to say the least. We were booked into, the then "Denny's Royal Hawaiian Hotel", complete with military discounts and a book of coupons upon arrival.

On the day before my departure, I was flown up to Saigon, Camp Alpha for my R&R processing and departure out of Tan Son Nhut. I enjoyed this flight aboard a "Huey", because I was only carrying my duffle bag and no "classified mail", most of all, I was headed to Hawaii and my love. Without a lot of fanfare, we landed at Camp Alpha and a few of us were directed to the R&R Center nearby. The chopper then took off with the rest of the poor bastards who were out on assignment.

We checked in and were given our billet assignment. There was an NCO / EM club within walking distance nearby. Off we went to catch a "cold-one". It was midafternoon and hot. We ventured in and the AC was quite welcome. The club was not very busy at this hour, there was maybe 25 troops or so in this large club. The juke box was playing all of our favorite tunes. Without really thinking we took up our positions at a rather large table. A very young and cute Vietnamese girl came over and took our drink orders. We got our beers in a short time and just kicked back and sucked up the cool AC and cold beer.

Not too much later, a group of Australian soldiers ("Aussies"), all wearing their "Aussie" bush hats, came in and asked us if they could join us at this large table. One "Aussie" asked, "Are you mates waiting for your other mates to join you?" I replied "No, we weren't.". Another "Aussie" then asked us if they might join us. In the spirit of good international relations, we answered positively. A group of about eight Australians got their beers and took up their positions around the table. A hearty toast was offered to our two nation's friendship and common cause in this war. They thanked us profusely for allowing them to sit with us at this large table.

The small talk ensued, mostly asking us about our units and what America was really like. It was fun to swap our "war stories" to our fellow "brothers-in-arms". They relayed their unique stories of their homeland, as we did ours. They also, were on their R&R, headed home to Australia. We all enjoyed each other's tales and company among our "Brothers-in Arms". It was not too much longer when one of our "mates" announced to all, "…gottta piss, mates ! ", and he ordered another round for the table. This pattern would continue throughout the evening. My traveling friends and I quickly finished our beers as the new round was served.

It was at this point that the fat Black club manager came over to our table and asked the Australians to please remove their headgear in the club, as it was proper protocol in American NCO clubs to do so. Just at that moment, a group of American Calvary troopers came in and upon seeing all these Australians wearing their headgear, merely kept theirs on and sat down at a table near us.

An Australian Sergeant Major stood up (complete with his "swagger stick") and confronted the club manager by saying"…and what about those blokes? They are wearing their 'cowboy' hats in your club." The shaken manager replied meekly, "…I'll take care of it. Remove yours !" The rest of the "Aussies" all stood up in unison and faced the Calvary troopers. The American troopers then also stood up. Me and my American Army friends who first entered the club with me and who sat at this table with me were caught in the middle. I said softly "Oh, shit. This is not going to end well. It will become an international incident among the Allies over an NCO bar's protocol in the middle of Saigon, in a foreign country." Both sides stood their ground and positions.

Needless to say, the club manager was beside himself, telling all involved to remove their offending headgear. There was a constant barrage of "…you go first !", "NO, NO, YOU GO FIRST !" Chairs were tipped over, along with a few beers on each side. "There is going to be a bar fight !". Me and my comrades were stuck in the middle. We then stepped back to give the "Aussies" some maneuvering room. One of the American troopers called for me and my friends to join them at their table, thus increasing the numerical odds for the American side. I stood there in bewilderment. We remained with our new-found friends and allied brothers-in-arms.

The club manager continued his sputtering and then announced in his best forceful voice that he was going to call the MPs. The drink service in the club ceased. Throughout the club people were getting ticked off as the stand-off continued. The Vietnamese staff then sought sanctuary behind the bar. Both sides, with hats still on, were shouting very creative insults to each other. The anger, adrenalin and a testosterone haze filled the club.

The "Aussie" Sergeant Major stood up and then strode up to the apparent leader of the American team, and merely said, "We do not want any trouble with you, YANKS !. In all fairness, let's resolve this conflict. I'll count to three and we ALL remove our headgear at the same time. In that way, no MPs, nobody gets hurt and we all save face. Most of all the drinks will be served again. What do you say?". Both sides looked at each other and nodded. The club manager had retreated behind the bar and was just bringing his phone to his ear.

The Australian Sergeant Major then in a proper British manner, clicked his heels, assumed the position of attention, and began his count, "Ok now mates, carefully, easy, now, ***ONE…TWO…THREE…****all together now!*". As if by magic, all the offending hats were removed at the same time. Another international incident was averted. The peace was restored by the "peacekeepers". The beer flowed once again.

The spilled beer was cleaned up and all returned to their beer drinking. When things were calm again, an "Aussie" sergeant walked over to the American troopers and offered them to join us. Soon the party was in full force on and in a very hearty brotherly manner. In between rounds, food was ordered from the grill. Few ate the Army chow over in the mess hall.

The Allies were once again on the same team and the beer was flowing again. We all were having a good time. In proper and polite form, as each "Aussie" got up to use the rest room, a round appeared at our table. At this point in time, me and my original crew were sadly behind the Australians in the beer drinking continuum. One "Aussie" stood up and ordered a stop to the festivities until the "Yanks" caught up and finished the beer before them. We did so, and the "Aussie" ordered the table another round. I really had to go pee !

At 1800hrs (6:00PM) sharp, the Sergeant Major announced in his best command voice: "ITS GIN TIME MATES!". What were we in for now? In proper British fashion, the group was obligated to be consuming gin instead of beer at this announced hour. By now I was quite drunk to say the least.

There we were, half-drunk from drinking a *lot* of beer, and the Australians now want to start on "the hard stuff", gin, no less. I thought to myself, these guys must be very much like the folks in our frontier days. Their being hardworking, professional and hard drinking fighters and lovers. I lost track of how many gin and tonics that we had put down. A bit later an Army medic came over and asked me if we were headed out on R&R. I told him, "…yes, we were." He then said in a very clinical manner, "Did you know that you will be tested for heroin use before you can leave on R&R? Go easy on the gin because the juniper berries used to make the gin will result in an altered or inconclusive result for heroin." "I did not know this." I replied. I told the table this news. The "Aussies" merely laughed and ordered another round. We Americans looked at each other very concerned. We did not want another potential international incident again by refusing to drink the "Aussie's" gin. This was going to be a long night. I probably had spent far more than I should have considering that Hawaii was in my future.

It must have been about 2200hrs. (10PM) or later when the three of us, quite drunk by now, had to excuse ourselves by explaining that we had to be up early and process out for our R&R in Hawaii. The "Aussies" all laughed and called us "their light weight mates". They understood and wished us all well and to have a "…merry good time on holiday, mates.". I slept like a baby. We were rousted at about 0600hrs.(6AM). We SS&S'd (Shit, Shower & Shave) went over to the mess hall and had breakfast. The flight was scheduled to leave at about 1100hrs (11AM).

We were then all packed up and bussed to the processing center to begin our R&R "out-processing. It all went very smoothly and did not take as long as I had expected. The first station was with the medics, who smiled and drew our blood. (Yes, he was the medic who warned us about the gin the night before.) When all was completed, and the blood tests came back negative for heroin, we were taken over to the terminal to await our flight. I was slightly hung-over, but very excited to be leaving Vietnam, even if only a week.

The air distance, Saigon to Honolulu is approximately 6,342.2 miles. We would be traveling at about 500 miles per hour. Depending on tail or head winds and altitude. This trip would take us about 13.6 hours, not counting re-fueling time in Guam. It was going to be a "time-warp" for us, in that Saigon is 17 hours ahead of Honolulu standard time. To the best of my recollection, we would land in Honolulu between 1400hrs and 1500hrs. In a strange way, I would relive part of a day because of this time difference.

I do not recall too much about the flight, except for a few points. Once the airplane made that first "jump" off of the runway there at Ton Son Nhut and it became airborne, there was such a loud cheer from all the servicemen on board that I thought that I felt the aircraft shudder. It was not until we were far out over the sea that we all felt safe and could relax because we could not be hit by any enemy fire. This was a government-chartered flight, so no alcohol would be served. We got a meal before Guam, and one meal between Guam and Hawaii. We would be landing at the Honolulu International Airport (now, the Daniel K. Inouye International Airport) midafternoon. I must have slept for most of the second leg of the flight after eating the second meal.

Hours later the captain came over the intercom and announced the decent into Honolulu International Airport. As we put our trays & seats in the upright positions and fastened our seat belts, the plane banked, and we could see Hawaii's lush green landscape and parts of Pearl Harbor. My ears popped as the plane leveled out and steadily descended until I could see houses and the tiny cars on the roads. Soon I saw the runway. When the plane made its first touchdown and the air-brakes screamed, all the GI passengers let out another cheer and a *"Thank God, We Made IT!, Safely"*. Yes, Hawaii is considered, in GI terms, a part of **"The World"**.

Soon, we were off the plane and bussed over to the R&R Reception Center at Fort Derussy. The airport was north west of Honolulu. I believe that we traveled down Ala Moana Blvd. to Kalakauna Ave and over to Fort Derussy. There, we were checked against the plane's manifest. We all made it ! Beautiful Hawaiian girls lei-ed us with colorful flower leis and a sweet kiss on our cheeks, "Welcome to Honolulu !" they said. "Honolulu, hell

THE WORLD! I said. Several feet ahead in a large lobby there were the waiting wives and families cordoned off with a red velvet rope which led to an open gate of sorts. Couples were hugging and kissing uncontrollably. Several guys simply hopped over the velvet rope barrier. These reunions brought a tear to my eye.

Soon, these couples were going off on their separate ways. I had yet to see my honey, Schar. It was a beautiful, bright and sunny spring afternoon in Hawaii, but I began to worry. I would give it a while. The crowd thinned out. Several of us were left in bewilderment, as our babes were not there yet. We looked at each other and perhaps thought the worst that the plane from San Francisco had gone down in the Pacific Ocean and we were not informed of it yet. The minuets seemed like hours when it came over the loud speakers that the San Francisco plane had been delayed and was just now taxiing towards the terminal. Our loved ones would be bussed over shortly. What a relief that was. We looked at each other smiling. There was about a dozen of us representing all the military branches and ranks. I sat down and waited very nervously.

Then all of a sudden we heard women yelling and shouting. Out of the door to the reception center was a herd of beautiful women walking at a fast pace towards us. Some of us jumped the red velvet rope to hug and kiss our honeys. There was my "Schar", ever so beautiful and dressed in tropical colors. What a wonderful sight and relief. We were together at last. We went to claim her baggage.

We stepped out into the tropical Hawaiian afternoon sun and hailed a cab. I told the cabbie which hotel, Denny's Royal Hawaiian. He jumped out and loaded our baggage and welcomed us to "his" island. He thanked me for my service as we pulled out into the Honolulu afternoon traffic. I held "Schar" tightly as this kamikaze driver weaved in and out of traffic. He then said, "Hang on *'brudder'*, Kami know what you two wanna do first thing." I get you there "chop-chop." "Schar" & I looked at each other, she giggled, and I had a *'shit eating grin'* on my face. Kami darted in and out of traffic, driving like a Roman charioteer. Buildings and other cars whizzed by, like we were jumping into "warp / light speed. Tires squealed as we rounded the street corners. It seemed that we were in all this heavy traffic for a long time.

With a screech of the aging cab's brakes, we halted in front of our hotel. Kami jumped out and unloaded our baggage onto one of those hotel luggage carts and even pushed it up to the front counter. I paid my fare and gave him a generous tip. Kami waved and said in his best Hawaiian, "…Mahalo, Brudder !"

We checked in and the desk clerk thanked me for my service. People in the lobby flashed me the "thumbs-up" hand gesture, others flashed me the "peace sign". A bell-hop did the same and brought our luggage up to our room many floors up.

We checked out our accommodations. On the desk there were many "R&R coupons and advertisements of "specials". All was beautiful and more than we had expected. The bell-hop opened the curtains, we had a small balcony overlooking Waikiki Beach and a lush patch of green. I asked the bell-hop what park that was down below. He replied, "Oh yeah, *'brudder'*, dat is Fort Derussy, you know?" I looked over and exclaimed "Shit, we could have walked over here! We were in that cab for quite some time." The poor bell-hop shrugged his shoulders and said, "Yea, man, gotta watch dose cab drivers here in Honolulu. Dey not all too honest. Be careful." I generously tipped the man anyway and thanked him for the "heads-up".

On the desk there was a stack of tourist literature promoting the many sights and destinations in and around Honolulu. Some of the top tourist destinations included, but not even remotely limited to:

- Pearl Harbor Memorial and the WW II submarine tour aboard the USS Bowfin.
- USS Arizona Memorial and navy boat ride over to the monument.
- Waikiki Beach.
- Diamond Head State Park.
- Hanauma Nature Preserve.
- Shangri La.
- USS Missouri battleship memorial.
- Koko Crater Railway Trail.
- The International Market Place.
- Helicopter Rides around the area. (I'll pass on that one.)
- "Duke's" Surfing museum and Hall of Fame.

…and about ten more equally fascinating locations. I wanted to see them all.

By now, it was getting close to dinner time. I was rather hungry after my long flight. "Schar" was also hungry in that she was really too excited all day to eat much. I called down to the bar and ordered a long-neck ice cold Budweiser and a Coke for my lady.(I was not even asked for my ID or age.. I do believe that 18 was the legal age here in Hawaii at the time.) While we were waiting for the drinks, I checked out the local TV stations and all the light switches in the room. We both bounced on the queen-sized bed. The bell-hop had also turned down the bedding for us. There were two mints on the pillows. There was a knock on the door. Our drinks had arrived. The barman placed our drinks on the desk. I paid for our drinks, and yes, another tip was in order.

That cold "Bud" was the second most beautiful sight that day. We talked over our drinks and I was brought up to date on the family and news from the world. It was decided that we would clean up and change before dinner. A hot co-ed shower was in order. With the soothing and erotic water and soap suds drenching and cascading over our young bodies; we made love right there in the shower. That was a first for us.

After a most refreshing and satisfying shower we were ready for dinner. I looked over the advertisements that were left in the room for us. "Schar" suggested that we go to a nearby Japanese restaurant that had come highly recommended. We then went down to the lobby and asked for directions to the restaurant. It was a joyful walk in downtown Honolulu. Even though I was not in uniform, I just knew that everybody knew that I was a GI (along with just about every short-haired young man in Honolulu today.) We enjoyed a wonderful meal and the first bottle of *sake* was on the house. After dinner we just wandered about town with no particular destination in mind. (I had no desire to take a cab.) Just being together and touching was Heaven in itself.

On the way back to the hotel we window shopped and wanted just about everything displayed. We laughed and talked about just about everything. We wandered in a few small shops and "Schar" picked out a few small souvenirs for the family. It was slowly getting dark as we returned to Denny's Royal Hawaiian. The desk clerk asked how our evening was going as he handed us the room key. I said, "All is well in Paradise." He smiled and then said, "Enjoy your R&R !" (I said to myself "...damn, everybody knows I'm on R&R...oh hell self, enjoy it !!")

I had the bar send up a bottle of champagne. That night between the "bubbly" and lovemaking we could not but help to regard this as our real honeymoon. The romance and lovemaking was rudely interrupted, when about 0300 (3AM) emergency vehicles with their sirens wailing away, red lights flashing in our windows roared by us down at street level.

That was it! Without thinking where I was or who I was with, I leaped out of bed ant took cover on the hotel floor. I yelled out *"INCOMING ! TAKE COVER !"* It took a few moments for me to realize where I was and that I was with my bride in Honolulu and that I was not in Can Tho under attack. We were safe. I sheepishly looked up over the side of the bed from the floor at "Schar's" puzzled look.

I was embarrassed to say the least. I explained to her, as I crept back into our bed, what the various sirens meant rocket attack, enemy fire, or a ground attack. I calmed her down and we went back to sleep in each other's arms. I was truly shaken. (PTSD reactions would not be recognized medically until the mid-1980s.)

We slept in the next morning, catching up on our lost sleep and the effects of "jet-lag". We went down to the hotel restaurant. After a late breakfast, it was decided that we would head out to the beach and spend the day on the beach.

Waikiki Beach has to be one of the most beautiful stretches of sand and ocean in the world. We got our things together and soon we were laying our beach towel on the hot sand. The sun was rather hot, but a warm ocean breeze blew over us. We rubbed sun lotion all over each other. That was very sensual. It was quite wonderful to be so young and carefree at this moment in time. We laid in the sand soaking up the warm sun rays, talking, kissing and just playing like a couple of kids in a big sand box.

The water was not very deep for about 50 yards out. There were many shades of blue as one looked further out to sea. Every now and again, we could see the fish just swimming by not even being afraid of all these strange creatures splashing and playing in their world. Far out to sea I saw the dolphins leaping and diving. It was breathtaking. For some strange reason, I thought of the "shades of green" of just a few days ago. After a while, we could feel the sun beginning to burn our skin. We took one last dip in that deep blue water. We packed up our things and headed back to the hotel. We made love for most of that afternoon.

That evening we ate dinner in a most fabulous restaurant. I do not recall the name of it, but it had something to do with an aquarium and diving. One entire wall of the restaurant was the glass wall of a huge sea aquarium. There were hundreds of tropical fish of all sizes, species and colors swimming all about. Sea plants and rocks decorated the seascape. Different colors of light accented the panorama before us.

During dinner a deep-sea diver was lowered down into the water. A stream of bubbles rose up from his helmet to the surface. He moved about feeding the fish. Soon he was joined by a young and beautiful Polynesian mermaid. She seemed so real. She was connected to the surface by a breathing tube which could hardly be seen by the customers. The lights were dimmed, and we watched in awe as the two moved about interacting with the fish and the audience. It was if we were in that wonderland below the waves with them.

There were a couple of rounds of drinks sent over to our table by the grateful citizens and customers of this great restaurant. It seemed so patriotic at the time in spite of how the majority of society viewed the war and America's military. It did feel good to be recognized and appreciated. Unknown to me at the time, but it would be decades later before I could feel this way again. "Schar's" last drink filled half of a pineapple. She was a bit tipsy after that. We returned to the hotel and our room rather late that evening. We then showered and made love well into the "wee" hours of the morning and fell asleep entwined in each other's arms.

The next morning, I went over the stack of brochures advertising all the sights in Honolulu and Hawaii in general. There was so much to do, so many tours to take, but it seemed so little time to do so. I had really wanted to go over to Pearl Harbor and go to the Arizona battleship memorial and pay my respects to my fallen Brothers-in-Arms from another war. We decided to walk along Waikiki Beach all the way to Diamond Head.

We set out later that morning after breakfast in the hotel's restaurant. We walked in the sands of Waikiki Beach hand in hand like two young lovers. (Oh yeah, at that time we were two young lovers.) We strolled carefree along the famed beach. This beach has to be one of the world's finest stretches of sand and surf. We talked endlessly about our past and our plans for the future especially when I was home from Vietnam.

We had almost made it to the base of Diamond Head when the heat and blaring sun forced us to turn back. The two of us were getting rather sun burned red. I reminded her that if I went to the medics for sunburn treatment, there was the possibility that I could get an Article 15 for damaging government property.

Later that evening we walked about the hotel's neighborhood and found a small Italian restaurant. It was small and well decorated to include the red and white checker board table cloths. In a way it reminded us of the little "mom & pop" place that we had so many wonderful meals and pizza back in San Francisco during the early days of our romance. We shared a bottle of "dago red" table wine with our meal. "Schar" was getting a little giddy and we returned to our hotel room and made love all through the warm Hawaiian night. Our honeymoon was drawing to a close in a couple of days.

"Schar" suggested that we make a romantic night on the beach this evening. We waited until it was dark. With a bottle of wine, cork screw, two hotel plastic glasses and our beach towel we headed down and out to Waikiki Beach. At first there were a few couples on the beach as we passed by. The moon was not full, so the limited light added to the secretive nature of our adventure. Shortly a secluded spot appeared, and we took full advantage of the shadows. The beach towel was neatly laid out on the still warm sand. I very unceremoniously opened the wine bottle and poured a glass each. I ignorantly stuck the unused portion of the wine bottle into the warm sand. We toasted each other to our future. Before we could finish a voice boomed out of the shadows, "Hey man how's it going? We're just headed down the beach a ways. Sorry if I disturbed you, man. Good night." (another GI on R&R) When the third couple did just about the same, we finished the wine and made out for a while before packing it all up. The mood was broken when a siren broke the still of the night. So much for being able to tell our grandchildren that we made love on the sands of Waikiki.

The next day we walked over to and spent most of the day at The International Market Place. It was like a whole city block sized Pier One Imports which, we were quite familiar with in San Francisco. There were products from just about every country in the world. The Asian section had many items that could only be special ordered in San Francisco. This was fascinating. "Schar" bought a few souvenir items for the family and we bought a small rug for our "home", (When we will have one of our own someday.) she had it shipped to her parents place. It was rather tiring, with all the walking that we had done in the last few days, so we had an early dinner in the area and returned to our room. "Schar" took a nice long hot bath. Needless to say, we made love again and fell into a deep restful and satisfied sleep.

We stayed around the hotel and explored more of the neighborhood. It was wonderful, all the sights and sounds of Honolulu. Even the smells took us on a world tour, from American steak house & grill, American BBQ to Korean BBQ, Chinese, Indian curry, Moroccan smoked lamb, Italian, and so many wonderful smells of the world's cooking. That afternoon as we were wandering about, a sudden tropical rain storm passed through with its warm rain. We got rather wet. "Schar" found the experience amazing because when it rained in San Francisco, it was cold.

The last full day was pretty much spent in our room together with only short trips out for meals. All of our great plans to tour the islands and Honolulu seemed to be postponed until we were out of time. There were no real regrets in that we made a lot of love and really enjoyed our "second honeymoon" in paradise. In the next morning we took a cab (no Kami this time) over to Fort Derussy to make our shuttle connections for our return flights to San Francisco and Saigon.

When the time arrived, we had to make our sad and painful farewells. For me, it was a long flight back to Saigon. The plane was just about all GIs returning from R&R. It was a pretty quiet and sad flight. Soon, I would be back in Can Tho.

CHAPTER THIRTY

ROCKET ATTACK: GROUND ATTACK

War has a strange way of changing the mundane into hell in a split second. That happened early one morning under a moonless night. I had worked the day shift, so I was sleeping during this time. Out of nowhere, the sirens blared like a screaming *"Banshee"*.

The pattern indicated a rocket attack was suspected. When the siren's pattern changed to "ground attack", I got worried. Now we are going to get the rockets first and then a Viet-Cong *"Banzai"* suicide attack. (Oh, SHIT).

My "battle station" was the Comm. Center. I was to oversee the set-up of the thermite grenades and the large document destroyers throughout the center. Along with the "trick-chief" (shift leader) would prepare the Comm. Center's defenses until the section OIC and NCOIC arrived.

Half-dressed and barefoot (Not too smart, I had tied on a good one that night.), I ran straight to the Comm. Center. Unknown to me, I had cut my foot quite badly on the M-8 PSP (Perforated Steel Planks) or Martson Mat, which were used to build the airfields since WW II.

The sirens were now sounding "ground attack". That meant that all non-critically assigned and off duty personnel were to draw their weapons and ammo and take up their pre-assigned posts along the perimeter.

After I arrived at the Comm. Center, I began directing the troops for both defense and destruction of the communications equipment and classified documents if needed. Shortly, the OIC & NCOIC arrived and relieved me of supervising the center's defense or destruction. The OIC asked who was wounded and pointed to the blood on the floor. It was not very long into this phase of operations, when one of the operators tapped me on the shoulder and pointed down to my bleeding foot. It was starting to hurt. I then noticed some bloody footprints on the floor.

I did not waste any time and got our medic pack out, cleaned and bandaged my wound. When all was set both in the Comm. Center and my wound, I mopped up the evidence of my arrival. The sirens were still blaring away. I went outside and checked the power generators and the two outside guards, posted front and back of the building. The messages were still pouring in and we were keeping the outbound messages flowing. Other than that, all else we could do is wait.

Off in the distance, outside, we heard a few explosions. I assumed that those were the RPGs fired at the airfield. The telephone switchboard was flooded with calls and we could not get ahold of our battalion. After what seemed like a millennium, the sirens went silent for several minutes. Nothing happened, and we still waited, not knowing what was going on outside. I went out to check. It was deathly silent with the exception of our generators humming along still providing power to the center. A couple of helicopters could be heard taking off. The guards were ok and there was very little other activity on the base.

Then when the sirens sounded the "all clear" signal we sighed a big relief. We stood down, restoring the Comm. Center to somewhat of its former "normal" state. In a while, we were able to contact our battalion HQ to find out what had happened. They were also rather confused and vague but conceded that the alarm was premature and probably was based on faulty intelligence. I thought, ("...*not here in Vietnam*"). No more explosions and most of all, no *"VC Banzai Charges.!"*

Before leaving, the OIC suggested that I go over to the medical clinic. He added, "You could get a Purple Heart because of your wounded foot.". I declined because, although throbbing, the foot was ok and well bandaged. Perhaps it was due to my youth and bravado that I refused, but I knew that the bodies of our KIAs went home with a Purple Heart. My flesh wound did not seem as equal. I went about my business and returned to the barracks.

A couple of months later we during an awards and decoration formation that we learned: the officers who were receiving the Purple Heart actually stumbled and fell while we were "under attack", exiting the Officers Club. They suffered at worse minor bruises, cuts and sprained ankles. One major was cited for urinating in their outside ice making machine.

THE LAST MISSIONS OF THIS "SPECIAL AIR COURIER":

After several months of basically routine missions, I reported for duty one morning and I was handed two sealed envelopes by the section chief. I was to be on a "special mission" today. One envelope was only to be opened by myself and the other was to be given to the flight operations personnel.

Upon arriving at the terminal and checking in with the flight operations sergeant, I was assigned my "bird". It was an UH-1 "Huey". I then opened my envelope and read the instructions carefully. These were my instructions:

1. Upon the arrival at the destination. I was to be dropped off on the ground.
2. I was to proceed to a bunker.
3. In that bunker, I would find a PRC-25 field radio and I was to "key" the microphone only three times, do not speak, proceed outside and wait under cover of the sand bags.
4. My sealed message was to be given _only_ to a Special Forces Major Thompson. It was a "Top Secret" FOR HIS EYES ONLY.
5. Once the message was delivered and the major returned into the jungle, if all was clear and secure, I was to "pop" a smoke grenade.
6. The chopper was to pick me up and return to Can Tho.
7. I would be under the strictest secrecy not to tell a soul anything about my mission.

I then headed out to the waiting chopper, (engine slowly idling) got on board, buckled in and handed the pilots the last sealed envelope. In a minute or so, after reading his orders, the pilot nodded to me and with a "thumbs-up" gesture; he burst the engine into life. We rose ever so slowly and in a heartbeat the bird pitched, lurched forward, and banked sharply to the west and we were off. After a steady climb to our cruising altitude, the flight leveled off and we headed west at a quick pace.

Riding in a helicopter always reminded me of those kid's toy, the flying saucer. (*Whirly-Gigs*). You held the launcher in one hand and pulled the string steadily with the other, which sent a three bladed plastic "saucer" airborne. It would hum and rotate as it flew. The aerodynamics were the same basically as the actual helicopter. This was especially true as when the chopper pitched and lifted forward. One's legs and feet were now behind and under the body. If one was sitting on the side seat or bench the legs went sideways.

I was somewhat used to the various flight times that I had flown around the Delta, but this flight was different. It seemed to me, after several checks of my wrist watch, that we had been flying 'way too long westwardly. I shrugged my shoulders and could only sit back and enjoy the ride.

It seemed like an eon or so, but the pilot came over the headset to inform me that we were very close to the LZ (landing zone) and for me to "get ready to bail". We began our decent. I thought over and over at this point, "…am I perhaps in Cambodia?". He informed me that they would "…be in the friendly skies above". I was to make my delivery and when the mission was completed, and all was safe, pop a smoke and I would be picked up. I had exactly 15 minutes to complete this action. If not, I was to destroy the documents and would basically be on my own until a rescue mission was dispatched. That was real assuring.

When the bird was only a few feet off of the ground, I jumped off and ran over to the bunker to the side of what seemed to be an old abandoned French airfield from the last war, but it there were new sand bags protecting the bunker.

I followed my special orders and keyed the mic three times, loaded my M-16, switched it to "auto-fire" (just in case), and stepped out and assumed a defensive stance, protected by the bunker wall. I waited, sweating in the tropical heat.

Off in front of me and this bunker was a clearing in the jungle overgrowth, a clearly cut path about 30+/- yards ahead. I had a full clear field of fire. I checked my watch, I had 13 minutes left. All of a sudden three Orientals emerged from the jungle. They all were armed and were wearing the "tiger-stripe" special forces fatigues of the elite South Vietnamese Army. I raised my weapon and halted them. They obeyed, which surprised me. I challenged them with the word of the day. I got no reply. This was odd; I began to feel afraid that things might go wrong.

The guy in the middle seemed to be the leader and in broken English yelled to me "You give me bag, Major Thompson, he very busy, sent Thran to pick up for him, OK, GI?". He took a couple of steps forward. I halted him again and chambered a round in my rifle. They all stopped. The "leader" tried again, saying"…hurry up, GI, No time, hurry, hurry, hurry. No be 'numba 10' foo me.". Major-San be beacoup mad if you numba ten me.". I looked even closer at the three with my sweat dripping onto my weapon.

One of them on the side was carrying an AK-47, the enemy's weapon of choice. The other on the side had an old M-14. The guy in the middle had a M-1911 .45Cal pistol. This did not look right. Upon a quick glance to their feet, I noticed that all three of them were wearing sandals (BF Goodrich Charlie Specials, J C Water Walkers.). They were not to be trusted, besides my messages were for Major Thompson's eyes only. I could not even give them to President Nixon if the president wanted me to. I did not have a lot of time to resolve this as my "ride" hovered overhead off in the distance.

The three stepped forward towards me and the leader continued to jabber in broken English about me giving him "the mail". I made a split-second decision that they were the enemy and as they raised their weapons towards me, I fired on fully automatic fire, sweeping left to right, dropping all three. I waited to see if they were still alive. With an empty magazine, I shouldered my rifle and pulled out my M-1911 and approached the three bloody and mangled bodies with my hand shaking. I delivered the "coup-de-grace" with one shot each in the forehead. The red ground became even redder. The gun smoke slowly cleared. The area was unusually quiet and eerie silence surrounded me. I made a quick check of the area, all was clear. I was definitely ready to catch my ride home.

I waited a few minutes and noticed that I still had five minutes to spare. My heart was still pounding, and I was drenched with sweat. I popped the green-colored smoke grenade. I still could see the chopper off in the distance just hovering just above the tree line, waiting for me. That was the longest five minutes of my life. I held onto the secure mail pouch with a "death grip", the documents were safe. I passed gas as a relief of this stressful situation.

Altogether, not too soon enough, the "Huey" dropped down on the LZ and I ran towards the waiting bird. I leaped on board and secured myself. I grabbed the headset as the chopper quickly rose vertically and turned east. The pilot asked me how it went. In a broken, panting dialogue, I briefly told the pilot what had happened. He told me not to say too much more and he would radio HQ and report the basics. He then told me to try and relax and that there would have to be a report made as soon as we landed.

It must have been my imagination working overtime, but the trip back to base did not seem to take so long as the trip out. That reflection went back to my younger years when that same phenomenon occurred during childhood road trips.

I studied the passing landscapes below me and wondered if I had done the right thing in greasing those "gooks". I kept telling myself that I did the right thing in that they were the enemy and my messages were for MAJ. Thompson's eyes only. Those documents were safe within my grip. The chopper bounced a few times, passing over the river due to an updraft. Before too long we were making our decent to the Can Tho Army Airfield.

We landed there at Can Tho. As I left the chopper and was headed towards the tower, two officers approached me and demanded that I identify myself. They both were packing the standard issued .45 Cal M-1911 semi-automatic pistol. I took out my ID card very carefully and the orders that I carried showing that I was a permanent Special Air Courier. They ordered me to come with them. I gripped the courier pouch even tighter.

Since these documents were for "eyes only" they would have to be destroyed upon my return to the Comm. Center. I said to the officers that I could not release the pouch to them and my protocol was to return them to the Comm. Center. They understood but were very forceful in demanding they "interview" me.

I was taken to a small office on the ground floor of the air terminal. We entered, and they told me to take off my pistol belt and put all of my weapons over on a small table off to the side. The captain shut the door behind us. The senior officer, a Lieutenant Colonel, took up his place behind a worn army standard issue desk. The other officer, a Captain took up his position on one side of the desk. They each held a clipboard and placed it on the desk in front of them, pens ready. I got a feeling very strongly that these two officers were MI (Military Intelligence) types.

The "light colonel" began the interrogation very simply and to the point by demanding; "Specialist, tell us what happened today." I cleared my dry throat and began to tell them of the flight out. The captain interrupted me and merely asked me what happened on the ground. I told them all that I could remember in detail. The captain went on with many more questions such as: what was the weather like?, what the ground was like?, any other signs of either enemy of friendly activity in the area?, were there any animals in the area?, he asked for a description of the bunker, did I notice any footprints other than one set going to the bunker from the jungle opening and back? any signs of trash in the area? He then went on to ask me point blank why I killed these three. This captain asked all the questions, the LTC merely sat there taking notes un- expressional.

I answered these questions over and over. Both officers seemed to be constantly taking notes during this entire interview. I knew from the cop shows, that they were trying to make me trip up somewhere in my story. I must have told them a dozen times how I had come to my decision to "fire". The interrogation lasted over an hour.

The LTC put down his pen and pushed his clipboard to the side, sat back, put his feet up on the desk and pulled out a fat cigar and lit it ever so ceremoniously. He asked me if there was anything else to add. I said "Yes sir, am I in trouble? Did I do something wrong?". He looked at his captain and they both nodded and told me that I would find out soon. "You are excused, carry-on.", said the captain. I saluted them, gathered up my gear and headed back to the Comm. Center. At least I was not arrested and those two were not MPs. I felt somewhat relieved, but still worried that I had messed up somehow.

Upon my return to my section in the Comm. Center, I relayed my story to my section chief, the Comm. Center NCOIC, the Comm. Center OIC, and the First Sergeant. I secured my weapons and accounted for the 30 rounds of ammunition that I had expended. (I'll probably be charged $1.00 each round for wasting them. > [bad pun], not intended.), I was totally burned out by this time and could not wait to slam a few cold "brew-kies". That I did upon reaching my "hooch". I skipped dinner and headed to the club. There I calmed down and tried to put on a calm exterior.

I only flew for about a week more. All of these assignments were very routine. Nothing had happened, although a few guys asked me in confidence what happened. I was very vague and could not understand what all the fuss was about. I never divulged any information about the mission, other than, perhaps that it was different than most. All was "Top Secret" stuff.

That Monday about on the eighth day after the "incident", when I reported for duty at the courier section, I was informed that I had been "grounded" and would be going up to battalion HQ in a little bit. I got a cup of coffee and sat back in the maintenance shop. All my friends kept asking me a thousand questions. I stuck to my guns, and did not say very much, but inside I was in terror. I said to myself "…this is **_IT!_.** I am going to be court-martialed, sent to LBJ (Long Binh Jail) and spend the rest of my life in a Federal prison, perhaps at Leavenworth, turning boulders into pea gravel for "Uncle Sam". My military career is over in disgrace, my life is over…ah SHIT!". I finished my coffee just as the Comm. Cen. NCOIC and a driver got me, and we went out to a waiting Jeep. We headed straight to the battalion HQ in Binh Thuy.

Much to my surprise, the sergeant was in a joyful mood and we passed the time in small but encouraging conversation. The sights, sounds and smells all too familiar along this stretch of the road as we passed us by. I was quite nervous and tried my best to maintain a calm exterior.

Soon we pulled into Binh Thuy's main gate and headed right to the 52nd Signal Battalion's Headquarters. I was directed to a conference room where three officers: the battalion commander, two staff officers, and the battalion sergeant major all sat behind a long table. There were two seats in front of the desk. We saluted the members of the panel. When their return salutes were completed, the SGM stood up and told me and my NCOIC to have a seat. We obeyed and sat motionless in anticipation. I thought *"… ah shit, this is it! "*

The LTC stood up and came around the desk and ordered me to stand up. I did so with trembling legs and a cold sweat. I thought to myself "Busted!, time to walk the gauntlet. As in the old westerns when a Calvary troop was 'drummed out'. My mouth went dry. The Sergeant

Major followed right behind the battalion commander. The battalion commander said, "You have done wonderful job in all aspects of your duties, keeping the communications flowing in the face of an armed and determined enemy. Your MOS test cannot be given in this field of operations, so you are hereby promoted to Specialist Fifth Class by my power as your battalion commander. This is a field promotion. In one week, you will take over as the Comm. Center Maintenance Section Chief. The present NCOIC will be going home. He will have that remaining time to brief you and bring you up to speed on all the duties expected of this position. Do you have any questions?". I said "NO,SIR." Then the two other staff officers stood up. (I was all of 19 years old.)

The Sergeant Major came up to me and removed my collar SP4 rank insignias and replaced them with those of my new rank. He shook my hand and gave me his brief congratulations. He stepped back as I saluted the commander. The other officers then came around and replaced the commander as he and the sergeant major walked out of the room. The staff officers in turn congratulated me. I saluted them. They also left and returned to their duties. My NCOIC further congratulated me, beaming ear to ear. I let out a huge sigh of relief. All this happened far too quickly for me to really grasp what had happened this week. At 19-years old, I was an Army NCO, 12 men to train, lead and be responsible for them. (They all made it home safely.)

The road trip back to Can Tho and the Comm. Center, went by too quickly, but in an entirely better frame of mind on my part. I relaxed as if a heavy weight was lifted off of me. I still did not really comprehend what went down out there in the field, even to this day, I do not really know.

{It was years later that when I was in re-hab, that I met an older retired Special Forces sergeant who served in the same years that I did in Vietnam as well as serving in the same areas of operations that I did. He recalled a similar incident but could not recall where or when. He ended by telling me that his team went through about half a dozen officers during his two tours and did not readily remember any "Thompson", maybe yes, maybe no, we don't know.}

We pulled right up to the Comm. Center. The sergeant and I got out of the Jeep and went straight in the center. The driver returned the Jeep to the motor pool.

We were greeted by the 1SG and the OIC of the Comm. Center. They both relayed their congratulations on my promotion. I went back to the shop and the current section chief shook my hand. I then began my week of training to be the "boss". All of the "tape apes" also congratulated me and all seemed happy that I got my stripe. I would have 12 men under my supervision. There was a "promotion party" at the club that night. As tradition had it everybody my rank of higher got to "pin" on my stripes. It was simple: one swift and hard punch on each of my upper arms. My arms would be black and blue for a couple of weeks.

That week went by real fast and I was a bit weary of my new responsibilities but was confident that my predecessor had trained me well. The routines basically remained the same, except now I was in charge and ultimately responsible for the section's operation and its success.

I was on call 24/7 and in the coming months would be spending time at both Comm. Centers, both as the supervisor as well as the shift repairman.

A huge issue came up over the assignments of guard duty. An *"acting Jack"* sergeant (a temporary stripe and position given, in spite of actually being a SP4 or Corporal.) would get the sergeant of the guard assignment, whereas us SP5s pulled regular duty as a sentry. We felt this was not really fair in that the regular sentry assignment rotated around more frequently and I was still expected to fulfill my NCOIC duties in the Comm. Center. On several occasions I received phone calls while in the guard tower asking me questions and seeking advice regarding operational issues. In general, the Army had this problem for years. The Army considered the "hard" stripe NCOs to be "real" leaders and we "specialists" were merely senior technicians. For a brief period during this time the "specialist" ranks actually went up to SP9 (equivalent to a Sergeant Major in pay.)

This guard duty issue was resolved and we SP5s were actually viewed as responsible as leaders and pulled sergeant-of-the-guard duty. (Perhaps a couple of smoke grenade "frags" hastened the decision.) In the next year or so this rank structure changed and a promotion to E-6 would require a "hard stripe" and proper leadership and NCO training. (I would eventually complete all the NCO training up to the senior and through the senior NCO level.)

The next couple of months went by busily and without any major issues; I ran a smooth section and we handled some very important issues and outages which resulted in circuit re-engineering. I really had no discipline problems, other than a few "chewing outs" and special "counseling sessions" with my subordinates. Overall the command was pleased, as I was.

One day during a special company formation, I was called out with several other troops and we were decorated. The Battalion Commander, oversaw the ceremony as Sergeant Major pinned on the medals. To my great surprise and total shock, I received the Bronze Star and the Army Commendation Medal. My citations were genetically worded and no "V" device was on the Bronze Star. Both awards were for meritorious service in the face of an armed and determined enemy. (no mention of air service or the "incident".) To this day I really do not know why, other that our classified communications were secure under "my watch".

Towards the end of my tour as the US forces were being reduced in Vietnam. Once when we had an over-abundance of maintenance personnel now we were short. Many units now were short of these specialists. The battalion then formed a "air-mobile maintenance team" and I was the "crypto-man" of that team. Once again I was in the air. The thrill was not gone. I went on several of these missions all over the Delta along with a radio repairman, a wireman and a teletype repairman. The team was led by a Staff Sergeant, who was extremely trained and versed in our tactical communication operations and equipment.

THE NIGHT OF THE GENERAL:

Late one night, or early morning (0200 + / -), I was at the "downtown" Comm. Center (Tran Le Loi) and even though I was maintenance, I was by fate, the senior enlisted man in the center. All of a sudden, as I was kicked back relaxing in my "shop", one of the specialists came running back and informed me that there was a general and a bunch of officers up front at the counter and were demanding to be let in. I rushed up front and asked the general what he wanted. The Comm. Center became quiet, except for a couple of teletypes chattering away. I saluted him sharply. The general said, "I am the new deputy commander of the 1st Signal Brigade and me and my officers want to inspect my Comm. Center." I told him,

"One moment please, "Sir, I need to check the access roster before I can let you or any of your men pass through that locked gate." One of his officers leaned over the counter and repeated the general's demand to be let in. I cleared my throat and then asked for each officer's identification card. In order they each produced their IDs. I could see the arrogance and contempt in their eyes.

By Army regulations, I had to check each officer's ID against the names and ranks on the access roster. None of these officers were on the access roster. I informed the general of that fact. He became furious and once again demanded entrance. This situation was getting uglier by the second. Two of the entourage leaned forward and also demanded that I allow all to pass. I said in no uncertain terms that until they are on the access roster, none would be allowed to pass, not even President Nixon.

There was a .45 Cal. M-1911 semiautomatic pistol just below the counter on a shelf; it was not holstered and was loaded. It remained on "safe" for the time being. I was most nervous, but confident that I was in the right. Between negotiations, the operators peered around the entrance door to the Comm. Center's operating room. The machines all seemed to burst into life with their chattering amidst their bell ringing. I said to the general, "I cannot allow you or any of your men to enter. None of you are on my access roster." The general turned beet red and demanded that I allow him access. Then as if out of nowhere, I demanded and told the group **"STAND FAST OR LEAVE IMMEDIATELY, SIRS !!"**

In less than a heartbeat I saw that this situation was not getting any better as I produced my pistol, took it off of the "safe" mode, and chambered a round. **"I cannot allow any of you to pass !"**, I said in my most stern NCO voice, but shaking below the waist. I then called to one of the operators and ordered him to call up to the battalion HQ and get the Staff Duty NCOIC on the direct field phone line to battalion. He did so for me. With a pistol in one hand and the phone in the other I faced the general. The general then asked who my battalion commander was. (...HELL!, I thought, he should know, HE is the deputy commander of the brigade...) I told him who my commander is, and told him to wait, in that they were getting my commander on the line.

The Staff Duty NCO came on the line. I explained the situation to him, never taking my eyes off any of this entourage, pistol at the ready.

After a ghastly long silent pause, he said, "Hold on for a few minutes, I will get the battalion commander on the line.". I could hear the clicking of the SB-22 switchboard as the call was forwarded and then the ring to the LTC. I nervously told the general that they were getting my battalion commander on the horn. The battalion commander came on the line, sleepily identified himself. I told him who I was and the basic situation, and that a general needs to speak with you, "...SIR !" (I thought to myself: "... Leavenworth, here I come !"). I handed the field phone to the general and anxiously awaited my fate. I then reminded myself how the other "incident" played itself out and felt briefly relieved.

We could only hear the general's side of the conversation. He repeated who he was and "... why-in-the-hell wasn't he on the damn access roster?". (His was a very new appointment, perhaps only a day or so old and the official order had not yet come down to my battalion.) He sputtered a few choice words and the last thing I heard him tell my commander, "...OK then, you get your ass down here ASAP! We'll be in the area until your arrival colonel. He handed me the phone. I checked, but our commander had already hung up. I hung up the "hot-line". The general and his group turned to leave. The general, still boiling mad, turned and nodded to me and said "This is not over Specialist..." He then exited the Comm. Cen in a huff. I was still sweating and shaking. I stood down and secured the weapon. The teletypes never missed a beat and continued to spew out messages. I sat down to catch my composure. My signal mates, patted me on the back and indicated that they never have seen an enlisted man stand up to a general as I just did. I felt somewhat better, but still worried.

In less than an hour, one of the "tape-apes" got me again saying in a loud voice, "THEY'RE BACK!" I went up to the front once again and there was the whole crowd. I allowed my battalion commander to sign for the general, but not the rest of the general's entourage. Our Battalion Commander signed the general into the Comm. Center for the general's "inspection". Before I led them back. There was a very awkward moment. The Battalion Commander shook my hand and merely said to me, "...well done Specialist, you followed your oral and printed orders to a 'tee'. You did what I would have expected of one of my NCOs." The LTC winked at me, unseen by the General. Then came the surprise of my life; the General shook my hand and told me that he was in the wrong and offered his apologies. I accepted and saluted him. Leavenworth would have to wait!

A month later, I was called into the company commander's office. The first sergeant was standing next to the commander's desk. I thought for sure that I was in trouble for something. I saluted the officer. He ordered me to have a seat, which I did. He said "I hate to inform you that your grandfather and guardian, Andrew Taylor has died and your grandmother Jessie Taylor, through the American Red Cross, has requested me to grant you emergency leave to return home to San Francisco as soon as possible. You will pack your gear and be on a special chopper this afternoon to take you to Saigon. Please accept mine and the first sergeant's deepest condolences. Any questions, Specialist?" I said "No, Sir, and thank you.". I saluted and was dismissed.

I returned to the barracks with a heavy heart. My buddies knew that something was terribly wrong with me. I told them what happened and began to pack. I gave a lot of my personal items away. They all extended their sympathies and wished me well. I told them to say good bye to the rest of my buddies for me. After chow and a few drinks, I was headed to the terminal with my leave and travel orders in hand. I was told not to worry about my personal things, they would be crated and shipped to my San Francisco home address as my "hold baggage.(That "Hold baggage never arrived. I would put in a claim when I reached my next permanent duty station.) At that point in time I really did not know if I would be returning to Vietnam to finish my tour after this emergency leave or be assigned to a new post elsewhere in the Army.

Soon, I was on board a chopper and headed north to Saigon. I would be home in just over 48+ hours. I spent the night at Camp Alpha and was on the "Freedom Bird" early the next morning. No partying at the club this trip, the day before pay day.

CHAPTER THIRTY ONE

SOME THOUGHTS AND REFLECTIONS OF MY VIETNAM TOUR: (THEN & NOW.)

Below are some of the statistics about the war which are disturbing. It is also curious that there is no definitive dates to the war's official beginning and ending. I am considering here the presence of the US military and / or civilian officials and contractors. Statistical numbers may vary depending on which dates are used.

The dates in question for the start of the war (2nd Indochina war, not including WW II.). These dates being: **1954?;** when the French were defeated at Dien Bien PHU, **1959?;** July 8, MSG Charles Ovnand & MAJ Dale R. Buis are killed in Vietnam and later become the first two names on "The Wall"; **1960?;** Official? start of the war, more US "advisors" sent. Date on the Vietnam Service Medal; **1961?** Based on VA eligible service dates. **1964?;** The Gulf of Tonkin Incident and Resolution, troop level is at 75,000 **1965?;** July 28, LBJ orders US troop level increased to 120,000;

The same issue also applies to the date that the war ended. **1973?;** Signing of the Paris Peace Accords: or **1975?;** The official "fall of Saigon", and perhaps: **July 11th, 1995,** When the US finally recognized the new government of Vietnam and established diplomatic relations.

There are some statistics regarding the Vietnam War that I found and still do find disturbing, these being :

- 9,087,000 served in the US military, Aug 5, 1964 to May 7, 1975.
- 2,709,918 served in Vietnam. 9.7% of their generation.

- 58,479 were KIA. / Average age was 23.1 years old.
- Deaths by rank, and average ages:

   Enlisted: 50,274 KIA 22.37 years old.
   PVT / E-1: 525 20.34 years old.
   Commissioned Officers: 6,598 KIA 28.43 years old.
   Warrant Officers: 1,276 KIA 24.73 years old.
   MOS, 11B (Infantry, light weapons) 18,465.

- 11,465 were younger than 20 years old.
- 17,539 were married.
- The 5 youngest were only 16 years old.
- Oldest was 62 years old.
- Overall Deaths, military & civilian, all sides: 2,122,744 (est.).
- US wounded: 304,000 (1 in 10).
- US severely wounded:75,000. (Amputations & severely wounded 300% higher than WW II)
- There were 18 US military hospitals throughout Vietnam.
- MEDIVAC missions: 500,000 (82% survival rate, one hour elapsed time from call).
- 2.6 % of Medevac'd died in the hospital.
- Number of airlifted: 900,000, ½ American.
- "Fragged" officers & NCOs: 788 / wounded, 714.
- The Air war: (Not counting Allied aircraft): 1,899,688 sorties: 6,727,084 tons of bombs, (Compared to 2,700,000 tons dropped on Germany during WW II.) 12,000 choppers were engaged, 4,864 were destroyed. Cost of bombing North Vietnam: $6,000,000,000.
- Chemical warfare: 3,500,000 acres were sprayed with defoliants, 19,000,000 gallons whose effects will last 100 years. (Agent Orange, perhaps?)
- Monetary cost: $352,000,000,000 to $738,000,000,000 Est. 2.3% of GNP in 1968 dollars.
- Since 2011 the VA has paid out over $39,000,000,000 in disabilities. (All wars.)
- The US military did not lose the war, the politicians did.

- In general, the US public did not support the war efforts.
- Vietnam Veterans were disgraced upon their return and it took decades to earn the public's respect.
- Was it worth it to have our "designer" apparel manufactured there and a location to "outsource" American jobs?

BACK IN "THE WORLD"

It was a long and tiring flight back home. The flight pattern was just the reverse of the trip over to Vietnam. We left out of Tan Son Nhut and flew to Guam to refuel. We then flew up to Yokota, Japan, refueled again and then it was over "the pond" to Anchorage, Alaska. Once again, were refueled and were on our way down to Travis AFB, California. It is approximately 1944 miles, Anchorage to Travis AFB.

This would be the strangest day of my young life. I actually lived the same date twice. There was about 24 hours of flying time east, crossing the International Date Line. Since Vietnam was a day ahead of the West Coast; I flew into "today". The actual elapsed time was the flight time between Anchorage, Alaska and Travis AFB, California. That was about 4 ½ hours, so I left Vietnam only 4 ½ hours ago by my watch and calendar.

There was a huge cheer aboard the plane when we lifted off from Tan Son Nhut. I also recalled the old saying used by the GIs: "You Ain't *'short'* (little time left in country or in-service.) until the 'NO SMOKING' sign comes on over Travis. They can always call that bird back !". Now when we touched down at Travis, there was such a cheer that probably could be heard all over California. After we were exited the plane, several guys ran out and actually kissed good old American terra firma.

The Air Force personnel welcomed us home. There was a big banner sign that read: **"Welcome Home", Job Well Done! MISSION ACCOMPLISHED !!".** Another sign informed us that Uncle Sam has a steak dinner waiting for us at the mess hall, courtesy of the US Air Force. The mess hall was closed when we arrived that evening. (Uncle Sugar; You Owe Me One!)

I went over to the American Red Cross desk and showed them my emergency leave orders and explained that I had only 25 Cents in military payment script on me and had to get home to San Francisco. They must

367

have felt sorry for me and gave me a one-way Greyhound bus ticket. They directed me to the bus stop. I shouldered my duffle bag and grabbed my AWOL bag and headed over to the bus stop. There would be over an hour wait for the San Francisco bus. There I sat, so close, yet so far. The distance between Travis AFB and San Francisco was 61 miles or so. It was a local bus route, so it would be making stops all along the way. It probably would take a couple of hours or so to make the trip. All I could think of was getting home to my family.

The bus trip down I-80 took me past many familiar towns: Fairfield, Suisun City, Cordelia, Richmond, Emeryville, Berkley and Oakland. The bus stopped at many of these as well as other small towns. Then it was over the Bay Bridge into downtown San Francisco. It was actually in the "skid row" section of the city, 3rd & Market / Townsend Streets, complete with an assortment of junkies, winos and hookers. I was in my khaki summer uniform. It was late at night and the San Francisco fog was settling in. I felt very cold, as the last year was spent in a tropical climate. I could almost feel the cold stares of the citizens as I walked through the terminal. I could hear their snide remarks as well as their curses and see their "one-finger salutes".

I went up to the ticket counter and asked the clerk if I could use his phone to call "Schar". He refused and referred me to the bank of pay phones across the terminal. I explained to him that I had just returned home from Vietnam and had no change or US currency. I had only $ .25 military payment script in my pocket. Paper money would not work in a pay-phone. He was not very helpful and cited some company policy preventing ticket clerks from letting customers use Greyhound phones. (Customer service, my ass !) That asshole could have at least welcomed me home. I was too proud to pan-handle, although many others approached me. By now, I was too pissed to even ask a cab driver to drive me to my destination and my wife would pay for the fare. I decided to walk the 3 miles to Laguna Street in the cold and damp. I figured that it was too late to go straight to my grandmother's, so I walked out of the dirty bus terminal headed to "Schar's".

No sooner than I crossed Market Street when a rather attractive hooker propositioned me for sex. Her price was $20 "for the time of my life". I told her that I only had 25, which was Ok with her until I produced my $ .25 "funny money". (That would have been "two-bits. Maybe she thought that I was calling her a "two-bit whore".). She was both insulted and angry at the same time as she walked on down the street, cussing me with each step. I had to laugh at that.

I even tried to hitch-hike across my hometown, and only got beer cans thrown at me along with even more cusses and insults. I wondered where in the hell did all that "Love, Peace & Happiness" of the 1960s go? Free love and understanding also went by the wayside.

There I was, walking through the fog alone late at night. I was cold and damp through my summer uniform. My duffle bag, with my jungle boots tied to the strap slung over my shoulder and AWOL bag in hand. I made it up to Geary Street, turned left and headed west to Japantown. Cars passing me honked at me. I did not really know if they were welcoming me home or simply harassing me. Off in the distance the old fog horns sang their sad refrains. I continued to march.

It must have been a lot past midnight, perhaps as the bars were closing at 02:00, when I was knocking on "Schar's" front door. I heard from above me, speaking out of an open window from her bedroom her voice asking, "... who was there? When I answered, "It's me !", all I could hear was her squeal of joy. Since I could not call anybody with my paper quarter no one knew when exactly my arrival time was. She ran down the stairs and after a very long hug and kiss on the porch, she let me in. All this commotion must have awakened the whole family. There at the top of the stairs were the whole family, as well as the neighbors.

I was greeted by "Schar's" parents, Yuriko and Junior with a hug and a handshake. They knew why I was home on emergency leave. Her sister Jane and young brother Willy also came over to welcome me home. We all went over into their living room and I finally put down my duffle bag and AWOL bag. I was very tired and must have looked a sight for sore eyes.

Junior offered me a beer and Yuriko went into the kitchen and came out with some "munchie snacks". Over beer and chips, I answered about a thousand questions about Vietnam.

We small talked and after about an hour, we broke up the party; "Schar" and I retreated to her bedroom. I had the alarm clock set because I wanted to call my grandmother, Jessie, in the morning and let her know that I made it home safely. Before long, we went to bed and embraced, my head hit the soft pillows, wisps of fog passed by the streetlight outside our window luminating their ghostly patterns. Soon, I was fast asleep.

We were up before the alarm because Yuriko had to go to work at the 5-Star, Ming Ga Ya Japanese restaurant. She worked as the sous chef, preparing the menu for the evening and dinner rush. Junior took her to work over on Union Street. He was retired by now. When he returned home, offered to drive me over to my home and grandmother out in "the avenues".

Over coffee we swapped "war stories". Junior was a medic in the Army just behind the first waves at Normandy Beach, 1944. (He retired from the Army in 1964 and went to work at St. Joseph's Hospital as an orderly. He retired from there when that hospital closed several years later.) "Schar's" brother and sister were fast asleep. Both had dropped out of high school and had no jobs or real schedules to keep.

I called my grandmother about nine and told her that I made it home safely late last night and spent the night with my wife. She was delighted to hear my voice and that I made it home from the war in one piece. I told her we would be over within the hour. After coffee Junior took "Schar" and me home.

It was quite an emotional reunion as Jessie's older sister, Catherine was there as well. There were hugs and kisses all around. We were ushered into the living room and over more coffee talked. I then took "Schar" on the grand tour of the entire house and back yard. For me it was like being reunified with an old friend. I took in every small detail of the house. Somehow it was not the same, or was I seeing it through different eyes and mind.

Andrew Taylor was 97 years old when he died. What happened was that, as usual, he sprung up out of bed early in the morning as he had done for all his years. Apparently that fatal morning, he got dizzy lost his balance, fell and hit his head on the window sill. That could have been the fatal wound, or perhaps he suffered a fatal stroke. Either way, the insurance company denied the accidental death benefits due to his advanced age. My grandmother and her sister had made all the final arrangements. Ironically the gravediggers at Colma and in San Mateo County were on strike. He would have to be cremated by Mt. Tamalpais Cemetery in San Rafael in Marin county and his ashes would be sent to Cypress Lawn in Colma.

We stayed there a couple of days and did all that we could to help the two sisters around the house and even went to the PX and commissary for them. The evenings were spent in conversation and the evening news updating us how "my" war was going. Before the funeral Catherine had to return to her apartment.

On the day of the funeral, the Taylor family came up and after all the "welcome home" hugs and a brief up-date on how we all were doing, we loaded into the cars for the trip to the Halsted Funeral Home on Sutter Street (Now Halsted N. Gray-Carew & English Inc.).That probably was the last time that I was together with the Taylor clan. (Glenhall Taylor Jr., Pat Taylor, cousins: Susan Taylor, Glenhall Taylor III <"Glenny">, James Taylor <Jamey> and Jim [the Taylor's adopted son]) We had an informal family dinner / buffet. After the meal we all departed company.

Throughout my childhood, I always referred to Glenhall Elmer Taylor Jr. as "Uncle Glen" and his wife as "Aunt Pat". He was a veteran of the Battle of the Bulge during WW II. He was awarded the Purple Heart Medal for his wounds in combat. After the war, he went on to college at the University of California, Berkley. He went on to help establish the credit card "Master-Card" for Wells Fargo Bank. He ended his career as the Vice Chairman of Credit Policy for the Bank of America. He was recognized by Wall Street as one of the top three loan specialists in the US. He also enjoyed the San Francisco sports teams. As a side line he wrote song lyrics.

The next week I made the rounds with neighbors and friends. I later went back to my high school with "Schar". (Most of these classmates remained estranged to me until only recently.) I went to visit my old bakery. They were glad to see me and I took home some "day-old" pastries. Overall, everybody seemed distant and cold upon hearing of my Vietnam combat experiences. Even the kids that I grew up with seemed distant. In some way all of my peers seemed very immature. I guess at 19, I was the old man. Often, I felt as if I was stranger in my own hometown. We spent most of my leave dividing up our time between the two households.

Eventually the Martins met my grandmother and her sister, only the second time since our wedding.

On one of my trips to the Presidio, to get paid and go to the PX and commissary, I checked in at personnel to see if my orders had come through, since it was getting close to the end of my leave. The orders came through: I was not to return to Vietnam (Which was a huge relief.) and was assigned to HHC 121st Signal Battalion, 1st Infantry Division (Mech) *"THE BIG RED ONE" !*, Fort Riley, Kansas. The NCOIC explained that that was the closest assignment available at the time since there at the Presidio, there were no tactical units where my specialties could be used. Ft. Lewis and Ft. Carson had no available openings in spite of having their tactical signal battalions with the 9th ID & 4th ID respectfully. "Big Red One", here I come.

The rest of my leave went well. I took in as much of the city that I could and treasured all the small things that I noticed and studied. There were emotional good-byes for all concerned. On the date of my departure, Junior took "Schar", Yuriko and me to the airport. More farewells and hugs. Soon San Francisco was fading behind me as I headed to Kansas City. In the air, once again. It was sad, yet not as emotional as my departure to Ft. Lewis for training for Vietnam.

CHAPTER THIRTY TWO

FORT RILEY KANSAS, "HOME OF THE BIG RED ONE"

I will be headed to a new post and units which have a lot of history. Fort Riley had a lot to do with the development of the American West. Fort Riley is located in the North-Central part of Kansas on the Kansas River. (also known as the Kaw River). It lies between Junction City and Manhattan, Kansas. (Home of the Kansas Bluejays) The military reservation lies in both Geary and Riley counties. It covers 101,733 acres and has a daytime population of 25,000. There is a residential population of about 8,000.

It was named in honor of Major General Bennet C. Riley who lead the first military escorts along the Santa Fe Trail, California, and Oregon trails. Originally in 1852, the same area was known as Camp Center, home to the 6th US Dragoons and the surveying parties of the US Army Corps of Engineers who were continuing to survey the vast west. The Fort Riley was established in 1853 and has served as a major US Cavalry post and school. Troops served there during the Civil War as well as during the Indian Wars. General George A. Custer was stationed there and to this day, no commissioned officer will live in the old house that Custer did (All commissioned officers who had lived there met disastrous fates and / or dishonored commands.). Today only warrant officers are allowed to reside there.

In 1887, it officially became the US Army's Cavalry School. The famed all Black 9th & 10th Cavalry Regiments were based there. These soldiers became known as *"The Buffalo Soldiers"* because of their hair that reminded people of the time of the hair on the buffalos. During WW II, the 9th & 10th were integrated, in name only, into the 2nd Cavalry (Armored) Division.

Troops were trained there during the Spanish-American War. (It is noted that Fort Riley was the "ground-zero" of the deadly Spanish Flu of 1918.) Over 50,000 troops were stationed there during World War One. Troops were trained there during WW II as well. Mechanized infantry tactics were developed, and troops were trained there. Over the years, various infantry units were assigned there. During WW II Fort Riley and 12 satellite installations were used to house German POWs. The 10th Mountain Division was activated there in July of 1948. (Any mountains in Kansas? We only had Custer Hill where the main troops were billeted.) During the Korean War, the base was used as a training facility.

From 1955 until 1996, Fort Riley was "home" to the 1st Infantry Division (Mech), "THE BIG RED ONE". (Between 1999 and 2006 it was home to the 24th Infantry Division (Mech) and "America's Warfighting Center" until the 1st ID returned from Leighton Barracks, Germany. Camp Whitside, as part of the base, was named in honor of Brigadier General Samuel M. Whitside who commanded company "B", 6th Cavalry Regiment between 1871 and 1874.

1st INFANTRY DIVISION: "The Big Red One"
(Sometimes called: 1st ID, "BRO" or "The Bloody One" or "The Big Red Un.)

The 1st Infantry Division is the longest continuously serving major unit of the Army. The division's motto is *"No Mission Too Difficult. No Sacrifice Too Great. DUTY FIRST !.*I would learn this quite well as time passed. The division's mascot in years past was "Rags", a mixed terrier. He was a "war dog", saving lives during the Argonne Campaign in 1918. He also carried messages warning of gas attacks. He died in 1936, an old "dog face" warrior.

The division was activated on 24 May 1917 as a combined arms division, a part of III Corps of the First American Expeditionary Force. The division marched through the streets of Paris on 4 July 1917. Captain C.E. Stanton of the 16th Infantry Regiment declared "Lafayette, we are here!". French and Allied morale was lifted by the appearance of the "Doughboys".

The division served with honor and gallantry throughout the various operations of the First World War. The division was highly decorated as well as the thousands of troops who served under The Big Red One. It has been noted that the troops of the 1st Inf. Div. were the first to have a shoulder patch sewn on their uniforms. The commanding general wanted all to know what unit these troops belonged to. Today, the Army soldier proudly wears on his left sleeve his unit of current assignment and on the right shoulder the unit that he served in combat with. (if he did). Otherwise his right sleeve was a "slick-sleeve", and he also was a "slick-sleeve".

The 1st Infantry Division's Service:

- World War One 1917-1919: Europe / France, Germany.
- Inter-War Reorganization of the Army: 1920-1941.
- World War Two: 1941-1945 England, North Africa, Sicily, Normandy ("D" Day), Germany: Combat & Occupation Forces 1945-1955.
- Korean War: Training Troops yet remained in Germany throughout the Cold War as a deterrent to the Soviet Threat.
- Vietnam 1965-1970:
- REFORGER: 1970 (Return of Forces in Germany & NATO Exercises yearly, of which I would participate.)
  {After my service, below} :
- First Gulf War: 1990-1991.
- Balkans:1996: Bosnia.
- Iraq: 2003 & 2004.
- Rebasing / Reorganization of US Forces.
- Iraq: 2006, 2007, 2008.
- Afghanistan 2008-2009.
- Iraq: 2008-2009.
- Iraq: 2009-2010.
- Iraq: 2010-2011.
- Afghanistan: 2011-2012.
- Afghanistan: 2012-2013.

- Operation Inherent Resolve: 2014, (500 troops supporting the Iraqi Army, WWOT.)
- Operation Freedom's Sentinel: 2016, (800 troops to Afghanistan with air support.)
- Operation Atlantic Resolve: 2017 (4,000 troops, rotation of forces in Europe.)

With that glorious military history and service behind the division, I proudly felt that I was becoming a part of a long-distinguished line of warriors.

THE REPLACEMENT COMPANY:

I managed to get through the terminal at the Kansas City International Airport and find a bus to Fort Riley. It is 139 miles to Ft. Riley, so if driven on I-70 it would take about 2 hours and 14 minutes if driven non-stop. Since I was on a Greyhound Bus and it was a local run, this trip took about four hours.

I was let off at the main gate along with several other soldiers. Only three of us wore our combat patches on our right shoulder. I still felt old for 19. Soon the MPs checked our orders and directed us to a bus stop, and we were instructed to tell the driver that we needed off at the replacement company. It was quite a quick tour of the base as other soldiers got on and off of the shuttle bus. Soon we were at the 1st Replacement Company. It was mid-afternoon when we signed in. We were sent to the supply room and picked up our bedding and then assigned our bunks. It was in a modern building and there were about 30 men in a large open bay. There was quite a range of ages and ranks. The highest rank was Staff Sergeant, E-6 and he was probably the oldest, being in his mid-twenties. The others were lower enlisted ranks about half of us wore our combat patches, the others were slick right sleeves, no combat experience. We were given all the basics, location of the mess hall and PX, snack bar and barber shop. The young buck sergeant giving us the briefing was a "slick sleeve".

We made up our racks and settled in these temporary quarters. We got to know some of these replacements. The routine would be simple: First call 0530, Chow 0600, first formation at 0700. Those with orders would be taken to their new units. Some lower rank personnel would be pulled out for various details around the company area or on post. The lowest ranks would pull some of the KP duties until their orders came through.

Since I had direct orders to the 121st Sig. Bn. I would only be here a day or so. We were not restricted to the company area at this time, so a few of us went over to the small snack bar and enjoyed a couple of pitchers of beer before the evening meal call. It was a relatively early night for me as I was quite tired from the travel and time differences.

I had a good sound sleep but was awakened rather abruptly when the lights were thrown on. That "slick sleeve" buck sergeant came through rousting the troops up. I looked at my bunk mate with disbelief that this young "buck" sounded as if he was rousting basic trainees. We all had been in the Army a while and half of us were combat veterans. I learned a bit later that many troops returning from Vietnam got into trouble here at the replacement company for "Mickey Mouse" offences, mostly for getting into it with these non-combat NCOs and officers. It was at times a rude awakening.

After chow, during the morning formation, I was assigned to lead a group of about six lower ranking troops, a detail to pull a complete police call (trash pick-up & removal.) around the company area and the motor pool. I was handed a large plastic trash bag. I immediately "delegated" the trash bag to one of the privates. I was somewhat surprised in that they had this Specialist Fifth Class leading troops. I recalled the "sergeant of the guard / sentry" debate from Vietnam. The other buck sergeants got similar assignments for other duties around post. Where need be, these details were bussed to their work areas.

When released from the morning formation, I walked my troops over to a clearing and then formed them up at "double arms interval", lined them up and we began our sweep of the company area. I stepped to the rear of the line to insure all was picked up properly. After a couple of passes around the barracks, I gave "my troops" a smoke break under the shade of a few trees. I reminded them to "field strip" their cigarette butts, or they would be picking them up as a part of this police call.

It was just about this time when our favorite buck sergeant appeared out of nowhere and called me over to him. He asked what in the hell I was doing. I politely told him that I was giving my troops a smoke break.

I told him in no uncertain terms that this was "my" detail and that I was in charge. I further told this "fuck of a buck" that we had made two passes around the company area and that we were headed over to the motor pool next. He seemed to turn red and his speech became rather nervous. I guess that he never had a Specialist address him in such a manner. I then challenged him to "inspect" our work area. He declined but added "It had better be all squared away, Specialist, or you'll answer to the company commander.". Big Deal ! what are they going to do? Send me to Vietnam? I just got back !

After an extended smoke break I formed up my detail and marched them across the road to the motor pool. I decided that we would sweep the outside perimeter and the fence line and then we would tackle the interior of the motor pool.

It took quite a while to police the perimeter of and then the interior of the motor pool. We took our time, but I made sure my troops did a good job. I could not but help to think that these people of the Replacement Company were slobs, knowing that there would be plenty of "newbees" to pick up after them. I had noticed a Coke machine outside of the motor pool garage building. Before leaving, I pointed this machine out to my troops and allowed them to go get a can, come outside for a break. This pissed off the Motor Sergeant, but it did increase the revenue from the machine to the motor section. By the time I marched the troops back to the company area for lunch, we had one quarter of a garbage bag filled. That was a lot of empty cans, bottles, paper and those disgusting cigarette butts.(even though I smoked at the time.) The next day, I was taken by Jeep to my new unit and permanent assignment, HHC 121st Signal Battalion.

121st SIGNAL BATTALION:
"The Army's Oldest and Most Decorated Signal Battalion"

Lineage

- Constituted 1916 July as a Signal Corps Battalion.
- Organized 1916 Sept. at Ft. Sam Houston, Tx. As the 2nd Field Battalion, Signal Corps, consisting of:
  1. Company "A" 1898 July, Signal Corps.

Re-designated 1910 as Field Company "A", Signal Corps.
Re-designated 1915 as Radio Company "A", Signal Corps.
Re-designated 1916 as Company "A", 2nd Field Battalion, Signal Corps.

2. Company "B" organized 1898, July as Company "D", Signal Corps.
Re-designated 1910, April, as Field Company "D", Signal Corps.
Re-designated 1916, Nov 11^{th,}as Company "B, 2nd Field Battalion, Signal Corps.

3. Company "C", organized 1917, 2nd Field Battalion, Signal Corps.

4. The Battalion was assigned 1917, May 24th, to the 2nd Field Signal Battalion.

- Reorganized and re-designated 1921 Feb. 09, as the 1st Signal Company.
- Reorganized and re-designated 1957 as Headquarters & Headquarters Company, 121st Signal Battalion, 1st Infantry Division, Fort Riley, Kansas. (inactivated in 1996)
- Reactivated 1996, Feb 02, Germany.
- Company "C", HQ & HQ Company, inactivated 2006, Apr. 10, Larson Barracks, Kitizingen, Germany.
- Company "B" inactivated 2005, Nov. 09, at Larson Barracks, Kitizingen, Germany.
- Company "A" inactivated 2006, Mar. 31, at Conn Barracks, Schweinfurt, Germany.

Campaign Participation Honors & Credits

- Spanish American War.
- Puerto Rico.
- World War One.
   1. Montdidier-Noyon.
   2. Aisne-Marne.

3. St. Mihiel.
4. Meuse-Argonne.
5. Lorraine 1918.
6. Picardy
- World War Two.
    1. Algeria-French Morocco w/arrowhead.
    2. Tunisia.
    3. Sicily w/arrowhead.
    4. Normandy w/arrowhead.
    5. Northern France.
    6. Rhineland.
    7. Ardennes-Alsace.
    8. Central Europe.
- Germany, Allied Occupation.
- Cold War.
- Vietnam.
    1. Defense.
    2. Counter Offensives II through VI
    3. Tet, 1968 & TET Counter Offensive.
    4. Summer / Fall 1969.
    5. Winter / Spring 1970.
- Balkans: Bosnia, Kosovo, Herzegovina.
- Southwest Asia.
    1. Defense of Saudi Arabia.
    2. Liberation and Defense of Kuwait.
    3. Cease Fire.
    4. Afghanistan / GWOT (Global War on Terror.)

MY TOUR WITH THE "BIG RED ONE"

A couple of us were assigned to the HHC 121st Sig. Bn. and arrived at the headquarters company. There was the usual processing in, both at the assigned company and at the battalion headquarters. Since I was an NCO, I got assigned a room with one other SP5. It was rather small, but a lot better than being billeted in a 60-man open bay. The next morning began the typical routine: Up at 0530, SS&S, chow, barracks cleaning &

maintenance, morning formation, PT (to include a 2-mile run because now the Army was getting fit & trim) The commanding General also had his pet project in having every troop in the division train and test to earn the EIB (expert infantry badge). That first PT session just about killed me, having been on a month's leave and Vietnam.

I was assigned to the Division Crypto Office. We were responsible for the maintenance of the crypto equipment of the entire 1st Infantry Division as well as those pieces of the 121st Sig. Bn.'s four companies. We also were responsible for the requests, storage and issuance of all the code books and materials.

Our shop was located in the basement of a multi-story old stone building on Main Post. The door to the shop was a huge vault door requiring a touch pad electronic code to gain entrance. It was, at the time, the home of 5th Army's NCO academy, where soldiers in the E-4 to E-6 grades were trained in leadership, tactics and military excellence. Right down the street were the long brick buildings that at one time housed the horse and mule stables during Ft. Riley's cavalry days. In the other direction was the main post PX.

We would make the daily trip from Custer Hill down to Main Post after the morning formation, drill, PT, and any other company business for our work and duty station. Some mornings, we would remain up on Custer Hill in the company motor pool to pull our operator maintenance on our section's motor vehicles. The section was allotted two "deuce and a half" cargo trucks each, one containing a shop shelter and the other, a GSQ-80 message distribution van. Power was supplied by two generator trailers, equipped with twin 5KW generators each. We also had the "chief's" ¼ ton Jeep and trailer. When all were present, the motor stables did not take very long, and we were glad to leave the company area for Main Post. (Less BS !)

The section's OIC was a warrant officer, CW3 Gonzalez. The NCOIC was a senior Specialist Fifth Class. He was the same rank that I had, only he had more "time-in-grade" than I. There was another SP5 repairman who also doubled as the division's crypto clerk. The last man in the section was a rather stout young Specialist Fourth Class. That young man must have been the most supervised troop in the division. (A CW3 & three SP5s over him.). There were always pieces of equipment to work on. In between that and the field exercises we all played mean games of chess.

The month that I arrived, the entire division was preparing to depart for Germany on REFORGER (Redeployment of Forces, Germany) and the NATO war games. We went to work clearing any backlog of repairs in the shop and going up to the battalion area and insuring that the commo vans all were in combat- ready condition. This would be the first time that I actually worked the tactical equipment mounted in the vans. Even though the actual equipment I serviced in Vietnam was classified as tactical, they were utilized in a fixed station configuration.

We also had to service our vehicles. Some would be shipped to Germany, others we would be issued at pre-staged equipment pools scattered throughout Germany for just the reason of quickly deploying the division from the States and picking up equipment in Germany, in route to "the front".

We also had to check and service our field gear, TA-50 (web belts, canteens, tents, mess kits, knap sacks, etc.) There was also the tedious task of inventory for all the shop equipment, tool boxes, and test equipment. We had to make sure that all of our repair parts were in good working order and stock levels were all up to date. There was a lot of priority ordering of parts and material needed in the field.

The division is being deployed in less than a month. The Division Crypto Support Section would be in the first waves of the deployment to insure that the division units would receive the proper code books and CEOIs (Communication Electronic Operating Instructions) upon their arrival. We were also to be able to provide almost immediate maintenance support.

I had the sad task of informing "Schar" that I was headed to Germany on REFORGER and would be gone for over three months. We would have to wait until December before we could get a place of our own. She was quite upset but understood. The rest of the time was spent in preparation for our deployment to Germany. I was getting used to the routine (*... sergeant, sergeant, can't you see all this PT is killing me?*) and learning my way around Fort Riley. I was making many friends and overall adjusting to life on the prairie.

About three weeks later we were boarding an army bus and headed to Mc Connell Air Force Base near Wichita, Kansas. Our duffle bags had already been loaded and our immediate shop equipment had already shipped ahead and would be waiting for us in Germany. Our section was a part of the division's advance party. We would be spending about a week or so more in Germany than the main body of the division.

This was really the first time that I had traveled any distance off of Ft. Riley. It is 131 miles between Ft. Riley and McConnell AFB. The trip normally would take about 2 ½ hours, but we were in a military convoy, so it will take much longer. As we rolled along, I could not but to be amazed at how flat Kansas really is. Custer Hill must seem like a mountain. It amazed me as we passed field after field of corn and other crops. The Mid-West definitely is America's "bread basket". Soon, we rolled through the main gate of McConnell Air Force Base. We would be flying to Germany in the relatively new Lockheed C-5A Galaxy heavy lift aircraft.

MC CONNELL AIR FORCE BASE:

The base is located four miles south-east of central Wichita, Kansas. The base is named after two brothers, Fred & Thomas McConnell decorated pilots from WW II. It is the home of the Air Mobility Command, providing world-wide airlift and re-fueling assets. It grew out of extensions to the Wichita Municipal Airport, which in June 1924 hosted 100,000 people for the National Air Congress exhibition. In August of 1941 the Kansas National Guard's 127th Observation Squadron was the first military unit to be stationed there as extensions to the airport continued. In March of 1942 the Army Air Corps completed leases from the city of Wichita and began expanding the facilities. Soon the Boeing plant nearby began delivering the famed B-29 Flying Fortresses. The Air Transport Division was based there, and the base was re-named Wichita Army Airfield. When the US Air Force was established in 1947. The base was re-named after the McConnell brothers in 1954.

During the Cold War, the base supported bombers of the SAC (Strategic Air Command) and the Titan II ballistic missiles. In 1964 the 23rd Tactical Fighter Wing was activated at the base. Later in 1965, three fighter squadrons were deployed to Southeast Asia in support of the war. In later years the base supported military operations world-wide by providing air-lift & re-fueling capabilities. As with this REFORGER operation, the Airlift Command provided troop and equipment deployments.

THE LOCKHEED C-5A GALAXY:

The C-5A is as of this writing, the world's largest aircraft. The Air Force began seeking a larger cargo aircraft in 1961. The C-5A has been in full service since 1970. Its prototype, the CX-X, first flew in 1968. It has a lift capacity of 190,000 lbs. The C-5A's cargo bay is one foot longer than the Wright brother's entire first flight at 121 ft. one foot longer than their flight. The cargo bay is 13.5 ft. high by 19 ft. wide. It is just over 31,000 cubic ft. in empty volume. It can accommodate up to 36 (463L) master cargo pallets. This huge bird can carry up to six AH-64 Apache helicopters. She can accommodate most armored vehicles as well, such as transporting five Bradley Fighting Vehicles in one load. There is a troop compartment on the upper deck which can seat 75 troops. The seats faced rearward, perhaps with the thought of better survival rates in the case of a crash landing. We could hear all the hydraulic fluids soaring through exposed lines and we could see the various cogs and gears turning, probably operating the rudder and stabilizer flaps or the rearward landing gears.

In fact, on our return trip back to McConnell AFB, we had to abandon the aircraft in emergency evacuation mode, once we landed, because one of the 26 landing struts and tire had caught fire. We were greeted home by the crash crew and a lot of foam. Another of the C-5As had to return back to Rhine Main because of a fuel leak from one of the RTT rigs.

CHAPTER THIRTY THREE

REFORGER:

REFORGER (Redeployment of Forces, Germany) was a yearly exercise to test and train the US capability to rush its forces in a minimum amount of time to Europe, should the Red Army pour through the Fulda Gap and her Eastern Block allies challenge all of NATO's borders and air space. The 1ˢᵗ Infantry would be the first to go, since it had a brigade permanently stationed in Germany. Our three brigades would mate up with the 4ᵗʰ Brigade and the entire division would be one of the first major units to defend Western Europe from the "red threat".

This also would be the time to test and service all the pre-staged equipment in the field depots.\ pre-staged in Germany. As well as our skills to rapidly return equipment to the "combat" front.

REFORGER would be a major test of tactics and logistics. At the end of the main exercise, all the NATO units would compete in gunnery competitions and other military contests. Above all it is designed to build a spirit of comradeship and esprit-de-corps among all the NATO military units participating. Hopefully in would demonstrate good will between the US military and the German civilians.

We would fly over to Germany aboard the C-5As to Ramstein AFB with our RTT (Radio Tele-Type) vans and equipment, and 75 troops per plane. We would then be sent to the equipment depots and check out most all of our vehicles and signal equipment prior to the main division arriving behind us.

There were six of us in the section and would be traveling together, mostly separate from division main. We would be a part of the war games and moved with the division and other NATO units. We were to observe all tactical disciplines while in the field. It goes without saying that we would be a very vital asset if captured by the OPFOR (Opposing Forces) since we had all the codes and crypto maintenance men and manuals. That is to also say, that in a "real" hot war we would be vital to enemy success, if captured. Our fate would be in question.

This experience would prove to be a lot different than my first tour in Germany, in that I would be traveling with two career warrant officers and a senior SP5, all who had multiple tours in Germany in the past. They not only did they know the customs and traditions, but all the great places to eat and drink. They spoke German a lot more than the rest of us. I would do all right with this crew.

We were all over central and southern Germany as the war games progressed. At one point we were too close to the border and had to make a hasty "re-directional retreat"; as in about an hour we would have been in East Germany (or was it Czechoslovakia?) with the division's crypto assets.

One evening while we were in a convoy, we were passing through a small town at dinner time. The streets were rather narrow and crooked. I had to urinate really bad, but the convoy could not stop at this time to allow me to relieve myself. I was riding in a "Deuce & ½" truck with commo shelter. The driver told me to simply open the door, step out on the running board, grab the frame of the side mirror and "drain the lizard". I stepped out onto the running board and began to piss just as the truck made a sharp turn passing by an outdoor patio of a guest Haus. Those German families were horrified at the spectacle rounding the corner standing outside of an US Army truck. All I could think of was to flash the "peace" sign, waving with my free hand, which released the "lizard" to finish peeing "free-style". As far as I recall there were no international incidents or calls to the US Embassy or State Department as a result of me "pissing" off the German civilians. Much relieved, I continued the mission.

I recalled one of the highlights of REFORGER was when we passed the Porche plant near Stuttgart. Our convoy was chugging along at about 45 MPH on the Autobahn which has no speed limit. There was a couple of miles to the rail head where the cars would be loaded on the trains for shipment. This stretch of highway was where the cars were "road-tested",

German style. Out of nowhere in the bright of day, the entire road was lit up with blinding headlights flashing. Those Porches sped by at almost 200 MPH., something out of "STAR WARS", jumping into light speed.

"Somewhere in Germany": The warrant officers found one of their guest Haus's, which had an outside patio. It was in a rather small village and the locals all seemed glad to see us. We stopped at dinner time and the weather was warm and sunny. We were led outside to the patio where we would be seated. A small stone fence separated us from the sidewalk. After our drinks were served, we ordered dinner. The warrant officers ordered for all of us in fluent modern German.

Two of my companions had never been to Germany. They ordered fried chicken. We began to eat our meal. These two were picking up their chicken and eating it with their fingers. This is a taboo in Europe, one must use the knife & fork to eat even chicken. At times I noticed the patio got very quiet and people walking on the sidewalk were stopping, pointing to the GIs eating chicken with the fingers. In rapid German, the parents were instructing their children proper table manners. The warrants were laughing hysterically as they told us what was really happening. In the name of international co-operation those two GIs finished their chicken very clumsily with their knives and forks.

Sometimes our section was on its own, wandering through the German countryside, while others were speeding down the autobahn. We also had out fast times on the autobahn. Still at other times we were locked into a convoy. Altogether it was a great experience, enjoying the landscapes, the culture, the history as well as the people. From both of my tours in Germany, I could not but to be amused when the older gentlemen would always tell me: "…oh, nine, I 'Vell", always fought on the Eastern Front, not against the Americans !". Or perhaps with a hint of being sinister: "….vell, ve vere merely following der orders of our superiors!". (Years later, a German Lieutenant Colonel once told me as he clicked his heels while returning my salute: "…Vell sergeant, des old vays die very slowly. Virstain? ".

When the official NATO war games concluded, we were sent to the training area known as Grafenwohr. (tent city) Many of the other division units not required to take part in the firing exercises returned home to

Kansas. We were there because we were Signal and laid out and maintained the communications on this live firing range.

Grafenwohr in German means, the Island of the Count from the 9th century. It is located between the River Creussen and the Stream Thum, in Bavaria. It covers an area of over 37 square miles.

As a military installation, construction began in 1908. The first artillery round was fired there on 10 June 1910. The Imperial German Army trained there during World War I. During the Second World War, the NAZI Wehrmacht expanded the training area to over 90 square miles. It was bombed by the Allies during the war. After the war it was rebuilt and reduced in size to only the 37 square miles of today. "Graf" has been continually used by German and NATO forces for training ever since.

There is also the Grafenwohr Airfield which supports the training area supplied by the 37th Airlift Squadron out of Ramstein AFB. Many other distinguished units from the Army and Air Force have been stationed there or have rotated in and out. Most every major unit in Germany has spent some time at "Graf".

First of all, "Graf" lives up to its nick name, "Tent City". The units rotating in for training were billeted in a huge bivouac area of field tents, to include their own mess tents. The post cadre occupies and lives in the fixed "brick & mortar" buildings. Many of these were used by the Wehrmacht during WW II. Some of the newer buildings were the PX, commissary, movie theatre, the medical clinics and the clubs.

Being that we were Division Crypto, we did not have a direct support role with the live fire exercises or the gunnery contests, other than maintain the code support and crypto support, should "the red flag" go up, for real while we were there. We basically kept up with our own crypto support activities. The cable crews laid out the field wire network and the telephone switchboards supporting the exercises. The various radio assets also were in direct support of the same.

I maintain three distinct memories of my time at "Graf". The first being the cold. We were there in November and towards the end of the exercise, I was freezing. I recall traveling in the back of the Chief's Jeep, without the "winterization" accessory kit installed, as the radio operator in my mountain sleeping bag. The next memory was the unique sound of the heavy artillery rounds making a deep, thundering, wobbling sound as they passed overhead. In contrast to the cold, my warmest memory was the comraderies and esprit-de-corps felt and shared among the various NATO country's troops. This was especially exhibited at the clubs, both on and off post.

After a week or so of these exercises at Grafenwohr the units began to pack up their tents and head home". The Germany based units to their own kasernes, other NATO soldiers back to their home countries. Most important was that we were to turn in the equipment that we drew from the pre-staged stockpiles from the German depots. We were ordered that that gear WILL be in better condition than we picked them up in. We may return !

Soon, but not too soon for me, we were headed towards Ramstein AFB for the trip home to McConnell AFB, Kansas.

After arriving at Ramstein AFB, we were billeted in a huge steel hanger building. There were several hundred troops in each of several of these massive hangers. These buildings were so big, I guessed a B-52 could easily be parked in there with room to spare. The Air Force fed us, which was great, compared to Army chow. I do believe that in 1971, the Air Force employed all civilian cooks and mess hall staff. (The Army would do so under the VOLAR (Volunteer Army) Program. The draft was expected to end in June of 1971 but was extended by Congress until June of 1973. (the draft officially ended 27 January 1973.) The Army was anticipating an "all-volunteer" force and began to make some changes.

It was a long flight back to the States and we were able to get some decent sleep, as by now we were accustomed to all the weird sounds inside of the C-5As. It was wonderful to be "back-in-the States" once again. Once we were back at Ft. Riley, we had a lot to do to get all the unit equipment cleaned and all maintenance performed and up to date. There was a lot of resupply and administrative functions to be completed bringing everything current after the deployment. I recall that the next weekend was a three-day weekend for us, courtesy of the Commanding General, just before the Thanksgiving holiday

EARLY MARRIED LIFE

It was not until mid-December that I was able to secure a small bungalow and have Scharlene come out to live as a married couple. It was a small place, one bedroom, living room, small kitchen, and a bathroom. It was partially furnished, and the rest of our initial household goods were either from the US Army or the Salvation Army.

We happily celebrated our first real Christmas together. Money was tight, but "Schar" kept teasing me that she had an expensive gift for me. I got rather upset, in that with the move together and all, my financial picture was rather dismal until the 1st. Never the less, we had a very small tree and a few simple gifts under the tree. We had each other and that was enough. As the Chesse' family tradition would have it, we opened our Christmas gifts on Christmas Eve. The Taylor side of the family honored the traditional, typical Christmas Morning routine.

At the stroke of midnight, we toasted to Christmas and our future with spiked egg-nog. "Schar" informed me that she was going to get my gift. She placed a blindfold over my eyes and demanded that I do not peek. She then disappeared into our bedroom and shut the door. After what seemed like an eternity of anticipation, I heard the bedroom door opening. She said, "You better not peek now, or I'll beat your butt.". I heard some rustling in the room, then silence. The radio was turned on and Christmas carols were playing softly. She told me that I could now remove the blindfold. I did so without any hesitation. The room was lit only by the tiny lights on the tree and several scented candles.

THERE SHE WAS WEARING ONLY A BRIGHT – RED VELVET RIBBON AND A SMILE.

That did it ! I was so overwhelmed with joy and happiness I could not contain myself. I slowly unwrapped my "present" and tasted the special "treats" that she presented to me. We made passionate love by the tiny Christmas tree. That was the best Christmas present in my entire life.

A week later we saw in a new year, 1972. That year would prove to be most interesting as we toasted in the New Year, but at least we were together at last. The events that would unfold in that year would have everlasting effects on my life.

Scharlene and I lived comfortably there in Junction City, Kansas. At first, I would catch a ride from our bungalow up to Custer Hill and after work catch the Army bus to the gate and walk home when I was off duty. We made many friends in the neighborhood, once the neighbors learned that my wife was not Vietnamese.

It was cold when it snowed as the wind off of the Great Lakes blew relentlessly across flat Kansas. Snow piled up everywhere on the windward side of things. "Schar" loved it, but I hated it, especially when we were in the field training.

A couple of months later, I was able to buy a car at a local "buy here, pay here dealer. I got a Fire Engine Red, black interior, 1968 Ford Mustang Coupe. I really loved that car. It made 3 trips between Junction City and San Francisco without any problems.

My military routine was pretty routine and living off-post made it all worthwhile. It was in May that I learned that my grandmother, Jessie, was terminally ill and the family had requested through the Red Cross to have me transferred to the Presidio of San Francisco to be nearer to my grandmother and family. I took a short leave and returned to San Francisco with "Schar". I returned to Ft. Riley alone and began my preparations to close up our house and make the transfer to San Francisco.

My wife returned to Kansas to be with me to finish up our business in Kansas. We drove together back to San Francisco. In June that year, my orders came through and I was ordered to the Presidio of San Francisco. I would be assigned to the Headquarters, 6th US Army, Special Troops.

CALIFORNIA, HERE I AM:

The trip between Kansas and California opened up a whole new experience and view of our country. We traveled from the extremely flat farm lands of Kansas to the Rocky Mountains of Colorado. We followed along the Green River and the many beautiful gorges along the river's path. The greenery and the sheer canyon drops were breathtaking.

We stopped at a small Bed & Breakfast outside of the Vail / Aspen resort area for breakfast one morning. We pulled into a log cabin style restaurant which was run by a "hippie" commune Since I was on orders to travel, I was in my summer khaki uniform. During the course of the meal a young couple tried to convince me to desert the Army and join their commune. They went on arguing against the war in Vietnam. The food was great, so I thanked them, settled our bill, but declined deserting the Army. We sped westward in the '68 Mustang I called "The Horse With no Name.".

Once we left the cities, the stretch between Utah & Nevada was the most desolate roads that I've ever driven. At night the heat, off of the desert. Would project the reflection of a car's headlights out in front of me, yet I would not pass that car for at least an hour. The eerie scene quite often were the tire skid marks that just left the highway with no signs of a car or wreckage. The buzzards constantly patrolled the highway, just in case. I kept a watchful eye on the gas gage. When we entered or left a small town there was always a sign saying something like **"NEXT GAS...135 MILES !"** or **"The Next Section of This Highway Patrolled by Aircraft Only"** They meant that for sure !

When we passed through Reno, Nevada and headed towards Sacramento on I-80, I realized that the interstate highway system was making quite a lot of progress, as there were eight lanes as we neared Sacramento. Once we crossed the California state line, I immediately felt that I was home again.

CHAPTER THIRTY FOUR

When I returned to San Francisco, I was assigned even further to the 6th Army Casualty Office. It was an interesting assignment, in that I was not working in any of my signal specialties. There were no tactical units stationed in San Francisco. The post Comm-Center had only fixed station crypto equipment. So, I took a correspondence course through the army for 72H20, Personnel Specialist.

Our office handled the active duty deaths and serious injuries case files, as well as supporting the surviving families that resided within the 6th Army Command area. (Western United States). We also took care of the POW / MIA cases that were in our jurisdiction. After I was OJT trained on the day shift, I was able to handle the office on my own and was transferred to the solo night shift. It was pretty good duty and I mostly worked nights, pulling a 15 hour shift, (1700hrs to 0800hrs.) Then I would have two days off. Every so often there would be a 24-hour week-end tour. It gave me a lot of time at home.

My grandmother's sister, Catherine Walker had converted the family living room into my grandmother's hospice room. There was always a nurse on duty for my grandmother. Catherine then had me & Scharlene move out of my own house to an apartment on Balboa Street that she would pay for. It was beneficial for all of us, but I still felt resentful for having to vacate my own home. We still bought groceries and things for the two sisters from the Presidio commissary and PX. My grandmother, Jessie Taylor died before my discharge from active duty. Catherine made all the arrangements very quickly and there was no service for us to attend. I felt cheated.

The Paris Peace Accords, officially ending the American involvement in the Vietnam War (Second Indochina War), was signed on 27 January 1973. In March of the same year, the US pulled out the last of the troops, leaving only a few "advisors" and limited ..diplomatic security personnel. We witnessed many of these troops being processed through 6th US Army facilities. I was on the night shift through these events.

I was on the night shift at the Casualty Office on the night of 12 February 1973 when the Senior US Military Liaison Officer in Hanoi came on a world-wide conference call. That phone conference call connected all the major US military commands, to officially announce the confirmed names and proven identity of over 600 US POWs from Hanoi. These POWs were often held for years in both North and South Vietnam in some of the most brutal and inhumane conditions.

With this task completed, Operation Homecoming officially began to bring our heroes home. I had the duty and honor of taking the names of the POWS who were from the 6th US Army command area, or their having their family members residing in our area. It was one of the most exhausting nights of my young life, yet today it represented my proudest hours. I spent the last part of my assignment there as a member of the Operation Homecoming Team. This operation lasted from 12 February until 4 April 1973, involving 54 C-141 air missions as well as other air transportation to return these POWs "Home" and to the various military hospitals around the country near their home towns for initial medical, psychological and intelligence de-briefings before being returned to military service or discharged from the military completely.

With this historic mission completed, I was getting "short" (90 days or less in the military). I was offered to enroll in <u>"Project Transition"</u>. This was an attempt by the military to safely transition service personnel back, "painlessly" into civilian life. The two paths open were a trade "apprenticeship" or a return to school. I choose to go the academic route at San Francisco State College. (Later accredited as a university, SFSU. I would receive my BA from SFSU in 1980 in International Relations, Asian Concentration, Minor in Business Management in 1980, thanks to the GI Bill.).

I began, in civilian status (no military requirements or duty) in the <u>Veterans Upward-Bound Program</u>. This program was to bring veterans up to college standards by a thorough academic curriculum and tutoring. The gap between our delayed academic profile and that of the recently graduated high school students was big. Most of us had two to six years (or more) absence from the academic world by being in the military. What we had experienced could not easily be transferred into college "credit or units". We began our college career at a distinctive disadvantage, although we had experienced more during our military tours than most all of these "kids" have in their entire lives.

I really enjoyed my last 90 days in the Army as a student, living at home with my wife, regular hours, home cooked meals, family and a distinct feeling of how a "civilian" lives and feels. The time at school was great, although there was a lot of negative words and feelings directed towards me, when other students and faculty learned of my military history.

As my ETS (expiration, term of service) date approached, I felt all the fears and concerns experienced by service personnel of the day returning to civilian life. The first major concern was income, finding a job. I knew that I would be going to school on the GI Bill, but there was a time delay involved in getting into the system on a regular timetable. I knew that the unemployment rate for newly discharged veterans was quite high. My other concerns were how society would or would not accept a 21 year old combat veteran and college student.

I further enrolled in San Francisco State's "Veterans Upward-Bound Program" for September's classes. This program consisted of 12 units of college entry level courses for one semester. Upon successful completion of that program, the veteran was guaranteed a position automatically in the college, regardless of past academic grades of scores.

As a part of Operation Transition, I went to an Army civilian "counselor" and took a series of tests to determine my best career paths after my discharge. To my amazement and later concurrence, I would become successful in the following fields: Undertaker / Funeral Director / Mortician, Minister (clergy) or a Teacher. None of these selections seemed to fit at the time. Later in life, at least parts of those careers did apply. (as a senior NCO, I taught and trained young troops, dealt with many deaths and over time, became quite spiritual.)

I was afforded a few days to clear post (clear all my various accounts, supply, medical, personnel, library, etc.) at the Presidio. On the day before by ETS date, I made sure that I had a good haircut, as I did not want the embarrassment at the last minute at the Oakland Army Base's discharge point. Early on the Friday morning of 3 August 1973, I drove the 15.7 miles from my house over to the discharge point on the Oakland Army Base. I was dressed in my sharply pressed Army dress-green uniform, complete with all my decorations.

In a strange way, getting released from the military seemed a lot easier that enlisting, even though it took most of the day. There was *a lot* of paperwork to go over and complete. There was a quick final physical exam. (Which in later years, proved to have overlooked a lot.)

I ate my last Army lunch at a nearby mess hall, where it seemed that all, but the cooks were getting out of the Army that day. We are "short" ! After lunch and some more "out-processing" we reported for our last pay at the finance section.

That final pay included 3 days of regular pay, and quarters allowance ($59.60) and one way travel pay (Oakland to San Francisco-12.4 miles @ $ .05 / per mile= $ .62. <bridge toll, one way was $ .50>.) I also had about three days of unused leave time, (@ $19.87 per day=$59.61). I was discharged with $ 119.22 to begin my new civilian life.

At the last minute, I decided to enlist in the US Army Reserve. The all the services had their reserve and national guard recruiters there to try to enlist these newly discharged veterans. I made this quick decision to help supplement my unemployment and GI Bill educational check. I enlisted with the 490th Signal Company (Support) stationed across the Golden Gate Bridge at Fort Baker. Unknown to me in 1973, I would wind up staying with that unit (as well,when it was re-designated, "B" Company, 319th Signal Battalion.) for the next 16 years.

I drove back to San Francisco as a civilian / week-end warrior at 21 years old after over 4 years of military service. Along the way, after a couple of *"Honey-Do"* stops at the stores. I still got the verbal and physical disrespect from some of the civilians, my fellow citizens. They did not know that I was recently discharged but required to wear the uniform because I was technically still on my travel / discharge orders for 24 hours after my discharge. Monday I would apply for my unemployment and be at least looking at the current job market for any future possibilities.

I pulled into the driveway outside my childhood home, 654 21st Avenue and all I could do was contemplate my life up to this point. The Martin family was now living in my house; I was now off of active military duty; I had a three year Army Reserve enlistment ahead of me; at least 4 or more years of college and many years ahead of me (God willing). I now had a family to think of and to care for now. Most of all I had a good future ahead of me and all that I had experienced up to this point in time seemed to be worthwhile.

I sighed and turned off the ignition in my "Horse With no Name" and got out of the car.

Scharlene saw me pull in and raced down the steps to greet me. I smiled and gave her a big hug and a very passionate kiss. When separated, and she took my hand to lead me inside. I looked up and down "my" block, the place of my childhood, and saw nobody was welcoming me home. I just then realized that there was a lot of truth in what a man much wiser than I, once said: "…once you leave home for the first time, you can never really go *"Home"* again." I walked up the stairs with Scharlene.

END OF BOOK ONE

APPENDIX, TIMELINES & NOTES

<u>San Francisco History Timeline</u>

- Prehistoric: 10,000- 20,000 years BC, estimated first human known habitation. The Native American tribe, the Oholone (Miwok for "western people") settle in the area. They live off of the bounty of the Pacific Ocean.

- 1579- English Captain Francis Drake enters the waters aboard the ship HMS Golden Hind. They name the area New Albion and stay five weeks, getting along just fine with the natives.

- 1769- 01 Nov. The entrance to the bay is named La Boca del Puerto, (mouth of the port.), by Spanish Sergeant Jose Ortega.

- 1776- The Spanish establish a colony by first building The Presidio of San Francisco (the fort) and then Mission Delores.

- 1820-1848 Americans trade with the Spanish and Mexicans in the Bay Area continues to grow, along with the cultural influences of both.

- 1846- A group of 200 Latter-day Saints settle in the area. Other religious and political groups find San Francisco a liberal city.

- 1847- The city's name is officially changed from Yerba Buena (beautiful herb) to San Francisco.

- 1848- January; gold is discovered at Coloma, in the Sierra Nevada foothills at Sutter's Mill. **THE RUSH IS ON !**

- 1849- The thousands of "49ers. Arrive and the City becomes a boom-town as the miners are supplied and serviced before their mad rush to the gold fields in the Sierra Nevada Mother Lode. The bay is clogged with the hulks Of abandoned sailing ships. The foundation of the San Francisco Financial District is the hulks of these ships and fill-in debris.

  The Saint Francis Hotel is built. The French bakery, Boudin Brothers Bakery begins its operation. (today the "mother-yeast" from the Gold Rush days is still used as the 'starter 'yeast.

- 1850- Statehood! September 9th. The City is incorporated.

- 1851- May 3 & 4, A major Fire burns a lot of the city. On June 9th, a man at Sidney Cove steals a safe from a merchant and runs to a row boat in the bay and begins to escape. A band of merchants overtake him. *"The 1851Committee of Vigilance"* is born.

- 1852- Ghirardelli Chocolates opens for business. (It still is in business today and its sweet products are shipped as a favorite worldwide.).

- 1853- California Academy of Science, and the YMCA, are founded.

- 1854- Lone Mountain (Laurel Hill) Cemetery is opened. (Later, Lone Mountain College for Women.)

- 1855- September 24th; The preserved heads of outlaws Joaquin Murieta & "Three Fingered Jack" were sold at an auction for $36.00. (in today's dollars.)

- 1856- Following The Committee's "cleanup" of crime, businesses poured into the City. On June 11th the city & county of San

Francisco is formed, and San Mateo becomes its own county. The City's population grows to over 30,000 and the city emerges from its "tent-city days of the Gold Rush to a moderate city of brick, stone and wood.

- 1856- James William, "King of William", editor of the Evening Bulletin is shot and killed by William Casey.

- 1857- State Convention of Colored People is held in the City.

- 1858- The Italian Benevolent Society is formed.

- 1858- Sutro & Company is founded by Gustav Charles and Emil Sutro. It will become the oldest investment-banking firm in San Francisco & California. The Italian Benevolent League is also formed.

- 1859- Joshua A. Norton declares himself *Emperor of These Here United States!* The story and legend of "Emperor Norton" is born. (Not to be confused with "Emperor Gene Nelson" of KYA Radio (AM).

- 1860- The Imperial Japanese Embassy arrives. April 03, The Pony Express begins trans-continental service. The "Pinoche Railroad" was begun by the Market Street Railway Company. (Forerunner to our present MUNI.)

- 1861- Fort Point is completed to protect the San Francisco Bay from Confederate (or any other's) invasion. Never was a shot fired in anger from Fort Point. The Overland Telegraph Company begins its trans-continental service.

- 1862- Herald's Business College is founded. The San Francisco Stock & Bond Exchange was founded.

- 1863- The San Francisco and San Jose Railroad begins operations.

- 1864- Hugh Toland founded the Toland Medical College. (It would later become the University of California, San Francisco.)

- 1868- On a spring day, banker James Sloan Hutchinson witnesses two horsemen dragging a squealing pig, mutilated behind them. They were taking the poor creature to market. He was so shocked by the bloody spectacle, that he and other wealthy citizens form The San Francisco SPCA.

- 1868-*"We propose to publish a bold, bright, fearless and truly independent newspaper, independent of all things, neutral in nothing!"* Two brothers, Charles and M.H. de Young, barely 20-years old each, declare the creation of a major newspaper: The Daily Morning Chronicle. They began their enterprise off of a borrowed $20.00 gold piece. Today, The Chronicle is still the morning paper in the City.

- 1869- The first westbound transcontinental train arrives in San Francisco. California Theatre opens. The San Francisco Yacht Club is founded.

- 1870- Rising out of the squalor of its "tent city" Gold Rush days, San Francisco becomes the 10th largest city in the United States. Golden Gate Park and San Francisco Microscopical Society established. The City's population rises to 146,473.

- 1871- San Francisco Art Association and St. Luke's Hospital are established.

- 1872- The Bohemian Club and San Francisco Bar Association are established.

- 1873- Clay Street Railroad Company begins its operations.

  The Polish Society of California is organized.

- 1874- California School of Design and Territorial Pioneers of California are founded. (My grandfather, Andrew Taylor is born near Yorkshire, England, in a small village named Doncaster.)

- 1875- The Palace Hotel opens its doors. The San Francisco Fire Patrol is established. (forerunner to the present fire department.)

- 1877- Anti-Chinese sentiments lead to full-scale riots. The population seems to forget that the Chinese build the railroads.

- 1878- The American Speaking Telephone Company issues its "phone book" of its subscribers. It is only one page long.

- 1878- The San Francisco Public Library, Pacific Yacht Club, YWCA are Established.

- 1880- Emperor Norton drops dead on California Street. His funeral and parade draws up to 30,000 mourners and revelers. Before his death, the emperor ordered that bridges be built north and east to span the San Francisco Bay.

  George Hearst acquires a small newspaper, The San Francisco Examiner, as payment for a gambling debt. The paper is a success and dominated the afternoon / evening news market. In the mid-1880s his eldest son, William Randolph Hearst takes over the paper, as the elder Hearst in now a US Senator from California. Today, the two papers: The Chronicle (morning) and The Examiner (afternoon / evening) are the last main papers in the City.

- 1882- During the 1840s & 1850s, Chinese laborers and businessmen flooded into California during the Gold Rush and the construction of the railroads. By about 1870, the Mother Lode gold fields were pretty much mined out. As the economy waivered, anti-Chinese and Asian sentiments grew. Congress passed the Chinese Exclusion Act, barring all Chinese immigration. That law was not repealed for another 60 years.

- 1883- "Black Bart" (Charles Bolton) the infamous "gentleman bandit", is revealed to have been a Wells Fargo bank clerk.

- 1887- Cogswell Polytechnic College is established.

- 1888- Associated Charities and San Francisco Business College are established.

- 1890- California Camera Club and University Club of San Francisco are established.

- 1891- Gregg Shorthand School established.

- 1892- The Hibernia Bank is built. The Sierra Club is formed by 182 charter members. John Muir is elected the president. Their first major environmental battle was to stop the reduction of the boundaries of the Yosemite National Park.

- 1893- Mark Hopkins Institute of Art is founded.

- 1894- Wilmerding School of Industrial Arts founded. (later merged with Lux Girls School and became 'Lick-Wilmerding' prep school.

  The Japanese Tea Garden is built.

- 1895- M.H. de Young Memorial Museum opens.

- 1896- The Sutro Baths opens.

- 1898- San Francisco Ferry Building opens. The City is re-chartered. The Buddhist temple opens. On Nov 19th, The American Anti-Imperialist is formed to oppose land gains of the US, resulting from the Spanish-American War.

- 1899- San Francisco State Normal School is established. (Later San Francisco State College and even later, San Francisco State University [this author's alma mater)

  San Francisco City Hall is built.

- 1900- San Francisco's population reaches 342,782.

- 1905- San Francisco graft trials expose political corruption in the City.

- 1906- April 18, The Great Earthquake & Fire. Most of the city destroyed.

- 1907- The City rebuilds. "Mutt" comic strip in introduced by the Chronicle.

- 1908- "South San Francisco is incorporated as a separate municipality.

- 1910- San Francisco Housing Authority created. Population, now: 416,912.

- 1911- The San Francisco Symphony is formed. Cort Theatre opens.

- 1912- Lux School for Industrial Training for Girls opens. The Book Club of California is established. James Rolph is elected mayor. Tadish Grill opens.

- 1914- California National Guard Armory is built.

- 1915- January 25, The first trans-continental telephone call is successfully made, S.F. to N.Y. Feb 20, Panama- Pacific International exposition opens. "Tower of Jewels is built. The San Francisco Labor Temple is built. San Francisco city hall is rebuilt.

(My grandfather, Andrew Taylor works on the ornate plaster.) Veterans Auditorium opens its doors.

- 1916- Preparedness Day bombing. Legal Aid Society is created. Buena Vista Café opens for business.

- 1917- Strand Theatre opens.

- 1922- The Golden Gate and Castro Theatres open.

- 1923- President Harding dies suddenly at the Palace Hotel.

- 1924- California Palace of the Legion of Honor opens.

- 1925- The Fleishhaker Pool is built.

- 1926- The Whitney Brothers "Playland at the Beach" opens. (amusement park).

- 1927- San Francisco Municipal Airport is dedicated.

- 1928- The Amazon Theatre opens to the public.

- 1929- The Stock Market crash; The Great Depression begins. The Fleishacker Zoo opens its gates. "Topsey's Roost" (restaurant) opens its doors.

- 1930- The Pacific Stock Exchange opens its doors.

- 1931- Stern Grove Municipal Park opens to the public.

- 1932- War Memorial Opera House opens.

- 1933- Jan 5th Construction begins on the Golden Gate Bridge. July 9th work begins on the San Francisco-Oakland Bay Bridge. San Francisco Opera / Ballet is founded. Coit Tower is built. (My uncle, Ralph Chesse' paints many of the fresco murals under the WPA program.)

- 1934- May 9, The General Strike begins. The Federal maximum-security prison on Alcatraz Island (in the middle of the bay) opens and takes in the government's worst criminals. Golden Grain Macaroni Company ("Rice-a Roni, The San Francisco Treat") begins its operations.

- 1935- San Francisco Museum of Modern Art opens as San Francisco Museum of Art in The Veterans Memorial Building.

- 1937- May 27, The Golden Gate Bridge opens for traffic.

- 1940- Holly Courts housing project opens.

- World War Two; San Francisco becomes a major hub for materials and troops headed to the Pacific theatre of operations.

- 1945- The "Tonga Room Opens"" (night club) opens for business. United Nations is organized and chartered.

- 1946- National Urban League, San Francisco Branch and The Marines' Memorial Club are established.

- 1949- The Presidio Theatre opens.

- 1951- *November 27, This author is born.*

THE EARLY TV LINE-UP

The "List"

San Francisco Beat	I Love Lucy
Death Valley Days (Twenty- Mule team Borax)	Gene Autry

The Rebel

Have Gun, Will Travel

Topper

The Honeymooners

Zorro

The Lone Ranger

Dragnet

Sky King

Lassie

This is Your Life

Cheyenne

The Lucy-Desi Comedy Hour

The Green Hornet

The Saint

Perry Mason

Get Smart

The Cisco Kid

The Outer Limits

Leave it to Beaver

My Three Sons

The Mickey Mouse Club

The Dean Martin Show

The Ed Sullivan Show

The Lawrence Welk Show

American Band Stand

Car 54 (where are you?)

Davy Crockett

Rawhide

Sea Hun

Amos and Andy

What's my Line?

Wagon Train

Batman

Wanted, Dead or Alive

The Man From U.N.C.L.E.

My Favorite Martian

I Spy

Voyage to the Bottom of the Sea

One Step Beyond

Father Knows Best

The Real Mc Coys

The Brother Buzz Show

The Saturday Line Up.

Captain Satellite

Captain Kangaroo

Captain Fortune's Funhouse

Tom & Jerry

The Roadrunner

The Jetsons

Dick Tracy

Mayor Art

Bozo the Clown

Popeye

Donald Duck

The Flintstones

Casper, the Friendly Ghost   Looney Tunes

Bugs Bunny   Dick Tracy

THE MUSIC LIST

The Partial List of the Bands and the Music of the Era

Big Brother & The Holding Company

The Grateful Dead

Moby Grape

Country Joe & The Fish

The Byrds

The Jimi Hendrix Experience

Quicksilver Messenger Service

Sagittarius

Jefferson Airplane (Starship, Jefferson in later years)

Commander Cody & the Lost Planet Airmen

Ultimate Spinach

The Steve Miller Band

Paul Butterfield Blues Band

Iron Butterfly

The Chambers Brothers

Ten Years After

Procol Harum

Spooky Tooth

Pink Floyd

The Doors

The 13th Floor Elevator

The Charlatans

Blue Cheer

Coven

The Human Beinz

The Seeds

Steppenwolf

The Velvet Underground

Spirit

Sly & The Family Stone

Creedence Clearwater Revival

Santana

Canned Heat

Blood Sweat & Tears

The Electric Flag

Moody Blues

Eric Burdon & The Animals (later, War)

The Allman Brothers Band

The Staple Singers

Malo (Carlos Santana's brother's band.)

Frank Zappa and The Mothers of Invention

Cream

Led Zeppelin

Taj Mahal

The Youngbloods

The Sons of Champlin

The Doobie Brothers

The New Riders of the Purple Sage

The partial list of Motown Groups and Artists

The Chilites

The Contours

The Elgins

The Four Tops

The Fantastic Four

Marvin Gaye

Brenda Holloway

Eddie Holland

Patrice Holloway

The Isley Brothers

Chuck Jackson

Mable John

Marv Johnson

Gladys Knight & The Pips

Shorty Long

Martha & The Vandellas

The Marvelettes

Barbara McNair

Smokey Robinson & The Miracles

The Monitors

The Originals

Barbara Randolph

David Ruffin

Jimmy Ruffin

Edwin Starr

Barrett Strong

Diana Ross & the Supremes

Bobby Taylor & the Vancouvers

R. Dean Taylor

The Temptations

Tammi Terrell

The Valadiers

Junior Walker & the All Stars

Mary Wells

Kim Weston

Little Stevie Wonder (Stevie Wonder, when he got older.)

Earl Van Dyke & The Soul   The Velvelettes
Brothers Syreeta Wright

<u>THE NEWSPAPER LIST</u>

- *The San Francisco Examiner*
- *The San Francisco Chronicle*
- *The Call*
- *The Bulletin (later these two became the Call-Bulletin)*
- *The San Francisco News*
- *The San Francisco Progress (later just 'Progress 'and a "neighborhood" rag.)*
- *The Socialist*
- *The Argus*
- *The Oracle (a Hippie paper of the 1960's.*
- These papers below may have been published later than my 1950-1980 timeline.
- Some may or may not be in print as of this writing.

- *The Chinatown Times (printed in Chinese)*
- *Asian Week*
- *The Argus*
- *El Mensajero (Spanish)*
- *Irish Herald*
- *Jewish News Weekly of Northern California*
- *Nichi Bei Times (Japanese)*
- *Noe Valley Voice*
- *Noe Hill Gazette*
- *Philippine News*
- *El Reportero (Spanish)*
- *Richmond Review*
- *SF Weekly*
- *San Francisco Bay Guardian*
- *San Francisco Bay Times*
- *San Francisco Bayview*
- *San Francisco Business Times*

1969 Partial Timeline

January 12th,   Super Bowl III, N.Y. Jets defeat the Baltimore Colts, 16-7

January 13th,   Elvis Presley begins his come-back album featuring: "In the Ghetto", "Suspicious Minds" and "Kentucky Rain".

January 14th,   An explosion aboard the USS Enterprise kills 27 and injures 314.

January 20th,   Richard Milhous Nixon was sworn in as the 37th President of the United States of America.

February 5th,   The Santa Barbara oil spill.

February 9th,   The Boeing 747 makes its historic maiden flight.

February 24th,   The Mariner 6 Mars Probe is launched; The supreme Court Rules that the First Amendment applies equally to public schools.

March 3rd,   Sirhan Sirhan admits killing Robert F. Kennedy.

March 10th,   James Earl Ray admits to killing Dr. Martin Luther King Jr. (He later retracts his guilty plea.)

March 13th,   Apollo 9 returns safely after its space mission.

March 28th,   Former General and President Dwight D. Eisenhower dies at the Walter Reed Army Hospital.

April 1st,   "April Fool's Day".

April (month-long)   A grass roots student and community movement in Berkley, Ca. seizes a parking lot and begin to transform it into "The People's Park". Police and protestors clash.

April 9th,   Students for a Democratic Society (SDS) seize the Harvard University's Administration Building. Before order is restored, 45 are injured many are arrested.

May 14th,	"Zip to Zap", a precursor to Woodstock Concert, was dispersed in Zap, North Dakota by the state's National Guard.
May 15th,	A teenager only identified as Robert R, dies in St. Louis of unknown causes which baffled the medical staff. It is not until 1984 that it is determined that he was the first to die of HIV / AIDS in North America.
May 20th,	The California National Guard sprays chemical skin irritants on anti-war Protestors from helicopters over Berkley, California.
May 22nd	Apollo 10 flies to within 15,400 miles of the moon's surface.
May 26th	Apollo 10 returns to Earth after a successful 8-day mission, testing components that will be needed for the upcoming moon landing.
June 3rd	The Australian aircraft carrier, Melbourne crashes into the USS Frank P. Evans, a destroyer in the South China Sea. 74 US sailors are killed.
June 8th	President Nixon and South Vietnamese President Thieu meet on Midway Island. Nixon announces a troop withdrawal of 25,000 by September.
June 18th-22nd	The National Convention of the SDS in Chicago collapses and the Weatherman faction seizes control of the SDS national office and any Further action from that office is Weatherman controlled.
June 23rd	Warren E. Burger is sworn in as the Chief Justice of The United States.
June 27th	This author is enlisted in the US Army, headed to Ft, Lewis for Basic Combat Training.

- Oct. 1: The Beijing Subway begins operations

- Oct. 2: A 1.2 Megaton thermonuclear bomb is tested on Amchitka Island, Alaska.

- Oct. 5: Monty Python's Flying Circus first is aired on the BBC.

- Oct. 9: "Days of Rage" in Chicago, the National Guard is called in to control the demonstrations.

- Oct. 11: The Mets defeat the Orioles in the World Series.

- Oct. 15: The Moratorium to End the War in Vietnam erupts into demonstrations across the country. (Formal Signal training is suspended for the day. We trainees are pulled out of class for the day to receive riot control training, complete with gas mask, M-14 & Bayonet.

- Oct. 17: At the Bell Laboratories, Willard Boyle-George Smith develop the CCD, used in digital cameras of today.

- Oct. 17: Fourteen Black athletes are kicked off of the University of Wyoming football team for wearing "Black Power" armbands to their coach's office.

- Oct. 21: Willy Brandt becomes the new Chancellor of Germany.

- Oct. 22: The Rock band Led Zeppelin releases the album "Led Zeppelin II "

- Oct. 25: The band Pink Floyd releases their album "Ummagumma".

- Oct. 29: The first message is transmitted over ARPANET, the forerunner of today's internet.

- Oct. 31: Wal-Mart incorporates itself as "Wal-Mart Stores, Inc."

- Nov. 1: Vietnam War: President Nixon addresses the nation, asking the "Silent Majority" to support his war efforts. Vice President Spiro Agnew calls anti-war protestors and resistors "an effete corps of impudent snobs and 'nattering nabobs of negativism'!

- Nov. 9: Richard Oakes leads a large group of Native Americans to seize Alcatraz Island in the San Francisco Bay. They hold the Island for 19 months giving rise to Native American Pride and power. The protestors demand Federal reform of Native American policies.

- Nov. 10: "Sesame Street" is first broadcast on the television network, NET.

- Nov. 12: Journalist Seymour Hersh breaks details and photos of the My Lai massacre in Vietnam. (Many of us are shocked at that horror.)

- Nov. 14: The second manned lunar mission is launched as Apollo 12.

- Nov. 15: The Soviet submarine K-19 collides with the American submarine USS Gato in the Barents Sea.

- Nov. 15: 250,000 to 500,000 protestors demonstrate in Washington DC against the Vietnam War. "The March Against Death". We are advised to be prepared for riot duty.

- Nov. 15: Regular color television programs are broadcast across Great Britain.

- Nov. 15: In an old former steakhouse, Dave Thomas opens his first restaurant in downtown Columbus Ohio. He names the new chain "Wendy's" after his 8-year old daughter.

- Nov. 17: SALT I negotiations begin in Helsinki with the Soviets.

- Nov. 19: Astronauts Charles Conrad and Alan Bean land on the "Oceans of Storms" (Oceanus Procellarum) on the moon.

- Nov. 19: Soccer great, Pele scores his 1,000[th] goal.

- Nov. 20: "The Plain Dealer" publication publishes very graphic photographs of the My Lai massacre.

- Nov. 20: Richard Oakes and the Native American occupiers offer to buy Alcatraz Island for $24. The protestors finally leave the island in January 1970.

- Nov. 21: President Nixon and Japanese Premier Sato agree in Washington DC to return Okinawa to Japanese control in 1972 The US would retain its military bases, but without nuclear weapons.

- Nov 21: The first ARPANET link is established around the world. It is the progenitor of the global internet.

- Dec. 1: The first Draft lottery is held in the country since WWII. One's draft order was drawn by birthday.

- Dec. 2: The Boeing 747 makes its maiden flight between Seattle and New York.

- Dec. 4: Black Panthers Fred Hampton and Mark Clark are shot dead by 14 Chicago police officers as the two slept.

- Dec. 5: The Rolling Stones release "Let it Bleed".

- Dec. 6: The Rolling Stones host the Altamont Free Concert in Northern California, amidst much violence. The motorcycle gang, The Hell's Angels was hired by the Stones as security. This concert was to be the "Woodstock of the West", but was noted as the death knell of the 1960's.

- Dec. 24: Accused mass murderer Charles Manson is allowed to defend himself in court in California and he turns the proceedings into a legal circus.

- Dec. 24: The giant oil company, Phillips Petroleum discovers a vast oil reserve in the Norwegian North Sea.

1970 PARTIAL TIME LINE

- Jan 2nd Secretary of State, Henry Kissinger gives President Nixon a memo which follows the NSA's policy option regarding South Africa, which became known as: "The Tar-Baby" option. It states, in part: "The Whites are here to stay and the only way that constructive changes can come about is through them. There is no hope for the Blacks to gain the political right they seek through violence, which will only lead to chaos and increased opportunities for the Communists." The NSA urges "…more economic assistance to draw the two groups [whites & blacks] together and exert some influence on both for a peaceful change.

- Jan 26 Mick Jagger of the Rolling Stones is fined £200 for possession of weed.

- Feb 2 British philosopher Bertrand Russell dies at the age of 97. (Same age that my grandfather, Andrew Taylor dies in 1971.)

- Mar 18 Cambodia's National Assembly removes Norodom Sihanouk from power. He is replaced by pro-western General Lon Nol, who is also anti-Vietnamese. Years later Vietnam and Cambodia would go to war.)

- Mar 29 Viet Cong and North Vietnamese troops launch an offensive against the Nol regime and loyal Cambodian forces.

- Apr. 1 (No joke.) Nixon signs a bill banning cigarette advertising on TV and radio, to take effect 1 Jan 1971.

- Apr. 1 The US Army charges Captain Ernest Medina for the My Lai massacres.

- Apr. 12 Down in Mississippi, a Black one-armed farmer, Rainey Pool is tortured, and beaten by a white mob and his body is tossed over a bridge.

- Apr. 30 President Nixon announces to the world on television, the "incursion" into Cambodia by US and South Vietnamese forces. ("This is not an invasion...") The mission is to drive North Vietnamese forces out of the sanctuaries in Cambodia.

- May 1 Protests erupt across America on college campuses over the "invasion".

- May 3 James A. Rhodes, the Republican governor of Ohio, calls the anti-war Protestors "...the worst type of people we harbor in America, worse than the brown shirts and the communist elements." He then orders the Ohio National Guard out to quell the protestors at the Kent State University.

- May 4 The National Guardsmen use tear gas and riot gear to try to quell the ensuing riot. When these tactics fail, a few untrained and nervous troops open fire on the crowd with "live" fire, killing 4 and wounding 11 others.
The nation and the world are shocked.

- May 5 Over 900 colleges and universities (as well as some high schools) are shut down in to protest the Kent State killings. Kent State itself will remain closed for six weeks.

- May 8 New York construction workers battle anti-war protestors. The nation is Divided over the war and the protests. At the Jackson State College in Mississippi, 100 protestors set numerous fires and overturn many vehicles on campus. Police open fire, killing two.

- May 20 Over 100,000 people from all walks of life demonstrate in the Wall Street district in support of the war.

- May 31 Alcatraz Island in the San Francisco Bay, remains occupied by Native American tribes. The Federal authorities shut off power and water to the island. Protests continue as the governor wants the island turned into a park.

- June 20 President Nasser of Egypt, King Hussein of Jordan and many other Arab National leaders fly to Libya to celebrate the US turning over the Tripoli Air Base to the Libyans.

- June 30 President Nixon orders the withdrawal of US troops from Cambodia, but warns that the US will continue to bomb targets in the north and along the Ho Chi Minh Trail.

- July 1 Over 5,000 South Vietnamese troops remain in Cambodia and they go on looting, raping, pillaging and other brutal actions against the locals.

- July 6 California passes the nation's first set of "no-fault" divorce laws.

- Aug. 1 Racial disturbances in Hartford Connecticut between Blacks and Puerto Ricans.
  Ricans leave one Puerto Rican man shot. Curfew and martial law is ordered. No one is identified as responsible for the shooting.

- Aug. 2 The Hartford police arrest seven Black Panther Party members. They are suspected of sniper activity in the area.

- Aug. 24 A bomb is exploded at the University of Wisconsin's Army Math Lab, Killing a 33-year-old researcher named Robert Fassnacht. Anti-war groups claim responsibility. No arrests were immediately made.

- Sept. 4 Socialist presidential candidate, Salvador Allende Gossens wins the Chilean presidential election. South America leans a bit to the left.

- Sept. 6-14 The Popular Front for the Liberation of Palestine, hijack five airliners. The Israeli airliner is boarded by Israeli security forces and thwarts the completion of the hijacking. The four other planes are forced to land at an airfield near Amman, Jordan. The last airlines are forced to Cairo, Egypt. The passengers and crew are allowed to leave the plane, but held as the Captors try to bargain for the release of many Palestinian prisoners. The plane is blown up on the tarmac.

- Sept 9 US Marines launch a ten-day search and destroy mission against North Vietnamese troops near the Da Nang Air Base.

- Sept 12 With the help of his wife, Rosemary, and members of the Weather Underground, LSD Guru, Timothy Leary walks away from a Federal Minimum prison. He was serving a sentence for the possession of marijuana.

- Sept 15 In an oval office meeting, President Richard Nixon says that he wants to stop president-elect Salvador Allende for taking office in Chile.

- Sept. 16 The Black September War erupts in Jordan. The Palestine Liberation Army which, was led by Yassar Arafat, attempts to seize power. Syria sends an armored force of 200 tanks and other armored vehicles to aid the PLA.

- Sept. 18 Rock icon and super-star Jimi Hendrix, dies in London of a drug overdose. He was only 27 years old and left far too soon. Janis Joplin gives a heartfelt eulogy to him.

- Sept. 20 *This author marries Scharlene H. Martin at the Post Chapel, Presidio of San Francisco.*

- Sept. 22 The League of Arab nations meets in an attempt to end the fighting between King Hussein's Jordanian forces and Yassar Arafat's PLA. Hussein accuses Arafat of trying to overthrow his government. Arafat responds, pounding the table and shouting obscenities. He goes on to call Hussein an agent of American imperialism and Israeli expansion. The Libyan leader, General (Colonel?) Mommar al-Gaddafi, accused the King of being a lunatic. Saudi King Faisal is quite disturbed my all the inner Arab fighting and vulgarity and declares all of them as being mentally unstable. (The world is still watching.)

- Sept 28. President Nasser of Egypt dies of a heart attack at the age of 52.

- Oct. 1 Egypt is in mourning. During Nasser's state funeral procession, the mob attempts to touch and carry the coffin. Police and soldiers have to beat the crown with rifle buts and batons. Many are seriously injured. Others are crushed to death in the confusion. The coffin is hastily loaded on a military vehicle and rushed off for a quick burial.

- Oct 4 Rock & Blues great, Janis Joplin, aged 27 dies from a combination of whiskey (Southern Comfort?) and heroin. An era in America is coming to an end of innocence. Two music legends die at age 27 less than a month apart. It is such a loss for my generation.

- Oct. 8 Soviet author, Alexander Solzhenitsyn is the winner of the Nobel Peace Prize in literature.

- Oct. 10 Quebec's Provincial Labor Minister, Pierre Laporte and British trade Commissioner, James Cross are kidnapped by the *Front de Liberation du Quebec.*

- Oct. 10 The island colony of Fiji becomes independent from France.

- Oct. 12 President Nixon announces the withdrawal of 40,000 troops from Vietnam. (Many well trained troops are "back-doored" from Germany. I was one of them,)

- Oct. 14 Moscow accuses the Nobel judges of being anti-Soviet in giving Solzhenitsyn the prize in literature.

- Oct. 18 Pierre Laporte, the Quebec labor minister, is found dead, stuffed in the trunk of a car. It was determined that he had been strangled to death.

- Oct. 23 Chilean Army's commander-in chief, General Rene' Schneider is assassinated. He voiced his opposition to the military's involvement in politics and stood in the way of the CIA's plan to have Allende overthrown by military force.

- Oct. 31 China describes Japan's "white paper" on defense as intending un-restricted expansion of Japan's military capability, armament acquisition and nuclear capability as preparation for a new imperial expansion.

- Nov. 3 President Salvador Allende of Chili is inaugurated after a victory of over 36.5 % of the electoral vote.

- Nov. 3 Governor Ronald Regan of California wins his second term. He defeated Democrat Jesse Unruh, the "tax & spend" candidate.

- Nov. 4 Russian nuclear physicist, Andre' Sakharov, forms his political arm: The Human Rights Committees.

- Nov. 9 French national hero, ex-president and general, Charles de Gaulle dies at the age of 79. The western world mourns.

- Nov. 20 An Algerian resolution before the UN General Assembly, to unseat Taiwan and make the Peoples Republic of China the sole representive of all of China passed with a majority vote.

- Nov. 21 56 elite US commandoes who were supported by 26 aircraft attempts to rescue and free the American POWs at the Son Tay camp near Hanoi. The prisoners had been moved earlier and the mission failed.

- Nov. 24 The Viet Cong's political arm, the Provisional Revolutionary Government of the Republic of South Vietnam to changes its name to: The Government of South Vietnam, which lasts until the fall of Saigon.

- Nov. 25 Japanese novelist, Yukio Mishima, breaks into the military headquarters in Tokyo. In a protest of current military policies, he commits a bloody hari-kari suicide.

- Nov. 26 The Nixon administration turns its attention to Chile as Allende seizes two American companies and announces to the Communist Party, his plan for even more large-scale nationalizations.

- Nov. 27 Alexander Solzhenitsyn decides not to seek permission from Soviet officials for travel permits to go to Stockholm to receive the Nobel Prize. His books are still not published in the Soviet Union. (My Birthday, 18 !)

MY BIRTHDAY !

- Dec. 2 With the stroke of his pen, President Nixon creates yet another Governmental agency: The Environmental Protection Agency. The new agency takes over functions that the Department of the Interior performed.

- Dec. 7 In Europe: German Chancellor, Willy Brandt signs a treaty in Poland normalizing the two countries relationships and allowing thousands of ethnic Germans to return to their Fatherland after being separated after W W II.

- Dec 18 Over five days of unrest comes to an end in Poland caused by: the political situation, shortages, unemployment, and rapidly rising prices. The Polish government admits that six people were killed by security and police forces during the riots and protests.

- Dec. 31 Thank God this year has come to an end and we are looking forward to the New Year.

1971, TIME MARCHES ON:

- Jan 25: Idi Amin takes power in Uganda, ousting President Milton Obote. The reign of terror begins.

- Feb 06: Great Britain recognizes the Amin government.

- Feb 07: Switzerland gives women the right to vote, but only in state elections.

- Feb 13: 12,000 ARVIN troops invade Laos (with US backing with air and artillery Support.). Communist forces retreat deeper into Laos, widening the war's front.

- Mar 01: A bomb explodes in a White House men's room. The Weather Underground claims responsibility.

- Mar 08: Four American airmen are released by leftist terrorists in Turkey.

- Mar 12: Hafez al-Assad becomes president of Syria.

- Mar 25: Pakistani president Khan launches "Operation Search Light", a military Offensive against East Pakistani separatists. Bangladesh is created.

- Mar 29: Army Lieutenant William Calley is found guilty of 22 counts of murder.

- Apr 06: In Phuqui, South Vietnam; the entire population is returned to their homes after being removed for two years due to American military operations. They are most hostile to the Saigon government and to the US.

- Apr 09: Charles Manson is sentenced to death in California.

- Apr 19: Public Radio begins broadcasting the Senate Foreign Relations Committee's Hearings on The Vietnam War.

- Apr 20: US Supreme Court rules that school bussing will be ordered to achieve racial desegregation.

- May 03: The Harris poll shows that 60% of Americans now oppose the war in in Vietnam and how President Nixon is conducting it.

- Jun 04: Secretary of State, Henry Kissinger says: "If East Pakistan becomes independent, it will become a cesspool…they're going to become a ripe field for Communist infiltration."

- Jun 10: The US ends its trade embargo against China, allowing two-way American trade and travel.

- Jun 13: *The New York Times* begins publishing The Pentagon Papers.

- Jun 30: The Supreme Court declares that the Nixon administration's injunction attempting to block the publishing of the Pentagon Papers is unconstitutional.

- Jul 03: Jim Morrison, front man for the Doors is found dead in his Paris apartment.

- Jul 22: In a taped conversation with Henry Kissinger, President Nixon says "We're doing the China thing to screw the Russians and help us in Vietnam.

- Aug 09: India signs a 20-year treaty of friendship with the Soviet Union.

- Aug 15: Britain increases its troop strength in Northern Ireland to 12,500+.

- Aug 15: The US abandons the Gold Standard and Nixon imposes a 90-day wage freeze.

- Aug 18: Australia & New Zealand decide to withdraw their troops from Vietnam. *My Vietnam Tour Ends as I return home on a compassionate re-assignment due to the death of my grandfather, Andrew Taylor in San Francisco.*

- Sept 12: After a four-day riot in the New York's Attica Prison, 32 prisoners and 10 corrections officers are left dead.

- Oct 25: The UN General Assembly expels Taiwan and admits mainland China to the United Nations.

- Oct 29: US troop strength in Vietnam falls to 196,700+, the lowest since 1966.

- Nov 10: The Cambodian Khmer Rouge gain in strength and power as their Offensive operations expand. Prince Sihanouk (a neutral during Vietnam.) flees to Beijing.

- Nov 12: Nixon (a year before the next presidential elections) announces the Withdrawal of another 45,00 troops from Vietnam, set for 01 Feb.

- Nov 23: The People's Republic of China takes its new seat on the UN Security Council.

- Nov 27: *This author turned 20 !*

- Nov 29: Scharlene H. Chesse' (the author's wife) turned 21 !

- Dec 3 & 4 India and Pakistan are at war.

- Dec 16: In Bangladesh, (East Pakistan) the Pakistani Army Surrenders; Bangladesh becomes independent.

TIMELINE 1972

Jan 29	Senator Adlai Stevenson criticizes President Nixon for supporting the Pakistani Government for its actions against East Pakistan (Bangladesh).
Jan 30	Pakistan withdraws from the British Commonwealth. British paratroopers kill 13 civilians in Londonderry, Northern Ireland during a street march and protest.
Feb 1	The first hand-held calculator goes on the market. Price: $395.
Feb 18	The California Supreme Court declares the death penalty "cruel & unusual Punishment. All death row inmates, including Charles Manson have their sentences commuted to "Life".
Feb 21-28	President Nixon and a huge entourage visit China, normal relations begin as Nixon recognizes Taiwan as a part of the Peoples Republic of China.
Feb 24	North Vietnamese delegates walk out of the Paris Peace Talks over the continued US bombing.
Mar 4	Libya signs an agreement with the Soviet Union to jointly develop oil exploration and refining operations. Military aid follows.
Mar 7	Presidential candidate Ed Muskie appears to "weep" on national television.

Mar 20	Soviet President Leonid Brezhnev declares that his country is concerned about "secret deals" between the US & China in the wake of Nixon's historic trip.
Mar 24	Britain closes the Northern Ireland Parliament and declares direct rule for the next year.
Mar 30	North Vietnamese forces launch its biggest offensive in four years.
Apr 10	The US, The Soviet Union, and 70 other nations sign an agreement banning the use of all biological weapons in the future.
Apr 16	President Nixon orders the bombing of North Vietnam to include Haiphong Harbor.
Apr 19	President Nixon tells his National Security Advisor, Henry Kissinger: "I'm the last president...I'm the only presidents, who has had the guts to do what we're doing...Reagan never could make president to begin with, and he couldn't handle it...I'm going to destroy [explicative] country, believe me. I mean to destroy it if necessary...We will bomb the "beejezus" out of North Vietnam and if anybody interferes, we will threaten the nuclear weapons. *oh shit, I'm still in the Army !*"
Apr 21	Kissinger in Moscow tells Brezhnev two US goals for Vietnam: Honorable withdrawal and a time interval to begin the political settlement.
May 8	Nixon orders the mining of Haiphong Harbor.
May 15	Presidential candidate Governor Mike Wallace is shot & wounded in Laurel, Md.
May 19	The Red Army Faction explodes three bombs in Hamburg, Germany.

May 24	Soviet President, Brezhnev pounds the table and calls Vietnam, "America's shameful war".
May 26	The US & Soviet Union sign the (SALT) Strategic Arms Limitation Treaty.
May 28	First attempt by Republican operatives to break into the Watergate Hotel.
Jun 1	Saddam Hussein, chairman of the Revolutionary Command Council, seizes international oil interests in Iraq.
Jun 2	Members of the Red Army (Bader-Meinhof Gang) faction are arrested after a shoot-out with police.
Jun 8	The tactic to bomb villages that supported the VC is filmed with terrified children running away, (The famous picture of the naked wounded little girl is shown world-wide.)
Jun 17	Five men are arrested at the Democratic National Committee at the Watergate Hotel in DC. They were planning to plant listening devices for the Republican Party.
Jun 17	The United States returns Okinawa to Japan.
Jun 23	President Nixon has a recording device in the White House. He and H.R. Haldeman are discussing using the CIA to obstruct the FBI investigating Watergate.
Jun 28	Nixon orders that draftees will not be sent to Vietnam.
Jul 14	Senator George McGovern wins the Democratic nomination got president.

Aug 3	The US Senate votes 49-47 to withdraw all US forces from Indochina within four months. (Providing all POWs are returned safely.)
Aug 4	In a Gallup Poll, 60% of voting-aged Americans oppose the Vietnam War.
Aug 12	President Nixon withdraws the last US combat units from Vietnam.
Aug 22	Jane Fonda's (Hanoi Jane) photo manning a North Vietnamese anti-aircraft gun goes world-wide.
Sept 5-6	Eight Palestinians of Black September murder eleven Israeli athletes in Munich, Germany during the Summer Olympics.
Sept 14	Germany and Poland restore relations.
Sept 21	President Marcos of the Philippines declares martial law.
Sept 29	Japan & China restore diplomatic relations.
Oct 2	Denmark joins the European Community.
Oct 25	First female FBI agent is hired.
Oct 26	In Kentucky, campaigning, President Nixon declares that cease-fire difficulties in Vietnam, … "can and will be worked out.".
Nov 1	President Thieu of South Vietnam declares that his country has been surrendered to the communists by the Paris Peace Accords.
Nov 7	Nixon won the election by 60% of the popular vote.
Nov 11	The US turns the huge military base of Long Binh over to the South Vietnamese.

| Nov 22 | US intelligence sources report that Hanoi has ordered all the communist forces to observe a cease-fire for 60 days and end terrorist retributions in the South. |

| Dec 7 | First Lady Imelda Marcos is seriously stabbed. Her body guards kill the assailant. |

| Dec 8 | The United Nations declares this day: International Human Rights Day. |

| Dec 16 | Henry Kissinger says that the negotiations with North Vietnam and the US have failed to reach "...a just and fair agreement" to end the war. |

| Dec 18 | President Nixon orders the resumption of the bombing of Hanoi. (Operation Linebacker). North Vietnam threatens to end the peace talks in Paris. |

| Dec 21 | East and West Germany finally recognize each other's governments. |

| Dec 22 | After five days of heavy bombing, Hanoi is a ghost town, heavily damaged, but the people are in vigorous spirits according to foreign correspondents. |

| Dec 24 | Former President Harry (Give them Hell Harry !) S. Truman die |

TIMELINE 1973

| Jan 1 | Britain, Ireland and Denmark join the European Economic Community. (The future European Union.) |

| Jan 7 | Mark Essex kills four civilians and three police officers during a siege at the Howard Johnson Motor Lodge in New Orleans. Ten hours later he is killed by the police from a Marine helicopter. |

Jan 14	Elvis Presley concert in Hawaii is televised worldwide. More watched this concert than watched the Apollo moon landing.
	Super Bowl VII: The Miami Dolphins defeat the Washington Redskins, 14-7.
Jan 15	Vietnam: President Nixon cites progress in the Paris Peace Talks and suspends offensive action in North Vietnam.
Jan 17	President Ferdinand Marcos declares himself President for Life.
Jan 20	President Nixon is sworn in for his second term.
Jan 22	President Lyndon B. Johnson dies, four years after leaving the White House.
	ROE vs Wade: The Supreme Court overturns states ban on abortion.
	George Foreman wins the World Heavyweight Boxing Championship by defeating Joe Frazer by a TKO, 2nd round in Kingston, Jamaica.
Jan 22	**US involvement in the Vietnam War ends** with the signing of the Paris Peace Accords. The US agrees to have all troops out in 60 days and in insured that elections will be held in the future.
Jan 30	Two of Nixon's "high command", G. Gordon Liddy & James W. McCord, Jr. are convicted of conspiracy, burglary and wire-tapping related to the Watergate break-in.
Feb 2	President Nixon is nominated for the Nobel Peace Prize.

Richard Helms, Director of the CIA is fired by Nixon for refusing to investigate the Watergate break-in.

Feb 4 The Suez Canal remains closed since the 1967 "Six Day War" as Israel still occupies Egyptian territory. Civil unrest erupts on both sides.

Feb 11 North Vietnam releases all the names of the POWs. (This author, on duty at the HQ, 6th US Army, Presidio of San Francisco and takes the names of the names in the command area.) The first "Operation Homecoming" flights begin.

Feb 13 The US Dollar is de-valued on the world market by 10%.Foreign goods cost US citizens more.

Feb 21 Point Mugu earthquake in Southern California injures several and causes over a $1,000,000 in damage.

An Israeli fighter pilot shoots down a Libyan passenger airplane, mistaking it for a military aircraft, killing all 108 on board. Tensions against Israel throughout the Middle East escalate.

Feb 22 Renewed Sino-American relations are restored following President Nixon's historic trip to China.

Feb 27 The hamlet of **Wounded Knee** is seized by the American Indian Movement (AIM). The conflict stems over the dis-satisfaction with current tribal leaders and the Oglala Sioux Tribal Chairman, Dick Wilson.

Mar 1	Eight members of the Black September Revolutionary Group seize the Saudi embassy in Sudan, demanding the release of the surviving gunman of the Lod Airport Massacre and the release of the Japanese Red Army members, jailed in Germany. Their demands are rejected, and they kill three diplomats. (Two Americans and one Belgian.
Mar 4	The Black September commandoes surrender to the Sudanese Army.
Mar 4	Israel's Prime Minister, Golda Meir lashes out at the European diplomats for surrendering to what she calls "Arab Blackmail" by releasing Arab terrorists.
Mar 8	Northern Irish voters endorse a referendum, remaining in the United Kingdom. Tensions grow between Catholics & Protestants.
	The IRA detonates several bombs in the London governmental district.
	Sudan's government talks of executing the Black September commandoes. And banning all Palestinian commando activity.
Mar 12	Gold has risen to $90.00 / an ounce. International markets pressure to dump the dollar being tied to gold prices. The US dollar is no longer tied to gold's price.
Mar 13	The newly enacted constitution in Syria, vests power in the Ba'ath Party with unlimited power in state and societal functions. The president is given vast powers and a seven-year term.

Mar 15	The Saigon government and the ARVIN begin seizing land in the Mekong Delta that the communist forces held as a hedge against any future aggression in the South by the NVA and VC forces.
Mar 17	Most all of the remaining US forces are leaving. The famous photo: *"Burst of Joy"* goes world-wide as a former POW is re-united with his family.
Mar 23	The Watergate scandal explodes: In his letter to Judge John Sirica, Watergate burglar, James W, McCord admits that he and the others convicted were pressured by the administration to *"remain silent"*. He goes on to name attorney John Mitchell as the "boss" of the operation.
Mar 29	The last soldier leaves Vietnam. (I hope that he turned out the light at the end of the tunnel.)
Apr 1	April Fool's Day. (Stories and film at 11:00.)
Apr 3	The first shoe box sized "cell phone" call is made by Martin Cooper in New York.
Apr 4	With a lot of fanfare and an elaborate ribbon cutting ceremony; The World Trade Center officially opens.
Apr 6	Pioneer 11 is launched on a scientific mission to study our solar system.
	Ron Blomberg becomes MLB's first designated hitter.
Apr 17	Six Native Americans / American Indian Movement members are wounded at Wounded Knee in a gun battle with Federal Marshals.
	Federal Express (Fed-Ex) begins national operations with a fleet of six small aircraft. Over 186 packages are delivered to 25 US cities.

Apr 29	Golda Meir, Prime Minister of Israel; Declares that Egyptian President Anwar Sadat is a *"leader in distress"*.
Apr 30	Watergate Scandal: Four of Nixon's aides resign. These being, Haldeman, Ehrlichman, Attorney General Kleindienst and his counsel, John Dean. The president accepts this bail out in anger. He goes on to claim "no white-wash" at the White House and accepts full responsibility of his subordinates.
May 3	The Sears Tower in Chicago is completed. It now becomes the tallest building in the world. (Record held until 1998.)
May 3-4	One of the six wounded by Federal Marshals at wounded Knee dies. Another gun battle ensues.
May 7	After talks the leadership of the American Indian Movement agree to stand down.
May 8	The 71 day stand-off at the Pine Ridge Reservation at Wounded Knee ends with the surrender of the militants.
May 10	The Nixon administration had been trying to control developments in Cambodia and Laos by continuing bombing. The House of Representatives with its democratic majority votes (219-188) to cut off military funding in Indochina.
May 11	Premier Thanom Kittikachorn of Thailand says that military assistance is still needed by due to the new situation in Vietnam, Cambodia and Laos.
May 12	Nixon's White House insists that despite the vote in Congress, the bombing missions will continue in Cambodia.

May 14	Skylab is launched as the US's first space station.
	The senate Approbations Committee votes, 24-0 to stop funding the Cambodian bombing.
	The British House of Commons abolishes capital punishment.
May 17	Watergate Scandal: The Senate hearings are televised.
May 20	President Nixon insists that Hanoi has persisted in violations of the Paris Peace Accords, as well as the status of the remains of American KIAs still unaccounted for. (NOTE: Recovery continues in 2019. As well as from Korea. WW I & WWII.
May 25	Skylab 2 is launched, with Pete Conrad, Paul Weitz and Joseph Kerwin on board to repair damages sustained on Skylab 1.
May 27	Several US Intelligence agencies report that the chances of North Vietnam and the Vietcong assets are greatly diminished and an offensive in the near future is slim to none.
May 31	The US Senate votes, 63-19 to prohibit funding combat operations in Laos or Cambodia.
June 16	President Richard Nixon and Soviet Leader Leonid Brezhnev begin a series of summit talks to improve relations.
June 19	Both the House & Senate pass the Case-Church Amendment, forbidding any further military action in Southeast Asia, to be effective 15 August 1973. (This act was "veto-proof." 274-124 House & 64-26 Senate.)
Jun 22	W. Mark Felt (aka: "Deep Throat") retires from the FBI.

Jun 23-25	Soviet Leader Brezhnev arrives in Washington to smooth over disarmament talks with Nixon.
Jun 25	Former White House counsel, John Dean begins to testify before the Senate.
Jul 1	The government adds a new agency: The United States Drug Enforcement Agency. (Aka: DEA, continuing Nixon's "war on drugs.")
Jul 2	The Congress passes the Education for the Handicapped (EHA)and proclaims it be mandated nationwide federally.
Jul 8	It has been reported that Colonel Kaddafi of Libya while speaking to Egyptian feminists, said *"women's liberation"* is **no good.**
Jul 10	The islands of the Bahamas gain full independence within the Commonwealth of Nations.
Jul 12	A major fire at the National Archives, in St. Louis, Mo. destroys most of the sixth floor and thousands of military records and other Federal records. (This author still has his life effected by that fire.
Jul 16	Watergate Continues: The former White House aide, Alexander Butterfield informs the US Senate that President Nixon has secretly records meetings in the oval office.
Jul 17	In Afghanistan, Prime Minister Daoud seizes power from his cousin, Shah Zahir, who has ruled since 1933 ending the Barakzai Dynasty, ruling since 1818. The new regime wants good relations between both the US and USSR. He is an economic progressive. There are only 50 miles of paved roads in the entire nation, but many palaces.

Jul 23	President Nixon refuses to turn over the "presidential tapes" to the Senate Watergate Committee or to the Special Counsel.
Jul 28	Skylab # is launched with Owen Garriott, Jack Lousma and Alan Bean to carry out medical and other scientific experiments.
Aug 3	**This author is released from active army duty and enlists in the Army Reserve.**
Aug 5	Two gunmen belonging to The Arab Nationalist Youth Organization for the Liberation of Palestine shoot and kill five and wound 55 disembarking Israeli passengers on a TWA flight landing in Greece.
Aug 8	The death of Dean Corli leads to the gruesome discovery in Houston, leading to the bodies of 27 boys, killed by three men.
Aug 11	In New York City, DJ Kool Herc originated a new music genre, known as *"Hip-Hop"*.
Aug 15	The US bombing of Cambodia officially ends 12 years of combat activity in Southeast Asia.
	(Author's note: When was the start of the American role in the war in Southeast Asia? 1954, Dien Binh Phu, Eisenhower, 1959 [1st two names on the wall.], 1960 (many Vietnam Service Medals, 1964, 1965 after the Gulf of Tonkin episode?
Aug 22	Down in Chile, inflation is running at over 500%. The parliament led by factions opposed to President Salvador Allende accused his government of unconstitutional acts and calls upon the military to restore order and constitutional following.

Aug 23	Egyptian President Anwar Sadat in speaking with Koranic references, has released Islamic activists from prison. He goes on to encourage Islamic students and institutions to counter Nasserites and the political left. Talks with Israel are stalemated regarding the occupied territories. Egypt prepares for war with Saudi King Faisal's pledge to use oil as a weapon.
Sep 2	Libya nationalizes 51% of its oil assets operating with foreign technology and capital.
Sep 11	Chile's military in a coup ousts elected president Salvador Allende who goes down fighting to his death with an AK-47 given to him by Castro.
Sep 15	Six Persian Gulf nations declare a negotiating front to prevent price increases and an end to support of Israel.
Sep 22	National Security Advisor to President Nixon, Henry Kissinger is appointed as Secretary of State. The South Vietnam military attack communist forces in and around Pleiku.
Sep 28	ITT is bombed in New York City by the radical Weather Underground. Their cause was the Chilean coup de etat.
Oct 1	President Nixon's former Security advisor, now Secretary of State, has had secret meetings with Egypt's President Anwar Sadat and has further been unable to convince Golda Meir that for eight months Sadat has wanted peace and resolve the territory disputes in Gaza and the East Bank of the Suez. The Israelis do not trust Egypt, now war looms close by.

Oct 6	Egypt launches offensive military action against Israel, supported by the armed forces of Hafez al Assad of Syria and King Faisal of Saudi Arabia. A surprise attack is launched against Israelite forces in the Golan Heights. Jordan has not joined in the war against Israel.
Oct 8	Israel launches its first major offensive in this war which in unsuccessful. The Israelites fear this is their downfall, as the USSR is airlifting military supplies to Syria.
Oct 10	The majority of the European nations under a threat of Arab oil embargos, stopped supplying Israel with munitions. President Nixon insures Israel that their military losses will be replaced by the US.

Spiro T. Agnew resigns in disgrace as Vice President and pleads "no contest" to tax evasion in Federal Court. He is fined $10,000 and given 3 years probation. |
| Oct 11 | Kissinger warns the USSR that if they send troops to the Middle East, so shall the United States. |
| Oct 14 | Responding to the military situation in the Golan Heights, Iraq & Jordan send troops.

A Thai student rebellion ends the military dictatorship of (now)Field Marshall Thanom Kittikajom and Prapas Charusathein. The Thais want to end the military alignment with the US and establish good relations with the People's Republic of China. |
| Oct 17 | Secretary Henry Kissinger and Vietnamese Le Duc Tho are awarded the Nobel Peace Prize. Tho refuses, and Kissinger touted Nixon's goal of everlasting peace. |

An Arab and OPEC oil embargo against all nations that support Israel, until the occupied territories are restored. cause major world economic problems and panic, thus we endure the dreaded *"GAS LINES"* This embargo will not be lifted until March 1974.

Oct 20   ***"THE SATURDAY MASSACRE"*** President Nixon orders Attorney General Elliot Richardson to fire Special Prosecutor Archibald Cox. Richardson refuses, and then resigns. Deputy Attorney General, William Ruckelshaus,. Solicitor General Robert Bock, (#3 in the DOJ.) then fires Cox. These events raise impeachment articles of Nixon foe obstruction of justice.

Israeli tanks & armor have succeeded against Syrian Armor and race to within 10 miles of Damascus.

Oct 21   Israeli forces have crossed over to the Egyptian side of the Suez Canal and have surrounded the Egyptian 3rd Army.

Oct 28   Due to the Arab side losing in the war so far, the UN, and the Soviet Union move to end the war. The Egyptian and Israeli leaders meet at Mile Marker 101 in the Sinai. This will be their first meeting in 25 years.

Oct 30   The bridge in Istanbul, Turkey is completed, connecting Europe and Asia.

Nov 1   Acting Attorney General Robert Bork appoints Leon Jaworski as the New Watergate Special Prosecutor.

Nov 3   Greek Students demonstrate against the country's dictatorship and clash with police and security forces.

NASA's Mariner Program: Launches Mariner 10 towards the planet Mercury. (On March 29, 1974 it will become the first space probe to reach that tiny planet.)

Nov 6	Vietcong and ARVN forces have been heavily fighting for weeks. Both sides claim the other is the aggressor and in violation of the Paris Peace Accords. No progress is made in resolving this issue.
	Donald De Freeze, a convict who escaped from Soledad Prison in California, joins a group of Urban Guerillas, calling themselves *The Symbionese Liberation Army."* (Later of Patty Hurst Fame.)
Nov 7	Congress overrides President Nixon's War Powers Resolution and limits the presidents power to wage war without congressional approval and funding.
Nov 11	Egypt and Israel sign a US sponsored cease fire accord.
Nov 16	NASA launches Skylab 4 manned by Gerald Carr, William Pogue, on an 84 day space mission.
Nov 17	Greek tanks and troops crash through the iron gates of the Athens Polytechnic University to help end the student occupation and protest of the government and dictator George Papadopoulos. Martial Law has been in affect since the night of the 17th.
	More Watergate: President Nixon, in Orlando Florida, tells 400 Associated press managing editors, **"I am NOT a Crook !"**
Nov 18	Greek students, police and security forces continue to clash. Many are injured.
Nov 21	President Nixon's attorney, J. Fred Buzhardt reveals the 18 ½ minuet gap in *"The Tapes".*
Nov 22	The Greek Chief of the Armed Forces outlaws 26 student organizations.

Nov 25	Papadopoulos is ousted in a military coup d'état. People in his hometown of Elaiohori in the Peloponnese are disappointed.
Nov 27	The US Senate confirms 92-3 Gerald Ford as Vice President.
	President Nixon signs the Emergency Petroleum Allotment Act to control prices and production as well as market controls.5
	This author turns 22 years of age and a student veteran.
Nov 28	The Greek junta, in order to gain public support, release many who were arrested during the uprising and protests.
	Scharlene is a year older.
Dec 1	Papua New Guinea gains self-rule and determination from Australia.
Dec 3	The Provisional Revolutionary Government of Vietnam (Vietcong) destroy over 18,000,000 gallons of fuel stored near Saigon.
Dec 15	The American Psychiatric Association removes homosexuality as a mental disease from the DSM-11.
Dec 23	OPEC doubles the price of a barrel of crude oil.
Dec 28	The US Congress passes the Endangered Species Act.

SAN FRANCISCO DEMOGRAPHICS

Note: Racial identify & classification collection data changes over the decades.

Source: San Francisco Census data base.

1950

Total Population:	775,357	100%
Households:	698,176	90%

Race:

Native White:	573,495	74.0%
Foreign-born White:	120,393	15.5%
Black:	43,502	5.6%
Other Races:		
Indians (East):	331	0%
Japanese:	5,579	0.7%
Chinese:	24,813	3.2%
White, Spanish:	31,433	4.1%

Sex:

Male:	389,866	50.3%
Female:	385,491	49.7%

1960

Total Population:	740,316	100%
Households:	713,321	96.4%
In Group Quarters:	26,995	3.6%

PAGE TWO (1960)

Race:

White:	604,403	81.6%
Black:	74,383	10.0 %
Other Races:	2,226	0.3 %
Indian (East)	1,068	0.1 %
Japanese:	9,464	1.3 %
Chinese:	36,445	4.9 %
Filipino:	12,327	1.7 %
White, Spanish:	51,602	7.0 %

Place of Birth

Native:	597,785	80.7 %
Foreign Born:	142,531	19.3 %

Sex:

Male:	363,424	49.1 %
Female:	376,892	50.9 %

1970

Total Population:	715,874	100 %

Race

White:	511,186	71.4 %
Black:	96,078	13.4 %
Indian:	2,900	0.4 %
Japanese:	11,705	1.6 %
Chinese:	58,696	8.2 %

Filipino:	24,694	3.44 %

1980

Total Population:	715,674	100%

Race:

White:	402,131	59.2 %
Black:	86,190	12.7 %
Native American:	3,566	0.5 %
Eskimo:	153	0.0 %
Aleut:	39	0.0 %
Asian & Pacific Islanders:	149,269	22.0 %
Japanese:	12,461	1.8 %
Chinese:	82,244	12.1 %
Filipino:	38,690	5.7 %
Korean:	3,442	0.5 %
Asian Indian:	2,704	0.4 %
Vietnamese:	5,078	0.7 %
Hawaiian:	1,048	0.2 %
Samoan:	1,568	0.2 %

PAGE FOUR

1990

Total Population:	723,959	100 %

Race:

White:	386,341	53.6 %

Black:	78,931	10.9 %
Native American:	3,354	0.5 %
Eskimo:	39	0.0 %
Aleut:	118	0.0 %
Asian or Pacific Islander:	211,000	29.1 %
Asian:	207,901	28.7 %
Japanese:	11,591	1.6 %
Chinese:	130,753	18.1 %
Filipino:	40,977	5.7 %
Korean:	6,538	0.9 %
Asian Indian:	2,891	0.4 %
Vietnamese:	8,952	1.2 %
Cambodian:	1,593	0.2 %
Hmong:	20	0.0 %
Laotian:	928	0.1 %
Thai:	592	0.1 %
Other Asian:	3,066	0.4 %
Pacific Islander:	3,099	0.4 %
Polynesian:	2,415	0.3 %
Hawaiian:	975	0.1 %
Samoan:	1,310	0.2 %
Tongan:	102	0.0 %

PAGE FIVE

2000

Total Population:	776,733	100 %

Race

One Race:		
White:	385,728	49.66 %

Black: 60,515	7.79 %	
Asian:		
Asian Indian:	5,24	0.71 %
Chinese:	152,620	19.65 %
Filipino:	40,083	5.16 %
Japanese:	11,410	1.47 %
Korean:	7,679	0.99 %
Vietnamese:	10,722	1.38 %
Other Asian:	11,527	1.48 %
Native Hawaiian & Other		
Pacific Islanders	3,844	0.49 %
Native Hawaiian:	473	0.06 %
Guamanian / Charro	305	0.04 %
Samoan:	2,311	0.30 %
Other Pacific Islander:	755	0.10 %
Some Other Race:	50,368	6.48 %
Two or More Mixed Race:	33, 255	4.28 %
Hispanic or Latino Race:	109,504	14.10 %
Mexican:	48,935	6.30 %
Puerto Rican:	3,758	0.48 %
Cuban:	1,632	0.21 %
Other Hispanic / Latino: 55,179	7.10 %	
White Alone:	338,909	43.63 %

PAGE SIX (2000)

Sex

Male:	394,828	50.83 %
Female:	381,905	49.17 %

2010

Total Population:	805,235	100.00 %

Race

White Alone:	390,387	48.48 %
Black or African-American alone:	48,870	6.07 %
Native American & Alaskan Natives:	4,024	0.50 %
Asian Alone:	267,915	33.27 %
Native Hawaiian & Other Pacific Island Alone:	3,359	0.42 %
Some Other Race Alone:	53,021	6.58 %
Two or More Races:	37,659	4.68 %
Population By Hispanic or Latino (Of any Race)	121,774	15.12 %
Persons not of Latino Origins:	683,461	84.88 %

Sex

Male:	408,462	50.73 %
Female:	396,773	49.27 %

PAGE SEVEN

2018-2019 Estimates

Total Population: 805,235   100 %

By the end of 2019, Estimated population growth reaches 864,816.

Race

White:	390,387	48.0 %
Black or African American:	48,870	6.0 %
Asian:	267,915	33.0 %
Hispanic or Latino (All races)	121,774	15.0 %
Some Other Race:	53,021	6.0 %
Two or More Races:	37,659	4.0 %
Native American:	4,024	< 1.0 %
Native Hawaiian / Pacific Islander:	3,359	< 1.0 %
Three or More Races:	3,349	< 1.0 %
Native Hawaiian:	410	< 1.0 %

Sex:

Male:	408,462	50.70 %
Female:	396,773	49.27 %

NOTE : All above Census Date is compiled from the US Census Bureau Records and the San Francisco Bureau of Vital Statistics and Records for the Decades and Years Listed. Statistical Standard Rounding is Taken Into Consideration in Calculating These Figures.

BIBLIOGRAPHY & FURTHER READING

FAMILY ORAL HISTORIES, AS TOLD TO ME.

Florence Scope Chesse'	(Deceased)
Roland Peter Chesse'	(Deceased)
Ralph Chesse'	(Deceased)
Dion Chesse'	(Deceased)
Andrew Taylor	(Deceased)
Jessie Mc Gregor Walker	(Deceased)
Catherine Walker	(Deceased)
Glenhall Taylor Sr.	(Deceased) Obituary: Los Angeles Times, Reprint, 08/20/2018
Glenhall Taylor Jr.	(Deceased) Obituary: Legacy.com / Crosby, N. Gray & Co. 08/20/2018
Milton Albin	(Deceased)
Yvonne Albin	(Deceased)
Roger Rush	(Deceased)
Leslie Rush	(Deceased)
Henri Arian	(Deceased)
Marcelle Arian	(Deceased)

TIMELINES

453

"Baby Boomer" Statistics:	Population Reference Bureau 2014	Kelvin M. Pollard, Paola Scommegna
"World History" Timeline, 1950-2000:	History of the World	08/03/2018
San Francisco History Timeline:	San Francisco History	08/03/2018
	Wikipedia	08/04/2018
Timelines, 1970,1971:	Wikipedia	08/04/2018
Timelines, 1971, 1972:	MACRO HISTORY	09/11/2018
Timeline 1973	MACRO HISTORY	05/05/2019
	WIKIPEDIA, 1973 in United States	05/05/2019
Oscar Lewis,99:	New York Times	03/10/2017
Books By Oscar Lewis:	Good Reads Inc.	03/10/2017

BASIC INFORMATION & DATA

Development & History of the Teletype:	Wikipedia: Teleprinter	08/14/2018
	History of Teletype Development:	10/1963
	Teletype Corporation Editors: R.A. Nelson, K.M. Lovitt	

Locations & History: San Francisco, Ft. Lewis, Ft. Monmouth, Ft. Dix, All Air Force

Installations, Germany, Vietnam; Cam Ranh Bay, Long Binh, Ben Cat (Lai Khe), Can Tho,

Mekong Delta, Ft. Riley, McConnell AFB, Grafenwohr: All complied from "Google",

Wikipedia, & on line searches, 2015-2018.

Teletype Message Format JANAP 128:	TM 11-5815-602-10,	
	TO 31W4-2UGC74-1	
	EE 161-DM-010/ E154UGC74	
National Route 1A (Vietnam)	Wikipedia	06/21/2018
Can Tho, Vietnam	World Guides.com	06/10/2018
	Can Tho, Vietnam, Britannica.com	06/10/2018
	Wikipedia	06/10/2018
United States Army Vietnam	Wikipedia	06/09/2018
Military Assistance Command	Wikipedia	06/09/2018
1st Signal Brigade	Army Historical Society Howard Bartholf	1983
Bin Thuy Air Base	Wikipedia	06/09/2018
	Vietnam Security Police Association: [	06/09/2018
Lai Khe	Wikipedia	05/29/2018
2nd Signal Group	scrubthe web.com	05/29/2018 / 1998
M-18 Claymore Mine	TM 9-1345-203-12	October 1995
	Wikipedia	06/05/2018
Phu Lam US Army Communications Base	Phu Lam History of / Phulam.com	1998
	Connie Chronister	

<u>1st Infantry Division (Mech)</u>	<u>Wikipedia</u>	05/18/2018
<u>121st Signal Battalion</u>	<u>Wikipedia</u>	08/21/2018
<u>Lockheed C-5 Galaxy</u>	<u>Wikipedia</u>	08/16/2018
<u>Grafenwohr</u>	<u>Wikipedia</u>	08/31/2018
<u>Riverine Operations in the Vietnam War</u>	Extract from the Vietnam 50th Anniversary 2015	
<u>The Brown Water Navy in Vietnam</u>	Robert H. Stoner, GMCM (Ret)	06/10/2018
<u>Vietnam War Facts, Stats and Myths</u>	SFC (Ret) David Hack	05/29/2018
<u>General Statistics of Vietnam War</u>	General On line search	06/13/2018
<u>R&R Rest & Recuperation</u>	1st Battalion, 50th Infantry Association	07/16/2018
<u>Vietnam War Casualties</u>	<u>Wikipedia</u>	06/13/2018
<u>Sobering Statistics Concerning Vietnam Vets As of April 2016</u>		April 2016
<u>Aircraft Flown During the Vietnam War</u>	Aircraft Flown During the Vietnam War 1968	
<u>The Most Expensive War in US History</u>	Alexander Kent, 24/7 Wall St.	05/25/2015
<u>US Casualties by Unit:</u>	The Patriot Files	11/19/2004

CPSIA information can be obtained
at www.ICGtesting.com
Printed in the USA
BVHW080811030719
552580BV00003B/44/P